A HISTORY OF
POSTCOLONIAL LUSOPHONE AFRICA

A History of Postcolonial Lusophone Africa

PATRICK CHABAL
with
DAVID BIRMINGHAM, JOSHUA FORREST,
MALYN NEWITT, GERHARD SEIBERT,
ELISA SILVA ANDRADE

INDIANA
University Press
Bloomington & Indianapolis

First published in North America in 2002 by

Indiana University Press
601 North Morton Street
Bloomington, Indiana 47404-3797 USA

http://iupress.indiana.edu

Telephone orders 800-842-6796
Fax orders 812-855-7931
Orders by e-mail iuporder@indiana.edu

Printed in England

Cataloging information is available from the Library of Congress.

ISBN 0-253-34187-6 (cloth)
ISBN 0-253-21565-X (paper)

ACKNOWLEDGEMENTS

This book is the outcome of an auspicious combination of factors, some personal and some institutional. I have been teaching the history of Lusophone Africa at King's College London for the last fifteen years and over that time have learnt a great deal from having to present complex material to students who were not familiar with Angola, Mozambique, Guinea-Bissau, Cape Verde and São Tomé e Príncipe. To them I owe a singular debt of gratitude not just for their interest in the field but also for their pointed questioning.

During that time the historiography of Portuguese-speaking Africa has grown considerably and there is now a significant body of scholarship that makes the present enterprise less hazardous. I have also been fortunate in benefiting from the work of several other scholars of Lusophone Africa, some of whom have been particularly generous of their time and knowledge but are too modest to admit it. I thank first and foremost my five co-authors—David Birmingham, Joshua Forrest, Malyn Newitt, Gerhard Seibert and Elisa Silva de Andrade for agreeing to join me on this somewhat perilous venture despite their own occasional reservations about any such 'general' volume on Lusophone Africa.

This book, like its companion volume *The Postcolonial Literature of Lusophone Africa* (London: Hurst & Co. /Bloomington: Indiana University Press 1996), has benefited greatly from the professional help given to me by Caroline Shaw, who has not only compiled the bibliography and produced the index but has also helped me immeasurably with the editing of the manuscript. Farzana Shaikh, as ever, has provided intellectual support and a critical gaze at a text that threatened at times to acquire a life of its own. I thank my colleagues in the Department of Portuguese and Brazilian Studies for providing a stimulating intellectual environment and for affording me the time to write.

Finally, I must express my continued gratitude to Christopher Hurst and Michael Dwyer for their unflagging support. The field of Lusophone African studies owes them a sizeable debt of gratitude for their ongoing interest in what are sometimes labelled as 'minority' areas.

King's College London   PATRICK CHABAL
November 2001

CONTENTS

Contents

PART II. COUNTRY STUDIES

NOTES ON THE CO-AUTHORS

Patrick Chabal is Professor of Lusophone African Studies, University of London, and Head of the Department of Portuguese and Brazilian Studies at King's College London. He is the author of numerous books, including, on Lusophone Africa, *Amílcar Cabral: Revolutionary Leadership and People's Wars,* (with others) *The Postcolonial Literature of Lusophone Africa,* and *Vozes Moçambicanas.*

David Birmingham is Professor of History, University of Kent at Canterbury. He is the author of a number of books on Portuguese-speaking Africa, among which are: *Portugal and Africa, A Concise History of Portugal,* and *Frontline Nationalism in Angola and Mozambique.*

Joshua Forrest is Professor of Politics at the University of Vermont. He is the author of a number of articles on Portuguese-speaking Africa and of *Guinea-Bissau: Power, Conflict and Renewal in a West African nation.*

Malyn Newitt is Charles Boxer Professor of Portuguese History, University of London. He is the author of numerous articles and monographs on Lusophone Africa, including the following books: *Portuguese Settlement on the Zambesi, Portugal in Africa,* and *A History of Mozambique.*

Gerhard Seibert is a researcher on contemporary Lusophone Africa, with a specialisation on São Tomé e Príncipe. He is the author of one of the few monographs on that rarely-studied country: *Comrades, Clients and Cousins: Colonialism, Socialism and Democratization in São Tomé e Príncipe.*

Elisa Silva Andrade is an economist and historian, currently a researcher and consultant in her home state of Cape Verde. She is the author of one of the most recent books on that country, *Les îles du Cap Vert. De la Découverte à l'indépendance.*

GLOSSARY

aldeamentos	strategic villages set up during the colonial wars and designed by the Portuguese military to contain the African population
aringas	fortified stockades (Mozambique)
assimilados	indigenous inhabitants of the Portuguese colonies considered to be assimilated into Portuguese culture and colonial socio-economic norms: *assimilado* status carried certain civic benefits including access to Portuguese law
bandidos armados	'armed bandits': description given especially to RENAMO, but also UNITA, suggesting a lack of coherent political motivation to violent activities
bermedjos	crioulo-speaking elite in Guinea-Bissau
chicundas	19th century slave soldiers of Afro-Portuguese and Swahili warlords (Mozambique)
civilizados	indigenous inhabitants of the Portuguese colonies considered to have reached a degree of integration into Portuguese culture and colonial socio-economic norms
colonatos	small subsidised farms set up to accommodate white Portuguese migrants (Mozambique)
cooperantes	volunteers, usually foreign
crioulo	Creole language (Cape Verde, Guinea-Bissau, São Tomé e Príncipe)
djulas	small-scale and informal traders active in west Africa generally and operating in the rural areas of Guinea-Bissau
Estado Novo	Portuguese regime 1926–74
fan bodja	authority group of male elders (Guinea-Bissau)
Flechas	special military force recruited from the African population by the Portuguese military

xi

forros	Creole elite in São Tomé e Príncipe
grupos dinamizadores	party activists in Mozambique involved in supervising production and working relations
grupos especiais paraquedistas	parachute troops recruited from the indigenous population by the Portuguese military
grupos especiais	military special forces recruited from the indigenous population by the Portuguese military
indígenas	indigenous inhabitants of the Portuguese colonies not considered to have become integrated into Portuguese culture or colonial socio-economic norms and subject to 'traditional' law
Katanga gendarmerie	rebel troops from the Katanga region of Zaire (now DRC)
mestiços	persons of mixed race
musseques	Luanda slums
poder popular	people's power
pontas	plantation-style trading farms in Guinea-Bissau
ponteiros	owners of *pontas*
prazos	estates originally founded by the Portuguese Crown in the Zambesi River region of Mozambique
roças	plantations on São Tomé e Príncipe
tabanka	Cape Verdean festival with origins in mainland Africa

ABBREVIATIONS

AD	Aliança Democrática
ADI	Acção Democrática Independente
ADNSTP	Acção Democrática Nacional de São Tomé e Príncipe
ANC	African National Congress
ANP	Assembleia Nacional Popular
AP	Associated Press
BBC	British Broadcasting Corporation
BCA	Banco Comerical do Atlântico
BCSTP	Banco Central de São Tomé e Príncipe
BNSTP	Banco Nacional de São Tomé e Príncipe
CAIL	Complexo Agro-Industrial do Limpopo
CFA	Communauté Financière d'Afrique
CIA	Central Intelligence Agency
CLSTP	Comité de Libertação de São Tomé e Príncipe
CNPC	Caixa Nacional de Poupança e Crédito
CODO	Coligação Democrática da Oposição
COMECON	Council for Mutual Economic Assistance
CONCP	Conferência das Organizações Nacionalistas das Colónias Portuguesas
CPI	Centro de Promoção de Investimentos
CPLP	Comunidade dos Países de Língua Portuguesa
DNS	Departamento da Segurança Nacional
DRC	Democratic Republic of Congo (former Zaire)
ECOWAS	Economic Community of West African States
FAIMO	Frentes de Alta Intensidade de Mão-de-Obra
FAO	Food and Agriculture Organisation

FARSTP	Forças Armadas Revolucionárias de São Tomé e Príncipe
FDC	Frente Democrata Cristã
FLING	Frente da Luta pela Independência Nacional da Guiné
FNLA	Frente Nacional para a Libertação de Angola
FPL	Frente Popular Livre
FRELIMO	Frente da Libertação de Moçambique
FRNSTP	Frente de Resistência Nacional de São Tomé e Príncipe
GD	*grupos dinamizadores*
GUMO	Grupo Unido de Moçambique
HIPC	highly indebted poor countries
IMF	International Monetary Fund
INC	Instituto Nacional de Cooperativas
JMLSTP	Juventude do Movimento de Libertação de São Tomé e Príncipe
MANU	Mozambican African National Union
MFA	Movimento das Forças Armadas
MLSTP	Movimento de Libertação de São Tomé e Príncipe
MLSTP/PSD	Movimento de Libertação de São Tomé e Príncipe / Partido Social Democrata
MNR	Mozambique National Resistance
MPD	Movimento para a Democracia
MPLA	Movimento para a Libertação de Angola
OAU	Organisation of African Unity
OJM	Organização da Juventude Moçambicana
OMM	Organização das Mulheres Moçambicanas
OMSTEP	Organização das Mulheres de São Tomé e Príncipe
ONUMOZ	Operação das Nações Unidas para Moçambique
OPEC	Organisation of Petroleum Exporting Countries
OPSTEP	Organização dos Pioneiros de São Tomé e Príncipe
PAICV	Partido Africano da Independência de Cabo Verde
PAIGC	Partido Africano da Independência de Guiné e Cabo Verde
PALOP	Países Africano de Língua Oficial Portugesa
PCD	Partido da Convergência Democrática
PCD/GR	Partido da Convergência Democrática / Grupo de Reflexão
PCP	Partido Comunista Português
PIDE	Policia Internacional de Defesa do Estado

PMI/PF	Protecção Materna-Infantil / Planeamento Familiar
PRC	Popular Republic of Congo
PRD	Partido da Renovação Democrática
PRE	Programa de Reabilitação Económica
PRGF	poverty reduction and growth facility
PRS	Partido para a Renovação Social
PSD	Partido Social Democrático
RENAMO	Resistência Nacional Moçambicana
RGB/MB	Resistência da Guiné Bissau / Movimento Bafatá
SADCC	Southern African Development Coordination Conference
SAP	structural adjustment programme
SWAPO	South West Africa People's Organisation
TEACR	Tribunal Especial para Actos Contra-Revolucionários
UD	União Democrática
UDENAMO	União Democrática Nacional de Moçambique
UDISTP	União Democrática e Independente de São Tomé e Príncipe
UM	União para a Mudança
UNAMI	União Africana de Moçambique Independente
UNDP	União Nacional para a Democracia e o Progresso
UNDP	United Nations Development Programme
UNICEF	United Nations Children's Fund
UNITA	União Nacional para a Independênica Total de Angola
UNSO	United Nations Sahel Organisation
UPNA	União das Populações do Norte de Angola
WHO	World Health Organisation
ZANU	Zimbabwe African National Union

PREFACE

This volume aims to furnish a comprehensive history of the five African Portuguese-speaking countries—Angola, Mozambique, Guinea-Bissau, Cape Verde and Saõ Tomé e Príncipe—since they became independent from Portugal in 1974–5.

This has been a demanding task. Indeed, there seems at first little to connect these five disparate African countries, other than the fact that they were once Portuguese colonies. They are on the face of it so different in size, geographical location and socio-economic profile as to defy easy comparison. Cape Verde is an the archipelago of ten islands 300 miles off the Senegalese coast. São Tomé e Príncipe consists of two remote west African islands sitting on the Equator. Guinea-Bissau is, like the Gambia, a west African micro-state, a colonial leftover, surrounded by much larger French-speaking countries. Angola and Mozambique, by contrast, are two of the largest African states, and both were colonies of white settlement. The former, one of the richest on the continent, is more akin to its Congolese (formerly Zairean) neighbour than to any other Portuguese-speaking country. The latter, stretching a thousand miles along the Indian Ocean, has always been as deeply influenced by its English-speaking neighbours (from South Africa to Tanzania) as by its Portuguese heritage.

Nevertheless, these five countries are bound by a long colonial history, going back to the fifteenth century when the Portuguese first rounded the continent, and this cannot but have had a strong influence on key aspects of their development. Furthermore, Portuguese rule linked these territories in ways which affected their evolution. To cite but a few examples: Cape Verdeans settled in Guinea and played a significant part in the administration and economy of the mainland colony in the twentieth century; Angolans were brought to São Tomé e Príncipe to work on the cocoa and coffee plantations from the last quarter of the nineteenth century; Indians from Goa settled along the Zambesi in Mozambique from the sixteenth century.

Everywhere, the legacy of the Portuguese presence left an indelible, if at times elusive, mark on the lands and peoples that came to form their African empire. The difficulty lies, therefore, in assessing how significant that Portuguese legacy is to an understanding of the present condition of these five, vastly different, independent nation-states.

To meet that challenge, this book has employed an original and iconoclastic approach. It differs from most other accounts of Portuguese-speaking Africa in at least four ways.

First, it presents the history of these five countries from two, complementary, angles. Part I of the book offers three analytical and thematic chapters which analyse what these countries have in common and how they differ from the rest of Africa. Part II provides a systematic account of what has occurred since independence in five specific country chapters, using a range of scholarly, official, semi-official and journalistic sources. Together they give the most extensive and up-to-date assessment of the evolution of postcolonial Portuguese-speaking Africa.

Second, this volume is set within a firm historical context. Both parts of the book aim systematically to link the precolonial and colonial past with the postcolonial period. In this aspect, therefore, it differs from most accounts of modern Lusophone Africa, where the emphasis is primarily on explaining current events. This makes possible an assessment of the contemporary situation of the five countries which takes into account their very specific historical trajectory, and the past they share, as Portuguese colonies. It also helps to explain how their precolonial past influenced their present condition.

Third, the book is comparative in scope. The objective here is to overcome the narrow Lusophone focus which afflicts most accounts of Portuguese-speaking Africa. The first part of the volume is organised around questions which are relevant to the understanding of all postcolonial African nation-states and the analysis provided aims throughout to show how the evolution of the five countries resembles, or contrasts with, that of similar African states. It offers a discussion of Lusophone Africa which sets the development of these five countries within the relevant regional context—western, central or southern African. For their part, the authors of each country chapter have also made every effort to set the history of the individual state within the appropriate local, regional or African context.

Fourth, this book was from the start a collaborative effort. Although several of the contributors might well have been able to write a history of postcolonial Lusophone Africa single-handedly, it was felt that the combination of specific country expertise and general comparative analysis would result in a far more searching and stimulating volume. My co-authors wrote on their area of specialisation in the ways they felt best suited to the task at hand—hence the marked differences in approach, style, scope and method adopted. Yet I believe that this diversity is one of the great strengths of this book and will enable the reader to understand better what marks out the contemporary Lusophone African world.

The country chapters are self-contained and can be read separately. Equally, the three chapters (and nine sections) forming Part I can be read singly or together. However, the overall logic and organisation of the book are such that the country chapters will be best appreciated if read in the historical and comparative context offered in the first part of the volume. The period covered is 1975–2000.

PATRICK CHABAL

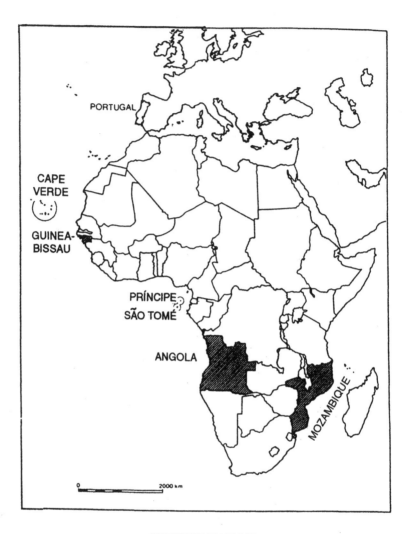

LUSOPHONE AFRICA

Part I

LUSOPHONE AFRICA IN HISTORICAL AND COMPARATIVE PERSPECTIVE

Patrick Chabal

1

THE END OF EMPIRE

COLONIAL WARS

'We, Portuguese military troops, who were sent to a war that we did not understand or support, have in our hands an unique opportunity to repair the crimes of fascism and colonialism, to set up the basis for a new and fraternal cooperation between the peoples of Portugal and Guinea if we are capable, at this late hour, of volunteering our disinterested collaboration [with the nationalists].'[1]

This statement, issued by Portuguese officers six weeks after the Movement of the Armed Forces (MFA) had overthrown the dictatorship in Lisbon (25 April 1974), illustrates both the contradictions and the futility of the colonial wars. It also helps to understand why the Portuguese regime was eventually overthrown by an army deeply politicised by their experience in the colonial wars.

Although there is understandable interest in the military aspects of the anti-colonial struggles in the three mainland African Portuguese colonies (Angola, Mozambique, Guinea), it is more useful to look at the wider picture for two reasons. The first is that there is as yet too little research both on the Portuguese colonial wars and on the colonial armies to present material comparable to what is available on the French, British or Dutch experiences. The second, and more important, justification for this broader approach is that, from the deeper historical perspective, the military and technical aspects of colonial wars are ultimately much less important than the political ones.

Discussing the colonial wars in Portuguese-speaking Africa is arduous for at least three reasons. First, because the Portuguese were involved in three colonial conflicts simultaneously: Angola (from 1961), Guinea (from

[1]Movimento das Forças Armadas (Guinea), 'Aos militares portugueses em serviço na Guinea', (Bissau, 5 June 1974).

3

1963) and Mozambique (from 1964). Even the most minimal account of these three conflicts requires more space than a volume of this nature affords. Second, military strategy in each colony was usually determined by complex local considerations which do not lend themselves to simple summary. Finally, and despite a resurgence of interest in this subject, we still lack both the historiography and the documentary evidence which would enable us to sharpen our analysis of the Portuguese colonial wars.[2] What follows, then, is a discussion of the nature of the anti-colonial wars in Portuguese-speaking Africa and some of the specific difficulties encountered by the Portuguese military in the prosecution of their counter-insurgency campaigns.

Who, then, were the nationalists challenging Portuguese colonial rule and why did they resort to violence? Taking the last question first, it is clear that the decision to launch armed action against the Portuguese in Angola, Guinea and Mozambique was practical rather than ideological. Indeed, the nationalist movements in these three colonies made it plain that they saw war as a last resort in the face of Portuguese intransigence and that they were prepared for a cease fire as soon as genuine discussions on independence were offered.[3] That the conflicts lasted so long is thus entirely due to the refusal of the Portuguese regime to contemplate negotiation towards decolonisation.

The nationalists in Portuguese-speaking Africa were similar in origin and outlook to their African peers. The singularities of the guerrilla wars in which they were involved are historically less significant for the understanding of their nationalism than the roots and political aims they shared with all other African nationalists.[4] What does matter, however, is that their anti-colonial struggle went on until 1974, at a time when most former British and French colonies had been independent for around a decade and a half. Hence, whilst the origins of Lusophone African nationalism were contemporaneous with those of the British, French or Belgian colonies, the endgame of decolonisation was played out in a very different African

[2]And this despite the recent publication of a book that focuses directly on the military aspects of the Portuguese counter-insurgency campaigns: John Cann, *Counterinsurgency in Africa: The Portuguese Way of War* (Westport CT: Greenwood, 1997). The book provides a mass of important details but it is based almost entirely on material issuing from the Portuguese military, thus affording a good summary of the metropolitan military view but not one as historically balanced as would be desirable.

[3]See here, for example, the documents published in the three volume collection: Aquino de Bragança and Immanuel Wallerstein, *Quem é o Inimigo?* (Lisbon: Iniciativas Editorais, 1978).

[4]A point which is obvious when reading, for example, the book written by the founder and first leader of the Mozambican anti-colonial front, FRELIMO: Eduardo Mondlane, *The Struggle for Mozambique* (Harmondsworth: Penguin, 1969).

and international context. There is in this way a huge time lag which can distort analysis and which it is important to take into account. For these reasons, and for reasons having to do with the specificities of Portugal as a colonial power, it is all too easy to over-emphasise or misread the so-called singularities of nationalism in Portuguese-speaking Africa.[5]

The fundamental divisions between the competing nationalists in Angola, Guinea and Mozambique were similar to those found in other African colonies at the time of decolonisation.[6] The anti-colonial movements fell into three broad categories: (1) the 'modernisers', imbued with an universalist political vision; (2) the 'traditionalists', attached to existing or imagined African socio-political realities and (3) the ethno-nationalists.[7] Here, again, these distinctions are useful for analytical purposes although in reality the boundaries between them were fluid and the extent to which they overlapped was significant. Nevertheless, they help us to map out the contours of nationalism in these three colonies and to place them in comparative African perspective.

Although there is no space here to discuss these three groups in detail, it is important to explain how they differed. The 'modernisers' were, for obvious historical reasons, those that mattered most for the colonial wars: in Angola the MPLA (Movimento para a Libertação de Angola); in Guinea the PAIGC (Partido Africano para a Independência da Guinea e Cabo Verde); and in Mozambique FRELIMO (Frente da Libertação de Moçambique). In their origins and outlook these 'modernisers' were similar in all African colonies.[8] They came from a younger generation, who were relatively well educated (often in the mother country), were assimilated or acculturated into the dominant colonial social and political 'mentalities', and were ideologically progressive, that is, in tune with the left opposition in the metropolis. Above all they were supra-ethnic nationalists. Their ambition was to fashion in Africa a modern secular nation-state on the (western or eastern) European model.[9]

---

[5]An argument which I develop further in chapter 2 of this volume.

[6]For a summary and comparative analysis of the main nationalist movements in Portuguese Africa see my *Amílcar Cabral: Revolutionary Leadership and People's War* (Cambridge University Press, 1983), chap. 7.

[7]I use these rubrics merely to distinguish, broadly, between these three groups and not because of any value judgement.

[8]Among some useful and critical books on these three movements see respectively, John Marcum, *The Angolan Revolution*, 2 vols (Cambridge MA: MIT Press, 1969); Thomas Henriksen, *Revolution and Counterrevolution: Mozambique's War of Independence, 1964–1974* (Westport CT: Greenwood Press, 1983); and *Amílcar Cabral*.

[9]For a discussion of nationalism which is relevant here see Ernest Gellner, *Nations and Nationalism* (Oxford: Blackwell, 1983).

The 'traditionalists' were, on the whole, less educated, less assimilated, less acculturated into the dominant colonial order. They remained more closely connected to the existing African socio-political order, either because they were of chiefly origin, had connections with chiefly networks or simply because their most important constituency was at the local level. As a result, they were often less urban oriented and more intimately linked with the rural world.[10] Their political discourse, though broadly anti-colonial, often emphasised the need to root the postcolonial nation-states into the 'traditions' of Africa. Their vision of independent Africa stressed the African rather than the modern or universal. Almost always they rejected socialism (as, often, all 'imported' ideologies) and they strongly distrusted the politics of the 'modernisers'.[11] Where these 'modernisers' were not black Africans, in that they included a mixture of *mestiços* (of mixed descent), Indians and whites, the 'traditionalists' questioned the legitimacy of their African and, by implication, nationalist claim.

In Mozambique and Guinea, the 'traditionalists'[12] were either co-opted into the 'moderniser' party (FRELIMO and PAIGC, respectively) or sidelined when they rejected nationalist union. Their original effectiveness as anti-colonial movements, largely due to their ability to operate freely in a neighbouring country, eroded as FRELIMO and the PAIGC asserted their nationalist credentials through political mobilisation and armed action. In these two colonies the relative success of FRELIMO and the PAIGC made it impossible for these 'traditionalist' rivals to establish themselves as credible nationalists. Their only recourse seems to have been to slide into ethno-nationalism.[13]

In Angola, the situation was more complex. The primary ethno-nationalist movement, the UPNA (União das Populações do Norte de Angola) was transformed into a 'traditionalist' nationalist party called FNLA (Frente Nacional para a Libertação de Angola) so as to compete with its chief 'moderniser' rival, the MPLA. However, the FNLA's weakness as a political

[10]Marcum's discussion on the FNLA (Frente Nacional para a Libertação de Angola) is here very revealing and probably relevant to all other similar groups.

[11]Some of their material can be read in a collection of nationalist material from Portuguese Africa published by Ronald Chilcote as *Emerging Nationalism in Portuguese Africa: Documents* (Stanford CA: Hoover Institution Press, 1972).

[12]The União Nacional Democrática de Moçambique (UDENAMO) and the Mozambique African National Union (MANU) from Mozambique, and the Frente de Luta pela Independência Nacional da Guiné (FLING) from Guinea.

[13]On Mozambique see Henriksen, *Revolution and Counterrevolution*, op. cit.; on Guinea see Ronald Chilcote, *Emerging Nationalism in Portuguese Africa: A Bibliography of Documentary Ephemera Through 1965* (Stanford CA: Hoover Institution Press, 1969).

movement, its enduring ethno-nationalist basis and the deleterious effect of exile politics on the party, all combined to weaken its effectiveness as an anti-colonialist front.[14] Although it had a well established political and military organisation in neighbouring Zaire, the FNLA never seriously engaged in armed action against the Portuguese nor did it try to establish 'liberated zones' inside the country. Its chief political aim seems to have been to wait for the time when the Portuguese would leave Angola. Its eventual defeat against the MPLA in the civil war which broke out in 1975 showed that it was too feeble to take over power by force.[15]

The deficiencies of the FNLA led in 1965 to the departure of its 'foreign minister,' Jonas Savimbi, who went on to found UNITA (União Nacional para a Independência Total de Angola), a more effective 'traditionalist' nationalist movement. UNITA, which was established in the heartland of Savimbi's own Ovimbundu country, sought from the beginning to create a political organisation rooted in the existing African socio-economic and political order. UNITA's nationalism was self-consciously the nationalism of the 'ordinary man and woman', embodying the desire of (mostly Ovimbundu) Africans to free themselves from colonial domination.[16]

Although in the early years Savimbi's need for foreign support led him to espouse a so-called 'Maoist' position, UNITA's politics were essentially anti-MPLA and above all pragmatic.[17] Savimbi, who has shown himself a shrewd politician as well as a capable military strategist, understood early that his most profitable course of action was to establish his 'African' legitimacy in Angola, to oppose the 'Marxist' and cosmopolitan (read: 'non-black') MPLA leadership and to get outside support wherever he could (from China to South Africa, including the USA). In Angola, then, the conflict between the MPLA and UNITA, which is still raging today, epitomises the political hostility between 'modernisers' and 'traditionalists' in Portuguese-speaking Africa. It parallels similar rivalries in other parts of black Africa, as it does in some sense the long history of tension in South Africa between the 'moderniser' ANC and the 'traditionalist' Inkatha.

The story about the ethno-nationalists is simpler since, at heart, their project in the transition of colonial Africa into independence was not viable. This is because there was a very broad consensus between the colonial powers and the nationalists that postcolonial Africa should be composed

[14]See Marcum, op. cit., vol. 1.

[15]Here see Marcum, op. cit., vol. 2.

[16]On the UNITA leader read here, among others, Fred Bridgland, *Jonas Savimbi: A Key to Africa* (Edinburgh: Mainstream Publishing, 1986).

[17]See here Marcum, op. cit., vol. 2.

of independent nation-states based on existing colonial boundaries.[18] The ethno-nationalist movements, therefore, recast their original claim to speak for one local group to a claim to speak for all.[19] Their attempt to do so, whether in Lusophone Africa or elsewhere, usually proved fruitless. The failure of ethno-nationalist movements during decolonisation, however, did not preclude their rebirth after independence as local (and sometimes even national) political forces.[20]

Although most anti-colonial movements resorted at some stage to violence, only the PAIGC, the MPLA and FRELIMO were able to organise, launch and sustain viable anti-colonial struggles—or at least relatively effective armed action.[21] UNITA, for its part, was able to use guerrilla warfare as a means, first, of establishing nationalist credibility and, after independence, of maintaining a plausible political challenge to the MPLA government. For this reason, the discussion below focuses on an assessment of the success of these three 'moderniser' movements. As there is ambiguity in the very notion of 'nationalist success', a few remarks may be appropriate at this stage. [22]

The nationalist wars in Lusophone Africa were primarily political conflicts. However protracted and sophisticated the actual military operations were, their ultimate aim was to force the colonial power to grant independence. Therefore, the appropriateness and effectiveness of anti-colonial military activity can only be judged in terms of the political results it achieved, namely, whether armed action made decolonisation on the nationalist terms more or less likely. It is thus meaningless to judge the success of the Lusophone nationalists' military campaigns in Guinea, Mozambique and Angola merely according to whether they were capable, or indeed ever likely, to inflict military defeat on the Portuguese armed forces—as, for example, the Vietnamese did against the French in Dien Bien Phu.[23]

---

[18]The most severe test of this consensus was the decolonisation of the Belgian Congo where United Nations intervention was used to maintain territorial integrity. See here Crawford Young, *Politics in the Congo* (Princeton University Press, 1965).

[19]See Marcum, op. cit., vol. 1 on the trajectory of the UPNA as it became the FNLA.

[20]Since independence, a number of different separatist political movements (e.g. in Sudan, Western Sahara, Chad, Somalia, Ethiopia) have resorted to armed action with some success.

[21]On other forms of anti-colonial struggles in Africa see Basil Davidson, *The People's Cause* (London: Longman, 1981).

[22]Here I draw from my 'People's war, state formation and revolution in Africa: a comparative analysis of Mozambique, Guinea-Bissau and Angola' in Nelson Kasfir (ed.), *State and Class in Africa* (London: Cass, 1984).

[23]Even here, the French gave up in Vietnam more for domestic political reasons than because they had been undone in Dien Bien Phu, although the psychological and political impact of that defeat in France cannot be underestimated.

Given the eminently political nature of these wars, it is possible to suggest some criteria to assess the efficacy of the anti-colonial struggle. They are (1) the extent to which nationalist unity was achieved and maintained; (2) the ability to mobilise the rural populations politically; (3) the degree to which armed action was profitably subordinated to political objectives; (4) the ability to defend the so-called liberated areas from counter-insurgency campaigns and (5) the capacity of the nationalists to use diplomacy to secure international (particularly United Nations) and, even, metropolitan support. Judged thus, it is possible to say that the Guinean nationalists were the most, and the Angolan the least, successful, with the Mozambican falling somewhere in between. Why was this?

The PAIGC was the most accomplished of the Lusophone anti-colonial movements primarily because it performed best on all of the above criteria. In particular, they were effectively able to maintain unity not only between different Guinean ethnic groups but also between Guineans and Cape Verdeans. They were adept at political mobilisation, managing to gain support in most of the country and to protect the liberated areas.[24] But above all, the PAIGC was outstandingly successful diplomatically.[25] The holding of its first national elections in 1972, following a UN mission into the liberated areas which upheld the party's claims, made possible a unilateral declaration of independence in September 1973 which was immediately recognised by a large number of countries. This in turn meant that, after 25 April 1974, the new Portuguese regime was prepared quickly to acknowledge the PAIGC's demand to lead an independent Guinea-Bissau and to form the transitional government in Cape Verde.

To be sure, the odds against nationalist progress in Angola and Mozambique were far greater—given the size and socio-economic complexities of the two colonies. Nevertheless, what happened there can also largely be explained in terms of clear political factors. In Mozambique, FRELIMO's early difficulties and its later achievements can be accounted for in terms of the extent to which it made progress on those five fronts.[26] Conversely, the failure to achieve nationalist agreement in Angola (which led eventually to a three-party civil war) was seriously detrimental to the anti-colonial struggle. Since anti-colonial unity was not objectively and inherently more difficult to achieve in Angola than in Mozambique, one

[24]See here Lars Rudebeck, *Guinea-Bissau: A Study of Political Mobilization* (Uppsala: Scandinavian Institute of African Studies, 1974).

[25]Here Cabral's role was fundamental, as I argue in *Amílcar Cabral*.

[26]For an account sympathetic to FRELIMO see Barry Munslow, *Mozambique: The Revolution and its Origins* (London: Longman, 1983).

must conclude that the Angolan crisis was largely the outcome of political failure.[27]

The establishment and maintenance of anti-colonial unity in Mozambique but not in Angola, made it possible for FRELIMO and impossible for the MPLA successfully to follow the 'Guinea model' of nationalist war[28] — that is, a successful campaign of political mobilisation before the beginning of armed action, allied with the ability to establish and protect 'liberated zones' and conduct a systematic diplomatic offensive internationally. Although by 1974 FRELIMO had not progressed as much as the PAIGC, it is likely that, despite the enormous difficulties posed by the large settler population, it would eventually have been in a position politically to challenge the hold of the colonial state.[29] The same, however, was not likely to occur in Angola where, in the absence of nationalist concord, the legitimacy of any one of the three nationalist movements could never fully prevail.

While it is true that in Angola only the MPLA sought to engage in a campaign of armed struggle along the lines pursued by the PAIGC and FRELIMO, its effectiveness as a movement of national liberation was seriously hampered by the factors which made unity impossible.[30] For reasons largely connected with the FNLA presence in northern Angola and in neighbouring Zaire, the MPLA could develop the armed struggle only in the Cabinda enclave and in eastern Angola. The relative success of its campaign, at least until 1970, can be explained by the ability of the MPLA to conduct a war on the 'Guinea model'.[31] But the situation in the field remained precariously balanced and the MPLA never seriously challenged the Portuguese either in the highlands or near the western seaboard.

Between 1970 and 1974 the Portuguese launched intensive counter-insurgency campaigns in the three colonies.[32] In all three they had initial

---

[27]For a defence of this argument see my article 'Un regard historique sur le devenir de l'Afrique Lusophone Australe' in Dominique Darbon (ed.), *Afrique du Sud. Les Enjeux de l'Après Mandela* (Paris: Karthala, 1999).

[28]What I call the 'Guinea model', again as a convenient peg, is the strategy of national liberation elaborated and put into practice in Guinea under Cabral's leadership as I explain in *Amílcar Cabral*.

[29]For a critical assessment of FRELIMO's potential see Henriksen, op. cit.

[30]One of the most revealing documents about the MPLA's armed struggle is the novel *Mayombe* written by the Angolan writer Pepetela. What makes this book extraordinary is not just that Pepetela was himself a guerrilla fighter in the Cabinda region where the novel is set but that he was able to discuss openly the most sensitive issues related to the MPLA's difficulties as a guerrilla army.

[31]For a sympathetic eyewitness account of armed struggle in the East see Basil Davidson, *In the Eye of the Storm* (Garden City NJ: Doubleday, 1972).

[32]On the thinking behind Portuguese military strategy it is instructive to read Escola

military success primarily due to the vigour of helicopter-borne assaults. In Guinea (and to a lesser extent in Mozambique), the nationalists were able to adapt and to counter the threat of these attacks.[33] They did this in two ways. First, they developed means to protect the population who supported them, essentially through effective anti-aircraft defence (including, eventually, ground-to-air missiles). Second, they intensified and diversified armed action against the Portuguese thus stretching their air and ground resources. This was achieved with most success in Guinea where, by 1974, the Portuguese virtually ceased to be able to use their air force for offensive operational purposes and even found it difficult to supply their outlying posts. Even in Mozambique, where the Portuguese campaign (the so-called Gordian Knot operation) was massive, FRELIMO eventually managed to regain the military initiative.[34]

In Angola, however, the precariousness of the MPLA's position was revealed by the Portuguese counter-insurgency campaign. And, again, the reasons why counter-insurgency was more successful and had more profound consequences in Angola than in Guinea or Mozambique are primarily to be found in the MPLA's political frailty. Ultimately, the serious military reversals which the MPLA suffered in eastern Angola led to increasingly acute internal divisions within the party (culminating, between 1972–4, in the Chipenda breakaway movement and the so-called Active Revolt) which nearly proved fatal.[35] Why?

There were three reasons for the MPLA's political fragility. The first had to do with the excessive gap between the external and internal leadership. The second concerned divisions within the leadership about the very nature of the armed struggle. The third was an excessive emphasis on 'correct' ideology at the expense of formulating a political strategy more appropriate to the conditions of the struggle. The result was that, unlike the PAIGC or FRELIMO, the MPLA was never able consistently to define, develop and implement a strategy of armed action in consonance with the experience gained in the field by its guerrillas. In turn, the guerrillas felt a lack of (political) support from the party leadership. This reduced confidence and

Práctica de Administração Militar, Secção Tecnica, *Táctica Guerra Subversiva*, 2 vols (Lisbon, 1966). See also John Cann, op. cit.

[33]For one interesting example of guerrilla organisation against helicopter attacks see Amílcar Cabral, 'Para o desenvolvimento da nossa luta contra os helicopteros' (Conakry: PAIGC, mimeo, June 1967).

[34]For a Portuguese viewpoint on the operation see the assessment by the Portuguese commanding officer in Mozambique, General Kaúlza de Arriaga in his *Coragem, Tenacidade e Fé* (Lourenço Marques: Empresa Moderna, 1973).

[35]See Marcum, op. cit., vol. 2.

induced a sense of vulnerability which was readily exploited by the Portuguese and which planted doubt in the minds of the population about the present strength and the future potential of the MPLA.

The party leadership seemed more preoccupied with holding on to power than making the ideological, political and policy compromises which might well have brought its armed struggle more success. Internal disunity continued to prevail. Consequently, when after April 1974, the Portuguese sought to negotiate the modalities of Angola's decolonisation, the MPLA was forced to concede parity with its two nationalist rivals, UNITA and the FNLA. The fact that the MPLA had been more successful in its military campaign against the Portuguese than UNITA and the FNLA put together was in the end not sufficient to counter the claim that its nationalist legitimacy was no greater than that of the other two parties.

Seen from the perspective of the Portuguese military, the colonial wars raise two sets of questions. First, what were the military constraints on the Portuguese armed forces and what were the main counter-insurgency measures taken over the years? Second, what were the political considerations which impinged most strongly on the course and ultimate outcome of the colonial wars?

Once it became clear that violence in Portuguese Africa was no mere disturbance but the beginning of anti-colonial campaigns, the Portuguese had to devise a counter-insurgency strategy. Whilst their immediate priority was to contain the initial violence unleashed by the nationalists, particularly in Angola, their overall concern was to put in place a military infrastructure to counter any future nationalist armed action. In this task they faced great difficulties.[36] The Portuguese armed forces, integrated as they were within NATO, were not trained for colonial wars. They now had to operate militarily in three different theatres separated by huge distances. The number of troops needed to guarantee the minimum viable deterrent force in the three territories was high. The transport capabilities required to ferry, equip, supply and service these troops were on a scale for which the Portuguese were not prepared. Nor, it must be emphasised, were the Portuguese armed forces combat hardened or even combat ready. Except for the minor and almost farcical episode of the Portuguese surrender to Indian forces in Goa in 1961, the army had not fired a shot in anger since the First World War.

There were thus three serious constraints to the development of effective counter-insurgency. The first was the lack of combat experience, particularly in conflicts of this nature. The second was the limited material resources at the disposal of a military suddenly committed to deploy its forces so far

---

[36]For a systematic discussion of these issues see Cann, op. cit.

from the metropolis. The third was the small size of the Portuguese armed forces, that is the lack of military personnel to mount effective military campaigns in the three African colonies. In retrospect, and perhaps paradoxically, it is clear that of the three, the last was the most significant. While the Portuguese high command was able eventually to devise relatively effective counter-insurgency measures and while they also managed to secure the military hardware which they needed, they could never satisfactorily resolve the question of the shortage of properly trained manpower. Indeed, it is this very problem which contributed most significantly to the failure of the Portuguese to 'defeat' the nationalists. And, as I explain below, it is this factor which helped bring about the Movimento das Forças Armadas (MFA) that restored democracy to Portugal on 25 April 1974.

Like other colonial armies faced with similar problems, the Portuguese developed their counter-insurgency campaigns according to well-defined criteria.[37] First, they improved the colonies' basic infrastructure, laying tarred roads (more difficult to mine) and constructed regional airfields. Second, they put together a string of fortified positions and set up 'free-fire' zones, cleared of population, as barriers to guerrilla infiltration. Third, they sought to cut off the guerrillas from their support bases by regrouping and controlling the African population inside the so-called *aldeamentos*, or strategic hamlets. Fourth, they shifted increasingly to airborne operations and to bombing raids against areas known to be sympathetic to the guerrillas. Finally, and most importantly, they set out to 'Africanise' their colonial wars, that is to recruit African troops.

It is not possible here to discuss these counter-insurgency measures in any detail except to say that, on the whole, the Portuguese never had the resources to maximise their effectiveness. Even in the very small colony of Guinea, a territory roughly the size of Belgium, they failed to contain the nationalist surge and found themselves in 1974, confined to a few fortified positions and the main cities. By that year, the PAIGC's increasingly successful use of anti-aircraft weapons (including ground-to-air missiles) had effectively neutralised Portuguese air superiority. That the Portuguese were more capable of countering the guerrillas in Mozambique and especially in Angola was due to nationalist weakness rather than counter-insurgency tactics. Both territories were huge and stretched the guerrilla supply lines enormously. In Angola, the Portuguese were able to regain the upper hand in the early seventies primarily because of the internal divisions among the nationalists. In Mozambique, however, this was not the case.

---

[37]The Portuguese high command knew about the counter-insurgency tactics used by the French in Vietnam and Algeria, the British in Malaya and Kenya and the United States in Vietnam.

Although the FRELIMO advance was very slow and, by 1974, had not yet seriously threatened the southern half of the country, Portuguese counter-insurgency measures had not managed to halt their progress.

After 1974, some Portuguese army generals, perhaps not surprisingly, argued that the colonial wars could have been 'won' had the government been prepared to allocate to them the necessary resources. This is very unlikely for at least two sets of reasons, above and beyond the fact that in the long run all colonial wars are lost. First, the armed forces were not, and could never have been, in a position to deploy the number of troops on the ground that a successful counter-insurgency campaign would have required. Second, the Portuguese troops eventually lost belief in their colonial 'mission', thus turning on themselves before sweeping the politicians from power.

The shortage of military personnel was critical. Although by the end of the war the Portuguese claimed that over half of all colonial troops were 'Africanised', the total numbers available for deployment in each colony was still far from sufficient.[38] While on paper it seemed simple enough to use African troops for frontline action, in practice such a policy was often fraught with danger. Most were not trained to the standards required for aggressive counter-insurgency. Those who were, like the Flechas, could (as the Selous Scouts in Rhodesia) be highly effective in search and destroy missions. But they suffered a relatively high rate of casualty. Furthermore, the degree of violence they inflicted against civilians (not least because of a *de facto* policy of 'no prisoners') often made them a liability in any campaign to regain 'the hearts and minds' of the local population.

The Portuguese armed forces were also weakened by the fact that the bulk of the metropolitan troops was made up of young Portuguese conscripts, drafted originally for two years but often serving for up to four. As the French found in Algeria and the Americans in Vietnam, the use of conscript troops in colonial anti-guerrilla warfare is undesirable, when not totally counter-productive. And so it proved for the Portuguese. By the early seventies, most conscript soldiers were disillusioned and unwilling to take risks. Since the success of counter-insurgency on the ground largely depends

---

[38]In the absence of reliable official figures, the secondary information available would indicate that by 1974 the Portuguese claimed the following number of troops: in Guinea, around 25,000 African and 33,000 European facing about 6,000 PAIGC guerrillas; in Mozambique, around 40,000 African and 20,000 European troops against roughly 10,000 FRELIMO fighters while in Angola they claimed 30,000 African and around 40,000 European soldiers pitted against around 4,500 MPLA fighters and a notional (and seldom hostile) 1,500 FNLA and UNITA guerrillas. See Douglas Wheeler, 'African elements in Portugal's armies in Africa', *Armed Forces and Society*, 2, 2 (1974), pp. 236–8. For more detailed background information see also Cann, op. cit.

on the effectiveness of infantry patrols, such low morale is highly inimical to anti-guerrilla warfare.

The shortage of military personnel became even more critical when it began to affect operational middle-ranking officers. However many conscripts the Portuguese could draft and however many African troops they could muster, the effectiveness of their armed forces depended ultimately on the quality of the officer corps. And in the end, the Portuguese simply did not have enough middle-ranking officers of the necessary professional calibre and operational experience.[39] This shortage of officers not only affected Portuguese counter-insurgency efforts, it eventually struck at the heart of the relationship between military and government. Indeed, the creation of the MFA in Portugal was precipitated by specific grievances within the officer corps. In July 1973, the government, in a desperate effort to increase the number of officers, passed a decree giving non-career officers with combat experience in Africa the possibility of obtaining commissions with the rank, pay and privilege to match those of professional officers. The outcry which followed forced the government to back down but the damage had been done and the MFA, now mindful of the futility of further war, went on to organise the coup which toppled the regime.

What, in the end, were the political considerations which impinged most strongly on the course of these colonial wars? Confronted, as they were, by low intensity guerrilla warfare in Africa, the Portuguese sought at first to contain what they viewed as mere 'emergencies'. Eventually, however, they came to realise that the conflicts in which they were engaged were primarily political and would require practical measures. In the early years of the colonial wars the Portuguese sought to improve political, social and economic conditions in the colonies so as to undermine the anti-colonial campaigns. The initiatives taken over time included: (1) giving a greater voice to 'indigenous' peoples on the various colonial consultative councils; (2) efforts to improve the quality of life in the colonies (particularly in the fields of health and education); (3) the provision of incentives to encourage white settlement in Angola and Mozambique; (4) the opening up of the colonies to foreign investment; (5) the forging of economic and strategic alliances with the two white-minority regimes of South Africa and Rhodesia;[40]

---

[39] While the number of class openings in the Military Academy (Lisbon) doubled between 1961–2 and 1971–2, the number of cadets admitted dropped by 300 per cent (from 257 in 1961–2 to only 88 in 1973–4). At the time of the April coup, over 400 places were left unfilled. The number of cadets competing for places also dropped from 559 in 1962–3 to 155 in 1973–4. Wheeler, loc. cit., p. 248.

[40] As is best illustrated by the construction of the Cabora Bassa dam on the Zambesi river, largely financed by foreign capital and intended to provide electricity to South Africa.

and (6) attempts to cultivate the support of those segments of the African population known to be hostile to the nationalists.

Some of these initiatives were successful, particularly in Angola and Mozambique where the sixties saw impressive economic growth and significant industrial progress. In Angola, the Portuguese were cleverly able to play on political enmity between the three nationalist movements ensuring, for example, that both the FNLA and UNITA would fight the MPLA rather than colonial troops. The counter-insurgency campaign undertaken in the early seventies could technically be counted a success. In Mozambique, however, the situation was more complex. The Portuguese did manage to seduce some FRELIMO dissidents but their much trumpeted Gordian Knot counter-insurgency drive had only transient effect. FRELIMO soon counter-acted the Portuguese military gains and opened new fronts in the centre of the country. Despite the claims of the Portuguese military commander, General Kaúlza de Arriaga, the colony of Mozambique could not be considered secured either politically or militarily.

But it was the situation in Guinea which exposed the weaknesses of Portuguese colonial policies, for it was there that the military realised both that the wars could never be won by force and that the Portuguese government would eventually have to negotiate with the nationalists. In Guinea, the Portuguese witnessed the limitations of their political campaign (the so-called 'Better Guinea' programme introduced by General António de Spínola), the failure of their effort to divide the nationalist movement between Cape Verdeans and Guineans[41] and, finally, the inadequacy of military counter-insurgency. It was in Guinea that General Spínola, one of Portugal's most senior and conservative military leaders, formulated the ideas later published in his explosive book *Portugal and the Future* about the need to find a negotiated political solution to the colonial wars. It was Spínola who, against the wishes of his own government, initiated secret talks with the PAIGC with a view to trying to settle the conflict in Guinea. It was Spínola too who was eventually to agree to take command of the 25 April 1974 coup and set in motion (though not to see through) the process of decolonisation.

As Colonel Carlos Fabião, military governor of Guinea after 25 April 1974, said, political consciousness was highest among those officers who had been posted in Guinea. 'The longer a subversive war lasts,' he added, 'the more one assimilates the ideas of the enemy, that is the oppressed.'[42]

---

[41]Which resulted in Amílcar Cabral's death following an attempt by Portuguese commandos to kidnap the PAIGC leadership in their headquarters in Conakry.

[42]Chabal, *Amílcar Cabral*, op. cit., p. 149.

DECOLONISATION IN HISTORICAL PERSPECTIVE

The decolonisation of Portuguese-speaking Africa stands out primarily because it was the outcome of two inter-related historical processes: protracted anti-colonial wars in three of the five Portuguese colonies; the overthrow of the Salazar-Caetano dictatorship and the transition to democratic rule in Portugal. The date 25 April 1974 thus not only marks the Portuguese revolution 'of the carnations' but also, in effect, the beginning of the transfer of power in the Portuguese African colonies. The aim here is neither to give an account of the end of the nationalist wars in Angola, Guinea and Mozambique nor to provide a chronology of the events that led to decolonisation,[43] but to ask some questions about the relationship between the dynamics of national liberation as it unravelled in Lusophone Africa and the politics of the postcolonial period which followed.[44]

First, how causally significant were the specificities of Portuguese Africa in the evolution of the nationalism which developed there? Second, what were the consequences for Angolan, Guinean and Mozambican nationalism of the experience of armed struggle? Third, how does one assess the importance of the 'socialist' or 'revolutionary' nationalist ideology propounded by the three nationalist parties? Finally, what is the relevance of this historical experience to the contemporary predicament of the Portuguese-speaking countries of Africa?

Although the focus here will primarily be on Angola, Mozambique and Guinea—the three mainland colonies where armed struggle took place—most of the analysis is also pertinent to a better understanding of the political evolution of the two island states—Cape Verde and São Tomé e Príncipe. This is so not just because the five parties which took power at independence had been linked within a common organisation, the Conferência das Organizações Nacionalistas das Colonias Portuguesas (CONCP), but also because their political outlook was very similar. Indeed, the PAIGC formed the government in both Guinea-Bissau and Cape Verde, while the Movimento de Libertação de São Tomé e Príncipe (MLSTP) came strongly under the influence of the MPLA.

A review of the literature on the end of the Portuguese empire in Africa would show that, for a number of historical reasons, Portuguese decolonisation has tended to be viewed through particularistic eyes. First,

---

[43]Issues to be discussed in the country chapters below.
[44]The most complete account of the decolonisation of Portuguese-speaking Africa is to be found in Norrie McQueen, *The Decolonization of Portuguese Africa: Metropolitan Revolution and the Dissolution of Empire* (London: Longman, 1997).

and perhaps most important, is that it took place a good fifteen years after the end of colonial rule in the French and British territories. By then, Africans and Africanists alike had a different perception of the realities of African independences. Portuguese decolonisation occurred against the background of an attempt to understand the growing problems of postcolonial Africa. This influenced the analysis of Portuguese decolonisation as well as the expectations of what postcolonial Lusophone Africa might become. In particular, it generated the hope that the new Lusophone regimes would avoid the pitfalls of their predecessors.

Secondly, decolonisation was brought about largely as a result of a struggle for national liberation which took the form of a guerrilla war in three of the five Portuguese colonies. Although there had been in Algeria one precedent for such an anti-colonial war and although there had been in black Africa instances of nationalist violence (for example, Cameroon, Kenya and Congo), the Lusophone experience of armed struggle was essentially new.[45] As such it called forth a different analysis of the process of decolonisation. It thus attracted the attention of a number of observers with greater interest in the process of the armed struggle than in the more complex realities of African history.

Thirdly, the decolonisation of the Portuguese territories went hand in hand with the nationalists' commitment to Marxism. This adherence to a policy of 'transition to socialism' took place against the background of an Africa where the first wave of so-called socialist experiments was recognised to have failed.[46] It also occurred at a time when socialism worldwide was entering a crisis from which, we now know, it was never to come out. Because of this, and because Portuguese-speaking Africa had achieved independence through people's wars, it was often seen as the last great hope of Third World 'socialism'.[47] As such, it attracted the attention of analysts more interested in the fate of socialism than in that of Africa.

Finally, the decolonisation of Portuguese Africa came intimately to be linked with the demise of the dictatorship in metropolitan Portugal. Quite clearly, the impetus for, and the political orientation of, the coup which eventually toppled the Salazar-Caetano regime owed much to the involve-

---

[45]For an insight into the differences between the Lusophone cases and some of the others compare Chabal, 'People's war, state formation and revolution in Africa', op. cit. with, for instance, a good study of one of these cases: Richard Joseph, *Radical Nationalism in Cameroun* (Oxford University Press, 1977).

[46]On the first wave of 'socialism' see Carl Rosberg and Thomas Callaghy (eds), *Socialism in sub-Saharan Africa* (Berkeley CA: Institute of International Studies, 1979).

[47]On the concept of people's war see Chabal, *Amílcar Cabral*, op. cit.

ment of the military in the African nationalist wars.[48] Hence, the history of Portugal's march to democracy is inextricably connected with that of the decolonisation of its African empire.[49] As a result, Portuguese decolonisation has attracted attention from historians more interested in Portuguese than African history.

Though all the factors mentioned above are important, it is perhaps the import of the 'socialist' perspective on Lusophone Africa that has most influenced the analysis of its decolonisation.[50] It virtually imposed an approach which not only took for granted the reality of Third World socialism but also assumed the feasibility of a 'revolutionary transition' in Portuguese-speaking Africa.[51] It had two constituent parts. The first considered the Portuguese-speaking countries from the perspective of those other countries (Russia, China, Vietnam, Cuba) where nationalism and revolution had combined to bring about a new 'socialist' order. The second deduced the viability of the 'transition to socialism' from the nature of the anti-colonial war. It established an historical causation between the development of people's wars proclaiming a 'Marxist' ideology in the former Portuguese colonies and the construction of a 'socialist' postcolonial order.[52]

While both perspectives had powerful historical and ideological roots, they both failed to ground their respective analysis in the realities of twentieth-century colonial and postcolonial Africa. Instead of studying the process by which these colonial struggles were adapted (more or less successfully) to an African setting, they read into them a revolutionary potential. Because the anti-colonial wars in Portuguese Africa had, as people's wars, strong resonance with those of China, Vietnam and Algeria, they were also taken necessarily to be pregnant with a 'revolutionary' future. Moreover, they were seen to presage a 'transition to socialism' not just in Angola, Guinea and Mozambique but also in Cape Verde and São Tomé e Príncipe, two countries otherwise totally distinct historically, socially, economically, politically and culturally.

---

[48]On the history of that period see McQueen, op. cit., and, among others, Richard Robinson, *Contemporary Portugal* (London: Allen and Unwin, 1979).

[49]Much as the Algerian war is linked with the transition from the Fourth to the Fifth Republic in France.

[50]On this approach see Patrick Chabal, *Power in Africa* (London: Macmillan, 1994), chap. 1, sect. 4.

[51]See as one example of this approach, James Mittelman, *Underdevelopment and the Transition to Socialism* (New York: Academic Press, 1981).

[52]I develop this argument in 'People's war, state formation and revolution in Africa', op. cit.

It is true that the process of the Lusophone people's wars was largely new to black Africa and that it did echo guerrilla struggles elsewhere. Yet, despite the apparent ideological commitment of the nationalist leaders, the context within which the Lusophone anti-colonial struggle took place made it improbable that it could ever engender full-fledged revolutions. There were no historical, structural or socio-economic reasons to expect in black Africa (except perhaps in 'feudal' Ethiopia) socio-economic and political change in the mould of the French, Russian, Chinese or even Vietnamese revolutions.[53] Thus, it was always highly unlikely that the Lusophone anti-colonial wars would bring about any 'transition to socialism', least of all on the Russian, Chinese, Vietnamese or even Cuban model.

While it is understandable why historians have tended to highlight the specificities of Lusophone Africa, a proper comparative understanding of its decolonisation demands that we re-anchor the study of the Portuguese-speaking countries into their proper African historical context.[54] We need to re-assess the ways in which the experience of armed struggle shaped the fate of independent Angola, Guinea and Mozambique within the general experience of postcolonial Africa. This in turn will help us approach the history of the two island states from a more realistic perspective. There are three areas which can help both to understand the history of the Lusophone countries and to compare their postcolonial evolution with that of the rest of Africa. First, how did the nationalist struggle affect the consolidation of national unity and the construction of the nation-state after independence? Second, what effect did the war have on the societies most directly affected by it? Third, how did the agendas of 'revolutionary' nationalism work themselves out in the policies of the postcolonial governments?

National unity and the nation-state

It has often been argued that the process of political mobilisation underpinning the anti-colonial struggle was conducive to greater nationalist unity and to a firmer sense of national identity. Where the affirmation of nationalism had to be defended by an armed struggle, it is claimed, unity must have rested on more secure foundations than were usually found in black Africa. Equally, since progress in the armed struggle depended on maintaining a united front against a colonial power seeking to divide, the war was bound to bring about a deeper sense of national unity than that generated by mere electoral politics.

This is true as far as it goes. Certainly, in Guinea the PAIGC's success

---

[53]See here John Dunn, *Modern Revolutions* (Cambridge University Press, 1972).
[54]This argument is one of the main themes of *Power in Africa*, op. cit.

was largely predicated on Cabral's ability to bring together not just most of Guinea's peoples but also Guineans with Cape Verdeans.[55] By contrast, in Angola, where nationalist unity was weakest, the achievements of the armed struggle were the most limited.[56] The question is, however, one of causality. Did the strategy of armed struggle make national unity more or less likely? Did the war bring about a more assured sense of nationhood?

In Guinea, nationalist unity, although not complete (the Fulas remained largely on the sideline) was both wide and enduring. During the period of the anti-colonial struggle the PAIGC brought together most of Guinea's peoples and integrated them into a party largely led by Cape Verdeans, despite an historically grounded distrust by Guineans of Cape Verdeans.[57] This unity survived the assassination of Amílcar Cabral in January 1973 which itself was the outcome of the attempt by the Portuguese to split Guineans from Cape Verdeans within the PAIGC.[58] Thus, Guinea, a territory only poorly integrated by colonialism, reached independence united and with a sense of nationhood.[59] It has since consolidated as a nation-state and does not at the moment face any serious crisis of national identity. Even the recent murderous civil conflict, pitting President Nino Vieira against his erstwhile minister Ansumane Mané did not rest on ethnic division and has not seriously threatened the national integrity of the country.

Angola and Mozambique, the two huge southern African Portuguese colonies, shared many common attributes and yet developed quite differently in respect of national unity.[60] Both were colonies of white settlement, both had substantial racial minorities (*mestiços*, Indians) who played a considerable role in the social and economic life of the colonies. Both had important links with neighbouring countries (Angola with the Belgian Congo/Zaire; Mozambique with Rhodesia and South Africa). Both, finally, had potential for nationalist disunity. Yet, the Mozambican nationalists under Eduardo Mondlane's leadership managed to bring together the three main nationalist constituencies into FRELIMO, to

[55]For a debate around my book on Cabral, see *Politique Africaine*, 19 (1985), pp. 95–117.

[56]See Marcum, op. cit.

[57]For a somewhat more critical view, see Rosemary Galli and Jocelyn Jones, *Guinea-Bissau* (London: Pinter, 1987).

[58]On the assassination, see Chabal *Amílcar Cabral*, op. cit., pp. 132–43.

[59]This unity survived into independence despite all the political problems faced by the country. For an analysis of the postcolonial period to 1986, including the 1980 coup and the break between Guinea-Bissau and Cape Verde, see Patrick Chabal, 'Revolutionary democracy in Africa: the case of Guinea-Bissau' in Patrick Chabal, *Political Domination in Africa* (Cambridge University Press, 1986).

[60]A useful (though purposely partial) comparative survey of Angola and Mozambique is David Birmingham, *Frontline Nationalism in Angola and Mozambique* (London: James Currey, 1992).

consolidate nationalist unity and to resist all subsequent fissiparous tendencies.[61] In Angola, on the other hand, not only did the two original nationalist constituencies (Luanda-based and Congo) develop two rival organisations (respectively the MPLA and the FNLA) but they failed to prevent the creation of a third, UNITA, rooted in central Angola and (originally at least) largely supported by the highlands Ovimbundu peoples.[62]

Why were there such disparities between the three cases? And how relevant was the fact of armed struggle to the issue? Despite the differing complexities of the three experiences, both the success of the armed struggle and the consolidation of nationalist unity were ultimately determined largely by the political skills of the nationalist leadership. It was political agency rather than contingency which made possible the bringing together of various ethnic and/or racial groups into one unified movement capable of developing a campaign of armed struggle against the Portuguese. The effectiveness of the anti-colonial war was thus a consequence (and not a cause) of nationalist unity. In turn, nationalist unity made the construction of nationhood more plausible, if not always easier.[63]

Where nationalist politics were predicated on divisions (as in Angola), the construction of the independent nation-state has been difficult and violent.[64] Where, on the other hand, the nationalists built on more secure foundations (as in Guinea), the consolidation of unity has been easier and deeper. In the Lusophone countries, as elsewhere in Africa, nationalism thus contributed both to the invention of a sense of national unity and to the exacerbation (or even the creation) of a number of divisions within the new nation-state. War in this respect was thus no more than the continuation of (nationalist) politics by other means. The extent to which armed struggle strengthened national unity and contributed to the consolidation of the nation-state was the result of the politics of the anti-colonial war(s). As in all African countries, the roots of unity or disunity are largely to be found in the long precolonial and colonial history of these nations rather than merely in the vagaries of nationalism. Or rather, the vagaries of the anti-colonial wars are themselves best understood in the longer perspective of precolonial and colonial history.[65]

---

[61]See the account of the difficulties in achieving nationalist unity given by Eduardo Mondlane, the FRELIMO's founding father, in his *The Struggle for Mozambique* (Harmondsworth: Penguin African Library, 1969).

[62]See Marcum, op. cit.

[63]On the construction of the postcolonial nation-state see *Power in Africa*, op. cit., chap. 7.

[64]For the general argument as it applies to Africa see ibid., chap. 11.

[65]As is perhaps best illustrated in Malyn Newitt, *A History of Mozambique* (London: Hurst & Co. 1995).

The effects of war

Although analytically armed struggle may be seen as a continuation of nationalist politics, in concrete terms it has a dramatic impact on the lives of those who have to suffer it. In this respect, the decolonisation of Angola, Guinea and Mozambique was traumatic. Prolonged anti-colonial violence can have very seriously deleterious effects on postcolonial politics, as became evident in Angola and Mozambique.[66] Above and beyond the obvious suffering which all such violence inflicts disproportionately on ordinary men and women, war had significant political effects in the three Lusophone countries.

The first and most obvious consequence of nationalist war is that it legitimises armed action and spreads weapons through the country. Whether this becomes an issue after independence, depends primarily on how tightly the political leadership controls the distribution and use of arms. Again, Guinea and Angola provide two extremes here—the first where weapons were used sparingly and for well-identified political objectives; the other where weapons proliferated throughout the country to many groups and factions and where they came to be employed much more indiscriminately against civilians and political rivals.

In Mozambique, FRELIMO was relatively careful to keep a close political grip on armed action. Yet, the climate of violence which the war engendered made it more, rather than less, likely that RENAMO's murderous challenge should result in the 'militarisation' of postcolonial politics. Although force is widespread in Africa, the singularly high and nasty level of violence found in Angola and Mozambique is, in part at least, the outcome of the degeneration of politics in a context where there has been armed action since the early sixties.[67] Savimbi's notion that he can claim power at the barrel of the gun is similarly the outcome of a political process where violence has become endemic.

The second effect of armed decolonisation is the greater opportunity it affords for those who seek to challenge the social and political structures of 'traditional' society. Historically, the process of decolonisation presented the younger political generations with the chance to confront their elders in ways which were inconceivable in precolonial and even in colonial times.[68] Armed struggle created a political situation in which it was both more legitimate and more feasible for a younger nationalist generation to resist and undermine pre-existing structures of power.

[66]See here Patrick Chabal, 'Pouvoir et violence en Afrique postcoloniale', *Politique Africaine*, 42 (1991).

[67]See Christian Geffray, *La Cause des Armes au Mozambique* (Paris: Karthala, 1990).

[68]I develop this argument in *Power in Africa*, op. cit., chap. 15.

The nationalist legitimacy of armed struggle endowed the younger generation of nationalist leaders with new and, where they were success-ful, greatly enhanced political legitimacy. In turn, such legitimacy made it possible for the fresh leaders to challenge 'traditional' power during and after the independence struggle. The case of the excessive zeal of Balante 'youngsters' during the anti-colonial war in Guinea illustrates both the opportunities and the pitfalls which an armed challenge to the elders can bring about.[69] Equally, FRELIMO's blatant hostility to 'traditional' leaders after independence was, in part at least, a result of the apparent ease with which the party had seen off the opposition of some such leaders in the areas which it controlled during the war.[70]

Although at the time it seemed that armed nationalism was better able to displace 'traditional' power in this way, events since independence have shown that this was a simplistic view.[71] Here again, violence is simply the instrument of the universal power struggle between 'younger' and 'elder' leaders which was exacerbated by decolonisation. As in other African countries, the outcome of such power struggles is played out after inde-pendence in a context where the new rulers often need to come to terms with the power which 'tradition' (and, hence, traditional chiefs) continues to exercise. This is a lesson which was learnt the hard way in Guinea and Mozambique. What can thus be said is that armed decolonisation sharp-ened even further conflicts which took place in all African colonies at independence.

Further, war led to the displacement of populations, sometimes on a massive scale. Again, this is a problem which now afflicts many areas of Africa, but clearly the anti-colonial wars were much more disruptive in this respect than peaceful decolonisation. In all three countries, there was a substantial proportion of the population which took refuge in or migrated to neighbouring countries. The consequences of such migration are not yet well understood but they certainly had a profound effect on postcolonial politics.[72] At the very least, the problems of having to accommodate large numbers of people who had lived in another country for many years presented the regimes with severe practical difficulties. Often, it created an atmosphere

---

[69]A number of Balante youth used the weapons given them by the PAIGC to advance their own, rather than the party's, political interests: they were severely censured at the Bafatá party congress in 1964. See *Amílcar Cabral*, op. cit., pp. 77–83.

[70]For evidence of such hostility in one region see Geffray, op. cit.

[71]On the relevance of 'tradition' to nationalism in the Zimbabwean armed struggle see David Lan, *Guns and Rain* (London: James Currey, 1985); for a different perspective see Norma Kriger, *Zimbabwe's Guerrilla War* (Cambridge University Press, 1991).

[72]Similar problems have arisen in Vietnam, Algeria and Cambodia.

of distrust between those who had remained and those who returned. Such distrust could be, and has been, politically significant, particularly in cities like Bissau, Luanda and Maputo.[73] Equally, the links with groups who remain outside the country after independence (in Malawi, Senegal or Zaire, for example) affect the relations both between groups inside the country and between the governments of the countries concerned.

Finally, the wars provoked internal migration, again sometimes on a large scale. Country dwellers sought refuge in the towns, particularly the capital cities. In Bissau, for example, the population increased around five-fold between the period before the war and independence (to reach around 10 per cent of the total population), creating huge social and political problems for the new administration.[74] Though, urban migration accelerated after independence in all African countries, in Angola and Mozambique it was massively amplified by the civil conflicts. Nevertheless, the fact that Angola, Guinea and Mozambique suffered such high migration before independence disturbed the balance between rural and urban areas and constrained their policy options afterwards.

'Revolutionary' nationalism and postcolonial politics

The most widely discussed aspect of nationalism in Lusophone Africa is undoubtedly its alleged revolutionary quality.[75] The main nationalist groups from Angola, Guinea and Mozambique (that is, the MPLA, PAIGC and FRELIMO) all claimed for themselves a 'revolutionary' or 'Marxist' perspective different from that tried and failed in the sixties elsewhere in Africa, and which would result in a 'transition to socialism' after independence.

There were three areas in which the theory and practice of 'revolutionary' nationalism affected postcolonial policies: first, in the impact it had on the ideological stance of the governments at independence; second, in the relation between party and state which it implied; third, in the development of economic policies, particularly in respect of rural areas.[76]

While the main Lusophone African nationalists were not the only socialists in Africa, it is fair to say that by the early seventies, they were among the most dedicated. That this was the case is, in part at least, the

---

[73]For one interesting example, that of the Kinshasa exiles returning to Luanda, see Birmingham, *Frontline Nationalism* op. cit., pp. 96–8.

[74]See Galli and Jones, op. cit., pp. 73–4.

[75]Discussed in my *Power in Africa*, op. cit., chap. 1, sect. 4.

[76]Themes which will be developed further both in the chapters and sections that follow and in the country case studies below.

outcome of the process of armed struggle, for it is undoubtedly in the course of the anti-colonial struggle that the PAIGC, MPLA and FRELIMO moved towards a more systematic commitment to socialism.[77] Had Portugal, like France and Britain, agreed to negotiate the end of its empire in Africa, it is likely that Lusophone African nationalism (even in Angola) would have embraced less 'Marxist' positions. However, in the face of Portuguese intransigence, moderate nationalist opinion tended to be swept aside. Furthermore, in Portugal itself active opposition to the regime was almost entirely confined to the Communist Party and its allies. As it was, the process of political maturation and mobilisation necessary for the prosecution of an anti-colonial war (and the need to find outside support, inevitably, among socialist states) led to a clear 'move to the left' among the main Lusophone African nationalists.

It is enough, for example, to follow the trajectory of FRELIMO's ideology in order to see how the armed struggle contributed to the emergence of a more radical, 'socialist' form of ideology.[78] Mondlane, FRELIMO's founder and first leader, was at first a nationalist in the classical 'liberal' mould—and certainly much influenced by Nyerere.[79] It is his experience of the sharpened political contradictions brought about by the armed struggle, as well as the growing influence of more Marxist colleagues and outsiders which contributed to his gradual adoption of a much more overt 'revolutionary' outlook.

Similar processes took place elsewhere. The nationalist wars produced regimes much more committed to a socialist ideology than would otherwise have been the case. Since the nationalists in Cape Verde and São Tomé e Príncipe were directly or indirectly influenced by the PAIGC, MPLA or FRELIMO, this meant that all five Lusophone countries were overtly 'socialist' at independence.[80] Of course, 'socialism' meant vastly different things in each one of those countries. Nevertheless ideology did impinge on real life both in terms of the political structures erected and the policies pursued after independence.

In respect of structure, such an ideology influenced the relation between

---

[77]Though it is fair to say that the MPLA was born of a particularly close association with the Portuguese Communist Party and its first leader, Agostinho Neto, it always had been connected with the world communist movement. This is not, however, the case of either the PAIGC or FRELIMO.

[78]For a perspective critical of FRELIMO's ideology see Henriksen, *Revolution and Counterrevolution*, op. cit.

[79]Mondlane, op. cit.

[80]See Tony Hodges and Malyn Newitt, *São Tomé e Príncipe: From Plantation Colony to Microstate* (London: Westview, 1988) and Colm Foy, *Cape Verde* (London: Pinter, 1988).

party and state. Not only did the five Lusophone African countries become (like all other African nations) one-party states but they became singularly 'statist' one-party states. Centralist, nationalising and intolerant of any opposition or even dissidence, the ruling elites set out to establish the means by which 'vanguard' parties would take charge of 'command economies'. The party congresses which took place in Angola, Mozambique and Guinea in 1977 laid down the new political principles to guide state–party relations.[81] Now, the notion of 'vanguard' party, unlike that of the more usual African 'mass' party, implied a degree of state control relatively new in Africa. The aim was to establish a socialist state not just to 'capture' the economy but also to transform society, that is to create the political and administrative structures to enable the party to control virtually all levels of society. This, in a context where it had already become clear that, in Africa, states simply did not have the means of realising their hegemonic ambitions.[82]

As we now know, the price paid in Angola, Guinea and Mozambique for this statism *à outrance* has been very high especially in the economic sphere, the area of government policy most obviously influenced by the 'revolutionary' aspirations of the newly-independent regimes. Although there have been in Africa a number of countries (for example, Ghana, Guinea-Conakry and Dahomey/Benin) where a sharp 'turn to the left' produced fairly unedifying economic results, it is in the Lusophone countries that the consequences of such 'socialist' policies were most pronounced. Indeed, despite the differences between Guinea and Cape Verde on the one hand, and the other three Lusophone African countries on the other, it is possible to see similar policies leading to similar results.

This is perhaps best illustrated by the gross failure of the three mainland countries' policies on rural development.[83] In Guinea, neglect of the countryside, state control of retail trade and investment in 'semi-industrial' concerns resulted in the virtual collapse of agricultural exports, widespread

[81]There were important differences between the three parties, discussed in the two other chapters, with the MPLA the most (and the PAIGC the least) committed to 'vanguardism', orthodox Marxist ideology and state control. See Luís Moita, *Os Congressos da FRELIMO, do PAIGC e do MPLA: uma Análise Comparativa* (Lisbon: Ulmeiro, 1979).

[82]My discussion of the state in postcolonial Africa is to be found in *Power in Africa*, chap. 4.

[83]See, *inter alia*, on Guinea-Bissau, Galli and Jones, op. cit. and my 'Revolutionary democracy in Africa', op. cit.; on Mozambique, John Hanlon, *Mozambique: The Revolution under Fire* (London: Zed, 1984); and on Angola, S. H. McCormick, *The Angolan Economy: Prospects for Growth in a Postwar Environment* (Washington DC: Center for Strategic and International Studies, 1991).

smuggling and a return to 'subsistence' agriculture in many areas. In Mozambique, the attempt both to implement a policy of 'villagisation' and of more collective forms of agricultural production not only failed to work but also generated strong rural grievances easily exploited by a RENAMO reborn of South African largesse. In Angola, crude attempts at 'primitive socialist accumulation' and the war with UNITA resulted in the absence of viable rural development policies and the wholesale abandonment of agriculture.

In all three countries, rural producers, the backbone of the armed struggle, were sacrificed at the altar of 'socialism'. The fact that all three countries eventually had to implement structural adjustment programmes makes the failure of their socialist aims all the more obvious. To be fair, both the Mozambican and Guinean governments eventually had come to admit that their policies were wrong and had shifted some resources to support rural development before structural adjustment. But this was a little too late for, by then, Guinea's agriculture had sunk very low and Mozambique was suffering the effects of one of the most vicious civil wars ever to afflict Africa.[84] As for Angola, until peace comes, there is little prospect of any improvement in its debilitated rural economy.

Nevertheless, it can be argued that the failure of 'socialist' economic policies in Angola, Guinea and Mozambique is not simply to be explained by the inherent defects of 'socialist' ideology. It is much more fundamentally a reflection of the economic crisis which is afflicting Africa generally. Whatever the interpretation of that crisis, one of its root causes is the inability of African states ('socialist' or 'free-market') and entrepreneurs alike to generate sufficiently productive economic activity to sustain growth for development.[85]

In this respect, then, as in all the others, it is now best to study the Lusophone countries from the perspective of the evolution of postcolonial Africa as a whole. Both the peculiarities of their decolonisation and the consequences of their 'revolutionary' nationalism are becoming less and less relevant to their present condition. A re-assessment of their present fate, as we shall see in the chapters that follow, demands a much more solidly Africanist comparativist outlook than has hitherto been usual.

[84]On RENAMO see Alex Vines, *Renamo: Terrorism in Mozambique* (London: James Currey, 1991).
[85]On Africa's crisis of production, see *Power in Africa*, op. cit., chap. 9.

2

THE CONSTRUCTION OF
THE NATION-STATE

POWER AND THE POSTCOLONIAL STATE

This section raises two distinct but inter-related questions which lie at the heart of the analysis of the contemporary politics of Portuguese-speaking Africa. First, how historically different is the Lusophone African postcolonial state from that found elsewhere in Africa? Second, what is the analytical relationship between understanding the postcolonial African state and explaining postcolonial politics in Africa?

The section is in three parts. The first reflects on why the history of Portuguese Africa and of Portuguese decolonisation has so often been confined to a discussion of its Lusophone specificities. The second reconsiders the question of how best to study the state in postcolonial Portuguese-speaking Africa. The last section is a more general argument in favour of the re-interpretation of postcolonial politics in Lusophone Africa.

The history of Portuguese Africa

For reasons having largely to do with the history of Portugal in Africa, Africanists have tended to view Portuguese-speaking Africa differently from the rest of the continent. This has had serious consequences for the study of Lusophone Africa, consequences which have had a profound effect on the interpretation of the postcolonial politics in Portuguese-speaking Africa.[1] The grounds which have led historians to focus on the singularity of Portuguese-speaking Africa come under three broad headings. The first has to do with the history of Portugal herself; the second with the history

[1]To gauge the change in focus, consider the advance made in the historiography of Lusophone Africa between James Duffy, *Portugal in Africa* (Harmondsworth: Penguin African Library, 1962) and Malyn Newitt, *Portugal in Africa* (London: Hurst & Co., 1981).

of Portuguese colonial rule and the third with the history of Portuguese decolonisation.

Ever since the mid-nineteenth century, and certainly from the time of the Berlin Conference, the Portuguese have considered both that their 'mission' in Africa was different from that of the other imperial powers and that the rest of Europe failed to understand how distinct that 'mission' was. From the Portuguese viewpoint this severe misunderstanding is perhaps best symbolised in the early years of colonial rule by the 1890 British Ultimatum and in the later years by the UN's refusal to admit Portugal because of its stance on its 'overseas provinces'.[2]

From the perspective of the other European powers, this sense of Portuguese difference is revealed in, for example, the history of the 'scandal' of forced labour in São Tomé and elsewhere in Lusophone Africa, as well as a widespread perception that the Portuguese colonial administration was utterly deficient.[3] Finally, both the Portuguese and their European rivals considered (from opposite moral perspectives) that the scale of miscegenation in Portuguese Africa was a symbol of the differences between the nature of their colonial rule.[4]

Of course, the history of Portugal since the nineteenth century, but particularly since the end of the Republic in 1926, provides good reasons for viewing Portuguese colonial rule differently. Portugal's political complexion, its economic backwardness, its reliance on mercantilism, its extremely slow industrial development, all made it inevitable that Portugal would have neither the inclination nor the resources to exploit its African empire like the other colonial powers.[5] Portugal, which dated its presence in Africa to the fifteenth century, did not easily accept that the criteria for 'effective' colonial occupation agreed at the Berlin Conference could in and of themselves reflect the realities of the Portuguese presence on the continent.[6] Conversely, Portugal's colonial rivals viewed the Portuguese claim of its special relationship with Africa as a smokescreen for excessive colonial ambitions and deficient colonial achievements.

[2]On the nineteenth century Portuguese perceptions see the views of the foremost Portuguese historian of his generations: Oliveira Martins, *Brasil e as Colonias Portuguesas* (Lisbon: Livraria Bertrand, 1881 2nd edn).

[3]On the issue of forced labour see H. Nevinson, *A Modern Slavery* (London: Harper, 1906).

[4]For a discussion of the ideology and realities of miscegenation in one colony see Gerald Bender, *Angola under the Portuguese* (London: Heinemann, 1978).

[5]On the nature of Portuguese imperialism see Gervase Clarence-Smith, *The Third Portuguese Empire* (Manchester University Press, 1985) and A. Castro, *A Economia Portuguesa do Século XX* (Lisbon: Edições 70, 1973).

[6]See here, for example, Marquês do Lavradio, *Portugal em África depois de 1851* (Lisbon: Agência Geral das Colonias, 1936).

While during the Republican era (1910–26), Portugal had sought to manage its colonial empire broadly on the lines followed by the other colonial powers,[7] from 1926 she isolated herself from the rest of the world and devised a colonial policy strictly in keeping with the Estrado Novo's narrow vision of its imperial mission.[8] After the Second World War and especially after the beginning of African decolonisation (from the mid-fifties onwards), Salazar's colonial policies (a narrow political and economic nationalism and a reluctance to contemplate self-governance in the colonies) seemed to set the course of Portuguese Africa completely at odds with the rest of the continent. Not surprisingly, therefore, the history of Portuguese Africa since the twenties has often been distinct from that of the rest of colonial Africa.

But perhaps the apparent singularity of Portuguese Africa was made most manifest in the years of decolonisation. If, from the fifties, Britain and France (although not yet Belgium and Spain) were preparing for the transfer of power to their African subjects, Portugal deemed its African colonies to be, and forever to remain, overseas 'provinces', integral parts of the motherland. This policy, dictated by the views of an ageing tyrant, was swayed neither by the French experience in Algeria nor by that of the Belgians in the Congo. It took over a decade of colonial wars, the collapse of the dictatorship and the return to democracy in Lisbon, before Portuguese Africa was set free. Here again, this singularly violent process of decolonisation marked out the Portuguese colonies from the rest of Africa.

Furthermore, the intellectual and repressive climate of the Estrado Novo made impossible the development of any serious Portuguese historiography of (both metropolitan and overseas) Portugal.[9] It also made it impractical for non-Portuguese scholars to have access to the kind of historical sources which they were able to use for the study of the British and French empires. Not only was it difficult for historians to study Portuguese Africa *per se* but the absence of any reasonable history of metropolitan Portugal meant that those who wanted to understand Lusophone Africa had first virtually to write such a history for themselves.[10] As a result, historians of Portuguese

---

[7]That is, the establishment of a modern infrastructure and colonial administration, the rational economic 'exploitation' of the colonies, and so on.

[8]Such as extreme centralisation of decision-making, the establishment of a Portuguese economic zone and the use of the colonies as labour reserves. See here Clarence-Smith, op. cit.

[9]For the best of these histories before 1974 see A.H. Oliveira Marques, *History of Portugal* (New York: Columbia University Press, 1972).

[10]See here, for example, James Duffy, *Portuguese Africa* (Cambridge MA: Harvard University Press, 1959). David Birmingham, originally a historian of central Portuguese Africa, eventually did write his own history of Portugal: *A Concise History of Portugal* (Cambridge University Press, 1993).

Africa tended to be Lusophone specialists, perforce more inclined to concentrate on the singularities of their area of study than of comparing Portuguese Africa with the rest of colonial Africa. In addition, few historians of colonial (British, French or Belgian) Africa had any serious knowledge of Portuguese Africa, thus reducing even further the probability of comparative colonial history. Add to this the fact that colonial history until forty years ago focussed more on the history of the colonial power in Africa than on the history of Africans under colonial rule and it becomes clear why our knowledge of Portuguese Africa has been severely curtailed.

Whatever their training, approach or ideological perspective, analysts of the five African Lusophone countries have had largely to rely on the histories of colonial Portuguese Africa extant. They too have felt the need to re-examine the history of Portugal in order to assess the relevance of Portuguese colonial history for the analysis of postcolonial Portuguese-speaking Africa. They too, therefore, have been inclined to view these countries from the perspective of their differences from the rest of independent Africa.[11]

Finally, as mentioned in the previous chapter, the study of Portuguese decolonisation reinforced further, if for different reasons, the analysis of Portuguese-speaking Africa from the viewpoint of its specificities. The fact that historians of Portuguese Africa, students of the Lusophone people's wars and analysts of the postcolonial 'transition to socialism' worked within totally different perspectives reduced the opportunities for meaningful analytical dialogue and led to excessive compartmentalisation. Indeed, it is striking how little continuity there is in the study of colonial and postcolonial Lusophone Africa. It is also notable how little interpretative interchange there has been between students of Lusophone and Francophone or Anglophone Africa.

The argument here is not that Portuguese Africa was not in many ways singular nor that a study of these singularities is unimportant. It is, rather, that the focus on these specificities has often been at the expense of the understanding of the realities of the postcolonial Portuguese-speaking African experience.

The postcolonial state in Portuguese-speaking Africa

There is scope, therefore, for a different approach to the study of Portuguese-speaking Africa. Instead of looking at the postcolonial Lusophone state

---

[11]Although to be fair, Newitt (who in this respect is somewhat of an exception) implicitly calls for a more comparative perspective in his 1981 volume.

from a Lusophone angle, we must look at the evolution of politics in Portuguese-speaking Africa from the perspective of the changes that take place in postcolonial Africa generally. From this viewpoint, what are the characteristics of the postcolonial state in Lusophone Africa in relation to those of the rest of Africa? Are there any grounds for thinking that the state in Portuguese-speaking Africa is in any fundamental way different from the postcolonial state elsewhere? What, finally, is the analytical relationship between understanding the postcolonial state and explaining postcolonial politics in Portuguese-speaking Africa?[12]

If we accept that it is analytically fruitful to consider the postcolonial state in black Africa from a comparative perspective, we must find a way of linking the development of the Lusophone postcolonial experience to that of the rest of Africa.[13] Although in the years immediately following the independence of the Portuguese colonies it seemed that they were to follow a different path, enough time has now elapsed to see that they did not do so. Today, over twenty-five years after Portuguese decolonisation, it is clear that, whatever the colonial specificities of Lusophone Africa, the evolution of their postcolonial politics is following an identifiable pattern.

We must also begin to recognise that, despite a common colonial past, there are analytically significant differences between the postcolonial history of the five Lusophone African countries. It is most useful to divide these countries into three groups. The first is that of Cape Verde and São Tomé e Príncipe, countries which in many crucial respects are better understood as Creole, rather than strictly African, societies—and in this way more similar to the Caribbean.[14] The second consists of Guinea-Bissau, a small west African country, whose history is best compared to that of neighbouring societies (in Senegal, Guinea and the Gambia).[15] There is finally Angola and Mozambique, the current political evolution of which has often been seen as parallel (if only because of their involvement in civil conflicts fuelled, wholly or in part, by South Africa) but countries which are in fact

---

[12]For an illustration of how I use this approach, see 'People's war, state formation and revolution in Africa' op. cit.

[13]I draw here from my general discussion on the postcolonial state in *Power in Africa* op. cit., chap. 4.

[14]On Cape Verde see, *inter alia*, Colm Foy, *Cape Verde: Politics, Economics and Society* (London: Frances Pinter, 1988) and Elisa Silva de Andrade, *Les îles du Cap Vert* (Paris: L'Harmattan, 1996); on São Tomé e Príncipe see Hodges and Newitt, op. cit. and Gerhard Seibert, *Comrades, Clients and Cousins* (Leiden: CNWS, 1999).

[15]See, *inter alia*, Galli and Jones, op. cit. and Joshua B. Forrest, *Guinea-Bissau: Power, Conflict and Renewal in a West African Nation* (Boulder CO: Westview, 1992).

most profitably compared with their immediate neighbours: Zaire, Zambia, Zimbabwe or Tanzania.

Even at this level of generality, it is immediately apparent how artificial the analysis is which consists in lumping these five Lusophone countries together. The fact they all share a Portuguese colonial heritage and that they all marched into independence committed to some form of 'socialism' is much too feeble a basis on which to generalise.[16] But there is more, for even the colonial history of these five societies is so different as to invalidate any generalisation about the similarities in the consequences of colonial rule.

Cape Verde was always apart, seen by the Portuguese as a special case and ruled accordingly. São Tomé e Príncipe was somewhat of a closed society, evolving as it did according to the rise and fall of its plantation economy. Guinea, always a Portuguese backwater, is best seen as the poor relation of the west African (French and British) colonies. Only Angola and Mozambique share many of the same features: from Creole and *mestiço* communities to settler colonies. Even here, however, it is not difficult to show that in many fundamental ways (for instance, in respect of concession companies, labour policies and the role of Indians) Mozambique is a case apart. It seems plain, therefore, that given these differences one must be cautious in looking for commonalities in the postcolonial development of the state in the five Lusophone countries which would be due to their shared colonial heritage.

Furthermore, there is a more fundamental historical reason why it is more profitable to study the evolution of the postcolonial state from an 'African' rather than from a strictly Lusophone perspective. One of the most significant lessons we can now draw from the analysis of postcolonial African politics is the importance of the process which I call (deliberately controversially) political Africanisation. By political Africanisation is meant the all important process whereby the political legacy—the ideas, practices and institutions—of colonial rule and colonisation was assimilated, transformed and re-appropriated by Africa. However significant the differences between various forms of colonial rule may have been, the outcome of political Africanisation is a process by which the sedimentation of postcolonial politics occurs along relatively similar lines in the various parts of Africa.[17]

If this is so, then it follows that the nature of the colonial legacy is less

---

[16]As is apparent from a book like David and Marina Ottaway, *Afrocommunism* (New York: Africana, 1981).

[17]For a development of this argument see *Power in Africa*, op. cit., chap. 12.

important than the ways in which it is Africanised after independence. It also follows that in order to understand Africa's postcolonial politics we need to grasp the nature of the links between its precolonial, colonial and postcolonial political history. Hence, it is more important to study the evolution of postcolonial African politics from the perspective of the evolution of the African societies which form these independent countries rather than simply from that of the postcolonial state as it was erected at independence on the foundations of (and in reaction against) the colonial state.

As time elapses, as the postcolonial period lengthens, as African societies recover their past and evolve according to continuities which link them back to their roots in the precolonial period, the significance of the colonial legacy is put into perspective. Over time, the process of political Africanisation shapes and re-shapes the political structures established at independence according to the vagaries and rhythms of the relationship between state and society. Constitutional arrangements and ideological pronouncements are adapted to and converted by the realities of postcolonial politics and economics. As this happens, the apparent similarities between the postcolonial politics of the five Lusophone countries evaporate, revealing underneath divergences in their political evolution which are best explained in terms of their (colonial, precolonial and postcolonial) history.

Two examples will serve as illustrations. First, comparing the postcolonial state in Guinea-Bissau and Cape Verde, one would expect major similarities. The two countries shared the same movement of national liberation, the PAIGC, in which both Cape Verdean and Guinean nationalists struggled together. At independence, they established a bicephalous single-party state in which the two countries were closely linked politically and even economically. They shared the same colonial and nationalist past and the same ideological outlook.[18] The common party, the PAIGC, was committed to closer integration between the two countries.[19] Yet, within a few years, the links between the two were broken and each country went its separate way.[20] Very quickly, it became apparent that Cape Verde's (relative) success

[18]The debate between Carlos Lopes and Lars Rudebeck on Guinea-Bissau about the nature of the PAIGC's ideology is in this respect very instructive. See Carlos Lopes and Lars Rudebeck, *The Socialist Ideal in Africa: A Debate* (Uppsala: Nordiska Afrikainstitutet, 1988).

[19]For an analysis of some of the issues related to the break between the two see the chapter, 'Revolutionary democracy in Africa: the case of Guinea-Bissau' in Chabal, *Political Domination in Africa*, op. cit.

[20]For an analysis of the events which led to the break between the two countries and in particular the November 1980 coup in Bissau see my series of articles in *West Africa*, 15 December 1980, 22–9 December 1980, and 12 January 1981.

in managing its colonial inheritance and in overcoming very serious postcolonial disadvantages was not to be repeated in Guinea-Bissau. Why?

With the benefit of hindsight it is easy to say that Cape Verde and Guinea-Bissau were very different, that their union was not viable and that it was unlikely that their respective postcolonial development would be similar. And yet, a narrow focus on the postcolonial state provides very little basis for explaining why the divergences were so wide. Indeed, it detracts from the analysis of the factors which most plausibly account for those political disagreements. Instead, an understanding of the evolution of state politics in Cape Verde and Guinea-Bissau presupposes an understanding of the relationship between the postcolonial politics of these two countries and their respective colonial and even precolonial history.

Second, an analysis of the political significance of UNITA and RENAMO in, respectively, Angola and Mozambique from a strictly postcolonial perspective would suggest important similarities.[21] Both movements were 'anti-socialist', 'anti-*mestiço*', 'black-oriented' and grounded in 'traditional' socio-political structures. Both used violence on a massive scale, both contributed to the collapse of the economy of their respective country and both single-mindedly sought to destroy the infrastructure and the trappings of state power. Both, finally, were supported by South Africa, the designs of which in the southern African region they have amply served. Yet, it is clear that an analysis along these lines would obscure rather than reveal the genesis and importance of UNITA and RENAMO in the postcolonial evolution of Angola and Mozambique.

Today, when the outcome of the peace negotiations in the two countries has proved to be very different, it might seem obvious how different UNITA and RENAMO are. Yet, it is not so long ago that there was near unanimity in the political analysis of these two movements as consisting of *bandicos armados*, bent on the mindless destruction of the nation. In fact, above and beyond the obvious similarities in some of the means employed by UNITA and RENAMO, these two movements have had little in common. Again, in order to meaningfully understand them it is necessary to relate the evolution of the postcolonial politics of Angola and Mozambique to their very different colonial and precolonial antecedents.[22]

---

[21]On RENAMO see Vines, *Renamo*, op. cit.; on UNITA and the war in Angola see W. M. James, *A Political History of the Civil War in Angola: 1974–1990* (New Brunswick NJ: Transaction Publishers, 1991) and Bridgland, *Jonas Savimbi*, op. cit.

[22]As I make clear in Patrick Chabal, 'Un regard historique sur le devenir de l'Afrique Lusophone Australe', in Darbon (ed.), *Afrique du Sud*, op.cit.

A discussion of the historical origins of UNITA and RENAMO will be offered in the next chapter. Suffice it here to point that in the early nineties Geffray's *La Cause des armes au Mozambique*[23] finally demonstrated that RENAMO was not simply a terrorist movement. It also offered one of the best examples of the kind of multi-disciplinary approach to the analysis of postcolonial politics which I advocate in *Power in Africa*. Finally, it showed concretely why an understanding of the postcolonial state in (Lusophone) Africa is best achieved by an analysis of its relationship with society.[24]

The state in postcolonial Africa

It is today not difficult to see that what has for the past twenty to thirty years passed for an analysis of African politics has largely been an analysis of the state in postcolonial Africa. There are, of course, good historical reasons why this has been so. First, decolonisation was largely about the conquest of the postcolonial state by the nationalists. Second, the postcolonial state replaced its colonial predecessor, a visibly strong and interventionist institution which had clearly been the paramount actor in colonial politics. Third, the state was recognised to have been central to the consolidation of the modern European nation-state and the realities of independent Africa dictated that it would be the postcolonial state which would create the African nation-state.[25] Finally, the European state after the Second World War was, quite rightly, seen to have been heavily instrumental in the reconstruction of western Europe, thus reinforcing the fairly popular 'socialist' notion of the planning state.

If it is easy to see why Africanists were at first prone to studying state politics[26] it is puzzling why they persisted for so long in believing that the postcolonial African state should evolve as it had in other parts of the world. The postcolonial African state, it is true, was usually constructed on the model of one or the other of the European states. Yet, the very divergent evolution of the various European states should have warned Africanists

---

[23]Christian Geffray, *La Cause des Armes au Mozambique* (Paris: Karthala, 1990).

[24]For another example of the importance of understanding historical continuities in the analysis of RENAMO see Newitt, *A History of Mozambique*, op. cit., chap. 20.

[25]On the construction of the African nation-state see *Power in Africa*, op. cit., chap. 7.

[26]Liberal and Marxist analytical traditions were both accustomed to focus attention on the nature and role of the state in national politics. Furthermore, the data necessary for the political analysis of the postcolonial African state was easily accessible. Sources were relatively abundant and convenient to locate, state politics was visible and the state's discourse was both voluble and understandable.

that the African postcolonial state was unlikely to follow any recognisable precedent. Further, the causes of such divergence in Europe were such as to suggest that it was the history of the relation between state and society, not constitutional frameworks, which determined the fate of the modern nation-state.

In retrospect it can be seen that Africanists were for too long led into believing that the vagaries of the African postcolonial state 'explained' African politics. In this respect it is strange that students of the Portuguese-speaking African countries—which only became independent some fifteen years after the French and British colonies—should so readily have repeated the mistakes of those who had studied French- and English-speaking Africa in the early years of their independence. Strange indeed, for it was precisely in the late seventies that the experience of these countries suggested that it was time to seek other interpretations of the postcolonial African state.[27]

As I have explained elsewhere, the African postcolonial state, although overdeveloped and hegemonically ambitious, is in fact both soft and over-extended.[28] Its violent and repressive nature is more properly the reflection of its political weakness than of its strength.[29] More importantly, in order to understand the postcolonial African state it is necessary to understand the complex and multiple ways in which the postcolonial political order has been Africanised since independence.[30] It is thus more profitable to conceptualise the African state today as an African(ised) state than to continue to view its evolution from a notional European state as deliquescent or pathological.

The interpretation of the relationship between state and society in postcolonial Africa has gone through at least three phases. The first consisted in believing that the postcolonial state was all-powerful and held the keys to the 'development' of the new African nations. The second viewed the political and economic 'crisis' which engulfed postcolonial Africa as the consequence of the collapse of the postcolonial state, by which was meant both its repressive excesses and dereliction in the discharge of its duties. One of the latest interpretation of the state's manifest failure is seen as

---

[27]For an early statement of a different approach see Jean-François Bayart, 'La politique par le bas en Afrique noire', *Politique Africaine*, 1 (1981).

[28]*Power in Africa*, op. cit., chap. 4. For an elaboration of my analysis of the African postcolonial state see Patrick Chabal and Jean-Pascal Daloz, *Africa Works: Disorder as Political Instrument* (Oxford: James Currey, 1999), chap. 1.

[29]See Patrick Chabal, 'Pouvoir et violence en Afrique postcoloniale', *Politique Africaine*, 42 (1991).

[30]*Power in Africa*, op. cit., chap. 12.

the 'revenge' of Africa's (civil) society.[31] This last interpretation was an important analytical advance on the other two in that it suggested that the evolution of the state can only be understood in its relationship with society. The African postcolonial state has indeed been shaped and transformed in the endlessly changing process by which it has sought to assert political and economic hegemony over society. But the dichotomies between state and society and the sharpness of the political competition between the two can be, and have been, overdrawn.

Echoing what I have written in *Power in Africa*, I would argue here that Africanists have hitherto largely inverted the political causalities between state and society in postcolonial Africa. The evolution of the postcolonial state is better understood as the process by which society has re-asserted control over the political order via the state rather than simply as the process by which the holders of state power have exercised their hegemonic powers. State and society are intimately linked by means of the neo-patrimonial political system which has prevailed on the continent since independence. In other words, politics is to be understood in terms of the patterns of political legitimacy, accountability, redistribution and abuse of power which mark those clientelistic networks.[32]

For this reason, the resilience as well as the deficiencies of the post-colonial state are best explained by the nature of the very complex links which tie, rather than simply oppose, state and society. While at the formal macro-analytical level it has often been convenient to view state and society as competitors for national resources, at the real but informal micro-level what matters are the strong complicities woven within the clientelistic networks that bind individuals, from top to bottom. In effect, then, the clientelist networks which link state and society are so numerous and so extensive that they guarantee the maintenance of a neo-patrimonial political system in which the state is only paramount over, in so far as it is 'colonised' by, society. Politicians, or Big Men, derive their legitimacy from their ability to placate their clients.[33] The political system is thus very largely informal.

Once the relation between society and the state is recast in this way, it becomes easier to understand both the endurance and the feebleness of the contemporary African state. In postcolonial Africa, then, the state is indeed at the centre of politics for it is at once the main agent in the construction

---

[31]See Jean-François Bayart, 'La revanche des sociétés africaines', *Politique Africaine*, 11 (1983).

[32]A development of these ideas about civil society is found in Chabal and Daloz, op. cit., chap. 2.

[33]For a comprehensive discussion of these issues see ibid., chap. 3 on elites.

and maintenance of the nation-state and the primary locus for the acquisition of resources. Nevertheless, however central and however resourceful (for those who have access to its various networks) the postcolonial state may be, its power to act upon society is severely circumscribed. Because the state survives only insofar as it is in symbiotic relation with society, its capacity to change that self-same society by means of social and economic 'engineering' is most severely limited.

In postcolonial Africa, therefore, it is largely an illusion to view the state as the agent for (socialist or capitalist) economic development. While in South-East and East Asia, for instance, the state has indeed often been directly responsible for bringing about impressive rates of economic growth, in Africa it has been the chief instrument of (individual and collective) neo-patrimonial drive. It has enabled the holders of state power and all those connected to them through multifarious networks to have access to the resources which the state commands. These resources have been utilised for purposes which on the whole have not contributed to sustainable economic development: exchange, consumption or accumulation rather than investment and production.[34] The notion that the Lusophone postcolonial state could bring about a 'transition to socialism' was thus never seriously plausible.[35]

Conclusion

If this argument is right, it follows that our understanding of the state in postcolonial Portuguese-speaking Africa is still in its infancy. Some have insisted on viewing it as specifically 'Lusophone', with similarities between the five countries which are largely figments of the imagination. Others have been blinded by the notion of the putative supremacy of the powerful, voluntarist, 'socialist' postcolonial state able to act upon and even transform society in ways which have failed to materialise anywhere else in postcolonial Africa. Many, consequently, have tended to attribute the manifest failures of the postcolonial state in Portuguese-speaking Africa to extraneous factors (such as South Africa, the Bretton Woods institutions, war, and drought) largely beyond state control.[36]

We need to rethink our approach and accept that, however different the history of Portuguese-speaking Africa may have been, the trajectory

[34]A more detailed discussion on the issues of production and on accumulation and inequality is in *Power in Africa*, op. cit., chaps 6 and 9.

[35]As is demonstrated in a recent study of Mozambique: Margaret Hall and Tom Young, *Confronting Leviathan: Mozambique since Independence* (London: Hurst & Co., 1997).

[36]For one example of such views see Hanlon, *Mozambique*, op. cit.

of its postcolonial states is not significantly distinct from that of the rest of the continent. Or rather, the differences which exist are no more (and no less) significant than the differences which may be found between any group of postcolonial African states. These are best explained by an historical analysis of the sedimentation of each individual postcolonial polity. Equally, the best way to understand what has happened in these five countries is to approach the study of their political and economic evolution from the comparative African perspective. Whilst the study of the colonial state understandably required, and indeed benefited from, a common Lusophone perspective, that of the postcolonial state demands that we shift the focus of analysis squarely to an interpretation of contemporary 'African' politics. The section that follow will show that such an analysis can enhance our understanding of the evolution of Portuguese-speaking Africa.

CREATING NATIONS

Although all newly-independent African countries faced the task of creating nations out of the territories they inherited from the colonial state, the former Portuguese colonies did so in singularly difficult conditions. What happened in those five countries provides in this respect as wide a range of experiences as can be found on the continent. From the relatively smooth organisation of the Cape Verde islands into a single national entity to the fiendishly complex and, to this day, unsuccessful attempt to bring together the peoples of Angola, there is in Portuguese-speaking Africa an array of distinct cases. The analysis of the process by which the regimes of these five countries sought to create viable nations enables us to come to some useful conclusions about independent Africa.

This section seeks to explain what happened in postcolonial Portuguese-speaking Africa with reference to the more general experience of nation-building on the continent as a whole.[37] Since, as mentioned, there is in the historiography of Lusophone Africa a tendency to view the experience of these countries as separate, different, almost *sui generis*, it is important to show how their experience fits in with the more common processes at work in postcolonial Africa. Or, to put it another way, there is merit in understanding how the specificities of Lusophone Africa affect the trajectory of these five colonies in ways which are consonant with what generally took place on the continent after decolonisation.[38]

[37]On the process of nation-building in Africa see Patrick Chabal, *Power in Africa*, op. cit., pt. III.
[38]It is interesting to note that there has hitherto not been a history of Lusophone Africa set within the comparative African perspective.

This section is divided into three main parts. The first casts a glance at the colonial legacy. The second discusses the obstacles to be found in each of the five countries to the formation of the postcolonial nation-state. The last analyses the process whereby the newly-installed regimes sought to consolidate their hold over the emerging nation.

The colonial legacy

As highlighted in the previous section, the formation of the postcolonial state, historically the first step following independence, was not significantly different in the Lusophone African countries from what it was elsewhere. The complexion of the five individual states was, of course, singular in that it derived as much from the colonial experience as from the concrete history of the particular territory. However, before discussing the specific nature of the nation-state in Lusophone Africa, it is useful to summarise some of the common features between the five territories. These can be traced to the roots of Portuguese modern colonial rule. In comparison with their French- and English-speaking counterparts, the Lusophone African countries started independent life with an exceedingly burdensome legacy. On the one hand, the postcolonial states inherited from their colonial masters a strongly authoritarian form of government. On the other hand, they took over a particularly inefficient bureaucratic administration. Both of these points need developing.

Although all colonial states were at once authoritarian and inefficient, the Portuguese ones proved more extreme in this respect, and this affected the extent to which, the postcolonial regimes succeeded in creating viable nation-states after independence. Both the influence of the Estrado Novo and the experience of decolonisation conspired to bring about in Lusophone Africa the development of rigid, cumbersome and autocratic political and administrative structures. There were, of course, important differences between the colonial government of the five territories—from a state in Guinea whose writ did not run very far, to the infinitely more sophisticated administration in Angola presiding over a buoyant economy and a relatively capable bureaucracy. Nevertheless, the five colonies shared some features which were to influence their political evolution after independence. Of these, three are significant: the absence of political representation, the heavily bureaucratised nature of the administration, and the outlook on economic affairs, particularly on the question of labour.[39]

---

[39]The most useful summary of these features will be found in Newitt, *Portugal in Africa*, op. cit.

The issue of representation is paramount in Africa. Even where there were democratic political structures (hastily) erected by the colonial powers before decolonisation, the trend after independence was towards the formation of one-party states.[40] In the Portuguese colonies, however, the legacy of the authoritarian Estrado Novo and the anti-nationalist campaigns bestowed on the colonial state a particularly unrepresentative type of government. No effort was made to allow for the expression of 'native' sentiments, other than in the most perfunctory of advisory 'representative' councils. No worthwhile elections took place, other than the ritual of the heavily undemocratic Portuguese presidential and legislative contests.[41] There was, finally, no attempt to set up political structures or to prepare African elites for the task of postcolonial government. In short, the peoples of these five territories had no experience of representative politics and no means of expressing their political views. Given that the anti-colonial movements all sought from the beginning to establish monopoly control of power, it can be seen that there was in Lusophone Africa very little chance that plural, or relatively free, expression of political representation would flourish after independence.

The legacy of the Portuguese colonial experience was also extraordinarily bureaucratic, in the most negative sense of the word. Portugal herself was until the seventies in the grip of an antiquated and cumbersome administration, which stifled private initiative and prevented social and economic, not to mention political, change.[42] It was only to be expected, therefore, that the colonies would suffer even more from the inflexible and inefficient hand of the administration. Although it is fair to say that by the seventies, Angola and Mozambique were experiencing relatively rapid economic growth, this was primarily due to the fact that the dynamism of foreign private capital managed to overcome, or bypass, the rigidities of the colonial bureaucracy. Nevertheless, even in these two colonies, there were structural and administrative obstacles which stood in the way of more sustained social or economic developments. The bureaucratic experience of the other three colonies—where such potential for growth did not exist and where most economic activity was, directly or indirectly, in the hands of the state or its financial allies—was in this respect, even more dire.[43] No Guinean, Cape Verdean or São Tomense could have believed at the time

---

[40]See Chabal, *Power in Africa*, op. cit., chap. 8.

[41]It is important to remember that, even in Portugal, there were no free and fair elections based on a universal franchise.

[42]See David Birmingham, *A Concise History of Portugal* (Cambridge University Press, 1993), chaps 6 and 7.

[43]See Bimingham, *Frontline Nationalism in Angola and Mozambique*, op. cit., chap. 2.

that the Portuguese administration had any other purpose than to make their lives as difficult and unpleasant as possible. Nor, based on their colonial experience, would any of the political elites of the five colonies have had clear notions of how a modern bureaucracy could be harnessed for purposes of (social, economic or political) development.[44]

The colonial state's outlook on economic affairs was equally constraining. Angola and Mozambique experienced rapid economic growth in the sixties and early seventies—growth which compared favourably with some of their southern African neighbours—but this largely took place outside the ambit (and in some ways against the wishes) of the Portuguese regime. In the other three colonies, where no such potential existed for private foreign capital, the colonial state's development plans brought little prospect for economic investment. In Guinea, the main activity centred on the traditional agricultural exports (groundnuts and rice).[45] In São Tomé e Príncipe, the colony's revenues depended on a declining cocoa and coffee industry, itself dependent on the import of labour from Angola.[46] In Cape Verde, no serious investment came to make up for the agricultural deficiencies and the lack of growth potential: emigration remained the only answer for the bulk of the population.[47] The Portuguese state thus carried on from the legacy of Salazar's plan that the colonies should serve either as labour reserves or as producers of primary agricultural exports such as cotton, sugar and coffee. There was thus a strong tradition of forced labour which permeated the colonial ethos. The role of the state was not to encourage local economic initiative but to ensure that production fitted in with the requirements of the empire, even if the costs to the local population or the local exchequer were onerous.[48]

The obstacles

The difficulties faced by the newly-installed independent regimes in constructing a viable independent nation were not equally daunting. Although they all started life with the burdensome colonial legacy of the state as it was established at the end of decolonisation, the ease with which they could use that political instrument to fashion the new nation according to

---

[44]Until Portugal joined the European Union, its bureaucracy remained an obstacle to economic development.

[45]On Guinea's socio-economic situation see Chabal, *Amílcar Cabral*, op. cit., chap. 1 and Forrest, *Guinea-Bissau*, op. cit., chap. 1.

[46]Here see Seibert, *Comrades, Clients and Cousins*, chap. 1.

[47]See Elisa Silva de Andrade, *Les Îles du Cap Vert de la 'Découverte' à l'Indépendance Nationale (1460–1975)* (Paris; L'Harmattan, 1996), pt. III.

[48]On the colonial economy see Clarence-Smith, *The Third Portuguese Empire*, op. cit.

their modernising (socialist) agenda varied greatly. Not only had their colonial history differed markedly but the experience of their decolonisation had been dissimilar. Here two important factors overlap and force an analytical distinction between the three mainland territories and the two island states. The former achieved independence following an anti-colonial armed struggle. The latter were able to negotiate decolonisation following the regime change ushered in by the coup of 25 April 1974.[49] This is, of course, directly connected to the fact that armed guerrilla war was impossible in the island colonies. The question is, therefore, how to assess the importance of the consequence of armed struggle for the construction of the nation? The previous chapter explained why the link between anti-colonial war and national unity was complicated. Here, we need to explore further the relevance of these wars to the evolution of Guinea, Angola and Mozambique.

The experience of the armed anti-colonial campaigns had mixed effects on the ability of the independent regimes of the three countries to consolidate the nation-state after independence.[50] On the positive side, the nationalist parties which took power were strongly motivated political organisations with a long experience in the field and relatively well-developed political structures. As usual, one must consider the differences between the three, with the PAIGC and FRELIMO much more homogeneous and better organised than the MPLA. Compared to many of the parties that emerged victorious at independence in the rest of Africa, the three possessed greater political resources, both in terms of their prominence during the anti-colonial struggle and in terms of their experience of managing a complex political organisation under difficult conditions. They were also endowed with a clear (socialist) development ideology which provided them with a practical blueprint for political and economic action after independence.

Crucially, however, they did not carry equal legitimacy in the eyes of the local population. The PAIGC was unquestionably recognised by the majority of Guineans as the only 'representative' nationalist party and started life with an enormous political capital.[51] FRELIMO, though nowhere near as successful in their armed struggle as their Guinean counterpart, faced no credible competitor during the decolonisation process and was thus ultimately in a position to takeover from the Portuguese unimpeded.[52] Their success as a nationalist party provided them with a relatively secure platform

---

[49]For a detailed account of the process of decolonisation in these countries see McQueen, *The Decolonization of Portuguese Africa*, op. cit.

[50]See Chabal, 'People's war, state formation and revolution in Africa', op. cit.

[51]See Forrest, op. cit.

[52]See Hall and Young, *Confronting Leviathan*, op. cit., chaps 1 and 2.

from which to set about creating (or inventing) the Mozambican nation. The MPLA, on the other hand, lacked political credibility both because its legitimacy as a 'national' political organisation was limited and because it had not managed to bring together the various nationalist strands in the country. In short, the position of prominence assumed by the MPLA at independence was contestable and, indeed, was contested by its main rivals, the FNLA and UNITA.[53] For the MPLA, then, the legacy of the anti-colonial struggle was mixed: positive in that it gained power but negative in that the history of bitter (and sometimes violent) competition between the three nationalist organisations undermined the very foundations of the emerging nation-state. On balance, then, except in Angola, the anti-colonial war made it politically easy for the victorious parties to undertake the construction of the nation.

War, however, did also have a negative impact in at least three ways. First, there was in the three mainland countries an opposition to the new regime with a history of strong hostility. In Guinea and Mozambique, there was a ready supply of discontented among those African forces that had fought with the Portuguese and who were mistreated after independence. There were also remnants of opposition groups, some with a history of violence, determined to remove the new governments at the earliest opportunity. In Angola, of course, independence was followed by civil war, and the country has been in conflict ever since.

Second, the anti-colonial wars polarised ethnic, religious and regional groups into support of or opposition to the new regimes. In Guinea, the Fulas were reluctant to accept the PAIGC dominance. In Mozambique, FRELIMO was confronted by a number of potential opponents from the northern Makua to the central Ndau. In Angola, the MPLA met hostility in large swathes of the interior of the country, particularly in the highlands. Such divisions, however minor, acquired momentum once the 'authoritarian' tendencies of the governing parties became clear. The experience of the nationalist struggle thus often fed strong feelings of hostility which all too readily could degenerate into violence.

Thirdly, the war gave the victorious nationalists the means to suppress dissent through coercion. Not only had the PAIGC, FRELIMO and the MPLA a long experience of guerrilla warfare but they were also familiar with the more mundane ways in which the wielders of weapons are able to ensure compliance. The extent to which violence was deployed during the armed struggle against internal opposition varied according to the ease with which the nationalists managed to garner support—most thoroughly

[53]See chapter 3.

in Guinea and least satisfactorily in Angola—but in all instances, the use or threat of violence had been part of the political armoury of these political movements. It was logical, if not inevitable, that such means would continue to be used after independence.[54]

Here, naturally, the experience of the two island states was different. Not only did they reach independence without an armed struggle but the dominant nationalist party in each country was forced by the Portuguese to demonstrate its political credentials in the election held before independence was granted. If the success of the PAIGC and the MLSTP was never seriously in doubt, despite the last-minute efforts among some Portuguese and their local allies to set up competitor political parties, the fact that elections took place was significant. In the eyes of insiders and outsiders alike, the two parties' legitimacy was thereby considerably strengthened. Added to this, the socio-cultural make-up of these two Creole societies was free from serious ethnic, religious and regional divisions. As a result, the prospects for the construction of the nation were infinitely better in the two island states than they were in the three mainland countries.

In the end, therefore, it is not clear that the armed struggle proved decisive in the overcoming of the difficulties faced by the nationalist parties in the construction of a viable nation-state at independence. If it provided the victorious parties with a large political capital and the means to ensure compliance through coercion, it also opened the way for the potentially violent sharpening of internal divisions. And since none of these parties ever countenanced either sharing power or seeking alliances to stay in power, it can be argued that their 'military' success, symbolic as it might have been, made it more likely that they would confront any opposition through force. Conversely, the manner in which the nationalist parties took over in the two island states, where in any event the very basis of the existing Creole society made family and social ties very much more proximate, augured rather better for a more peaceful and pragmatic political future.

It was clear, therefore, that the nature of social relations in Cape Verde and São Tomé e Príncipe facilitated the establishment of a working nation-state after independence. Indeed, the obstacles faced by the two new regimes were almost exclusively linked to the economic fragility of their country and not, as in most mainland African countries, to the potential divisions within a poorly consolidated and far from homogeneous society. Of course, the new Cape Verdean government had to take into account the differences, and imbalances, between the islands that formed the archipelago.

[54]See here Patrick Chabal, 'Pouvoir et violence en Afrique contemporaine', *Politique Africaine*, 42 (1991).

Similarly, there were in São Tomé e Príncipe potentially fractious divisions between the local elites, or *forros*, and the plantation workers or their descendants, whilst the inhabitants of Príncipe had always felt neglected.[55] But these social and geographical divisions never threatened either the integrity of the country or the legitimacy of the regime in place. In sum, there were in the two island states few obstacles to the consolidation of the nation-state after independence.

This was not the case in the other three territories. Above and beyond the impact of the guerrilla war, the legacy of Portuguese colonial rule was not overly favourable to the construction of the independent nation. Whatever the circumstances of decolonisation in Africa, it is generally accepted that the transition to independence was easiest in those colonies where the political, social, economic and technical infrastructure was the most developed. An educated elite, a minimum degree of literacy, functioning devolved political institutions, proper means of transport and a relatively healthy local economy made it easier for the new regimes in place to construct the new nation. On all these counts, the Portuguese colonies were deficient. Although Angola and Mozambique in the years before independence experienced an economic surge forward, this was based almost entirely on foreign capital and a settler Portuguese population—a fragile base on which to build, especially after most of the settlers and almost all foreign capital fled the country prior to independence.

If Guinea was, without contest, the least developed of the Portuguese colonies, Mozambique and Angola were perhaps even less consolidated as national territories. The former suffered from a lack of integration between the regions north and south of the Zambesi, and it lacked the administrative or transport infrastructure to bring together its disparate parts. Furthermore, it was historically divided into three 'zones'—south, centre and north— which were locked into economic relations with their English-speaking neighbours: South Africa, Rhodesia/Malawi and Tanzania. In many significant ways, the newly-independent Mozambique was an economic satellite of South Africa because of its reliance on the remittances from migrant mine labour and on the transport fees garnered on rail traffic from the Witwatersrand. On paper, certainly, it can safely be said that the new Mozambican regime lacked most of the basic means of consolidating its territory into a functioning, not to say viable, nation-state. It was always going to have to struggle to bring together the various regions and peoples of this vast, 'geographically challenged', country.

Angola, for its part, was split into three main socio-economic zones—

---

[55]For details on these social divisions see the chapter on São Tomé e Príncipe below.

a 'Creole' Luanda and its hinterland, the north-west and the central highlands—the modern (nineteeth and twentieth centuries) history of which had conspired to separate and bring into competition or conflict. The fact that those three areas came to be represented by three different nationalist parties—respectively, the MPLA, the FNLA and UNITA— only made politically concrete a division that had already marked out the evolution of the colony under Portuguese colonial rule. Since political competition greatly increased the hostility between these three socio-ethnic and geographical groups, the march into independent statehood took place under the worst possible auspices. From 11 November 1975, Angola's 'national' foundations were rotten at the core. The nationalist war degenerated easily into a civil war, from which the country has not recovered. In some fundamental way, Angola does not yet exist as a nation-state.

Guinea, finally, faced somewhat different difficulties. Although, there was at independence no strong tension between the various ethnic groups, there were two potentially divisive obstacles to overcome. The first was the lack of support for the PAIGC in the Muslim north-eastern areas controlled by the Fulas and their allies. The second was the dominance of the Cape Verdeans and *bermedjos* (the Creole-speaking elite) over the main economic and political sectors of society.[56] Since the PAIGC was the party in power in both Guinea-Bissau and the Cape Verde, the resentment at Cape Verdean supremacy was potentially dangerous, especially as the first government of independent Guinea was largely in the hands of politicians of Cape Verdean origin. By far the greatest obstacle to the consolidation of the country into a viable, working, nation-state, however, was its socio-economic and infrastructural backwardness. Indeed, the legacy of Portuguese colonial rule was so minimal that the administration hardly controlled the countryside, where the notorious Companhia União Fabril (CUF) conglomerate had enjoyed a position of economic (and administrative) monopoly dominance.[57] Most of the territory's inhabitants had had only minimal contact with the colonial authorities. Education and other social services were virtually non-existent; roads were in short supply; and the economic fabric of society had been shattered by the colonial war. In short, despite the success of the anti-colonial struggle, Guinea-Bissau was one of the African colonies least prepared to enter independent nationhood.

[56]The expression *'bermedjo'*—there are other possible spellings of the word—derives from the Portuguese *'vermelho'*, or red, and refers to the Cape Verdeans and their descendants on the mainland.

[57]The CUF was one of the largest Portuguese conglomerates, that is large-scale business concerns with interests in many areas, ranging from trade and banking to agriculture and shipping.

Although it is clear that all colonies had a difficult transition after independence, it can be argued that the Lusophone African territories faced an unusual array of problems. Where, as in Angola and Mozambique, both the size and economic potential of the country were promising, the colonial history as well as the circumstances of the anti-colonial struggle raised serious obstacles to the erection of viable nation-states. Their violent birth set in motion a political and military dynamic that made laborious the task of national construction. Where, as in Guinea, the anti-colonial campaign had brought a large degree of unity, the lack of socio-economic development imposed crippling limitations on the postcolonial regime. Since, additionally, the administrative capacity of the PAIGC government was minimal, the outlook for nation-building was not particularly good. Where, as in the two island states, the socio-political framework for independence was auspicious since it provided a solid basis for the construction of a unitary state, the economic foundations of the newly independent countries were virtually incapable of sustaining the country's population, let alone improve their well being. For all five countries, therefore, the road into independence was fraught with danger.

The making of the nation

If the five Portuguese-speaking countries faced rather different obstacles in the construction of the independent nation, they resorted to somewhat similar instruments to achieve their aims. Like all their African counterparts before them, the five newly-installed governments sought to use the state and the party to erect the political and administrative structures required for their autonomous existence. Where they differed is that they set out with a relatively well-defined ideological framework—socialism—within which to operate politically. The next section will discuss in greater detail the import of this ideological choice for the economic development of the five Portuguese-speaking countries—known collectively as the Países Africanos de Língua Oficial Portuguesa, or PALOP. This section focuses on some of the political consequences of the socialist agenda.

For comparative purposes, it is useful to first give a brief overview of the process of nation-building as it took place in the French and British colonies, which became independent between 1957 and 1964.[58] With few exceptions, those other colonies decolonised peacefully and entered autonomous statehood endowed with a multiparty parliamentary system.

---

[58]For a discussion of this process in Africa as a whole see Chabal, *Power in Africa*, op. cit., chap. 7.

The victorious nationalists usually owed their position, in part at least, to their electoral success and they set out to consolidate their power under constitutional arrangements that favoured the separation between the legislature and executive, the independence of the judiciary and the rule of law. Party and state were originally discrete, although the overlap in political elites in practice made that distinction artificial. Finally, they all had a functioning market system, even if many of them rapidly set about asserting state control over key sectors of the economy.

However, the hallmark of the evolution of these postcolonial African countries was undoubtedly their transformation into one-party states within the first decade of independence. The reasons why the one-party state became the norm in Africa is not, as was widely argued by the nationalists at the time, primarily because the postcolonial order demanded cohesion and unity rather than political competition—which, of course, it did. It is essentially because the African state at independence became patrimonial rather than institutionalised (in the Weberian sense).[59] What this meant is that, despite its Western democratic appearance, African politics operated differently. At the core of the formal political system there developed a logic of patronage (neo-patrimonialism) which relied almost entirely on networks of personalised and vertical relations between rulers and ruled, elite and populace. Hence, the arena of politics became more and more informal. By the time the Portuguese colonies became independent, the rest of the continent was well in the throes of one-party neo-patrimonial political systems.

Since the newly-installed Lusophone African regimes were all in some fundamental way committed to 'socialism', they naturally considered that the path ahead required not just a one-party state but the dominance of the party over the state. For them, the model of nation-building was not primarily what had taken place in the rest of Africa but, more significantly, what had occurred in the 'socialist' world beyond the continent. As a result, the constitutional arrangements of the five countries started from two fundamental premises: the first, that nation-building and socio-economic transformation went hand in hand; the second, that the party was the 'leading' political force. What this implied was that the task of creating the nation-state could not be dissociated from that of transforming society (dubbed the 'transition to socialism') and that both would be achieved by a state firmly controlled by the ruling party. Right from the beginning, then, there was an emphasis on the leading role of the nationalist party, upon which

<hr />

[59]For more on the state in Africa see Chabal, *Power in Africa*, op. cit., chap. 4 and Chabal and Daloz, *Africa Works*, op. cit., chap. 1.

all responsibilities now fell. The nation, therefore, would be in the image of the party.

Of course, there were differences between the political complexion of the five parties in power, which the first few years of independence made clear. Broadly, the PAIGC (in power in both Guinea-Bissau and Cape Verde) was markedly less 'orthodox' in its socialism than the others. Although the political structure set in place did give absolute power to the ruling party, the PAIGC never claimed—as did the MPLA and FRELIMO— that it was the vanguard of the progressive alliance of the working class, peasants and revolutionary 'intellectuals'. Nor did it ever advocate the form of African 'socialist accumulation' taken for granted by the other two.[60] The party congresses of the three parties, held in 1977, made explicit the more rigidly 'orthodox' political blueprints of the MPLA and FRELIMO. As for the MLSTP, it followed in broad ideological terms the lead of the MPLA, to whom it turned for political and practical support.

Nevertheless, the governments of the five PALOP all set about constructing the new nation-state according to a fairly clear, if rather rigid, notion of what they intended to achieve. Here, again, we need to distinguish between the experience of the three mainland countries and the two island states. In Cape Verde and São Tomé e Príncipe, both homogeneous Creole communities, there was little need to be concerned about the architecture of the new nation. These two countries were obviously self-contained 'national' entities with no socio-political division liable to threaten the integrity of the territory. Differences between islands, or between social groups, never put into question the overall consensus about the state's national identity. The inhabitants of these two island states knew who they were and knew what configuration they wanted their country to have. The debate was not about the nation but, more prosaically, about the type of politics to be followed.

There was, however, one controversial issue which was potentially divisive within the PAIGC: the nature of the link between Guinea-Bissau and Cape Verde. Whilst there initially was very little dispute about the right of the PAIGC to take power in both territories, there was serious (if originally subdued) opposition to Amílcar Cabral's plan to bring the two together into a bicephalous nation-state. For reasons having to do with the history of the relations between the archipelago and colonial Guinea, there was on both sides much to make that aspiration unpalatable. The Guineans had long resented the role of the Cape Verdeans as successful

---

[60]These issues are examined in greater detail in chapter 3.

entrepreneurs and colonial auxiliaries. The Cape Verdeans considered themselves a Creole, rather than African, society and they valued their close links with Portugal. They also believed that union with Guinea-Bissau, though theoretically economically profitable for them since the archipelago was so devoid of resources, might become a political liability.

The future of the bi-territorial nation-state envisaged officially by the PAIGC was thus in question right from the start and it did not survive the 1980 military coup in Bissau in which Luiz Cabral, the (Cape Verdean) president of Guinea-Bissau, was overthrown by his (Guinean) prime minister, João Bernardo (Nino) Vieira. The break thus formalised important political differences between the two countries which had partly to do with a struggle for power between Guineans and Cape Verdeans but which also touched on the different political aspirations of the two regimes. The PAIGC government in Guinea-Bissau had rapidly become functionally neo-patrimonial whereas in Cape Verde it had achieved a degree of political institutionalisation that favoured the consolidation of the nation-state and the relatively sound management of the (admittedly very weak) economy.

The failure of the PAIGC to achieve Cabral's ambition to bring the two territories into one single nation-state points to a number of difficulties faced by the PALOP as they set about nation-building. Indeed, one of the reasons why Cape Verde and Guinea-Bissau did not merge is that the notion of nation in the two territories was vastly different. In the former, the population at large considered that they were primarily Cape Verdeans and thus needed a state to reflect their national identity. In the latter, there was little 'national' identity to bring the various peoples of Guinea-Bissau together, above and beyond the fact that they had been colonised by a very remote Portugal and that they took pride in the PAIGC's achievements as an anti-colonial movement. It was in the process of national liberation and in the construction of the postcolonial state that the Guineans were now forging a new 'national' identity. As they were doing so, they had reasons to be suspicious of the historical dominance of the Cape Verdeans on the mainland.

In other words, nation-building in Cape Verde—as in São Tomé e Príncipe—was primarily about erecting political institutions to reflect the interests of the nation as a whole. In Guinea-Bissau—as in Angola and Mozambique—it involved additionally, but crucially, coming to some agreement within the country about what the 'nation' was. Inevitably, such a quest for a 'national' identity on mainland Africa was more demanding. The three mainland countries lacked many of the attributes of 'nationhood' already present in the two island states, of which the most significant were:

a common language and oral culture, a shared history, a sense of community, a single religion (Catholicism) and an identity strongly linked to the geography of their country.[61]

Such was, however, not the case in Guinea, Angola and Mozambique. In those three countries, as in the whole of postcolonial Africa, the construction of the nation-state involved three distinct, but crucial, steps. The first was to mobilise support for nation-building behind the ruling party. The second was to neutralise internal (political, ethnic, religious or regional) opposition. The third was to establish a political system able to balance the demands for representation with the need for consolidating 'national' unity. As is evident, the three Lusophone regimes were unequal to the task of fulfilling such an agenda. To some extent, the historical circumstances under which they came to power at independence determined how easy it would be for them to engage in nation-building. Yet, above and beyond these contingent factors, it is clear that the ideological and political orientations of the three governments influenced strongly the way in which they went about their work.

In terms of the historical context of independence, Guinea-Bissau was the most favoured. Not only had the PAIGC achieved the highest degree of national unity, it had also managed to establish its credentials as a nation-building party. At independence, it faced no credible rival, no serious regional or ethnic opposition, and the party was seen legitimately to represent the aspirations of the population at large. FRELIMO was equally successful at establishing its overwhelming 'nationalist' credentials but it had to countenance much more political, regional and ethnic antagonism. Whilst it benefited from an enormous political capital, due in large measure to its success in negotiating independence and running the transitional government with the Portuguese, it had still to prove its ability to bring together the peoples of Mozambique into one single nation-state. The MPLA, as has been pointed out, was bereft of most of these attributes. Its legitimacy, such as it was, lay in its having seized power on 11 November 1975 and having successfully beaten off the opposition (FNLA and UNITA) political and military challenge.

Although these historical factors were important, and in the case of Angola ominous, they did not necessarily determine what happened after independence. If the PAIGC had little difficulty in garnering support for nation-building behind the party, FRELIMO showed it too could mobilise

---

[61]Even if there were in São Tomé e Príncipe strong social divisions between the local elites (*forros*), the plantation workers, and the descendants of escaped slaves (*angolares*), there was widespread agreement about the national 'identity' of the two-island states.

the whole country for the same purpose. Despite a fairly large degree of scepticism, or outright opposition, the ruling Mozambican party was able rapidly to convince the population as a whole that it was legitimately entitled to expect the new government to build the Mozambican 'nation'. Indeed, the first three years of independence saw the party consolidate its hold over the whole territory and put in place an administration with a clear, though unsanctioned by elections, mandate. The situation was different in Angola, where the MPLA never succeeded in gathering unambiguous support for its national project, even if (with the aid of its international allies) it managed to defeat the FNLA and push UNITA to the far south-eastern corner of the country. Owing to its lack of nationalist legitimacy, its blueprint for nation-building was always suspect to a large proportion of the population.

Equally, in terms of the second factor—neutralising internal (political or regional) opposition—Angola stood out from the other two. Even when it believed that it had vanquished both opposition parties, the MPLA government never could claim that it had eliminated them politically. UNITA, with South African support, succeeded in re-implanting itself inside the country and, gradually, asserted strong military resistance to the central state. Since it received important support from a number of Western countries, UNITA represented (until at least the 1994 Lusaka agreement) a credible political alternative to the government in place. The MPLA regime was never rid of this legitimate rival, who put forward very different plans for the future of Angola. The PAIGC, for its part, was able (despite the 1980 coup which exacerbated divisions between Guineans and Cape Verdeans inside the country) to neutralise all opposition until the 1994 multiparty elections. It was thus in a position to assert the supremacy of the party-state throughout the country.

For FRELIMO, the situation was more complex. Whilst the regime remained secure both in terms of its 'national' legitimacy and the coherence of its political and economic programme, it faced increasing opposition from RENAMO, an internal enemy which originally had been no more than the puppet of the Rhodesian secret services. This externally-funded opponent never gained sufficient national and international legitimacy to challenge the regime's 'national' credentials but it proved an obdurate adversary who could not be eliminated. The consequences of the civil war that ensued was to impair the government's action and to reduce its capacity to meet the demands or, even, the expectations of the population. Ultimately, the FRELIMO state was forced to concede that the armed opposition had made normal life in the country impossible and thus to agree to peace negotiations. The result of the subsequent elections, in which FRELIMO was returned to power despite RENAMO's very strong (albeit regionally concentrated) showing, demonstrates (in part at least) that the regime continues to be endowed with the legitimacy of a 'national' party, whose ability to re-build the country still carries some conviction.

The third step—to establish a political system able to balance the demands for representation with the need for consolidating 'national' unity—turned out to be the most difficult. Even in Guinea-Bissau, where the question of unity did not become unduly salient after independence, the political system has failed either to allow for proper representation or to deliver meaningful economic development. As a consequence, there have been strong regional and ethnic tensions, which have hitherto not degenerated into overt civil strife. The recent armed conflict between the president, João Bernardo Vieira, and his former minister, Ansumane Mané, which devastated the country, was due more to political rivalry and general discontent than to a well-focussed challenge from a particular ethnic or regional opposition.[62] In this respect, there continues to be a strong sense of 'national' unity in the country. The problems facing Guinea-Bissau are due to the malfunctioning of the present polity and are common to, if perhaps not quite as acute in, all west African countries. Of course, such problems could in the long run—especially given increasing regional tension—lead to a disintegration of national unity.

In Mozambique, nation-building proved much more formidable. Not only had the territory been very poorly integrated as a 'unit' under colonial rule, but the challenge posed by RENAMO to the FRELIMO regime prevented the consolidation of the country as a nation-state. For all its nationalist legitimacy, FRELIMO was unable to establish a political system that would reconcile the basic requirements of government with the demands for representation. The state's strength was its unity of purpose and its unbending will to build a Mozambican 'nation' that would accommodate all ethnic, racial, regional and religious groups. Its weakness was its determination to impose a political framework that neglected history and opposed rural socio-political traditions.

The Marxist ideological blueprint, which was wholly inappropriate in the African context (even if it was believed to have been successful in other non-African settings), conspired to alienate large segments of the population, thus enabling RENAMO to capitalise on discontent, and to undo the party's original political capital. Indeed, the imposition of a 'vanguard' Marxist party onto the realities of the country was almost entirely counter-productive since, *inter alia*, the nationalisation of the economy, the strong hostility

---

[62]The details about this conflict are given in the country chapter in this volume.

to 'traditional' political customs, and the attempted forced villagisation of the countryside, proved a complete political disaster. Although in the early eighties the party leadership realised that it had to alter course, by then the political and economic damage had been done and RENAMO had become an intractable problem.

It is difficult, even with the benefit of hindsight, to state with certainty whether the obstacles faced by the newly-independent regime were beyond the capability of any government. It is much easier to assert that the political choices made by that government made nation-building infinitely more problematic than it need have been. One can but conclude that FRELIMO did not satisfactorily manage to create a Mozambican 'nation' before the civil war made that ambition impossible. It is only now, a few years after the peace settlement and the elections which have followed since, that the process of nation-building can resume.

The situation in Angola is far worse, and this for well-understood political reasons. While there have always been deep socio-economic, regional and ethnic divisions in the country, the fact that the nationalists remained bitterly disunited until independence ushered in a period of civil conflict that continues to this day. It is by now a moot point to argue that such divisions were not inevitable and that the 'objective' barriers to national unity in Angola were not as problematic as in Mozambique.[63] The failure of the MPLA to find a *modus vivendi* with its nationalist opponents, allied with the strong support given to the opposite sides by the Cold War rivals, made it inevitable that there would not be a consolidation of the territory into a single nation-state until peace was restored. Although neither the MPLA government nor UNITA have ever envisaged the partition of the country, and in this way continue to recognise the legitimacy of the 'nation' as it is geographically defined, the civil war makes it impossible to lay down the foundations for a unified political entity.

Indeed, the war may make less explicit the failure of the Angolan regime's blueprint for the construction of the nation. Since both its ideological commitment to 'orthodox' Marxism and its attempt to impose a Stalinist political system were even more extreme, and certainly more enduring, than in Mozambique, it can safely be concluded that, regardless of the civil war, the government would have found it most taxing to consolidate the country on such a political basis. Fundamental opposition to the MPLA would have remained strong. The recent political transition towards multiparty elections—which in any event has had very mixed results

[63]See chapter 3.

elsewhere in Africa—must be seen primarily as a tactical move to ensure financial support from the Bretton Woods institutions. The present situation in the country is one in which a narrowly based presidential neo-patrimonial system is maintained through a combination of severe repression and very selective clientelism.[64] Without the oil resources, the present MPLA regime would not have survived the pressures it would have faced from a population it has essentially left to fend for itself. Conversely, without the sale of diamonds, UNITA could not have resisted the government's military campaigns. The construction of the Angolan nation is thus in abeyance, and will remain so until the conflict has come to an end. The tragedy is that it now suits both parties to continue the war, regardless of its effects on the Angolan people.

BUILDING SOCIALISM

The construction of the nation-state in Lusophone Africa was inextricably bound with the use of Marxism as a guiding ideology. Whereas most of the governments of the former British and French colonies had, with few exceptions (such as Guinea), entered independent statehood without an entrenched political outlook, the regimes in the PALOP were committed to 'socialism'. It is true that, by the mid-seventies, there were in Africa a number of ostensibly left-wing or Marxist regimes in place, so that the ideological direction taken by the five Portuguese-speaking countries did not appear so singular. However, there had never before been on the continent such a large group of states moving immediately after independence to set up Marxist, or neo-Marxist, polities. For this reason alone, the experience of the PALOP presents us with a unique case study in the use of socialism for the purpose of nation-building.[65]

The fact that these five regimes were committed to such an ideology may, in retrospect, appear of little consequence—now that Marxism has been abandoned in the former Soviet Bloc and that capitalism is making huge strides in China and Vietnam, where socialism is still the official credo. Indeed, since the five regimes have now firmly turned their back on their socialist past—opening up their markets and privatising most of the state concerns as well as introducing multiparty electoral systems—it may seem that the ideological orientation of the PALOP's governments are supremely irrelevant. This is true as far as it goes. Yet, it would be difficult

---

[64]See Tony Hodges, *Angola: From Afro-Stalinism to Petro-Diamond Capitalism* (Oxford: James Currey, 2001).

[65]For a discussion of socialism in Africa see Chabal, *Power in Africa*, chap. 1.

to understand their postcolonial history without taking into account the importance of ideology for the construction of the nation-state after independence. What is more, the ideological transformation of these regimes in the last twenty-five years is itself of substantial historical relevance.

This section gives attention to the role of socialism as an ideology of nation-building—that is, not just as an economic blueprint but also as a framework for the organisation of the political institutions of the newly-created states. It seeks to explain why such an ideology had a greater impact on society because it was imposed immediately after independence rather than, as in most other African countries, a number of years after the consolidation of the nation. Finally, it discusses the important differences between the ideological orientations of the five states and assesses the extent to which these differences mattered for their postcolonial development. This section is in two main parts: first, it presents the nature of the ideological choices made by the nationalist parties; second, it evaluates the practical socio-economic and political consequences of their socialist orientation.

Socialist ideologies in Portuguese-speaking Africa

In chapter 1, we considered the link between the anti-colonial struggles and the move towards a socialist perspective. It is important to stress, again, that such an ideological inclination had more to do with the circumstances in which the nationalist leadership found itself during the anti-colonial campaigns than with a deep-rooted political choice. Here two factors were crucial. The first is that Portugal was a dictatorship, under which all political parties were banned. As a result, most of the opposition to the regime, both in Portugal and in the colonies, gravitated around the only solidly organised political organisation: the Portuguese Communist Party (PCP). For this reason, the African nationalists, who had virtually all studied in Portugal in the forties and early fifties, came under the influence of Marxism, at that time the only coherent ideology that opposed the Salazar regime. Additionally, they forged links with the Portuguese opposition, most of whom were of a communist or socialist disposition. Their ideological schooling as well as their political alliances thus placed them, broadly, in the Marxist camp.[66]

The second is that the Portuguese, unlike the other colonial powers, refused to enter into negotiations about the decolonisation of their overseas territories. Because of this, the nationalists were forced to resort to armed

[66]For an account of Portuguese politics on the eve of decolonisations see Kenneth Maxwell, *The Making of Portuguese Democracy* (Cambridge University Press, 1995).

struggle and in the process of waging war against a right-wing authoritarian regime they readily embraced a left-leaning ideology. Over time, they moved to a strongly-held socialist position both because they came to believe that radical socio-economic change would be required after independence and because they found in the socialist world their only secure allies. If some of them, like Agostinho Neto (the MPLA leader), always were close to the PCP, others like Amílcar Cabral (the PAIGC head) were more inclined to take a socialist posture somewhat askance from the Soviet variant. A few, like Eduardo Mondlane (the FRELIMO founder), had little knowledge or experience of Marxism and only evolved into convinced socialists in the course of the anti-colonial campaign.[67]

Because of these diverse origins, the nationalist leaders represented a wide range of ideological tendencies and it would be simplistic to see them as all fitting one indistinguishable Marxist mould. If we are to understand the differences between the regimes they established after independence, it is important to be mindful of the distinctions between their political outlook and, indeed, understand the extent to which they believed ideology to be relevant to the postcolonial politics of nation-building. The diversity of opinion was here as wide as could at the time be found within the socialist world. Furthermore, there is plenty of evidence that the parties in question evolved politically over time, both before and after independence. The key question here is thus to understand both the nature and the relevance of such dynamic diversity.

At one end of the spectrum, the most 'orthodox' Marxist of the five parties was without doubt the MPLA. Why was that and what did it mean in the context of Africa? Within the Marxist ideological perspective of the sixties and seventies, the reference to 'orthodoxy' would have highlighted two distinct areas: the first having to do with the type of socialist blueprint adopted by the party; the second indicating that the party was most closely associated with the Soviet Union and its allies rather than with China and her supporters. Leaving aside the international diplomatic aspect, what does 'orthodox' socialism mean in concrete terms? Originally, it referred to the proximity of the selected ideology to the model adopted after the Soviet revolution in Russia. In the African context, self-evidently very distinct from the Russian one, the emphasis must essentially be put on three aspects: the type of party, the role of the party within the country's political system and, finally, the economic priorities adopted.

The 'orthodox' Marxist party was endowed with the characteristics

---

[67]See here, *inter alia*, Chabal, *Amílcar Cabral*, op. cit. and Eduardo Mondlane, *The Struggle for Mozambique* (London: Zed Press, 1983).

of the Soviet model, that is, a vanguard party run on the principles of 'democratic centralism', and maintaining strict control over every aspect of the political system in place.[68] What this meant in Angola was that the MPLA was conceived as an elite organisation charged with the wholesale overview of the whole range of socio-economic and political changes envisaged by the regime. The government itself was in effect an arm of the party. Such an ambition was new in Africa, where most socialist parties had been conceived as mass organisations charged with the mobilisation of the largest number of followers in order to carry forward the task of nation-building. Indeed, the experience of those former French and British colonies that had adopted Marxism after independence was that there was little scope for such an all-encompassing party in Africa. Whereas mass parties enabled the leadership to seek maximum support throughout the country and maintain a relatively stable neo-patrimonial equilibrium, a vanguard party became in effect a self-serving clientelistic network which aroused considerable opposition. Nevertheless, the MPLA (especially after the 1977 Nito Alves coup attempt)[69] turned itself into a closed Marxist party relying on ideological purity and repression to assert its control. The existence of internal enemies (the FNLA and UNITA) helped it in this respect to portray itself as the embattled keeper of 'national' integrity.

The change that took place in 1977, in the wake of the post-coup purge, making the MPLA an even more 'elitist' vanguard party aiming to oversee all aspects of the polity and of society, was a forlorn venture. Angola in the seventies did not possess the means, particularly the security apparatus, which the Soviet regime had deployed in the thirties and forties to 'domesticate' the Soviet Union. Nor was it in a position to take control of the 'commanding heights' of the economy so as to spur a process of forced industrialisation by means of 'primitive socialist accumulation'.[70] In

---

[68] A vanguard Marxist party is a party run by a 'revolutionary' elite on behalf of the proletariat. Democratic centralism refers to a political practice consisting of reaching policy decisions supposedly on the basis of open discussion within the party but then allowing the leadership to implement them with total ruthlessness.

[69] Nito Alves, a former guerrilla commander in the Dembos region near Luanda, was a 'radical' member of the MPLA leadership who had ambitions for a more thorough 'revolution' in Angola. Allied with other left-leaning members of the party, and enjoying strong support in the *musseques* (slums) of Luanda, he took the fateful decision of trying to overthrow the regime. His attempt, which failed largely because the Cubans supported the government in place, was repressed with extreme violence. Although there are no reliable figures, best estimates are that hundreds were killed.

[70] The term 'commanding heights' refers to the key sectors of the economy, particularly industry. 'Primitive socialist accumulation' refers to the Soviet policy of squeezing the agricultural sector as hard as possible in order to help finance industrial development.

practice, the evolution of the MPLA into the MPLA-Partido do Trabalho (Workers' Party) had only two purposes. The first was to re-state strongly Angola's place on the Soviet side of the Cold War. The second was to use ideology as a political weapon to assert stronger dominance over the only relevant sector of the economy, that is, petroleum. Since Angola's regime was sustained by the oil export revenues, it was in a position to avoid having seriously to worry about how to attempt to engineer an economic 'transition to socialism' in the country. The MPLA's economic blueprint, though formally dedicated to the development of a nationalised industry and the creation of a more 'collective' agriculture, did not in the end amount to much more than the use of the oil dividend to nourish the restricted political elite on which the regime dependent for survival.

Although FRELIMO also dubbed itself a vanguard Workers' Party at its 1977 conference, the similarity in ideological vocabulary concealed vast differences with the Angolan case.[71] In the first place, the party's leadership was both less 'orthodox' and more pragmatic. Mondlane, unlike Neto, had not been a communist sympathiser but much more of a Third World socialist. His successor, the charismatic former guerrilla commander Samora Machel, was not an ideologue and was prone to follow the advice of his closest associates, among whom there was no obvious consensus on the party's preferred political orientation. The move towards an 'orthodox' Marxist position must thus be seen primarily as an instrumental, rather than ideological, move. In the circumstances in which Mozambique found itself in the late seventies, with strong hostility from the West, the regime decided to seek support from the Soviet Bloc—going as far as to apply for membership of Comecon in 1981—and marked that policy choice by endorsing the appropriate 'socialist' programmatic package.[72]

Nevertheless, the choices made at the 1977 party congress had important consequences for the people of Mozambique. In political terms, the government did set about reshaping the party and making it more central within the administration. FRELIMO was no longer conceived as a broad 'front', such as it had originally been, but became the political arm of the envisaged 'transition to socialism'. Although there was no political purge,

---

[71]For a comparative analysis of the MPLA and FRELIMO 1977 congresses see Luís Moita, *Os Congressos da FRELIMO, do PAIGC e do MPLA* (Lisbon: Ulmeiro, 1979).

[72]Mozambique's application to join Comecon was turned down by the Soviet Union for economic and political reasons. Economically, Mozambique was seen as being too weak and would have been a drain on the Comecon's finances. Politically, integrating a non East European country into Comecon membership would, in the Cold War context of the time, have been interpreted as a very hostile act on the part of the Soviet Union. For this reason, Vietnam's application was also turned down.

as in Angola, there was a tendency to remove those who were dubbed the 'opportunists' (political free-riders) and to require of party members a more rigorous commitment to the socialist aims of FRELIMO. In particular, party members became the enforcers of the new 'socialist' economic policy and even of 'socialist' morality, which were now implemented with vigour throughout the country.[73] The result or such changes, as we shall see below, were not positive.

The situation in the other three PALOP was somewhat different, in that they did not adopt an 'orthodox' position. Even the regime most influenced by Angola, that of São Tomé e Príncipe, did not commit itself to the same ideological path as the MPLA. The MLSTP did embrace a fairly clear socialist programme, including the nationalisation of the economy, but in the context of a small Creole country there was little scope for the formation of a 'vanguard' party. In a setting where family and community ties cut across political affiliations and where in any case the ruling party was already small, the notion of a vanguard elite would have made little sense. Furthermore, the MLSTP regime could not, for obvious reasons of international diplomacy, afford simply to join the Soviet side. Its continued links with Portugal, its dependence on (largely Western) foreign aid, as well as its position within a central African region where some key pro-West states, like Gabon, mattered greatly, all conspired to limit the regime's enthusiasm for Cold War rhetoric. Where the MLSTP was influenced by its socialist ideology was primarily in its views on the future of the country's economy.

The PAIGC, for its part, differed in some important respects from the other three nationalist parties. Not only did its position as the ruling party of two separate countries induce a fair degree of pragmatism, but its ideological stance never acquired any 'orthodox' complexion. The 1977 party congress was in this respect quite revealing, as the political programme adopted stood in contrast to that chosen by the MPLA and FRELIMO.[74] If there was no difference in terms of the 'leading role' of the PAIGC—that is party control of the government and of the administration—there was a distinctly less sectarian tone to the document. There was a recognition that the situation in both countries was not such as to justify the type of socialism that might have been appropriate in other parts of the world. Following Cabral, whose writings had made clear that there could be no political 'model' for Guinea and Cape Verde, the PAIGC was obviously reluctant to

---

[73]For instance, those deemed to be trading illegally were treated very harshly and a few were executed.
[74]See Moita, op. cit.

define an ideological line that could be associated too firmly with the Soviet or Chinese variant.[75] Diplomatic considerations were also important: the PAIGC committed itself more strongly to the Non-Aligned movement rather than to the socialist camp. In any event, the 1977 programmatic intentions were overtaken by the events which followed the November 1980 coup in Bissau. The rift between Guinea-Bissau and Cape Verde, followed by the creation of a separate party for the archipelago, the Partido Africano da Independência de Cabo Verde (PAICV), formalised a political split which left little space for ideology. Whilst Guinea-Bissau became a one-party state on the west African model, Cape Verde evolved firmly away from the socialist model and adopted more pragmatic 'social-democratic' policies.

What such ideological contortions meant in practice for the PALOP is not entirely clear, as it could be argued that political pronouncements essentially derived from foreign policy objectives. This is partly true: it is easy to correlate the ideological evolution of the five parties with their diplomatic self-interest. Equally, it is not difficult to show that socialism waned markedly after the fall of the Berlin Wall in 1989. Nevertheless, to explain away ideology in this way would be an excessively reductive position to take, for the adoption of socialist policies had very consequential effects for the development of the five countries after independence.

Socialist policies in Portuguese-speaking Africa

It is easy to over-emphasise the importance of ideology—as did many sympathetic observers of the regimes in question—and even more to be tempted to explain the development vagaries of the PALOP merely on the basis of the pronouncements of their political elites.[76] In Africa generally it has long been clear that the formal programmatic orientations of governments have had limited relevance to actual events on the ground. Politics on the continent operate very largely in the realm of the informal, in ways which habitually make ideology a mere instrument of the search for neo-patrimonial dominance.[77] One should clearly be careful about examining postcolonial Lusophone Africa through an ideological lens.

Yet, it is undoubtedly the case that the socialist proclivities of the five regimes impinged, to a greater or lesser extent, directly on the manner in

[75]On Cabral's political thought see Chabal, *Amílcar Cabral*, op. cit., chap. 6.

[76]For one example of an approach which deduces the developmental failings of Mozambique from the changes in ideological outlook see Michel Cahen, *Mozambique: la Révolution Implosée* (Paris: L'Harmattan, 1987).

[77]For a full-scale development of this argument see Chabal and Daloz, *Africa Works*, op. cit.

which they endeavoured to construct the nation-state—and did so in ways which were novel on the African continent.[78] With the possible exception of Guinea Conakry, no other country in Africa embarked at independence on a recognisably socialist course. But even in that French-speaking state, the experience of decolonisation had been so markedly different from the Lusophone as to make its socialist project almost wholly distinct. What defined the PALOP as a special case in this respect was precisely the combination of the experience of the anti-colonial struggle allied to a resolutely socialist perspective, that is the practice of harnessing active (and sometimes armed) political mobilisation for the purpose of achieving well-defined programmatic aims. For this reason, the decision to implement socialist policies at independence, however unrealistic it might have been, was significant.

So was the fact that the newly-installed regimes, unlike almost all their previous counterparts in the former French and British Africa, did not envisage that the political institutions bequeathed to them by the Portuguese could in any way serve their postcolonial aspirations. In so far as the new regimes believed, however naïvely, that they would have to reconstruct the nation-state without relying on the colonial administration, their actions after independence acquired an even greater 'revolutionary' potential. The five regimes behaved, at least for a time, as though it was incumbent upon them to design a new political architecture that would not only replace the hated colonial one but also enable them to fulfil their more overtly socialist aims. In this way, they all came to power with a very full agenda. The pressure on them to replace what they had inherited was further increased, in some cases dramatically, because of the effects of the chaotic, not to say vindictive, manner in which the Portuguese departed. If in Guinea and Cape Verde, the transition was orderly, in Angola and Mozambique it was potentially catastrophic given the combination of massive settler flight and deliberate sabotage of some of the infrastructure. São Tomé e Príncipe too was gravely affected by the wholesale departure of the Portuguese.

The scene was set, therefore, for a greater political upheaval than had occurred in any other African colony. What happened was not on the 'revolutionary' scale proclaimed by the victorious nationalists but it was more structurally significant than might have been expected in view of what had taken place on the rest of the continent. Of importance here is the need to analyse the (admittedly) distinct ways in which such an ideological orientation determined the main political, social and economic policies adopted,

---

[78]With the single but most significant exception of Ethiopia, where a genuine (socialist?) revolution did take place in 1974.

if not always implemented, by the Lusophone African regimes. I propose to summarise briefly what occurred in this respect in the five countries.

If the constitutional frameworks of the PALOP differed little, there were strong and significant contrasts between what happened in practice. The Angolan and Cape Verdean cases stand at the two extremes of the spectrum. In the former, the regime rapidly put in place a singularly 'Stalinist' or 'orthodox' one-party state.[79] The main features of such a system were: the concentration of power in the hands of a very small group at the apex (the party's central committee and political bureau run with an iron hand by the president); the absolute dominance of the party over the organs of government (including the prime minister and his ministerial colleagues); the supremacy of the party within all essential state, administrative, military and economic institutions; the reliance on ideology as a weapon of political control; the re-shaping of the economy according to the rigid principles of nationalisation and 'primitive socialist accumulation'; and, finally, the attempt to exert total (party) political control over the principal (religious, social, academic and cultural) institutions of civil society.

Although it is clear that the MPLA regime never succeeded in imposing the type of socialist dictatorship experienced in the Soviet Union or China, it did manage to massively re-shape the country's political infrastructure. The tightening up of party control which followed the Nito Alves coup attempt and the resumption of the civil war in the country was intensified by José Eduardo dos Santos, Neto's successor as president. Furthermore, the evidently detrimental effects which such policies were having on the country did not result in any serious political reform until the mid eighties, when Angola's economic crisis as well as the pressure exerted by the West to settle the Namibian conflict forced the regime to begin a process of economic and, perforce, political liberalisation. For well over a decade, therefore, Angola suffered from the imposition of a severely authoritarian socialist political system which presided over the intensification of the civil war, the collapse of the economy, the flowering of massive corruption at the top, and the gradual immiseration of its population. Whilst a socialist ideology is not required to achieve such distinctly catastrophic results, its use made it easier for the MPLA regime to implement its policies of choice without opposition. Socialism in Angola, for all the idealism which genuinely moved a large proportion of the party militants at independence, turned out in the end to have been the eminently practical instrument for an intensely neo-patrimonial and economically unproductive authoritarianism.

[79]For a summary of the Angolan political system see Keith Somerville, *Angola: Politics, Economics and Society* (London: Frances Pinter, 1986).

If Angola's oil reserves enabled the regime to survive, there is little doubt that the socialist policies adopted were detrimental to the other sectors of the economy. The first few years after independence saw a rapid decline in agricultural production and exports, due in large part at least to the government's attempt to use nationalisation and collectivisation as the twin instruments of its economic policy. The failure to support rural producers and the inability to ensure proper transport throughout the country rapidly destroyed internal trade. Once the civil war resumed in earnest, the whole basis of the agricultural system began to collapse. But even in the face of such catastrophic developments, the government soon ceased to consider rural production an important part of its economic responsibility.

The continuation of the war provided the justification for a callous neglect of food, let alone export, production. Increasingly, the country relied on imports, paid out of the oil dividend, to sustain the population, especially in the urban centres. The rest of the country was virtually left to its own devices. The 'transition to socialism' meant, in the Angolan case, a political system which enabled the party to consolidate its hold on power whilst maintaining sufficient coercive control to fend off any realistic challenge to the growing enrichment of the party leadership. If the neglect of agricultural production could be explained away in (simplistic) Marxist terms,[80] the stark reality was that the oil revenues made it possible for the regime to ignore the acute problems of its rural population—who were, in addition, suffering the brunt of the civil war. As a result, there was a massive displacement of population from the countryside towards the urban centres, particularly the capital Luanda.[81]

The situation in Mozambique was both similar and very different. It was similar in that the ruling party also went down the 'orthodox' socialist path in the first few years after independence. Both in political and economic terms, FRELIMO adopted policies akin to those of the MPLA: a more compact 'vanguard' party designed to lead the 'transition to socialism'; the gradual extension of party control over political institutions and much of civil society; the adoption of a 'socialist' economic programme, based on an attempt to force villagisation, collectivise agriculture and develop industry; and the war against an increasingly disturbing internal enemy. It was different in that FRELIMO never instituted as authoritarian a political

[80]Marxist theory posits the gradual disappearance of the peasantry as the economy becomes increasingly industrialised. The Soviet experience was, of course, based on the destruction of individual household agriculture and the forced collectivisation of the rural workforce.

[81]By far the most provocative analysis of the changes that have taken place in Angola over the last twenty years is Hodges, op. cit.

system as the MPLA; in that it inflected its socialist economic policies when it realised that they had proved ineffective; and in that it recognised early on that political unity was more important than repression. It also had to face hard economic realities very soon after independence: Mozambique was not endowed with oil or other mineral resources on which it could live; and it remained singularly dependent on its economic relationship with South Africa. Since in the end its commitment to socialism failed to earn it the economic backing of the Soviet Union, the Mozambican regime was left to take up a rather more pragmatic political and economic approach than Angola.[82]

It is, of course, true that the FRELIMO leadership was never as committed as that of the MPLA to the full rigours of the 'orthodox' socialist blueprint. Machel, for all his fiery left-wing rhetoric, was not an ideologue and he quickly realised that the party's socialist option had grave limitations. By the late seventies, it was the president himself who started campaigning against the pernicious effects of the government's policies. Whilst never questioning the basic commitment to socialism, Machel went out of his way to point out the shortcomings of the increasing politicisation of the social and economic spheres. He berated bureaucratic inefficiency and decried the poor performance of the economy and of the social services, particularly health and education.[83] Furthermore, the manifest failure of the government's rural policies brought changes. When it became obvious that the attempt to set up large collective farms and to bring about 'communal' farming in the countryside had resulted in a serious decline in production, the FRELIMO regime sought to steer a more realistic course. An attempt was made to give ordinary family-based rural producers the support which they had hitherto lacked. By then, however, it was too late, for the RENAMO challenge had reached most parts of the country and rural production, for too long neglected by the government, was now at the mercy of the civil war.

In Mozambique, then, socialism had a more patchy impact than in Angola. It resulted in the establishment of a one-party state that was far less coercive than the MPLA in several important respects. First, there always was a wide variety of political views accepted within the party leadership, from 'orthodox' Marxist to social-democratic. Second, ideology was not paramount and, more importantly, was not systematically used as an

[82]The most complete summary of Mozambique's postcolonial political evolution is Hall and Young, *Confronting Leviathan* op. cit.

[83]On Machel see Iain Christie, *Samora Machel* (London: Panaf, 1989); see also Machel's writings in Barry Munslow (ed.) *Samora Machel: An African Revolutionary. Selected Speeches and Writings* (London: Zed, 1985).

instrument of repression. Third, the party did not acquire the same commanding role in non-political (civil) institutions as in Angola. Finally, the regime never sought to control and gag civil society: if overt opposition to the regime was not allowed, much leeway was left in religious, cultural, literary and social circles.

Where the party's ideology had a profound impact on society, however, was in the regime's relentless hostility towards the so-called 'traditional' rural socio-political institutions. If many postcolonial governments were keen to neutralise the political weight of chiefs and other 'traditional' authorities, few were as relentless as FRELIMO in the attempt to do away with them. This attitude stemmed in part from the experience of the armed struggle, when the party had suffered from what it saw as the opposition of 'traditional', or more likely, colonially-appointed chiefs. But it was also due to a political analysis that deemed 'traditional' authorities to be incompatible with the construction of a modern 'socialist' postcolonial nation-state. To the party leadership—some of whom were either of Creole, Goan/Indian, or white origin—African 'traditional' authority was not just incompatible with the process of nation-building, it was positively backward, or reactionary, and in this way had to be eliminated. The consequence of such a militant view against 'tradition' was that the FRELIMO regime was soon perceived to be antagonistic to the rural population, which already felt undermined by the party's socialist economic blueprint. Such grievances, allied with rural economic decline, proved a fertile ground for RENAMO when, in the early eighties, it sought to infiltrate larger and larger areas of the country. The regime's ideological straightjacket alienated a significant proportion of the rural population and thus managed to considerably set back the process of nation-building.[84]

In Guinea-Bissau, ideology played a far less significant role. If the regime did set itself firmly against the so-called *régulos*, or 'colonial' chiefs, it very rapidly settled for a policy which, in practice, left substantial leeway to local 'traditional' authorities. For this reason, the attempt to establish party 'village committees', on the model of what had been done in the liberated areas during the armed struggle, did not really succeed. Or rather, the village committees were taken over or replaced by locally-selected representatives who paid scant attention to the centre. Nor did the PAIGC's supposed socialist orientation fundamentally affect the *de facto* power of the Fula Muslim leadership, with which the government eventually had to come to terms. In the end, the regime's nation-building was guided by a relatively pragmatic outlook, which allowed 'traditional' local authorities

---

[84]For more details on these issues see the country chapter in this volume.

autonomy so long as they did not challenge the overall position of the party within the state.[85]

Because the PAIGC was in power in both Guinea-Bissau and Cape Verde, its original socialist outlook was rapidly diluted by the differing realities it faced in the two countries. Whereas in Guinea-Bissau, the party developed an economic policy influenced by its ideology, in Cape Verde this did not happen—if only because the conditions on the archipelago made it impossible. On the mainland, the regime was inclined to pursue the twin goal of more 'collective' agriculture and agro-industrial growth. This was underpinned by a legal framework which placed economic power in the hands of the party and allowed for a nationalised economy. In practice, what this meant was that internal and external trade was controlled by state monopolies and that the bulk of the aid-funded investment was lavished on agro-industrial and other import-substitution projects for which the country was ill-equipped and which, in any event, did not fit in with its development requirements. The results were as unedifying as they had been in Mozambique. The industrial aspirations were essentially stillborn; agriculture suffered grievously from under-investment and poor transport facilities; exports declined; the nationalised trade network failed to deliver the goods; the formal economy began to shrivel whilst the informal sector, sustained by massive smuggling into Senegal (giving access to the convertible CFA Franc), thrived.

Although it can safely be said that ideology ceased to be politically relevant in Guinea-Bissau from the early eighties, the foundations of the regime remained structurally socialist until the constitution was changed on the eve of the multiparty elections in 1994. What is true, however, is that socialism did not materially affect nation-building, as opposed to state-building, both because the legitimacy of the party was not initially in question and because formal politics did not have a significant impact at the local level. To a very large degree, the evolution of the postcolonial regime conformed to that found in the neighbouring west African countries: an authoritarian (but not highly repressive), though highly inefficient, one-party neo-patrimonial state. The change of leadership that took place in 1980, when the prime minister overthrew the president, did not materially affect the nature of the political system. The split within the party, and the creation of the PAICV, made it easier for the Guinean leadership to accelerate the transformation of the PAIGC into a vehicle for patrimonial politics.

In Cape Verde, however, the impact of ideology on nation-building was very different. If in structural terms, the political system put in place on the

---

[85]As is explained in depth by Joshua Forrest in the country chapter in this volume.

archipelago was similar (one-party state, 'rubber stamp' parliament, state control of the commanding heights of the economy, and the rest), the realities on the ground were very dissimilar. There was in Cape Verde a clear congruence between society and nation. The country's national identity did not depend, as it did in most mainland countries, on the creative travails of the party in power. No one doubted the unity of the country, the legitimacy of the government or, even, the need for a single-party regime—after all the PAIGC had been elected virtually unopposed into office. Where the regime's ideological position mattered was in terms of its economic outlook. Socialism did not sit easily with a people long accustomed to roam the world, seek employment abroad, freely to use their earnings and invest their savings. Here, the government's initial attempt to nationalise the banking system, to impose restrictions on currency transactions, and to control the emigrants' remittances, all met with hostility. Similarly, the commitment to land reform sat uneasily with the landed classes and the Catholic church (which also opposed more liberal legislation on abortion).[86]

As a result, the PAIGC (later PAICV) regime moved with great caution. Whereas it asserted its political control over the country, and brooked little opposition, it readily adjusted its economic outlook according to circumstances. The controls on emigrants' capital were eased, the land reform was not as radical as first envisaged, and retail trade was not nationalised. Furthermore, the government set about building a relatively effective, and surprisingly incorrupt, administration which did much to implement a desperately-needed programme of economic improvement—among which water-retention schemes and reafforestation were paramount. The regime's commitment to schooling and social services was also welcome by a population long used to colonial neglect and who now enjoyed the fruits of a 'social-democratic' (rather than 'socialist') social policy. In sum, the relevance of ideology to nation-building in Cape Verde was minor, limited as it was to the role of state institutions and the determination to improve living conditions for the mass of the population. In terms of its foreign relations, the country remained strongly non-aligned, giving equal attention to its relations with the Cold War adversaries but refusing to be drawn into either one's sphere of influence.

In São Tomé e Príncipe, by contrast, the commitment to socialism had more profound, if ultimately evanescent, effects. As in Cape Verde, there was in the equatorial island state little debate about the country's national

---

[86]For an analysis of these processes in historical perspective see Elisa Silva de Andrade, *Les Îles du Cap Vert de la 'Découverte' à l'Indépendance* (Paris: L'Harmattan, 1996), pt. III, chap. 3.

identity, even if sharp social divisions continued to determine the place of most inhabitants within the new political order. The state institutions put in place after independence were also similar in that they led to the establishment of an authoritarian one-party regime with all its ancillary social and economic bodies. São Tomé e Príncipe, like Cape Verde, pursued a relatively pragmatic foreign policy based on a non-aligned stance. By contrast, however, the MLSTP's ideology had a more profound impact on the economic evolution of the country. True, the situation in the two island states were markedly different and São Tomé e Príncipe was singularly vulnerable to the swift and massive departure of the Portuguese at independence. Left with an economy based on the export of cocoa and coffee, with plantations in sharp decline, and without the managerial or technical resources to improve production, the regime had little option but to take over the plantations.

Nevertheless, given the choice of nationalising and running the plantations or bringing outside private investment and expertise to resume production, the government believed its socialist blueprint was preferable. In the event, this proved a disastrous choice, from which the economy has still not recovered. Although the regime did not interfere with private agricultural production or fishing, of which there was little, it failed (partly because of ideological blinkers) to evolve economic policies that would have spurred a diversification of production and a more vigorous internal market. Since, otherwise, it committed itself to a large expansion of the bureaucracy and an improvement in health, education and social services (little of which materialised), the budget rapidly went out of kilter. It is, obviously, difficult to be certain that the trajectory of postcolonial São Tomé e Príncipe would have been different under a regime with a divergent political outlook, but it seems reasonable to infer that the ideological proclivities of the regime made worse a situation that was already precarious at independence. The fact that the MLSTP regime indulged in large-scale patrimonial corruption in the years that followed independence clearly did little to ensure that, as in Cape Verde, the country succeeded in managing well the scarce economic resources it possessed. The chief difference between the two island states, in this respect, was less one of ideology than of integrity and proficiency. If the regime in São Tomé e Príncipe achieved the establishment of an independent nation-state, it did little to enhance its economic well being.

THE INTERNATIONAL DIMENSION

A single-minded focus on Lusophone Africa could easily detract attention from the fact that the five countries' postcolonial trajectory has been intimately bound up with regional and international factors. Indeed, it could scarcely be otherwise given the geographical and geopolitical situation of each one of the five countries. Guinea-Bissau is part of a sub-region of west African French-speaking territories, with contrasting international interests. Cape Verde is linked both to west Africa and Europe and it sits astride important sea and air routes. São Tomé e Príncipe's closest neighbours are Gabon, the two Congos and Angola—countries with distinctly diverse political outlooks. Mozambique is surrounded by English-speaking nations (including South Africa), all of which have had a profound impact on its evolution. Angola, for its part, belongs to a central African constellation of states that share access to some of the richest mineral resources on the continent.

The five countries form an official grouping of African Portuguese-speaking countries, the PALOP, which seeks to speak with a single voice within some important international institutions such as (and most notably) the European Union. They are now also members of the Comunidade de Paises de Língua Portuguesa (CPLP), which includes Brazil and Portugal—a recent diplomatic grouping which, because it has largely been bereft of resources, has hitherto achieved little of note.[87] Nevertheless, these five countries have pursued their own regional and international goals according to their own perception of their national self-interests. Thus, any proper understanding of their place in the international system must analyse the evolution of their foreign policy in terms of their own historical development. In short, the existence of these very visible Portuguese-speaking associations can all too easily divert attention from the key domestic, local, regional or international determinants of their foreign policy.

This section will examine the international dimension from two different angles. The first will focus on those aspects that are common to the PALOP. The second will discuss in more detail the specific considerations which have influenced each country's foreign policy.

The historical context

The single most important factor which influenced the PALOP's postcolonial international position was its socialist ideological commitment and its concomitant connection with the Soviet Bloc. Although all five countries retained important political and commercial links with Portugal, these were not in the first few years after independence as influential as had been the ties which the former French and British colonies had maintained with

[87]See, among others, Manuel Ennes Ferreira, 'Les contours économiques de la CPLP', *Lusotopie* (1997), pp. 11–34.

the former colonial power. The PALOP were, to varying degrees and for different reasons, reluctant to become too close to Portugal and they all sought, in so far as possible, to set up an independent foreign policy.[88] Since during the period of the anti-colonial campaigns, they all had had sustained relations with the Eastern Bloc, as well as with the more supportive Western countries (Scandinavia, the Netherlands, Canada), they set out at independence to consolidate their international links.

They were not, however, able to do so in the same way. There is an important distinction here between the three smaller states and the two southern African giants. The PAIGC's foreign policy—common, at least until 1980, to Guinea-Bissau and Cape Verde—was decidedly non-aligned.[89] In the context of the seventies, this consisted of two main policy objectives. The first was that it rejected any overt alliance with either of the two superpowers (the USA and the Soviet Union) and that it sought to diversify its international relations as much as possible. The second is that it supported the Non-Aligned movement, which was at the time a coalition of (largely) Third World countries, broadly hostile to the 'imperialist' West but wanting to maintain autonomy from too close an association with either one of the two competing socialist blocs—one linked to the Soviet Union; the other with China.[90]

Thus, Guinea-Bissau's and Cape Verde's socialist 'identity' did not prevent them from establishing fruitful relations with the widest range of foreign partners. Because both refused to grant the Soviet Union special facilities, they received a relatively warm welcome from the West, which agreed to provide foreign aid almost from the beginning. There were in any event historically-important links between the Cape Verde islands and the USA—a large number of Cape Verdeans having settled in New England between the mid-nineteenth century and the First World War. If the USA was more doubtful about Guinea-Bissau, it nevertheless recognised the

[88]The legacy of the anti-colonial wars as well as the disagreements between various post April 1974 Portuguese governments and the nationalists during the period of decolonisations all bore heavily on the relations between Portugal and her former African colonies after independence. In addition, there were tensions between some of the main actors. Samora Machel, for instance, felt slighted by the Portuguese and kept his distance.

[89]It did not change much after the two broke: both continued to pursue a relatively non-aligned foreign policy, at least until the whole international context altered with the collapse of the Soviet Union—with Guinea-Bissau keeping closer links with a number of socialist countries and Cape Verde much closer to the West.

[90]A further controversy dogged diplomacy: whether to have diplomatic links with the People's Republic of China or with Taiwan, both of which offered foreign aid in exchange for recognition.

regime whilst most other Western countries provided aid. The Scandinavian countries, as well as the Netherlands and Canada, were favourably inclined towards the two PAIGC states and soon offered very substantial aid. Portugal, for its part, was content to keep closer relations with Cape Verde, the one colony it had always considered distinct from the others.[91] Both countries were within the broad Francophone area and both, therefore, drew closer to their French-speaking neighbours and thus to France.[92]

São Tomé e Príncipe's situation was somewhat different. Although it too subscribed to a non-aligned foreign policy, its international position was distinct. In the first place, as we have seen, the regime was markedly more 'orthodox' in its socialism and thus ideologically closer to the Soviet Bloc. Second, it was very broadly aligned with Angola, whose foreign policy was largely determined by Cold War factors. As São Tomé e Príncipe's regime had obtained special armed protection from Angola against (real or imagined) coup plotters since 1978 and as it received petroleum at highly preferential rates (well below market prices), it was inclined to follow that country's foreign policy injunctions. Within limits, however, São Tomé e Príncipe sought to maintain good relations with Portugal and the rest of the Western world. As Eastern Bloc assistance was limited, the bulk of foreign and technical aid did, in the end, come from the West. In any event São Tomé e Príncipe was too insignificant geopolitically to deserve special attention in the international arena.[93]

São Tomé e Príncipe's foreign policy was more pointed, however, when it came to relations with its closest neighbour, Gabon. Because opposition to the regime was based there and because the archipelago's regime believed that country to be supportive of its armed opponents, it was episodically hostile to it. This would have been of little consequence had it not been for the fact that, deprived of links with Gabon, São Tomé e Príncipe was even more dependent on Angola. As Angola itself was at odds with Zaire, such hostility prevented closer association with the other sizeable French-speaking central African country in the region. This in turn presented the regime with some difficulty since, under strong French influence, it was

---

[91]During the colonial period, Cape Verdeans were all considered to be automatically 'assimilated', unlike in the other colonies where the status of *assimilado* was difficult to obtain. Moreover, there were in Portugal a large number of Cape Verdeans: both professionals and migrant manual labourers.

[92]France quickly sought to establish a strong presence in the two countries by setting up French cultural centres or providing facilities for teaching French, and supporting a number of cultural initiatives.

[93]For details see country chapter below.

otherwise drawing closer to the Francophone zone of influence.[94] Following the end of the Cold War and the change of government in São Tomé, the rapprochement with the Francophone bloc became more pronounced.

Mozambique's situation was complex. On the one hand, the FRELIMO regime was ideologically close to the Soviet Bloc. On the other, it had long-established relations with its English-speaking neighbours, from Tanzania in the north to Rhodesia in the west and South Africa in the south. The government was thus caught between an official foreign policy aligned with the east and myriad economic ties to its two, virulently anti-communist, settler southern African neighbours. Here, the government pursued two distinct policies. FRELIMO's political hostility to the Ian Smith regime led it to close off its border with Rhodesia and actively to support Robert Mugabe's ZANU. The outcome of this militant policy was that the Rhodesian security forces created a rebel force, which eventually became RENAMO, as a subversive outfit used to destabilise the central regions of Mozambique.[95]

On the other hand, economic self-interest induced a degree of caution that aimed not to allow ideology to jeopardise the country's revenues accruing from South Africa (through the mineworkers' remittances and the fees paid to Mozambique for the use of the Johannesburg–Maputo railway). Nevertheless, RENAMO activity and economic crisis eventually forced the government to sign the Nkomati Accord in 1984, by which it committed itself to stop aiding the ANC in exchange for South Africa's agreement to cease assistance to the Mozambican rebel movement. Although the Pretoria regime failed to honour that commitment, Mozambique was in no position to adopt a more hostile position vis-à-vis its southern neighbour.[96]

At the same time, the government tried to increase the support it received from the West, which it eventually managed to achieve because of two specific factors. The first is that FRELIMO had strong historical links with Scandinavia and other Western countries supportive of the liberation struggle. The second is that it was able to play on the powerful anti-apartheid sentiments to be found right across the Western world. Additionally, Samora Machel's role in convincing Mugabe to sign the Lancaster House Agreement, which brought the war in Rhodesia to an end, earned him the gratitude of

[94]Here too the French played the cultural card, setting up a cultural centre, subsidising tuition in French and supporting a number of literary and cultural activities.

[95]On the origins of RENAMO see Vines, *Renamo*, op. cit.

[96]Partly because Pretoria's policy of hiring fewer Mozambican mineworkers had a deleterious effect on the revenues which this vital 'export' sector had long provided for the country's economy, the Mozambican government simply could not afford to alienate the South African one.

Margaret Thatcher's government. Thereafter, Britain's benign sponsorship facilitated the FRELIMO regime's overtures to the West and Mozambique received much more substantial Western foreign aid. And despite its continued close links with the Eastern Bloc, it also obtained diplomatic support against RENAMO. Even if the rebel movement had allies in the West, particularly among right-wing organisations, it never acquired proper legitimacy in the eyes of Western governments. This alone ensured that RENAMO did not receive overt, or even covert, aid from them.[97]

Angola's predicament was, from the beginning, much more significantly affected by international considerations. The very circumstances of its decolonisation, which involved both a South African invasion and Cuban deployment, ensured that the country's fate was profoundly marked by Cold War politics. Because of this, the MPLA regime was firmly cast by the United States into the Soviet camp, was denied diplomatic recognition, and (political as well as material) support was provided to its adversaries. Conversely, the Soviet Union considered Angola to be one of its key African allies and, accordingly, provided ample diplomatic, economic and military assistance. The result was that the country became prey to superpower rivalry and its conflict with UNITA came increasingly to be interpreted in the light of Cold War calculations. So long as there were Cubans in Angola, the United States and South Africa would aid UNITA, overtly or covertly. So long as South Africa threatened the Luanda regime, the Cubans would remain in Angola and Soviet aid would flow.[98]

The civil war in Angola also enmeshed the regime in complicated regional politics, which further contributed to the destabilisation of the area. The MPLA's historical hostility to Mobutu's Zaire, its ambiguous relations with Kaunda's Zambia, and its active support of the Namibian liberation movement, all contributed to difficult bilateral relations with its neighbours. South Africa's active support of UNITA and its progressively bold incursions into Angola, ostensibly to suppress the Namibian nationalist party, the South West Africa People's Organisation (SWAPO), maintained a state of *de facto* undeclared war. UNITA's use of Zambia as a rear base raised Angola's suspicion towards that country and made for tense relations between the two states. Finally, Mobutu's very pragmatic alliance with Jonas

[97]The 1988 Gersony Report, which documented RENAMO's appalling atrocities, made it impossible for the United States, or indeed any other Western country, to give the rebel movement any official support. See Robert Gersony, *Summary of Mozambican Refugee Accounts of Principally Conflict-Related Experience in Mozambique* (Washington: Bureau for Refugee Programs, 1988).

[98]See here Fernando Andresen Guimarães, *The Origins of the Angolan Civil War: Foreign Intervention and Domestic Political Conflict* (Basingstoke: Macmillan, 1998).

Savimbi enabled UNITA to use Zaire as a conduit for military supplies. The MPLA government retaliated by giving every possible support to Mobutu's 'Katanga' opponents who, twice, attempted to invade Shaba Province from Angola.[99]

The relationship between international factors and domestic policies

The extent to which each of the five PALOP was affected by international factors varied over time and, in this instance, it is important to follow the chronology of events. Equally, it is useful to bear in mind that there were no hard and fast divisions between the political and economic considerations of diplomacy. For this reason, it is more profitable to discuss them together than to try artificially to separate them. Finally, it is well to remember that matters of foreign policy were affected directly by the momentous changes which took place from the late eighties onwards with Gorbachev's reforms, the fall of the Berlin Wall, the collapse of the Soviet Union and the end of communism in Eastern Europe. These events triggered large-scale mutations in international relations which affected, directly and indirectly, almost every aspect of the PALOP's political and economic life. The remainder of the section will not discuss systematically the international policy of each country but will seek instead to contrast and compare what happened in the five PALOP.[100]

To follow the order adopted thus far, we turn first to Guinea-Bissau and Cape Verde. Although the two countries were governed by the same party until 1980, after independence they soon followed their own foreign policy path for reasons having to do as much with domestic needs as with diplomatic considerations. Cape Verde's situation was constrained by two major factors. First, it was a country with such limited natural resources that it could not hope to be self-sufficient or even economically viable, and thus had to rely on foreign aid. Second, a large proportion of the country's men (as well as some women) worked abroad, especially in Portugal, whilst a number of Cape Verdeans are permanently settled in foreign countries, the bulk of whom are in the USA.[101] Additionally, there are Cape Verdeans living intermittently elsewhere, including in several African countries. For

---

[99]The 'Katangais' had been exiled into Angola following the unsuccessful Katanga secession in the sixties and they had remained Mobutu's implacable enemies. Their attempt to re-conquer Katanga (later renamed Shaba) was foiled on both occasions through Western (mainly French) intervention on the side of Mobutu's forces.

[100]For details on the foreign policy of each of the five see the country chapters (pp. 137 ff.)

[101]Which by now is greater than the current population of the archipelago. In the United States alone, it is estimated that there are around 500,000 Americans of Cape Verdean origin.

this reason, the government's foreign policy options were determined as much by the need to maximise income from foreign aid and emigrants' remittances as by the obligation to maintain good relations with these various constituencies, hence with the countries in which they lived.

Cape Verde thus followed from the beginning an eminently pragmatic foreign policy, seeking to establish and uphold profitable links with the widest range of countries. Portugal has been the dominant economic partner since independence both in terms of the proportion of trade and as regards political, diplomatic and cultural relations. Although there was initially tension between the PAIGC and the government in Lisbon, this was rapidly overcome and a pattern of close relations was formed. The break with Guinea-Bissau in 1980 did not seriously affect these links. The change of regime in 1990, when the MPD came to power in Praia, was favourable to even closer ties with Portugal since the party had received support from the governing metropolitan right-of-centre party. The MPD was resolutely anti-socialist, pro-Western, keen to strengthen ties with Europe and the USA and willing to distance itself from Africa—as was made obvious by the change of national flag.[102]

Although symbolically, there were major shifts in ideology when the MPD took power, in practice it is clear that the same constraints on the country produced the same foreign policy. Other than a greater emphasis on Cape Verde's American community and some reluctance to cultivate equally close relations with Africa, the MPD's diplomacy has been marked by continued pragmatism. While the present regime sees its future in association with the European Union, it is not in a position to neglect any of the country's diplomatic links, including with Africa since there are substantial Cape Verdean communities in Senegal and in the other African Portuguese-speaking countries. Furthermore, it must continue to cultivate good relations with those countries outside the European Union—such as Switzerland, Norway, Canada, the United States and Brazil—which provide continued aid to the country. As the Cold War divide has vanished, the MPD's inclination to link with the West is no longer of momentous international significance. What is true, however, is that the archipelago remains an important strategic staging post off the west coast of Africa, with modern air and sea facilities, and is for this reason of interest to NATO (of which Portugal is a member) in respect of its south-western flank.

As regards relations with the other Portuguese-speaking African

[102]The MPD government's decision to introduce a new flag was very controversial, both because it seemed to strike at the heart of the country's identity and because it was obviously intended to loosen the PAICV links with Africa, as symbolised by the red, yellow and green colours. The new flag was blue and white, very clearly 'European' colours.

countries, Cape Verde has always been an active player. Despite the trauma of the 1980 coup in Bissau, which led to a split between the two countries and the creation of the PAICV, Cape Verde resumed contact with Guinea-Bissau rapidly. Here too, practical considerations were the order of the day as there are on the mainland a large number of Cape Verdeans and there is constant movement of population between the two countries. Further afield, Cape Verde was instrumental in facilitating the negotiations leading to the withdrawal of Cuban troops from Angola and to the independence of Namibia. Aristides Pereira, the former PAICV president, played a crucial, if discreet, part in easing contacts between Angola, South Africa, Cuba, Portugal and the United States.[103] Furthermore, as the country closest to the former colonial metropole, Cape Verde has always been involved in helping to maintain, or restore, working diplomatic relations between Portugal and the other PALOP members. Finally, Cape Verde has lent its considerable diplomatic weight, both in terms of personnel and experience, to the establishment of special working relations between the European Union and the PALOP, now a recognised African 'grouping' in Brussels.

Guinea-Bissau was in a very different situation. Firmly anchored in a French-speaking west African sub-region, the country has from the start needed to cultivate good relations with its neighbours. At the same time, the PAIGC regime was more closely tied, at least in the early years, to the socialist bloc. Finally, like Cape Verde, it sought to diversify the sources of foreign aid. Because these three determinants of its foreign policy were not easily compatible, the Bissau government went through several 're-orientations'. During the Luiz Cabral presidency (1974–80), the regime held fast to a friendly attitude towards the socialist world (particularly Cuba and Eastern Europe) while making every effort to integrate itself into the Western sphere of influence. Over time, it became clear that most assistance would come from the West and diplomatic efforts in that direction were intensified. This transition towards a more Western-oriented foreign policy was strengthened during the presidency of João Bernardo (Nino) Vieira (1980–99). This is not surprising since the country's 'socialist' identity rapidly lost all political significance and, in any event, Guinea-Bissau continued to pursue a non-aligned foreign policy.

Guinea-Bissau shared with Cape Verde a history of strong support on

---

[103]Cape Verde had always had some links with South Africa (despite Africa's boycott of the country) because it had allowed South African Airways to use Sal airport as a stop over for its longest transcontinental flights. Since Sal was also used by Cuban Airways, the airport provided a convenient meeting place for the two sides.

the part of the more 'progressive' Western countries (Scandinavia, the Netherlands and Canada) that had offered aid to the liberation movements before independence. This help, which originated in the very successful diplomacy undertaken by Amílcar Cabral during the sixties and early seventies, served the two PAIGC-led countries well but it was particularly beneficial to Guinea-Bissau. Indeed, such solidarity on the part of some of the wealthiest European countries helped to make the country the largest recipient of foreign aid per capita on the African continent. From the very first years of independence, therefore, and until the mid-nineties, substantial bilateral aid from Europe continued to flow at a rate that many other African countries might have envied. Despite the coup d'état in 1980, and even after, it became clear that the regime had failed to induce any sustained development, some countries, particularly Sweden, were reluctant to cut off assistance. Only the disappointment of the events which followed the 1994 multiparty elections and the most recent civil strife (1998–9) brought to an end that remarkably long history of 'solidarity' aid.[104]

Guinea-Bissau's international commitments have on the whole been determined by the more immediate economic, political and diplomatic problems it has faced since independence—rather than by ideology. Of these the two most pressing have been its search for foreign aid and its attempt to join the Francophone zone. If the country became the largest per capital recipient of foreign aid in Africa, it made very poor use of that aid, as Joshua Forrest explains in the country chapter below, and found itself in increasing need of outside funding. By the early eighties it became clear that the regime's economic policy—an attempt to develop agro-industry whilst neglecting rural production—had failed to achieve any of its development targets. Faced with growing economic problems, the regime initiated a privatisation programme and took steps to meet the advice of the IMF and the World Bank. As a result, structural adjustment programmes started in 1987.

The other major factor in Guinea-Bissau's foreign policy turned around the country's need to live in harmony with its French-speaking neighbours. If Guinea (Conakry) had long been supportive of the PAIGC, Senegal had been more wary of a 'socialist' regime on its doorstep. Relations with Senegal, though ostensibly friendly during both Luiz Cabral's and Nino Vieira's tenure of power, were often fraught. The first bone of contention was a dispute about off-shore oil exploration, for international maritime boundaries were unclear. Here a compromise was reached under the auspices

---

[104]Sweden's special support of Guinea-Bissau originated in the sixties and early seventies when Amílcar Cabral visited the country and generated a wave of enthusiasm for the PAIGC.

of international arbitration and Bissau was granted substantial rights. The second problem, the secessionist movement in the southern Senegalese region of Casamance, turned out to be much more intractable. As there are close links between the peoples of Casamance and northern Guinea-Bissau, Senegal has long been suspicious of Bissau's intentions. Although no evidence has ever been produced to show that Guinea-Bissau actively supports the secessionist movement, the continued activities of the armed movement created a serious strain in bilateral relations and, indirectly, led to the outbreak of the recent civil strife in Guinea-Bissau which pitted Nino Vieira against his erstwhile military commander, Ansumane Mané.[105]

Guinea-Bissau's troubled relations with Senegal were, paradoxically, not improved by Bissau's rapprochement with the Francophone zone. If Nino Vieirá was close to Senegal's president, Abdou Diouf, as was amply demonstrated by the support he received from Dakar during the recent civil war, there were in Bissau as well as in Francophone Africa opposition to Bissau's entry into the club. Many in the country resented France's growing influence and members of the CFA Franc Zone feared that Guinea-Bissau's economic fragility could destabilise the Francophone area. In the end, Vieira rode roughshod over internal opposition and managed to convince his Francophone partners. Bissau became a member of the Zone in 1997 and the national currency (peso) was replaced by the CFA franc—the main attraction of which is that it is a fully convertible and stable (though recently devalued) currency.[106] Such a move has, of course, cut back the profits of smuggling into the neighbouring (CFA) Francophone countries and provided Guinea-Bissau with a firm currency. It is not clear, however, that it has made improvement of the economy any easier. Nor, finally, is it certain that it ushers in an era of closer cooperation with France, given that the present administration is less keen than the previous one to follow that course and that Portugal is making overtures to Bissau in order to ensure that all the PALOP remain linked to the former metropole through the CPLP.

If São Tomé e Príncipe shared with Cape Verde and Guinea-Bissau a close association with France—as observer members of the Francophone summits—it was very much more constrained internationally. As we have seen above, the socialist proclivities of the first MLSTP government (1975–91) and the need to placate Angola were the two mainstays of the county's foreign policy. Difficult relations with Portugal and tensions with its

[105]Details of the civil war that ensued will be found in the country chapter below.

[106]The CFA franc is tied to the French franc, and hence to the Euro. Before the devaluation, 500 CFA francs were worth 1 FF. The devaluation halved the value of the CFA franc: today 1,000 CFA francs equal 1 FF.

African neighbours, Gabon and Zaire, seriously limited the government's options and inevitably meant that, during that period, São Tomé e Príncipe was isolated diplomatically. Although the country had good relations with the socialist world (Cuba, Soviet Union, Eastern Europe, and even China), these did not bring much by way of foreign aid.[107]

Yet, as the country chapter below shows clearly, 'socialist solidarity' was of limited use and did not provide sufficient resources for the regime to improve the economic viability of the country. By the early eighties, the crisis was all too visible and the regime began a slow conversion towards more 'liberal' economic policies, while at the same time seeking closer relations with the West. As in Guinea-Bissau, this resulted in the opening up of the market to foreign capital (particularly into the much-neglected coffee and cocoa plantations) and, in 1987, led to the first structural adjustment programme. This opening to the West was accelerated in the late eighties, for international and domestic reasons. In the foreign field, the end of the Cold War transformed the international situation. Internally, the MLSTP, like the PAICV before, faced increasing discontent by the younger party members with the rigid ideological outlook of the leadership. These changes brought about multiparty elections in 1991, in which the regime was swept from power. As in Cape Verde, the new rulers were much more favourably inclined towards the West. Since then, and despite several further changes in government, São Tomé e Príncipe has pursued an entirely pragmatic foreign policy, sustaining links with those countries (like Portugal or France) which are most prepared to provide assistance.

If the three micro-states were able to adjust their foreign policy to the constraints they faced, Angola and Mozambique were confronted with infinitely more severe problems. Many of the similarities and differences between the civil war in the two countries will be discussed in the next chapter. Here we look more especially at the impact of the interaction between international and regional factors, most notably the role of the local superpower, South Africa. Clearly, that country was intimately involved with the evolution of its two Lusophone neighbours from the time of their decolonisation. Although South Africa's (overt and covert) foreign policy affected Angola and Mozambique equally strongly, there were significant differences between the two which need to be explored in some detail since they go a long way towards explaining what happened in these countries.

South Africa was embroiled as a party to the civil conflict in Angola right from 1975, when it made an ill-fated attempt to help wrest Luanda

---

[107]Students received scholarship to study in many of these socialist countries and China financed the construction of the building for the national assembly.

away from the MPLA. There were several reasons for this. First, the South African regime feared the MPLA's 'Marxist' orientation and its close alliance with the Soviet Union. It felt that the consolidation of Angola as a 'communist' state would pose a serious threat to the region. Second, South Africa sought to remain in south-west Africa, where it had economic and strategic interests, despite its international obligation to grant that territory independence. As the Namibian nationalist movement, SWAPO, was closely allied with the MPLA, the new Angolan regime was seen to pose a most serious threat to South Africa's control of the former German colony. Finally, South Africa had reasons to believe that it could help UNITA to take power in Angola and thus to set up an administration that, it supposed, would be friendly. Whether that hope was realistic, given the nature of Savimbi's political trajectory, is a moot point.[108]

By contrast, South Africa considered Mozambique a less serious menace to its regional hegemony. First, the two countries had long had very close links and there were at independence a large number of Mozambican mineworkers working in South Africa. Whatever its ideological inclination, the FRELIMO regime could not ignore its economic need to maintain these links. Second, the Mozambican government appeared to South Africa to be much less stridently 'socialist' and much more pragmatic, seeking a profitable *modus vivendi* rather than confrontation with its southern neighbour. It is towards Rhodesia that Mozambique quickly became hostile. And, as a result, it was from Rhodesia that armed opposition to the FRELIMO government was unleashed. Lastly, the South African regime did not consider that there was a serious alternative to the FRELIMO government in Mozambique. Its aim was to blow hot and cold, so that Maputo would remain compliant with South Africa's regional interests. Not until Rhodesia's independence, did the South Africans opt to relocate RENAMO to the northern Transvaal and support armed opposition to the Mozambican regime.[109]

While South Africa maintained an implacably hostile attitude towards the Angolan regime until the end of apartheid, it was less extreme in its support of destabilisation in Mozambique. During the period 1980–84, it backed the expansion of RENAMO but at the same time made overtures to Maputo. Under the combined pressure of economic crisis and armed violence, Mozambique was compelled to sign the Nkomati Accord in 1984, renouncing thereby active assistance to the ANC. Although South Africa

---

[108]On South Africa's role in Angola see Guimarães, op. cit.
[109]See Vines, *Renamo*, op. cit.

failed to keep its promise to rein in RENAMO (there is, in fact, clear evidence that it continued to supply them), it did not encourage the rebel movement to overthrow the FRELIMO state for the simple reason that it was unsure about their ability to govern and it preferred a chastened FRELIMO regime to an unpredictable RENAMO one. In any event, by then much of RENAMO's 'success' was due to the alienation of large sections of rural Mozambique from the regime and not to South African prompting.[110]

In Angola, the situation was different. Between 1975 and 1987, South Africa made every effort, including repeated armed incursions, to support UNITA's bid to take power in Luanda. That it failed was due in part to the unreliability of UNITA, in part to Cuba's dogged military assistance to the MPLA government and in part to the improving fighting capacity of the Angolan armed forces. Furthermore, South Africa could count on the (unofficial) support of the United States, for Cold War politics dictated that Soviet support for the Angolan regime should be met by implacable American hostility. Only from the mid-eighties onwards, when it became clear that South Africa could not sustain its military involvement in Angola (largely because white casualties kept increasing), was it forced to enter into serious negotiations about the future of Namibia. International pressure compelled Angola to agree to an accord that linked the removal of Cuban troops to South African withdrawal from south-west Africa and the transition to Namibian independence where SWAPO won the elections and took power. However, until the end of apartheid, South Africa continued to give full support to UNITA, thus prolonging the conflict in Angola.[111]

The international context, therefore, encroached upon Angola much more systematically than it did upon Mozambique. The former was, until the early nineties, classified as a close ally of the Soviet Union and Cuba, thus earning the obstinate wrath of the United States. If European countries adopted a much more cautious and pragmatic attitude towards the MPLA regime, they were hampered in their efforts to bring about a settlement (which would then allow them economic access to the country's riches) because of the US position. Mozambique, by contrast, was able to diversify its diplomatic contacts sufficiently rapidly to earn foreign assistance from a wide range of sources. And, following the 1984 Nkomati Accord, there was widespread international condemnation, even in the United States, of RENAMO's extreme violence.

Mozambique was also forced to consider changes in its economic policy

[110]See here Geffray, *La Cause des Armes au Mozambique*, op. cit.
[111]Simultaneously, the United States provided unofficial backing to the UNITA.

earlier than Angola, which could survive and continue to fight the war against UNITA because its oil income was so great. However, by the mid-eighties both countries eventually came to recognise that they must change economic course. They did so because of the awareness that rising indebtedness and continued civil strife put intolerable strain on their economies; debt was growing, and they needed to have access to Western aid. Both produced plans for economic liberalisation and both eventually met the conditions for structural adjustment programmes, though they viewed the SAPs differently. Angola was essentially concerned about dwindling financial reserves but had little interest in the reform of the economy implied by structural adjustment. Mozambique, on the other hand, was forced to comply more fully with the conditions imposed, for it had few other sources of revenues and, thus, few other options. Given its international profile, however, Mozambique managed to secure foreign aid from a number of countries, including most European states and the USA. Angola, for its part, could rely on fewer allies, especially after the end of the Cold War.

The political transformation of South Africa had an immediate impact on the sub-region. Now committed to peaceful co-existence with its neighbours, the government in Pretoria began to exert pressure on the rebel movements in Angola and Mozambique to enter into negotiations. The effect was more pronounced on RENAMO than it was on UNITA, both because the former was more dependent on material and strategic South African support and because it lacked the political legitimacy credibly to challenge the FRELIMO regime. UNITA, a wealthy outfit, was able to continue to obtain supplies from the open arms market and to have them delivered through Zaire. In Mozambique, as we have seen, the two sides were compelled to come together for peace negotiations. After the ANC was elected into office in 1994, South Africa's role in the region became even more conciliatory: the government now saw itself as an honest broker aiming to help resolve regional conflicts.

If the peace process in Mozambique was a success, in no small part because the UN operation[112] was well conceived and well executed, central Africa was soon engulfed in a series of violent conflicts about which South Africa could do little. The resumption of the civil war in Angola, the genocide in Rwanda, the continued killings in Burundi and, above all, the collapse of the Mobutu regime in Zaire, set fire to the Congo basin area and engulfed Angola further into regional conflicts. The fall of Mobutu meant, of course,

---

[112]For details of the United Nations role in the transition to peace in Mozambique see the country chapter below.

that UNITA had lost its strongest ally in the region. For this reason, it is not surprising that Angola sided with Laurent Kabila, the president of the Democratic Republic of Congo, formerly Zaire, and sent troops to support him when it seemed that Rwanda, his regime's original patrons, were about to overthrow him in the second Congo 'liberation war'. However, the newly re-christened Democratic Republic of Congo (DRC) is still in conflict and much of its vast territory is under the control of rebel armies, loyal either to Rwanda or to Uganda. UNITA continues to be able to use some of the regions bordering Angola as conduits for its supplies.

Angola intervened militarily even further afield when it came to the help of Sassou-Nguesso, the former president of the Popular Republic of Congo (PRC), as he tried to reclaim by force of arms the control of a country he had previously lost in multiparty elections. Whatever the merit of that dispute, the fact that Angola was willing to send its troops militarily to support a political ally in another central African country was most significant. It meant that the Luanda regime was now behaving as the local 'superpower', prepared and able to step in to act as the region's policeman in order to further its foreign policy objectives. There is clearly today competition in the central African region between several ambitious and aggressive regimes—among which are Uganda, Rwanda and Zimbabwe—and Angola is undoubtedly acting as though its considers itself to have become an 'arbiter' of these potentially dangerous-regional conflicts.

This regional foreign policy objective is consistent with the Luanda regime's present ambition to wipe out UNITA, militarily and politically, and assert total control over its national territory, once and for all. That aim, however unrealistic it may well be, requires that Angola neutralise support for UNITA in the sub-region. And in order to achieve that goal, the MPLA government is bound to intervene more and more overtly in the politics of its neighbouring countries. As history shows, however, this is a dangerous policy since it is by no means clear that Angola will ever be able to ensure that UNITA is prevented from operating in adjacent countries. Ultimately, the source of the conflict lies inside Angola and, until there is a viable peace settlement between the two parties, violence is likely to fester on. In the meantime, Angola's active involvement in the sub-region may bring it into friction with some of its neighbours and bring about greater tension in the area. Given the DRC's continued instability, and the limited prospect of a resolution of its internal conflicts, it is fair to say that Angola will continue to be enmeshed, directly or indirectly, in regional conflicts.

3

THE LIMITS OF NATIONHOOD

THE FAILINGS OF ONE-PARTY STATES

If the PALOP regimes were singular in their choice of socialism as the founding ideology of the new nation-state, they quickly evolved a pattern of politics familiar in Africa. Admittedly, their political creed presupposed the dominance of the ruling party so that, unlike their French- or English-speaking counterparts, they did not need to justify the establishment of one-party states. Nevertheless, after a few years, there was little to distinguish these regimes politically from their counterparts in the rest of the continent. Indeed, by the first half of the eighties, there were in Africa only a few (nominally) multiparty democratic states.[1] As one-party states, the PALOP were thus no different from the bulk of other African countries.

There were, as noted, marked differences in the types of regimes established in the five countries but, again, these differences were also to be found elsewhere in Africa. Although more recently independent and ostensibly more committed to a 'socialist' agenda than French- and English-speaking Africa, it is clear that in the eighties the PALOP began to evolve, politically and economically, along similar lines. The defining features of all African countries at that time were: ostensibly authoritarian but in reality neo-patrimonial (or clientelistic) political systems; the inability of the state to function effectively and in particular to spur development; the concomitant decline of the economy; and, in consequence, an increasing competition for power at the top.

For this reason, it is useful to analyse what happened in the five Lusophone countries within a comparative framework. As the relevance of the armed struggle declined, as the 'transition to socialism' faltered, the PALOP came to resemble more and more their African neighbours: with more problems, perhaps, but in essence not so distinct. Hence, the understanding of their

---

[1]For example, the Gambia, Mauritius, Senegal and Botswana.

evolution between the consolidation of the nation-state in the mid-seventies and the transition to multiparty politics in the early nineties is best achieved comparatively. During that period, all African countries displayed what I call the failings of one-party states, that is, the state's inability to bring about sustainable economic development. Although the reasons for this are complex, it is useful here to highlight a few key issues related to the emergence in Africa of neo-patrimonial polities.[2]

In a neo-patrimonial system, political accountability rests on the extent to which patrons are able both to influence and meet the expectations of their followers according to well-established norms of reciprocity. Although in Africa most of the political leaders at independence were new (young graduates), rather than 'traditional' (chiefs), elites, the parameters of the neo-patrimonial systems which developed after independence owed a great deal to what might be called 'traditional' principles of legitimacy. Among those, the most significant had to do with a notion of accountability which involved a direct link with the delivery of resources to clients. In other words, the legitimacy of political leaders was perceived by all (from top to bottom) to rest on their ability to provide for their own personal constituents. What mattered politically, therefore, was principally whether patrons were able to meet their obligations in respect of their own clientele, rather than on their performance as 'national' leaders, particularly in terms of spurring the country's economic development.

Although such a neo-patrimonial system worked well in many countries after independence, it was inherently unstable. First, it required the delivery of state or other national resources to buttress private patronage. However, the situation of relative economic well being enjoyed by most countries— useful colonial assets and stable export prices—was shattered by the world economic crisis in the seventies. As revenues declined and debt increased, African patrons began to run out of means. In a situation where the search for resources became ever more difficult, political competition increased. Since in the African neo-patrimonial systems access to governmental assets is paramount, struggles for power intensified and violence escalated.

Second, the neo-patrimonial system that evolved in postcolonial Africa was essentially inimical to economic development as it took place in the West, or later in Asia. This is because it failed to foster, and in many ways totally undermined, economic growth—by all accounts the prime basis for sustainable development. Political legitimacy was rooted in the maintenance of a situation in which patrons had simultaneously to uphold the image of

[2]The remarks that follow are drawn from Chabal and Daloz, *Africa Works*, op. cit., pt. I.

substance which they required and to feed the networks on which their position depended. Thus, they needed to spend with ostentation and to provide resources to their clients. In such circumstances, they could scarcely defer consumption and expenditure for the longer-term purpose of 'national' development. For this reason, African states as well as entrepreneurs rarely invested in economically-productive activities.

The crisis which crippled African countries in the eighties was thus a result of the combined effect of diminishing economic wealth and the dissipation of political accountability which it brought about. As political elites competed in an increasingly desperate bid to have access to central power—still the fount of most resources—force became widespread. This led to a steady deliquescence of the existing systems of neo-patrimonial political legitimacy and engendered further discontent, even chaos. As neo-patrimonial political accountability was eroded there was an ever more frantic search for the means needed to assert power.

This section outlines the ways in which this process occurred in the PALOP, bearing in mind the significant differences to be found between the five countries. Indeed, it is evident that the limits of one-party states were reached in vastly distinct historical, social, political and cultural contexts and that the manner in which this occurs was of significance for their subsequent evolution. I discuss first the experience of the two island states, then of Guinea-Bissau, before coming to the more complex cases of Angola and Mozambique, for, it is surely no coincidence that it is in that chronological order that the five moved away from socialism to become, at least in principle, multiparty polities.

The main reason why the one-party state was adjudged a failure in Africa is not principally because it was undemocratic—which it was, at least in Western eyes—but because it presided over widespread economic failure. Ideology was in this respect of little significance, since in the end all African countries were faced in the eighties with declining revenues and acute economic problems. Nevertheless, it seems in retrospect clear that overtly socialist regimes reached their limits even earlier than their more market-oriented counterparts.[3] From this point of view, the experience of the PALOP confirmed a trend already noticeable elsewhere on the continent. What seemed to matter, above and beyond ideology, was how effectively governments were able to discharge the formal state functions, of which the most important are the maintenance of peace, the upholding of the rule of law and the management of an operative bureaucracy. Here, the contrast between the five Lusophone countries was great.

---

[3]Benin, a relentlessly Marxist state during that period, is a good example of such early failure.

Cape Verde was from the beginning in a league of its own. The PAIGC government on the archipelago was composed of the elite of the nationalist movement that had waged the anti-colonial war in Guinea and it was in this respect made up of ministers well able to master their brief and discharge their responsibilities. For reasons having to do with Cape Verde's colonial history, there was in the country a reasonable supply of potentially competent and dedicated civil servants.[4] The PAIGC was thus in a position from the beginning to set up an effective administrative infrastructure able to manage the state and carry out the policies endorsed by the politicians. Although the dominance of the party was total, there was relatively little political interference with the day-to-day running of the administration. The regime was dedicated from the outset to try to tackle the enormous problems facing the newly-independent country and, as it confronted little serious political opposition, it was able to channel its energy wholly into the fulfilment of these ambitions.

Since the PAIGC held power in Cape Verde and Guinea-Bissau, it is instructive to analyse the reasons for relative success in the former and undoubted failure in the latter. Here the explanation cannot be found either in the ideology or the leadership of the party, which were common to both. Rather it must be sought in the main political, social, economic and cultural distinctions between the island Creole state and the west African country. Put in its simplest terms, Cape Verde did not evolve the neo-patrimonial system found in the rest of Africa. In other words, the notions of political legitimacy and accountability at the heart of the political system in Cape Verde did not move towards the clientelistic form which characterised Guinea-Bissau.[5] As the Bissau regime was also very largely in the hands of Cape Verdeans, rather than Guineans, it is obvious that the extent to which neo-patrimonialism prevailed was less a question of individuals than of system.[6] Why then did Cape Verde prove the exception to the rule?

The answer, though somewhat intricate, lies in the fact that Cape Verde is a Creole island rather than an African society. What this means is that

---

[4] Bureaucratic efficiency, however, is not simply due to highly-qualified personnel, it is primarily the result of an ethos of public service that comes from the acceptance of the institutionalisation of the role of civil servants. And this derives in large measure from the attitude of the political leadership.

[5] Indeed, Luiz Cabral's administration was notorious for its patrimonial behaviour. Since Luiz Cabral was Amílcar's half brother and since Amílcar was seen by the PAIGC as the political role model *par excellence*, Luiz's behaviour appeared shocking to many in the party, especially in Cape Verde.

[6] This is an important point. The notion that 'black Africans' are more patrimonial than others is clearly wrong as is evidenced by the supremely patrimonial nature of the multi-racial regime in Luanda.

the ways in which the archipelago's inhabitants conceive of their own identities, interact as families and communities, work and earn a living, all create a public sphere thoroughly distinct from that found on the African mainland. The following characteristics are of paramount importance. Creole societies have a single language used for all aspects of social and cultural life. People relate on the basis of concepts of individuality, family and locality which differ fundamentally from those of community and ethnicity, as found on the mainland.[7] Their religious beliefs are more firmly anchored in an Europeanised form of Christianity. For this reason, the main social divisions are related to economic or geographical distinctions rather than, as on the mainland, to communal or ethnic ones.[8] Because of this, the type of clientelism that develops in small Creole island societies like Cape Verde, or São Tomé e Príncipe for that matter, is one that seldom crosses the boundaries of 'family and friends' and is thus crucially distinct from the neo-patrimonialism extant on the African mainland.[9]

The Cape Verdean wing of the PAIGC thus set about constructing the nation-state on the basis of a single-party political system that was more akin to that found in other parts of the world, notably in Eastern Europe or in East Asia, than in the rest of the African continent. Like the East European regimes, the government had a clear idea of its main policies, ensured the running of an administration able to implement them and, above all, committed itself to the specific improvements in living and working conditions that the country most needed. Its achievements were considerable, as can be seen in the country chapter below, and should cause us to reflect on the impact which a relatively efficient and uncorrupted state with clear objectives can have on the development of a country as wretchedly unsuited to independent life as Cape Verde was.

The measure of the regime's success can be gauged by the fact that it was considered by donors to be the continent's most adept at managing its economic resources (including foreign aid) and was thus never required by the Bretton Woods institutions to implement a structural adjustment programme. Furthermore, Cape Verde was one of the very few countries in Africa to maintain a consistent, if necessarily limited, record of economic growth. This was not sufficient to sustain its population, of course, since

---

[7]See here Deirdre Meintel, *Race, Culture and Portuguese Colonialism in Cabo Verde* (Syracuse University Press, 1984).

[8]As is best evidenced by a reading of Cape Verdean literature which, since the thirties, has built on the development of a singularly 'national' cultural identity. See here Patrick Chabal *et al.*, *The Postcolonial Literature of Lusophone Africa* (London: Hurst & Co., 1996), chapter on Cape Verde by David Brookshaw.

[9]A point which is developed at length in *Africa Works*, op. cit., chap. 1.

the archipelago cannot be self-sufficient in food and is not inherently economically viable, and it could not have survived without the remittances of its large emigrant population. But there is no gainsaying the most impressive progress made by the government in providing its people with a better life than they ever had under colonial rule.

Nevertheless, despite this impressive record, the regime (both president and party) was voted out of office when the first multiparty elections took place in 1991. This outcome, which took most observers by surprise, requires some explanation.[10] Above and beyond the more contingent issues of the success of the anti-PAICV campaign, the simple answer is that, in a context where the voters were free to express their opinion, they chose to point to the limits of the one-party state. In trying to explain the defeat of the former nationalist party, which has now been re-elected into office after a ten-year stint in opposition, we thus need to consider what these limits are and why they led to the defeat of a regime that had appeared more able than most in Africa to govern in the interests of the country, rather than simply of its own political clientele. There are three sets of factors which are relevant not only to the understanding of Cape Verde but of the other PALOP.

The move to multiparty politics came about under the impetus of a younger, more technocratic, generation which was frustrated both at its lack of prospects within a rigid party organisation and at the reluctance of the leadership to adopt more 'liberal' policies. The fact that it prevailed is evidence that the leadership was willing to test the party's popularity against the opposition, even if at that time no one—not even the younger party members—believed that they would be defeated. The second is that there was a swing against the socialist ideology which underpinned the party's policies, even if such an ideology no longer had much influence on domestic decisions. The younger generation in the country, and the emigrants abroad, had little time for an allegiance to what was by then, after the fall of the Berlin Wall, the discredited creed of the past. Finally, the opposition (well financed by emigrants abroad and well advised by right-of-centre parties from Portugal and elsewhere) managed to mount a very successful electoral campaign, using to the full the modern Western electoral panoply (from T-shirts to negative campaigning). The PAICV, with no experience of such electioneering, was completely out of its depth.

In Cape Verde, then, the political opening up revealed that the legitimacy of the one-party state had run its course. Necessary as it was to unite the country at independence and in order to chart the country's postcolonial development, the PAICV's very success exposed the closed nature of the

---

[10]This is discussed in more detail in the final section of this chapter.

political system, the rigidity of the party, the reluctance of the leadership to alter policies and, inevitably, the government's lack of response to public demand for reform. The population, in other words, was ready for a change, not primarily because it felt that the PAICV had failed in its historic task but because it became convinced that the existing political order was not open and flexible enough. The emphasis, therefore, was on the need for the system to evolve: it was now required to mature from a single-party to a multiparty state. The irony is that the PAICV's successor, the Movimento para a Democracia (MPD) began to exhibit some of the features of the single-party state after a decade in power and that, again, probably was one of the key factors in its recent defeat.

Although the case of São Tomé e Príncipe is, on the surface, very similar, there are some important differences—differences which are quite enlightening about the process of political change in the PALOP. The similarities lie in the fact that São Tomé e Príncipe also underwent a transformation into a multiparty system in 1990, which also resulted in the defeat of the incumbent government and president.[11] Since then, there have been several more government changes. In São Tomé e Príncipe too, there was clearly a willingness to remove the regime in place and give the opposition its chance. Yet, the fact that governments have changed so rapidly, before even they might have made a difference, points to some important contrast between the two countries. In Cape Verde, the PAICV was voted out of office primarily because of dissatisfaction with the political system. In São Tomé e Príncipe, the MLSTP lost the elections chiefly because it had failed to fulfil its promises.

This was partly a question of ideology, as was discussed above, in that the MLSTP exhibited some of the worst features of a socialist administration: rigid in its economic outlook and politically sectarian. But it was much more the result of the type of politics that prevailed in the country. Where the Cape Verdean government had worked with diligence and probity, the MLSTP was both relatively inept and corrupt. Within a few years of independence the regime had become patrimonial and was perceived as such by the bulk of the population. The state, therefore, was not seen as the engine of development, as it was in Cape Verde, but rather as the fount of the resources that fed the clientelistic networks on which the political elites depended.

However, since São Tomé e Príncipe is, like Cape Verde, a small Creole community, the form that patrimonialism took and the effects it had were

---

[11]Indeed, the two Portuguese-speaking island states were the first two countries in Africa to experience a multiparty regime change.

distinct from that found in the three mainland countries. In São Tomé e Príncipe, competition for resources took place within the ambit of a small population where family and community ties mattered more than political affiliation.[12] Multiparty competition, therefore, was almost a 'friend and family' affair, rather than the deadly 'zero-sum game' it is on the continent. Consequently, the repeated regime changes reflects less a sanction against the failures of a given government—and no government has hitherto outshone its predecessor—than a means of ensuring that resources are not always concentrated in the same hands.

In São Tomé e Príncipe, then, the limits of the single-party state were not so much systemic as patrimonial—by which I mean that they point less to the dissatisfaction of the population with the failure of the political system *per se*, deficient as it certainly was, than to the impatience of sections of society for the spoils of government. The socialist complexion of the ruling party had enabled it to take control of the country's economic assets and to direct the flows of foreign aid into the rapidly expanding administration—and thence to its clients. Those who failed to benefit from such largesse objected less to the 'ideology' of such a regime than to the fact that a monopoly of power made possible a patrimonial system that benefited only those members of the community most closely associated with the regime. As for the *de facto* abandonment of socialism, it was no more than a consequence of the country's need to meet the conditions for structural adjustment in the post-Cold War age.

Guinea-Bissau, for its part, represents a more typical west African example. There, the limits of the one-party state are identical to what they are in most other similar mainland countries. The most significant factor in Guinea-Bissau's postcolonial evolution is less its adherence to socialism than the rapid transformation of its erstwhile militant PAIGC into the mainstay of the emerging neo-patrimonial system. The first phase (1974–80), during which Luiz Cabral was president, saw the dominance of the Cape Verdean 'clique' and its allies. Following the coup in November 1980, the new Guinean president, João Bernardo (Nino) Vieira, sidelined the Cape Verdeans and put in place a new clientelistic network. From then on, Vieira ruled, largely uncontested, and he presided over the rapid development of a neo-patrimonial political system. The consequence of the political behaviour of the two successive presidents is that the PAIGC, which had once mobilised large sections of the rural population, gradually lost

---

[12]Here too literature is a good guide to understanding society. See, Chabal *et al. The Postcolonial Literature of Lusophone Africa*, op. cit.; chapter on São Tomé e Príncipe by Caroline Shaw.

legitimacy, not to say relevance, in the countryside. From the much idealised party of political mobilisation it had been during the anti-colonial struggle, it now became akin to most other ruling parties across Africa: that is, an instrument of patron-client politics.

As in other African countries, therefore, the limits of the one-party state were reached when the government's economic shortcomings began to impinge more seriously on the bulk of the population. The shrinking of the resources available centrally, despite massive foreign aid and structural adjustment funding, led to increasing disaffection within the country. Unlike São Tomé e Príncipe, for instance, where economic activity beyond the shores of the island is virtually impossible, Guinea-Bissau is well placed for its inhabitants to invest their energy into the transborder parallel economy. The failings of the neo-patrimonial system prompted by the economic crisis from which the country suffered, were countered by the shifting of productive activities into the informal sector. Since there had been in colonial Guinea so little economic development that had benefited the rural population, agricultural producers adjusted to the failure of the state to provide the support needed to boost food production and exports by ignoring the formal sector altogether. As the government's economic policies were largely irrelevant to them (except when producer prices were raised), the rural population managed its own affairs—politically and economically.[13]

The shift to multiparty politics thus came about very largely because of outside pressure, in particular IMF/World Bank political 'conditionalities', and not primarily because of domestic demand. True, there was within the PAIGC a cohort of younger technocrat modernisers who, as in Cape Verde, deplored the ossification of the political system. But its influence was not such as to prompt the leadership to test the limits of their neo-patrimonial legitimacy. The 'democratic' transition took place haltingly, virtually under duress, and the regime worked hard to neutralise the opposition. The result of the 1994 elections, in which the PAIGC retained power, was not a token of support for the party. It was, rather, an indication of the division within the opposition and of the calculation on the part of a large part of the population that there was still more to obtain from the patrimonial largesse of the party in power than from the impecunious opposition.[14] Indeed, the recent civil war, following which Vieira was finally ousted, revealed the depth of feeling against his much-maligned regime.

The experience of Guinea-Bissau is instructive because it highlights

[13]See Forrest, *Guinea-Bissau* op. cit., chap. 3.
[14]For details about the elections see the final section of this chapter.

the failings of an African micro-state with restricted administrative competence and few natural resources. A comparison with the Gambia, another west African micro-state, would show that Guinea-Bissau suffered from a grave handicap in terms of its colonial heritage and the capacity of its political system to generate economic growth. It would also make plain that the success of the anti-colonial campaign, for all the political capital it bestowed on a party endowed with great legitimacy at independence, did little to obviate the rapid neo-patrimonial transformation of the regime. It was as if the 'traditional' political complexion of the territory had merely been put into abeyance, masked by the modernist discourse of the victorious party, only to resurface after the nationalist takeover. The limits of the single-party state in Guinea-Bissau had in the end more to do with the deliquescence of the neo-patrimonial system than with the failure of the 'socialist' transition. The party's 'socialist' legacy, whatever it had ever been, had long dissipated when the first multiparty elections took place in 1994.

The cases of Angola and Mozambique are historically more complex but not analytically so distinct from that of Guinea-Bissau. The main differences lie in the nature of the political systems put in place and in the effects of the civil wars. We shall discuss the origins and implications of the armed strife in greater detail in the next section. Here, the focus is on an analysis of the impact of these conflicts on the political evolution of the two states, with a view to explaining the deficiencies of the one-party system in the two large southern African PALOP. From that perspective, the most useful starting point is a double comparison: one with Guinea-Bissau and the other with some of their neighbouring countries.

The similarities with Guinea-Bissau have to do with the transformation of an ostensibly militant socialist party, with a pedigree of active political mobilisation in the countryside. Admittedly here, as we know, the achievements of the MPLA were in this respect far less impressive. Nevertheless, all three parties shared structural and mobilisational attributes at independence and all three had gained considerable, though unequal, political capital. Where the MPLA and FRELIMO differed from Guinea-Bissau's ruling party was in the extent of their reach. The PAIGC had support from the bulk of the country, even if it was eyed with some suspicion among the Muslim Fulas who had traditionally been in competition with the coastal peoples supporting the PAIGC and who viewed the party's socialist inclination with concern. FRELIMO had more limited backing, both politically and geographically, in that it brought together in a disparate coalition people from widely different regions (north and south but little in between) and distinct social backgrounds (rural in the north and urban in the south). The MPLA's constituency was even more limited—essentially

Luanda and its hinterland—though it did include support from both the urban Creole and African communities and from the surrounding rural areas. Although FRELIMO and the MPLA were committed to supra-ethnic, non-racial politics, the gaps they suffered in political support reduced their legitimacy and made opposition easier.

In other respects, however, the two regimes had much in common with those of the neighbouring countries (Zaire, Zambia, Zimbabwe, Namibia, Kenya or Uganda). First, like them, they claimed to speak for the whole nation but had clearly demarcated constituencies (whether ethnic, regional or racial) which mattered more. In that sense, they faced the difficulty of balancing competing, or even conflicting, interests. Second, they faced serious infrastructural problems both because of the deficiency of the administration and because of the size of the territories over which they claimed to rule. They were here not unlike Zaire. Third, they needed to use the party to attempt to bring, and maintain, unity in the country and were in this way destined to evolve a centralising one-party state. Finally, they were confronted with internal opposition almost from the start, again a feature common in large central African countries.

The limits of the single-party states in Angola and Mozambique, therefore, were tested in three areas: one having to do with the socialist framework put in place; the second connected with the management of such huge territories; and the final relating to the civil conflict which broke out, or intensified, a few years after independence. All three are, of course, inter-related in their effects and explain why the two regimes experienced great difficulty in consolidating the nation-state. We have seen how the attempt to set up a socialist system was socially and economically counter-productive. Let us here examine more carefully how it affected the evolution of the political system in a context where the administration was over-extended and the internal opposition was becoming ever more threatening.

In Mozambique, the first few years after independence saw a vigorous development of the FRELIMO state, with the party reaching down into the local level. Because of the difficulties faced by the regime after 1975—when the Portuguese departure had crippled administration, trade, industry and transport—the party quickly took charge in all these areas. Since this deployment went hand in hand with the strong (socialist) politicisation of the body politic and of society, the impact of the newly established party-state was both dramatic and far reaching. From the *grupos dinamizadores* (party activists involved in supervising production and working relations) in the workplace to the party cells in the villages, FRELIMO was suddenly ubiquitous.[15] Its impact was felt at all levels of society—including in areas

---

[15]For a development of this important point see the country chapter in this volume.

such as health and education where politics now became an integral part of the working environment.

The model applied derived from that of the 'political commissar', first used during the Russian revolution: that is, a party member responsible for ensuring the proper political 'orientation' of the designated group (whether, for example, soldiers, teachers, or health workers). Whilst it was understandable that the party should have wanted to maintain political control of the armed forces during the anti-colonial war, it is clear that the extensive party interference that occurred after independence engendered considerable difficulties. Not only did politics frequently interfere with the effective operation of the enterprise in question (factory, hospital, school, municipality, etc.), but it led to a two-tier hierarchical system which was not propitious to good working relations. The notion that a factory director or a surgeon should be 'supervised' by a semi-educated FRELIMO cadre could not but lead to widespread disruption and growing resentment against a party that had taken over with a great store of political capital.

Since the qualified were not infrequently white Portuguese who had committed themselves to FRELIMO's Mozambique and since the party cadres were often young black militants, the tension created by such combative politics sometimes brought about racial tension. A number of white Mozambicans lost heart and left the country, thus compounding the economic and organisational problems caused by the flight of those well-qualified Portuguese (and *mestiços*) who could not accept the FRELIMO victory in 1975. The pernicious effects of such policies were acknowledged by the party leadership—Machel embarked on a series of key speeches on the issue—and policy was modified. From the mid-eighties, therefore, the regime gradually abandoned such party interference.

At the other end of the social spectrum, the implantation of the FRELIMO state administration into the rural areas was also problematic. This, as we have seen, stemmed from the party's ideological outlook and its socio-political ambitions. The socialist future which the regime envisaged had no place for the so-called 'traditional' structures of social, religious and political authority. These were deemed backward, reactionary obstacles to the construction of a modern, forward-looking and efficient nation-state. There was at the core of the FRELIMO political blueprint a very strongly Jacobin centralising project which required the imposition of party control from the top. Such political objectives did not sit well with the experience of Mozambicans in the rural areas. Where FRELIMO had received strong backing during the liberation war (chiefly among the northern Makonde) and where it was popular (in the south), villagers were taken aback by the party's sudden transformation into an intolerant structure of political control. Elsewhere, particularly in the rest of the northern and central provinces where FRELIMO had less support, the imposition of such a political system was perceived as an attempt to carry on from where the colonial state had left off. [16]

Unlike Guinea-Bissau, where the ruling party allowed 'traditional' authorities to continue functioning, or Angola, where the MPLA rapidly ceased to attempt to govern the countryside, the Mozambican party-state sought to maintain a strong grip on the rural areas. When the RENAMO challenge, initially dismissed by the government merely as the action of 'armed bandits', became more pressing in the eighties, the state made every effort further to tighten its control of the countryside. The civil war turned the party into an armed protagonist and caused it to forfeit its political capital in the eyes of large groups of rural dwellers, who now came to see both sides as equally objectionable. In sum, the FRELIMO policy of anti-tradition, 'collective' agriculture, villagisation, its efforts to 'tame' the rural authorities, and the attempt to eradicate RENAMO, all conspired to make the party appear oppressive, rather than liberating. Consequently, it rapidly lost legitimacy in large swathes of the country and the leadership's ambition to use the party as an engine of social and political mobilisation ran into the ground.[17]

From the early eighties to the early nineties, the regime was involved in a vicious civil war which precluded any but the most summary activity in the rural areas. Where the state still exercised control, its energies were concentrated on beating off the repeated RENAMO attacks and providing for the population displaced by the conflict. Where control was lost, the government's efforts were usually in vain, since it found it impossible to dislodge the rebel fighters from the rural areas they had invested. The result was that the bulk of the countryside found itself engulfed in a fluctuating conflict which, though mostly low level, made impossible the continuation of normal life. The economy and transport were in chaos, with a large proportion of the population forced to flee to towns in order to avoid starvation. The administrative, social and political infrastructure put in place after independence was almost entirely destroyed. The countryside was effectively reduced to 'year zero'. Whilst it would be historically inaccurate to attribute the war to FRELIMO policies, it would be naïve to deny that the failings of the one-party state installed in the country after

---

[16]In those areas, particularly in the central areas, there was too a long historical memory of southern Gaza domination which made many suspicious of FRELIMO's 'imperial' behaviour. See here Newitt, *A History of Mozambique*, op. cit., chap. 20.

[17]See here Christian Geffray, *La Cause des Armes au Mozambique*, op. cit.

independence contributed significantly to discontent in the rural areas and, in this way, made RENAMO opposition more plausible.

The FRELIMO party-state, however, retained national legitimacy throughout the period of civil war and continued to receive strong support in the south of the country as well as in the main urban centres. The MPLA, for its part, was in a very different situation. Victorious in November 1975, the regime found itself shorn of legitimacy both because its internal enemy had not been completely eliminated and because its links with the Soviet Bloc deprived it of Western recognition. Its attempt to consolidate party rule throughout the country met with armed opposition from UNITA and from a large degree of mistrust in the north and central (highlands) provinces. Furthermore, the regime's 'orthodox' ideology was contested—on the right as well as on the left—within the MPLA itself. This lack of national credibility and this internal division provided a weak base from which to try to establish in the country a credible and effective single-party administration.

Although the MPLA regime managed to bring under control the bulk of the country after its defeat of the FNLA and UNITA in 1975–6, it rapidly lost ground in the rural areas once the civil war resumed. From then on, the government's writ effectively stopped running outside the main urban centres. Nor did the regime make efforts to support the rural population, a large proportion of which was forced to flee to the cities in order not to perish in the conflict. The MPLA political infrastructure, therefore, was largely confined to the urban world. The early years after independence saw the same type of political control asserted over the economy and civil society as in Mozambique. Differently from FRELIMO, however, the Angolan ruling party never lessened its use of ideology as an instrument of repression. Until the late eighties, the regime maintained direct party control over the administration, the armed forces, industry, education, culture and most other areas of civil society.[18]

The one-party state in Angola thus became the mechanism by which the ruling elite imposed its domination over the politically-significant segments of society: the armed forces and the population of the main urban centres. The party soon lost both the limited nationalist capital it had inherited at independence and the goodwill it had received among its urban constituents in the early years. Nevertheless, the threat of UNITA—particularly to the whites, *mestiços* and the Luanda Creole community—was such as to induce

---

[18]With the exception of the Catholic church which, despite suffering heavy political pressure, managed to remain relatively independent.

the majority to support the MPLA when the first multiparty elections were held in 1992. The vote, therefore, must be interpreted largely as an indictment of UNITA, which did not manage to convince the electorate of its superior political pedigree other than in the highlands areas where it had always been well implanted.

The difference between the electoral victories of FRELIMO and the MPLA reflects the contrast in the ways the two single-party states reached their limits. In Mozambique, the regime eventually agreed to sign the peace accord and allowed, if grudgingly, the UN to oversee the transition to multiparty politics. The population, desperate for the war to end, recognised the ruling party's achievements, even if it voted against the government in large parts of the country. FRELIMO had been chastened and RENAMO came to accept its place as 'official' opposition within the new political dispensation. In Angola, on the other hand, the MPLA secured victory primarily because the fear of UNITA was greater than the disapproval of the regime's repressive and corrupt behaviour. Neither the government nor the opposition was totally committed to the peace process and both remained prepared to resume war if the electoral verdict did not accord with their ambitions. The main outcome of the 1992 elections has been to endow the MPLA regime with the national and international legitimacy which it had long craved in vain. It has done nothing either to make more likely the end of the war or the 'democratic' transformation of the one-party state which the MPLA controls with an iron hand.

While the evolution of the three mainland PALOP made manifest the limits of single-party regimes, the changes which have taken place since multiparty elections have been held do not augur well for the future of democracy as it is conceived in the West. If the economic and political failings of the regimes in place were ruthlessly exposed, the outcome of the elections held so far is ambiguous. As elsewhere in Africa, there seems to be no obvious connection between the record of a regime and its ability to be re-elected. The reasons for this are complex but they hinge on two key factors. The first is that the neo-patrimonial model of politics continues to hold sway. The second is that political culture in these countries continues to favour the incumbents since it is they, rather than their competitors, who have access to the state's resources, on which the survival of so many depends. The contrast between the two island and the three mainland states does point to politically significant differences between the culture, social customs and religious beliefs which go a long way towards explaining why similarly conceived one-party regimes have met distinct ends.

ANGOLA AND MOZAMBIQUE: SOCIAL DIVISIONS, POLITICAL
RIVALRIES AND CIVIL WAR

In trying to explain the civil conflicts which have ravaged Angola and
Mozambique, most observers have focussed their attention on the
specificities of each case. This section will consider whether a more
comparative approach would help to shed some additional light on these
events. The aim, therefore, is not primarily to give an account of the internal
wars in these two southern African Portuguese-speaking countries.[19] It is
to consider whether their much troubled postcolonial fortune can be made
more intelligible by means of a comparative historical analysis.[20]

The two main questions are: (1) why has the situation in Angola become
so intractable? and (2) why is it that Mozambique has managed to resolve
a conflict which in many respects appeared worse than in Angola? The
most common response to the first is that the situation in Angola was
always bound to be delicate because of the historical division of the country
between the three main ethnic constituencies (Bakongo, Kimbundu and
Ovimbundu). The standard reply to the second is that, following the end
of apartheid in South Africa, RENAMO simply ran out of steam and had
to settle. There is some truth in both of these points but I will show here
why they are over-simplifications.

The section is in three parts. There is, first, an examination of the recent
situation in Angola and Mozambique. There follows a discussion of a
number of issues connected with the history of the colonial period and of
the anti-colonial struggle. Finally, there is an attempt to provide a re-interpretation of what has happened since independence in the light of that
history.

*The recent situation in Angola and Mozambique: hypotheses
and causalities*

The present condition of Angola remains precarious. Following the 1991
peace agreement, elections were held in 1992 under United Nations
supervision.[21] Contrary to expectations, they returned a majority for the
government in power since independence. The leader of the opposition

---

[19]Which will be found in the two country chapters in this volume.

[20]For useful background to the historical situation of Angola and Mozambique see, *inter
alia*, Newitt, *Portugal in Africa*, op. cit. and Birmingham, *Frontline Nationalism in Angola
and Mozambique*, op. cit.

[21]For details on these elections see the final section of this chapter.

refused the electoral verdict.[22] War started again. Another peace accord (the Lusaka Protocol) was signed in November 1994.[23] Again, a ceasefire was agreed and its implementation was overseen by a much strengthened UN presence—until war resumed again in late 1998.[24]

Between 1994 and 1998, an attempt was made by the international community to facilitate the execution of the 1994 Lusaka Protocol: consolidating peace and establishing power-sharing arrangements. UN supervision was intended to make possible the stage-by-stage implementation of the Protocol, encouraging both the government and UNITA to conform to the terms of the agreement. UNITA forces were at the time believed largely to have demobilised and the new integrated national army was supposed to have been set up. The distribution of posts at the local, regional, provincial and national level had been agreed and both sides showed some willingness to conform to the letter, if perhaps not the spirit, of the accord. UNITA agreed to take its place in the national assembly. Even Jonas Savimbi was at one time reported to have accepted the position of 'leader of the opposition.'

The reality, unfortunately, was utterly different from this edifying assessment. Although formally there had been progress in terms of de-militarisation and political integration, the situation was very far from stabilised. First, UNITA had not fully demobilised. Although it had disarmed a number of its soldiers, there is evidence both that it had kept its best troops in reserve and that it was actively re-arming. Second, the country was neither safe nor integrated. There remained areas controlled by UNITA in which normal political and economic life could not resume. Conversely, the government was slow in implementing power sharing in regions of the country where it was in control. In short, there was still too much violence throughout the country and too little effort made to allow any consolidation of peace.

Third, there was little evidence that power sharing, such as it was, at the regional and national levels led to collaboration, even less to reconciliation. The structure of political authority in Angola is such that, despite the notional place of UNITA in the national assembly and other administrative bodies, authority lies firmly in the hands of the MPLA. Power sharing was simply not an effective reality—nor, perhaps, could it be. Finally, Savimbi remained as elusive as ever. There was much evidence, abundantly confirmed

---

[22]For an inside account of the failures of the UN see Margaret Anstee, *Orphans of the Cold War: The Inside Story of the Collapse of the Angolan Peace Process* (Basingstoke: Macmillan, 1996).

[23]Although significantly it was not signed by either of the two leaders.

[24]Evidence of the difficulty of the peace process in Angola can be found in Keith Hart and Joanna Lewis (eds), *Why Angola Matters* (London: James Currey, 1996).

since, that the UNITA leader had no intention of accepting the offer of opposition leader and vice-president and that he was simply biding his time until he was in a position to re-launch his military campaign to seize power outright. The fact that he had refused to sign the Lusaka Protocol personally was an ominous token of his intentions.[25]

Moreover, and despite the overwhelming desire for peace throughout the country, there were strong indications that the government was not unanimous on the question. While the official policy was clearly geared to showing that the regime was complying scrupulously with UN injunctions and working hard for the success of the Lusaka Protocol, there were perennial reports of a faction within the MPLA which favoured eliminating UNITA militarily once and for all. From their perspective, the mistakes of 1992—when the MPLA began to disarm following the first peace accord— were not to be repeated. In short, then, there were within both the MPLA and UNITA powerful 'war parties' whose ultimate aim was to defeat the other side and assert sole control of the country.

The resumption of war in 1998 was ample confirmation that the Lusaka Protocol had little chance of success, even with strong UN support, because neither side was willing to sacrifice supremacy for peace. The recent government assault on the UNITA armed forces has marked a decisive breakthrough in that the rebel movement has been ejected from the cities it held and its 'conventional' heavy weapons (such as tanks and large artillery pieces) have been largely destroyed. Furthermore, it has lost control of most of the diamond fields, thus drastically reducing its revenues. From the government's point of view, it is now a matter of 'mopping up'. Yet, there is little doubt that UNITA has not been destroyed as a guerrilla force and that, despite the enormous military setbacks he has suffered, Savimbi is fully prepared to continue his armed opposition by all possible means.

Nor is it clear that regional and international factors are favourable to peace. It is true that the United States has for some time now been putting pressure on Sayimbi to settle and, to that end, has renewed sanctions against UNITA.[26] It is also true that the South African government has used its influence to support the peace process. Yet, there is no doubt that UNITA continues to be supplied in arms, in part at least through US dealers and in part by means of air supplies originating in the Democratic Republic of the Congo (DRC) or, even, South Africa. Moreover, there are conflicting pressures on the Angolan government, with substantial foreign interests worried about the prospect of a UNITA regime and thereby giving tacit

[25]See here, among others, Karl Maier, *Angola: Promises and Lies* (London: Serif, 1996).
[26]But the UNITA leader undoubtedly still has powerful backers in the United States.

support to those in the MPLA who seek to defeat the enemy. Unlike in 1992, few businesses now bank on a UNITA victory. Finally, the long-term implications for Angola of Kabila's takeover are not yet clear: ostensibly, Savimbi has lost Mobutu's unconditional support but in practice UNITA still seems to be able to operate from the DRC—large areas of which are scarcely under central control. The recent Angolan involvement in Congo (Brazzaville) will also affect regional stability.

Angola's outlook, then, is at best uncertain and at worst unpropitious. Although the country's economic potential is enormous and, at peace, it could rapidly develop into one of the economic giants of Africa, the political situation is far too unstable to justify much hope. Civil war has not ended. The country is still poised on a knife edge and it will take the greatest efforts on the parts of those, both inside and outside, who want peace to make it happen. Unfortunately, it now looks more and more as if war will continue until the government has achieved its aim of 'eliminating' UNITA—a forlorn hope since, as history shows, guerrilla movements are rarely 'defeated'. In the end, and despite the present bullish statements made by the MPLA, there will be a need for a peace agreement at some stage—unless, as many suspect, the regime is concerned to maintain a 'credible' enemy so as better to justify its ruthless hold on power.

The situation in Mozambique is, on the other hand, radically different.[27] Here the 1992 peace accord, signed by the leaders of both FRELIMO and RENAMO, led to an orderly end to the war, the disarmament of RENAMO soldiers, the integration of both armies and the holding of successful multiparty elections—all under UN supervision. The experience of the failures of the transition to peace in Angola meant that the UN was given a mandate to support more strongly the consolidation of the ceasefire and the preparation of elections in Mozambique. These elections were held in October 1994 and, as in Angola but not as unexpectedly, they returned the same government and president to office.[28]

In Mozambique, the armed opposition accepted the peace accord and organised itself into a political party capable of contesting the national elections and prepared to function as an opposition afterwards. Perhaps because Dhlakama and RENAMO did better than most had anticipated,

[27]For an exhaustive history of Mozambique since the fifteenth century see Newitt, *A History of Mozambique*, op. cit. The most recent and up-to-date account of the postcolonial history of Mozambique is Young and Hall, *Confronting Leviathan*, op. cit.

[28]For an inside account of the electoral process see the book written by the Chairman of the Electoral Commission: Brazão Mazula, *Elections, Democracy, and Development* (Maputo: Embassy of the Kingdom of the Netherlands, 1996). See also the Mozambique chapter in this volume.

the party was willing not just to concede electoral defeat but also to come to terms with FRELIMO's refusal to set up a post-election coalition government of national reconciliation. It did so, moreover, without resorting to the threat of resuming violence. RENAMO, therefore, completed a most remarkable mutation from armed outfit bent on destruction to party machine geared to carving for itself a legitimate political place in today's Mozambique. The December 1999 elections confirmed the balance of political strength and the outcome was similar to that of 1994.[29]

Of more long-term concern is the extent to which the government has been able to re-build the country and initiate a process of economic growth which might in due course lead to sustained development. The odds here are not good. Mozambique is devoid of substantial mineral resources and, although its agricultural base for export is potentially good, its present economic condition remains alarming. There is evidence that the constraints of structural adjustment are so severe as to jeopardise the very viability of the country and thereby make virtually impossible the kind of massive investment which its reconstruction requires.[30] There is evidence too that NGO involvement in the economy is so massive as to discourage government economic policy and derail its long-term initiatives.[31] The question for Mozambique, then, is whether it will be able to weather the stringency of structural adjustment while laying down the foundations for economic rebirth.

How can we best explain the different outcome of Angola's and Mozambique's postcolonial transitions to peace? Can a comparative historical analysis of the precolonial, colonial and anti-colonial history of these two countries help us answer that question?

The weight of history

This section considers some of the historical factors which are most relevant to an understanding of the civil conflicts in the two countries. The main concern here is to analyse the extent to which those factors explain both

---

[29]Chissano once again gained an absolute majority, 52.3 per cent, but Dhlakama increased his share from 33.7 per cent in 1994 to 47.7 per cent. FRELIMO won 133 seats with 48.5 per cent of the vote while RENAMO won 118 seats with 38.8 per cent. RENAMO took six provinces with FRELIMO secured five. FRELIMO increased its share of the vote but only at the expense of minor parties.

[30]On the impact of structural adjustment on Mozambique see Joseph Hanlon, *Peace without Profit: How the IMF Blocks Rebuilding in Mozambique* (London: James Currey, 1996).

[31]On the impact of NGOs in Mozambique see Joseph Hanlon, *Mozambique: Who Calls the Shots?* (London: James Currey, 1991).

Patrick Chabal

the similarities and the differences in their postcolonial trajectory. In particular, did the differentiated effects of colonial rule determine the complexion and effectiveness of the anti-colonial movements which sought independence from Portugal?

What is noteworthy about colonial Angola is the extent to which the formal colony evolved in continuity with what had happened prior to the Scramble for Africa.[32] Angola had been since at least the sixteenth century linked with Brazil through the slave trade. During that period there emerged in Luanda a commercial and administrative Creole elite—Portuguese-speaking, mixed race, Catholic, and cosmopolitan—involved in the triangular Atlantic trade. This Creole society lived in Africa but its connections with the interior of the continent were limited to the commerce which sustained the local economy. They had their representatives inland who dealt with local Africans. The slave trade was the main, but not the only, commercial basis for this relationship between Luanda and the hinterland. Other commodities were also traded but, until the nineteenth century, it was the business of slavery which underpinned the relationship between Creole and African societies.

The effects of the slave trade on inland African communities varied enormously, between those which raided and traded slaves and those which were raided. It was Africans who sold the slaves to the traders acting as intermediaries for the Luanda Creole merchants. This Creole community lived in some considerable separation from the interior, turned as it was towards the Brazilian and Portuguese societies of which it felt a part—and with which indeed it had complex family, social and economic links. It is clear, therefore, that most inland Africans would, long before the colonial period, have viewed these city-based Creoles as quite 'alien'.[33]

The abolition of the slave trade coincided with the beginnings of the modern colonial period, culminating with the partition of Africa at the Berlin Conference in 1884–5. The history of Angola thereafter is that which was common to all colonial territories, namely 'pacification', the establishment of an administrative colonial structure and the development of a colonial economy to serve the metropolis. The effects of formal Portuguese colonisation on Angola were obviously many but perhaps the most crucial was the enforced decline of the Luanda Creole community

[32]There is no single satisfactory history of Angola but see here, among others, David Birmingham, *The Portuguese Conquest of Angola* (Oxford University Press, 1965) and Gerald Bender, *Angola under the Portuguese* (London: Heinemann, 1978).

[33]For a useful discussion of race relations in the Portuguese empire see Charles Boxer, *Race Relations in the Portuguese Colonial Empire* (Oxford University Press, 1963).

within the newly-created colonial order. By the twenties it had become clear that the former Creoles were to be used as mere adjuncts to the new Portuguese colonial masters. Socially and economically, their status was diminished. Furthermore, colonial rule created other elites, both *mestiço* and African, who rose through the ranks of colonial society to challenge the supremacy of the older established Creole society.[34]

The beneficial effects of colonial rule on the bulk of the African population of Angola were relatively minimal. Compelled to work by colonial legislation, Africans had little choice if they wanted to avoid forced labour or, worse, 'contract' work in São Tomé. They could either transform themselves into proper 'farmers' and become integrated into the colonial economy or they had to hire themselves out as labourers in Portuguese agricultural or commercial concerns—of which the most successful were the coffee plantations in the northern Congo area. For historical reasons, the Ovimbundu (of the central highlands) had to seek employment on the coffee plantations as their agricultural economy was not sufficiently strong to sustain their relatively large population. As for the Bakongo, those who did not work as agricultural labourers were chiefly associated with the business and trade which had developed in the Belgian Congo to the north. Some of them became substantial businessmen, a few owning plantations in northern Angola.[35]

Finally, Angola was a colony of settlement—but of a nature which marked it off from British Africa. Other than the coffee plantation owners, clearly an elite among the colonists, the Portuguese settlers were poor, unskilled, uneducated and, on the whole, they failed to succeed as agriculturists. Unable to compete with Africans and without resources, they moved to the cities and survived as best they could by doing menial jobs. Although in the sixties more dynamic Portuguese businessmen and entrepreneurs did settle in Angola, the bulk of the white population in the colony remained relatively poor and unskilled. Their presence was a continuous bar to the progression of Africans into the kind of jobs which they might have expected to have in other, non-Portuguese, colonies. Their presence too was conducive to an atmosphere of petty discrimination and racism which affected the ordinary Africans and the Creoles of the cities.

It can be seen, therefore, that the development of Angola as a colony

[34]See Christine Messiant, 'Angola, les voies de l'ethnisation et de la décomposition' in *Lusotopie*, vols 1–2 (1994) and 3 (1995).

[35]For an exhaustive account of colonial Angola see René Pélissier's two-volume history: *La Colonie du Minotaure (1926–1961)* and *Les Guerres Grises (1845–1941)* (Orgeval: Pélissier, 1978).

was both relatively smooth and potentially divisive. It was smooth because the Portuguese consolidated their hold over the colony (relatively) rapidly and integrated the whole territory under one functioning administration. It was potentially divisive because the colonial order induced—as it did elsewhere in Africa but in Angola on a larger scale—sharp dichotomies between social and, inevitably, ethnic or racial groups. Of those, the most significant was that between the Creoles and the Africans of the interior— whether in the centre or north of the country—since the Kimbundu were used to living in much closer proximity with the Creoles of Luanda.

Such divisions were sharpened by considerable social, cultural and religious factors. The Creoles were Portuguese-speaking, often (but not always) of mixed race, Catholic and urban-based. As they lost ground in the colony to the newly-established colonial elites, they sought to maintain their superior status by stressing even more than before those characteristics which set them apart as the true elites of the country. Though less prominent than they had been in the nineteenth century, they remained at the heart of the colonial order and were, not unnaturally, seen by the Africans of the interior as 'collaborators'. Theirs was indeed a very Lusophone world— in culture, language and outlook. Inland things were different. Influences from foreign Protestant and Catholic missionaries, from other colonies (either Belgian or British) where many worked, were more important than those coming from Luanda. Furthermore, local African socio-political and cultural institutions, left relatively untouched by Portuguese colonial rule, continued to preside over the day-to-day life of the population.

In short, Angola was characterised by one sharp dichotomy—between the Creole community and the Africans of the interior—and a relatively well-integrated if poorly developed colonial order, in which the economy was very largely in the hands of the white settlers. This meant that, by the 1950s, there were two deeply frustrated social groups: the Creole elites, distinct but enfeebled; and the Africans of the interior, poor, uneducated and neglected at the bottom of a fairly rigidly stratified social order.

Mozambique was different in many significant respects.[36] First, its precolonial history had been linked with that of Portuguese India and had (up to the last quarter of the nineteenth century) relatively little to do with the slave trade. Portuguese East Africa consisted, until the Scramble, of the Ilha de Moçambique, stagepost to India, the estates or *prazos* of the Zambesi river region, and a few Creole communities on the coast. The

---

[36]See Newitt, *A History of Mozambique* op. cit. and Thomas Henriksen, *Mozambique: A History* (London: Rex Collings, 1978).

prazos became, in Isaacman's famous phrase, Africanised.[37] As for the Ilha de Moçambique and the other coastal towns, they had neither the economic resources nor the social clout to compete successfully with the local Afro-Arab trading communities that dominated the region. With the decline of Goa, the Portuguese presence in eastern Africa weakened. There was nowhere in Mozambique remotely the equivalent of the strong, cohesive, self-contained and dynamic Luanda Creole society.

Second, the clash between South African and Portuguese colonial interests, following the British Ultimatum of 1990, resulted in the creation of a Portuguese colony whose geography was inimical to easy integration. Not only was Mozambique very elongated from south to north, but its various provinces had less in common than they had with the regions immediately to the west prior to the Scramble. Indeed, except for the impact of the post-Mfecane Ngoni migration from south to north (up to the Zambesi), the main lines of trade and migration had in the past always been from east to west. As a result, therefore, the colony of Mozambique started life on very weak historical and geographical foundations.

Third, the consolidation of Portuguese colonial rule comprehensively demolished the precolonial Creole elites. The *prazos* were subdued by force of arms during 'pacification' and the capital of the colony was moved in 1903 from the Ilha de Moçambique to Lourenço Marques, at the opposite end of the country.[38] There it developed very largely as an adjunct to the Transvaal. At a stroke, therefore, the south of the country became the heart of the colony and the new capital was created in deep symbiosis with South Africa.

Fourth, Mozambique was never properly consolidated as a colonial territory. Unable to colonise the north of the country, the Portuguese leased it to a number of concession companies charged with its pacification and 'development', in exchange for monopoly control of its economy. The result was that northern Mozambique became a labour reserve, without even the meagre benefits which Portuguese colonial rule bestowed on Africans by way of administration, education and health provision. The populations of the north, many of whom emigrated to the British territories in search of better working and living conditions, were thus further separated from those of the south, who in their turn were looking west to

---

[37]See Allen Isaacman, *Mozambique: The Africanization of a European Institution* (Madison WI: University of Wisconsin Press, 1972).

[38]See Allen Isaacman, *The Tradition of Resistance in Mozambique: Anti-Colonial Activity in the Zambesi Valley, 1850–1921* (London: Heinemann, 1976).

Rhodesia and South Africa. The main southern urban centres, Lourenço
Marques and Beira, not only serviced these two interior countries but came
very largely to resemble their segregated cities.

Fifth, Mozambique was more racially complex than Angola. In addition
to the mixed race and white settler population, there were in the colony
Indians and Chinese. The Indian community consisted of long established
Goan Portuguese and of western Indian traders who settled everywhere
in eastern Africa during the twentieth century. The Chinese came as
labourers or traders. As for the white population of Portuguese settlers, it
was both less numerous and more differentiated than that of Angola.
Although the bulk of Portuguese immigrants were, as in Angola, poor
and uneducated, there were in the fifties a number of businessmen and
professionals whose influence on the cultural and political life of the colony
was far from negligible. [39]

Finally, Mozambique was never as rich as Angola. Although endowed
with reasonable agricultural and fishing resources, it was devoid of the
serious mineral wealth of Angola—of which oil and diamonds were, and
remain, the two most important. Nor, by the end of colonial rule, was
Mozambique as economically advanced as Angola. Moreover, whereas
Angola had become a rapidly growing self-standing economy, Mozambique
remained intimately dependent on the revenues remitted by labourers in
South Africa or Rhodesia and those generated by the use which these two
countries made of Mozambican railways and ports.

This, thus, is the context within which anti-colonial movements grew.
On the face of it, the complexities of, and the divisions within, Mozambique
were far greater than those in Angola. Although both colonies appeared ill-
prepared for the demands of a unified anti-colonial movement, Mozambique
seemed in this respect far worse off—and this for at least three sets of
reasons, which we know from the general experience of colonial Africa
to have been crucial in the formation of nationalism. First, the colony was
very poorly integrated as a single territorial entity. Second, there was no
strong internal economy to bring Africans together in occupational
groupings: the working population of Mozambique was scattered in
different British colonies and in South Africa. Third, there was no cohesive
educated elite capable of leading the anti-colonial movement.

And, indeed, the early stirrings of anti-colonialism seemed to confirm
this view. In Angola, the MPLA was founded already in 1956 on clear

---

[39]See here the chapter on Mozambique in Chabal *et al., The Postcolonial Literature of
Lusophone Africa,* op. cit.

nationalist, supra-ethnic and ideologically-coherent lines.[40] In Mozambique, there were several anti-colonial groupings based in the British colonies of Kenya (MANU), Malawi (UNAMI) and Rhodesia (UDENAMO)[41]— somewhat similar in this respect to the ethnically based Bakongo UPNA, which eventually became the FNLA.[42] There was in addition a small band of politically conscious (anti-colonial) secondary school students in Lourenço Marques (UNEMO).[43] The key historical question, then, is why the anti-colonial movement in Angola remained divided between the MPLA and the FNLA, and eventually UNITA, while in Mozambique the majority of these relatively disparate groups of anti-colonial forces came together in 1962 into one broad coalition, FRELIMO?[44]

This is a fiendishly complicated question, a complete answer to which would require access to documents which we simply do not have and are now unlikely ever to have. There are, however, some key explanatory points. These can be divided between external and internal factors.

In terms of external influences, the four most important factors are the following. First, the crucial outside country had opposite influence: Zaire supported the FNLA and opposed the MPLA whereas Tanzania applied the strongest pressure on Mozambican anti-colonial movements to form a single alliance. Second, the two Angolan movements were backed by the two opposing super powers whereas no such strongly dichotomised international constraint applied in the case of Mozambique. Third, both the MPLA and FNLA had networks of support among individual, and often ideologically opposed, African countries whereas, again, the situation was not nearly as sharply divided in the case of the Mozambican groups, who merely had tacit acceptance in their host country. Finally, the FNLA was able to get early endorsement by the newly created OAU, which in Mozambique, however, supported the coalition of nationalists represented by FRELIMO.

---

[40]The most exhaustive account of the nationalist movements in Angola remains Marcum's two-volume, *The Angolan Revolution*, op. cit.

[41]MANU: Mozambican African National Union; UNAMI: União Africana de Moçambique Independente; UDENAMO: União Democrática Nacional de Moçambique.

[42]UPNA: União das Populações do Norte de Angola; FNLA: Frente Nacional para a Libertação de Angola.

[43]UNEMO: União Nacional dos Estudantes de Moçambique.

[44]For a sympathetic account of the formation, development and success of anti-colonialism see, among others, Allen Isaacman, *Mozambique: From Colonialism to Revolution, 1900–1982* (Boulder CO: Westview Press, 1983); for a more critical approach see Henriksen, *Revolution and Counter-Revolution*, op. cit.

The internal factors are, to my mind, even more significant. They too can be reduced to four. The first has to do with the strength of the historical divisions between competing anti-colonial movements. In Angola, the FNLA and MPLA represented totally distinct sets of interests: respectively, the Bakongo 'African' elites of the North and the Luanda Creole community and its regional Kimbundu supporters. In Mozambique, the various ethnic anti-colonial groupings were brought together by a relatively young southern elite with little previous contact, or antagonism, with the others. The simmering hostility between the northern Makonde people (integrated within FRELIMO) and their Makua neighbours (who were not), though never resolved, did not result in the formation of credible rival anti-colonial movements. Nor did the expulsion from the party of the prominent Makonde leader, Lazaro Nkavandame, lead to the creation of a viable rival Makonde party to challenge FRELIMO.

The second turns around a fairly clear sense of real, or imaginary, racial difference. The FNLA liked to consider the MPLA Creole leadership as a 'non-African' mixed race group disconnected from the 'real' Africa— even if a substantial number of the MPLA leaders (including its head, Agostinho Neto) were in fact black African. In Mozambique, on the other hand, the FRELIMO leadership—though it included *mestiços*, Indians and whites—was never perceived to be made of an equally homogeneous and historically distinct 'Creole' group.

Third, the role of ideology in the anti-colonial struggle movement was different. In Angola, the MPLA was from its inception strongly ('orthodox') Marxist and the FNLA equally vigorously anti-Marxist. For this reason, a number of Western countries (most notably the USA) never wavered in their support of the FNLA and their implacable opposition to the MPLA. In Mozambique, the situation was not so clear cut. The various anti-colonial groupings had little overt ideology and although the bulk of the FRELIMO elite was 'socialist', the movement was founded by Eduardo Mondlane, an US-trained black Mozambican who worked for the United Nations.

Finally, but perhaps most importantly, there were strong differences in leadership. It can readily be seen that in Angola the anti-colonial movements were set up by the 'old' colonial elites, representing respectively the Creole and northern African communities. By contrast, the anti-colonial leadership in Mozambique issued very largely from a 'new' generation of southern and *mestiço* politicians. Furthermore both the MPLA and the FNLA were in the hands of leaders with little taste for compromise: after the failure of the attempt in 1962 to merge the two parties, there was little chance that either Agostinho Neto or Holden Roberto would ever work with the other. Savimbi's decision to leave the FNLA and his rejection by the MPLA led directly to his decision to create UNITA, thus greatly exacerbating the situation.[45] In Mozambique, Mondlane had the vision and the skill to bring and keep together the bulk of the anti-colonial leadership, no matter how strongly the divisions between some of them might have been, or indeed remained, within the new coalition.[46]

In Mozambique, FRELIMO pursued an inclusive nationalist campaign, seeking to bring on board all anti-colonial forces, and conducting a guerrilla campaign on what I call the Guinea model—that is, the strategy followed with great success by Amílcar Cabral in Portuguese Guinea, of which the three key elements were: unity at all costs, political mobilisation of the countryside, and political control of armed action.[47] In Angola, on the other hand, the two nationalist rivals were immersed in exile politics and in continuing internal power struggles—a policy of exclusion rather than inclusion—and they were unclear about guerrilla strategy.[48] Although in due course the MPLA did attempt to follow the Guinea model in eastern Angola, this too was ultimately undermined by the intra-party political struggles which culminated in the two grave factional splits known as the Active Revolt and the Chipenda break-away.

To conclude this broad historical survey, then, it is simply not the case that the prospects for nationalist unity and anti-colonial success were historically better in Mozambique than in Angola. The differentiated outcome of the anti-colonial campaign in the two colonies can be explained in terms of the degree to which the respective nationalist leadership managed to overcome the most potentially damaging political constraints they faced. It is human agency rather than circumstance which explains FRELIMO's greater success in this respect.

The postcolonial roots of conflict

The consequences of those differences were profound.[49] In Mozambique, FRELIMO, however poorly implanted it was in many regions at independence, undeniably embodied the country's national aspirations.[50] It was the single legitimate voice of independent Mozambique, as was demonstrated

---

[45]See here Marcum, op. cit., vol. 2.

[46]One will here read with profit Mondlane's own account, reprinted as *The Struggle for Mozambique* (London: Zed, 1983).

[47]On Cabral and the anti-colonial struggle see Chabal, *Amílcar Cabral*, op. cit.

[48]See Marcum, op. cit., vol. 2.

[49]See here Birmingham, *Frontline Nationalism in Angola and Mozambique*, op. cit.

[50]In 1974, FRELIMO was only seriously politically active in three provinces and had little real impact in the cities.

by the imperious manner of its negotiations with the post-1974 Portuguese regime. In Angola, however, the MPLA—though it held the capital on independence day and managed to gain control over most of the country in the following twelve months—was never endowed with the nationalist legitimacy it claimed. Right from the beginning, its historical right to rule the country was contested. The problem in Angola, then, was not so much one of nationalist plurality, a situation which was found in many countries at independence, but rather an inherent lack of legitimacy in the eyes of many, both in and outside the country.

The strength of FRELIMO as the ruling party of a newly-independent country was reinforced by the unity, coherence and collective will of the leadership. By contrast, and in direct continuation with the past, the MPLA was from the start riven by divisions, both personal and ideological, and eaten by political rivalry. The extent of the differences between the two was illustrated in the early years after independence. Although, as we have seen, both parties were to identify themselves officially as Marxist-Leninist in 1977, that political move had different implications for each.[51] In Mozambique, it was primarily a practical political decision meant in part to placate Eastern donors and in part to initiate ('socialist') modernisation. In Angola, it was above all a way for the ruling clique to mark out their ideological differences with their political competitors. The result of such intolerance was the 1977 Nito Alves coup attempt which split the MPLA asunder, unleashed savage repression, fed political paranoia and moved the party firmly in a Stalinist direction.[52]

In Mozambique, ideology was viewed pragmatically: when it proved to fail, it was discarded, as it was by 1979 in respect of a collectivising approach to agriculture. In Angola, ideology was a weapon for power and served to identify those who were close to the regime and those who were dangerous to it. Thus, although in 1977 the two parties were ideologically and politically at one, by 1980 they had very little in common except their position as a single ruling entity. The government in a Mozambique had by then already embarked on some radical changes in policy while in Angola it was entirely preoccupied with what might be called the 'politics of hegemony'. In comparing the MPLA and FRELIMO, then, ideology is of little consequence. The main difference lay instead in the nature of the political systems established and in the extent to which they differed in

[51]On the 1977 party congresses that led to these changes see Luís Moita, *Os Congressos da FRELIMO, do PAIGC e do MPLA* (Lisbon: Ulmeiro, 1979).

[52]On the coup attempt see David Birmingham, 'The twenty-seventh of May', *African Affairs*, 1978.

terms of the coherence, unity and quality of their respective leadership.[53]

Of the four factors which best explain the differences in the postcolonial evolution of both countries, and consequently the distinct outcome of the civil war, the most important one is undoubtedly that which separates the two parties in terms of legitimacy and coherence. Throughout this period, FRELIMO worked as a united and cohesive ruling party, and for this reason overcame the death (in 1986) of Samora Machel with relative ease. They were able to adjust policies as the situation required of them. The MPLA ruling elite, by contrast, were forced to assert their view against both external and internal opposition, defining policy more in terms of the 'correct line' than in respect of what was best for the country. No change of policy could be made without attacking those who were supposed to be against it. In short, despite its socialist ideology FRELIMO was essentially pragmatic whilst the MPLA remained obdurately Stalinist.

Beyond this crucial difference, there were three other specific sets of factors which impinged on the postcolonial fate of the two countries: their economy; their position in regional and international relations; and the nature of the armed opposition. Economically, first, the Angolan government could exploit its most valuable asset, oil, throughout the civil conflict and was thus always able both to sustain its (largely urban-based) client population and to finance the astronomical cost of the war. It could ignore all other sectors of the economy and still survive. Even when it lost control of the diamond fields to UNITA, it was still able to uphold its considerable military budget. Conversely, UNITA found in diamonds the means to increase military expenditures for its campaigns. As a result, the government only considered a move towards more liberal policies when it became economically necessary and politically expedient to do so—particularly in terms of the changing foreign policy of the Soviet Union.

Mozambique, by contrast, was bereft of serious mineral resources and was left at independence with a wrecked infrastructure. Although in the first three years the government managed, with much foreign aid, to increase agricultural production, the economy began to collapse thereafter under the repeated assaults of a RENAMO bent on wanton destruction. Drought, misguided policies and war virtually brought the regime to its knees, prompting thereby the signing in 1984 of the Nkomati Accord with South Africa. The regime in Mozambique was thus compelled to temper its socialist ambitions according to the very considerable economic constraints under which it laboured—all the more so when, in the mid-eighties, it

---

[53]On Angolan politics see, *inter alia*, Keith Somerville, *Angola: Politics, Economics and Society* (London: Frances Pinter, 1986); on Mozambique see Young and Hall, op. cit.

became obvious that the Eastern Bloc was no longer going to continue to bankroll the economy of its far-flung ideological friends. From 1986 onwards, Mozambique entered the long road to Damascus that was eventually to lead to the IMF and structural adjustment.

The second determinant had to do with the fact that Angola had been from the beginning a pawn in Cold War politics whereas Mozambique, although seemingly in the socialist camp, was never viewed in the same light. The effect was that, as soon as UNITA had been embraced as the champion of anti-communism, it was supported, armed and supplied by the West as a counterforce to the 'Soviet-backed and Cuban-protected' MPLA state. Once the US had adopted 'constructive engagement' vis-à-vis South Africa, the conflict in Angola was only ended by Gorbachev's change of foreign policy—leading to a settlement in Namibia, the departure of Cuban troops from Angola and the opening of negotiations between the MPLA and UNITA. Nevertheless, and this gives a good indication of US intentions, the MPLA government was not recognised until UNITA's resumption of the civil war in 1992. UNITA, however, continued to be able to rely on Zaire's support and supplies from, or via, South Africa.

The situation of Mozambique was different. For a host of historical reasons, some of which undoubtedly subjective, the West never construed the FRELIMO regime as ideological foe, an ally of the Cold War enemy. Nor did South Africa, even at its most aggressive under P.W. Botha, consider removing the FRELIMO government. It used RENAMO to weaken the country so that it would settle down as a docile neighbour and, following the 1984 Nkomati Accord, stop giving the ANC logistical support. Finally, Machel was able to cultivate the 'Thatcher connection'[54] to gain access to the US and seek aid for his desperately poor country. In sum, then, Mozambique was wooed by the West, not ostracised, so that the move towards economic liberalisation and political pluralism occurred gradually under the leadership of a party increasingly keen to end the conflict with RENAMO. The changes in South Africa ushered by the release of Nelson Mandela put pressure on RENAMO to negotiate with FRELIMO and stop the war.

Finally, the factor which most influenced the evolution of the civil conflict in both countries, was the very different character of the two opposition forces: UNITA and RENAMO. Although UNITA was born a genuine anti-colonial political organisation and RENAMO a foreign bred armed engine

---

[54]Margaret Thatcher was grateful to Samora Machel, who had been instrumental in persuading Robert Mugabe to accept the Lancaster House Accord for the independence of Rhodesia, and she repaid her debt in diplomatic terms.

of destruction, their evolution was to turn them into their very opposite.[55] UNITA eventually became a military machine, bent on seizing power at the barrel of a gun, while RENAMO transformed itself into a political party willing and able to compete in the electoral game.[56] There are essentially three reasons for this, of which the first, Savimbi's absolute will to power, is paramount. The other two—UNITA's access to foreign support and its control of Angola's diamond resources—merely served to fuel the instrumental purpose to which the party was put: namely, making Savimbi the undisputed ruler of Angola.

Above and beyond this undoubtedly critical personal factor,[57] there is little doubt that Savimbi's unbending determination to overthrow the Luanda regime stems, in part at least, from the fact that the MPLA was never endowed with full legitimacy at independence. By contrast, however much RENAMO sought to destroy Mozambique's infrastructure and eliminate FRELIMO cadres, it never serious entertained the belief that it could itself challenge FRELIMO's historical place in contemporary Mozambique.[58] Indeed, politically RENAMO always defined itself in relation to, as a mirror image of, FRELIMO. Its future acceptance as a legitimate political organisation depended entirely on its eventual recognition by the FRELIMO state. UNITA wanted to eliminate the MPLA; RENAMO wanted to be given its place in the political order established and dominated by FRELIMO.

It is for this reason that the two sets of peace negotiations had such radically different outcomes. UNITA only settled because Savimbi believed that the elections, which he was utterly convinced he would win, would be the most economical way of seizing power. Once it became clear that UNITA had lost the electoral contest, he resumed war. By contrast, RENAMO saw the elections as the best means of legitimising its place as opposition party and thus to gain access to the resources which political participation was likely to make available. Savimbi wanted total power; Dhlakama wanted a share of the spoils. This difference is likely to continue to affect the future of both countries.

[55]On UNITA and the war in Angola see W. James, *A Political History of the Civil War in Angola: 1974–1990* (New Brunswick NJ: Transaction Publishers, 1991) and Bridgland, *Jonas Savimbi*, op. cit.

[56]On RENAMO and the Mozambican war see Geffray, *La Cause des Armes au Mozambique*, op. cit. and Vines, Renamo op. cit.

[57]Some argue that Savimbi's death would put an end to UNITA's political and military ambitions and would make possible a swift transition to peace.

[58]See here an intriguing article on RENAMO's political discourse: Michel Cahen, ' "Entrons dans la nation". Notes pour une étude du discours politique de la marginalité—le cas de la RENAMO au Mozambique', *Politique Africaine*, 67 (Oct. 1997).

Although these contrasts in opposition leadership appear merely to be idiosyncratic, it can be argued that they have much to do with the weight of history. The division of Angola's nationalists into enemy political factions was not, as is so often argued, the inevitable outcome of the colony's ethnic 'divisions' but rather the result of the inability of its elites to form a broad anti-colonial coalition. Conversely, the unity of nationalist purpose in Mozambique was achieved against considerably larger odds than in Angola and it was maintained as the absolute priority throughout the war. Consequently, the two parties which took control at independence (the MPLA and FRELIMO), though superficially similar in ideology, were in fact endowed with distinct political attributes, of which nation-building legitimacy was cardinal.

It is to be feared that the weight of history will continue to blight Angola's future for years to come. Mozambique, though weakly integrated and economically destitute, can at least set about re-building a country on more solid foundations. Angola may well have to see its very political foundations destroyed before it can begin reconstruction.

THE TRANSITION TO MULTIPARTY POLITICS

The main question being asked today about black Africa is whether the transition to multiparty elections that has taken place will usher in political systems which are recognisably more democratic. As it turns out, the recent history of the five Portuguese-speaking African countries provides us with a most interesting range of experiences, the analysis of which may hold some insights into the more general question of the putative democratic transition in Africa.

This is so for two sets of reasons. The first has to do with what these five countries have in common. Most obviously, they share the Lusophone colonial heritage, a heritage quite distinct from that of the other two main colonial powers: Britain and France. Whether it is the long legacy of Afro-Portuguese contact, the creation of Creole societies or even the influence of a severely bureaucratic dictatorship since 1926, this patrimony cannot but have had a profound impact on these five societies and, hence, on their potential democratic future. Moreover, the PALOP have in common a history of militant anti-colonialism in which the parties which eventually took power at independence were all committed to socialism, even if there were some crucially important differences in their ideological position.

The second, and perhaps even more instructive, reason has to do with what makes Lusophone Africa so diverse. Indeed, if one were to try to find a cross-section of countries representative of the continent's socio-political complexities, one could hardly improve on the sample of the five furnished here—as has already been made clear.

This section reviews the modalities of the move to multiparty politics in the PALOP, focusing especially on the change that occurred as their governments abandoned the single-party system and adopted a new 'democratic' framework. The main concern is to explain the nature of these transitions in historical and comparative terms.[59]

Let us begin with Angola and Mozambique, where the shift to multiparty politics was intimately associated with the peace process. For a long time, the governments in Luanda and Maputo refused to negotiate with their enemies (respectively, UNITA and RENAMO). Eventually, as we have seen, exhausted and their countries largely destroyed, the Angolan and Mozambican governments settled with their opponents. Peace agreements were signed in May 1991 in Angola and October 1992 in Mozambique.

The elections were held in 1992 in Angola under United Nations' supervision. Somewhat surprisingly, they returned a majority for the government in power since independence. The ruling MPLA obtained 53.7 per cent of the votes while UNITA got 34.1 per cent. The presidential results pointed in the same direction. In the first round, the incumbent, José Eduardo dos Santos, polled 49.5 per cent and the UNITA leader, Jonas Savimbi, 40.07 per cent. A second round was due to be held since dos Santos was short of the 50 per cent mark. Savimbi, however, rejected the electoral verdict. War started again. Another peace accord (the Lusaka Protocol) was signed (although, significantly, not by the two leaders themselves) in November 1994. Again a ceasefire was agreed and its implementation supervised by a much strengthened UN presence. To this day, the Lusaka Protocol has not been implemented and the war is raging once again. New elections have still not been held.

The experience of the failures of the transition to peace in Angola helped the UN to support more strongly the consolidation of the ceasefire and the preparation of elections in Mozambique. These elections were held in October 1994 and, as in Angola but not as unexpectedly, they returned the same government and president to office. FRELIMO polled 44.3 per cent of the votes and got 129 seats (a majority) in the national assembly; RENAMO received 37.8 per cent and got 112 seats. In the presidential elections, the sitting president Joaquim Chissano was re-elected with 53.3 per cent of the votes as against his main RENAMO opponent, Afonso Dhlakama, who received 33.3 per cent. The 1999 elections confirmed the 1994 results although the opposition made gains. Chissano gained a

---

[59]A fuller account of the elections will be found in the five country chapters in this volume.

slimmer majority of 52.3 per cent against Dhlakama's 47.7 per cent. In the elections for the national assembly, RENAMO took six provinces with FRELIMO winning in five—Niassa shifted its support to the opposition. FRELIMO won 133 seats with 48.5 per cent of the vote while RENAMO won 118 seats with 38.8 per cent.

The political outlook for Mozambique, though precarious, is immensely more favourable than it is in Angola, if only because RENAMO has accepted the electoral verdict and committed itself to working as a 'loyal' opposition. Dhlakama has always denied rumours about a RENAMO coup or the possibility of renewed violence. Events since the elections confirmed that the peace had been consolidated, RENAMO made the move to legitimate political organisation and is now attempting to consolidate its not inconsiderable electoral success. It is, of course, much too early, to say what the democratic future of Mozambique actually is, or even whether there can be a 'democratic' future for the country. Nevertheless, even if the transition to multiparty politics had brought nothing other than permanent peace in Mozambique it would already have been a most significant achievement.

The history of the transition in Cape Verde and São Tomé e Príncipe is at once interesting and complex. In Cape Verde, the ruling PAICV was forced to confront openly the issue of political liberalisation. Domestic pressure and internal debate led to the momentous decision in September 1990 to introduce the constitutional amendment abolishing the one-party system and paving the way for multiparty politics. This decision was historic in that Cape Verde was one of a handful of African countries not to have had a structural adjustment programme and, therefore, not to have made the move to multiparty politics under strong outside political pressure or political conditionalities. Opposition parties were set up and were allowed to campaign for the legislative and presidential elections to be held early in 1991, the former preceding the latter. By then the sitting president, Aristides Pereira, had resigned as PAICV leader and had sought to assume a position 'above politics'.

The main opposition was organised around a coalition, the Movimento para a Democracia (MPD), led by a dynamic lawyer, Carlos Veiga. The campaign was vigorous and open. The MPD swept to victory on a wave of anti-PAICV sentiment, obtaining 56 of the 79 seats at stake; the PAICV was humbled with a mere 23 seats. The presidential elections which followed were even worse for the incumbent, Aristides Pereira, a widely respected figure at home and abroad, was defeated—74 per cent to 26 per cent—by his opponent, António Mascarenhas Monteiro. The verdict was clear: a large majority of the population had had enough of the single-party regime.

Since then, politics in Cape Verde has been energetic. The PAICV reorganised to face the challenges of working as an opposition and pressed for the MPD to introduce a true, as opposed to 'symbolic', parliamentary system in which the opposition could play its full and constructive role. For its part, the MPD found it difficult to make good its electoral promises on economic liberalisation and reducing unemployment, by far the single most important problem in the country. It was also racked by internal dissension and a number of its prominent members left to form another opposition party.[60]

Moves for greater decentralisation, certainly a key requirement of democratisation in Africa, have been very slow. However, local elections did take place and all parties were able freely to prepare for the subsequent legislative and presidential elections. The 1995 legislative elections returned the MPD to power with an absolute majority of 50 out of 72 seats.[61] Although the PAICV complained that the MPD had abused its dominance over the mass media and communications to gain unfair advantage in the campaign, it accepted the electoral verdict. The presidential elections that followed also led to the re-election of the incumbent. The most recent elections, held in late 2000 and early 2001 finally ended the MPD's reign and brought the PAICV, and its leader, back to power. Multiparty politics in Cape Verde had thus come full circle and these changes are a token of the fact that the country has now entered a phase of greater democracy.

By the standards of the rest of Africa, then, Cape Verde's transition to multiparty politics was an unqualified success, Although the opposition PAICV was scathing in its attacks on government inefficiency and corruption, itself a sign of the existing freedom of expression, the picture is more complex. True, the MPD behaved rather petulantly against the opposition and was not slow in taking advantage of its hold on power. Nevertheless, there were genuine reforms towards greater openness and accountability and efforts were made to implement the aims of economic liberalisation which had been promised. As a result, there are signs that foreign investors are now looking more seriously at Cape Verde as a country with a cheap but well-qualified labour force and an attractive climate of political peace and social cohesion.

São Tomé e Príncipe's story of political reform is equally startling. After independence, the dominant MLSTP, as we have seen, moved to establish

---

[60]Of course, it is well to remember that, from the beginning, the MPD was a broad coalition of very diverse political forces.

[61]The MPD obtained 61.3 per cent of the votes, the PAICV 29.8 per cent and the second opposition party, the Partido da Convergência Democrática (PCD), 6.7 per cent.

in the country a socialist one-party system. Faced by a calamitous economic situation, due in part to the departure of the Portuguese and in part to the collapse of the cocoa and coffee plantation economy, the government was eventually forced to turn to the World Bank for succour. By then both Angola and Mozambique had also initiated plans for economic reforms. Under strong pressure to democratise, the MLSTP introduced in September 1990 a new constitution providing for a multiparty political system. Opposition parties soon formed and legislative elections were held early in 1991.

The results, as in Cape Verde, were emphatic. The sitting MLSTP was swept away by its main opposition rival, the Partido de Convergência Democrática/Grupo de Reflexão (PCD/GR). The MLSTP obtained 30.5 per cent of the votes and 21 out of 55 seats while its competitor received 54 per cent and took 33 seats. Having felt the winds of change and fully aware of the humiliation of President Aristides Pereira in Cape Verde, the incumbent, President Manuel Pinto da Costa, withdrew from the presidential contest, allowing his long-time opponent, Miguel Trovoada to be elected unopposed—with 81 per cent of the vote—but abstention was at a very high 40 per cent.

The situation in São Tomé e Príncipe, however, was quite different from that of Cape Verde. The country was in a ruinous economic state and was firmly in the grip of structural adjustment. The new government did not have either well-defined policies or the administrative capacity to institute fundamental reforms. Although there were a number of moves to follow World Bank recommendations and liberalise the economy, few outside investors were interested in taking over long-neglected and poorly-productive plantations. Progress was slow to non-existent. Disillusion with the new regime grew rapidly into active discontent. The 1992 local elections gave the government early warnings as, overall, it lost out to its opponent, the MLSTP.

Given the poor record of the government and the growing sense of dissatisfaction throughout the country, President Trovoada eventually resolved to dissolve the national assembly and to call for fresh legislative elections. Held in October 1994, the elections registered an unambiguous vote of no-confidence in the PCD/GR government and returned the MLSTP to power with a majority of seats.[62] Thus, São Tomé e Príncipe became the first African country to bring back a formerly non-democratic ruling party to power by democratic means—much as several East European

---

[62]The MLSTP obtained 27 seats out of a total of 55; the third opposition party, the Acção Democrática Independente got 14 seats while the PDC/GR came last with 13 seats.

countries have now witnessed the return of former communist parties to government through democratic elections. Since then, elections have been held at regular intervals according to the established procedures. Results have been accepted by winners and losers alike and there now exist a system in which multiparty politics is an accepted way of life on the islands.[63]

Although such a course of event may appear to bode well for the health of democracy in São Tomé, it is important to point out the very specific conditions which have made such an outcome possible. As Gerhard Seibert shows clearly in the country chapter below, multiparty politics and changes in government have not resolved the country's deep problems. Successive administrations since 1990 have followed very similar policies with fairly similar, and relatively unimpressive, results. The country suffers from deep structural economic problems not amenable to simple solutions.

Political competition is in principle to be applauded but in the absence of concrete improvements in the quality of life of ordinary men and women there is always a danger that multiparty politics itself will become discredited. The 1995 attempted coup in São Tomé may have been prompted primarily by grievances within the armed forces but it may also have reflected more ominous moves among the military to do away with 'inefficient and corrupt' politicians who have achieved very little.[64] At the very least, it could be seen as a danger signal. Although it appears today that the military is no longer in a position to meddle in politics, this is due to the fact that it has been co-opted by politicians rather than to its greater professionalisation.

Guinea-Bissau's transition to multiparty politics is instructive in ways different from those of the four other Lusophone countries. It follows a pattern found in several other African countries like, for example, Côte d'Ivoire, Cameroon or Kenya. Guinea-Bissau had been under structural adjustment since 1987 and, consequently, had experienced strong outside pressure to open up the political system and to organise multiparty elections. Although the constitution was changed in 1991, abolishing the single-party system, the moves towards genuine multiparty competition were exceedingly unhurried. Legislation to remove the impediments to multipartyism was passed at leisure and many obstacles were put in the way of the legalisation of parties by the supreme court. Whether this contributed to the mushrooming of political parties and to their inability to coordinate their action is not

---

[63]For details of later elections see the country chapter below.

[64]During the coup the conspirators detained the prime minister, attempted in vain to find a suitable civilian replacement and, having failed, eventually had to restore the incumbent to power with apologies.

entirely clear. What can be said with more certainty, however, is that while the many opposition parties quibbled, the ruling PAIGC got on with the job of campaigning.

At the same time, there were continuous disagreements between government and opposition as regards the timetable for the presidential and legislative elections as well as the constitution of the electoral commission. Although the obstacles were slowly overcome, the elections were delayed repeatedly and only took place in 1994. Voter registration and the actual organisation of the polls left much to be desired but, to the surprise of many inside and outside the country, the elections were relatively efficiently dispatched and took place without violence. Despite strong protest by the opposition about irregularities, the international observer corps declared the polls free and fair. In time, the opposition accepted the results.

The legislative elections saw the not entirely unexpected (given opposition divisions and ineffectual campaigning) return of the PAIGC to power with 46 per cent of the vote and 64 of the 100 seats in the Assembly.[65] The presidential contest was much closer. Although President Vieira had formally disassociated himself from the ruling PAIGC to stand as a 'national' candidate, his main opponent, Koumba Yalla, ran a particularly vigorous, effective and forthright campaign against the president's record. The result was that, much to his surprise, Vieira failed to secure the 50 per cent vote required to be elected on the first round.[66] A second round was held amid allegations of intimidation by Yalla. Vieira in the end won a narrow 52 per cent victory which Yalla, despite early protests of vote rigging, was persuaded in the end to accept—as observers rejected claims of malpractice. Nevertheless, there is little doubt that President Vieira's position had been seriously weakened.

The main question following the elections was about the complexion of the new government and whether it would include opposition members. In the event, and after much protracted debate within the PAIGC and with the opposition, the government remained decidedly single party. Although a large number of ministers lost their jobs and were replaced by a relatively younger PAIGC personnel, power continued to rest with the party that had been in office since 1974. Equally, President Vieira remained firmly in command of the government—the prime minister, Manuel Saturnino da Costa, was his choice—and the cabinet changes reflected his view of what was best for the PAIGC in the aftermath of the polls.

[65]The main opposition, Resistência da Guiné Bissau/Movimento Bafatá (RGB/MB), led by Domingos Gomes won 17 seats while the Partido para a Renovação Social (PRS), led by Koumba Yalla, got 12 seats. Two other parties shared the balance of seven seats.

[66]Vieira got 46.17 per cent of the votes cast and Koumba Yalla 21.89 per cent.

The elections that took place after the end of the recent civil conflict have finally seen the end of the PAIGC domination.[67] However, because the circumstances under which they were held were so special, it is difficult to assess the extent to which, without the civil war, dissatisfaction with the ruling party would have been translated into a regime change under purely electoral competition. Equally, it will be interesting to see whether discontent with the new government will in time induce the electorate to return the PAIGC into office. For now, the country is faced with the difficult task of reconstruction under conditions where foreign aid is much less plentiful.

What conclusions can one draw from the experience of the political transitions in the five Lusophone countries? And how useful are these conclusions for the comparative analysis of 'democratic' transition in the rest of black Africa? Artificial as the exercise may appear to be, the analysis of the recent political history of the five Lusophone countries is in fact quite instructive. There are three separate sets of issues here: (1) the apparent success of the political changes in Cape Verde and São Tomé e Príncipe; (2) the significance of the Guinea-Bissau case and (3) the lessons to be learnt from the contrasting outcome of the elections in Angola and Mozambique.

The relative ease and smoothness of the transition in the two island mini-states would seem to confirm the hypothesis that multiparty politics comes more easily to such countries. Why should that be? In the case of Cape Verde and São Tomé e Príncipe, the following factors were certainly important in facilitating the transition. First, as has already been indicated, these are two fairly homogeneous societies with a common language, common history and common culture. There are, of course, significant social cleavages, but those do not coincide with separate ethnic identities *per se*.[68] Political differences, differences of opinion and ideology, are not associated with any well-defined social, ethnic, religious or regional grouping. The expression of political disagreement does not automatically assume socially divisive forms.

Secondly, and equally importantly, the formation of political parties is largely a reflection of political opposition, political ambition, or even programmatic differences. Parties may be seen as the instrument of prominent politicians but they are not primarily the vehicle for the promotion

[67]Details are to be found in the country chapter in this volume.
[68]With the possible exception of the *angolares* in São Tomé who, because they were isolated from the rest of the islanders until the twentieth century, do still consider themselves a 'separate' social (though not ethnic) group. But these divisions have begun melting away in the post-independence period.

of distinct social, ethnic, religious, regional or racial interests. The population at large considers the different parties more or less from the individual(ist) instrumental perspective which is the hallmark of democratic politics: that is, what will this party do for me? In both countries, people were simply tired of the arrogance which the prolonged exercise of power induced in the politicians who had been in power since independence. In São Tomé e Príncipe, they offered the opposition a chance but, in the absence of tangible results, resolved to sanction the government and give the former ruling party the opportunity to learn the lessons of multiparty politics. Since then, the elections have been used as instruments of patrimonial politics.

Thirdly, in Cape Verde at least, there is a tradition of administrative efficiency and of relative political probity which makes it rather more difficult for politicians widely to abuse power and state resources for purposes of patronage. Cape Verde, for example, is one of the rare African countries consistently to be praised for its proper management of foreign aid. São Tomé e Príncipe is not in the same league in this respect but there are strong social bonds and pressures which make it difficult for politicians to plunder the state for their own ends. It is simply too small a country, where information circulates too easily, for such action to be either concealed or ignored. For this reason, regime changes are seen as a way of 'distributing' opportunities more fairly. In São Tomé e Príncipe, it is not uncommon for members of the same family to support opposite parties, thus putting an immediate check on the misdeeds of family members. Of course, this is not to say that family interests might not easily override political affiliation, even less that there are no patron-client networks. It is simply to say that clientelistic politics is, as it were, out in the open.

Finally, there has not been in either country a slide from authoritarianism to violent repression. In Cape Verde, despite rumours of a 'leftist' coup in the late seventies, the ruling party did not as a rule jail political dissidents. Nor did it harass its opponents in the ways most commonly found in the rest of Africa. In São Tomé e Príncipe, the 1978 and 1980 alleged coup attempts led to political trials of dubious legality but although the judgements handed down were quite severe (especially given how flimsy the evidence was), those sentenced were able to leave the country after some time. Political repression did not degenerate into violence, even if power was firmly abused. Eventually, the MLSTP was forced to recognise the failure of its authoritarianism. Furthermore, those who had been hounded earlier and thrown out of the party (chief of whom was Miguel Trovoada) did not seek revenge when they returned to power. There was no witch-hunt.

The case of Guinea-Bissau is much more typical of what has been happening in black Africa for the last ten years. Although there was in the country much dissatisfaction against the regime, there was no organised and systematic pressure for changes to a multiparty system. The only seriously active opposition party, the RGB/MB, was (perhaps inevitably) based abroad in Lisbon and commanded only limited support in the country. There were, of course, divisions within the ruling PAIGC but President Vieira had managed over the years to use those to his advantage and to maintain a firm grip on power. Much as the opponents to the PAIGC regime called for democracy, there seemed no immediate prospect that their demand would be considered, let alone met.

It was outside pressure which forced Vieira to accept the transition to multiparty politics. Indeed, it was only when the World Bank refused to continue structural adjustment payments, for reasons ostensibly having to do with Bissau's inability to carry out the SAP, that the regime initiated the reforms necessary for political transition. Vieira, in other words, only acted when he had no other choice. By the time the constitution was amended in May 1991, the president had had the opportunity to study at close quarters the outcome of the elections in Cape Verde and São Tomé e Príncipe, two countries with which Bissau had close links. No doubt, he drew the appropriate lessons from the rout of the ruling parties (especially the sister PAICV) and the humiliating defeat of the sitting presidents (especially his 'elder' and mentor, Aristides Pereira).

Over the next three years, the Bissau government moved with great care, and a distinct lack of urgency, through the steps required to make possible multiparty politics. At every step of the way, the regime had to be pushed by the opposition to concede the minimum constitutional, legal, institutional and political space needed for the transition to be more than an empty shell. Applications for the registration of parties were often delayed for the most trivial of reasons. The excesses of the secret police were curbed only slightly and the opposition failed in its attempt to do away with it entirely. Opposition politicians were harassed in subtle and not so subtle ways. Obstacles were constantly placed in the way of their campaigning—permission for which was only conceded gradually and grudgingly. Finally, only concerted demands from the opposition parties and outside pressure secured the government's agreement over the composition of a relatively neutral and generally acceptable electoral commission, without which the elections could not take place.

Furthermore, throughout this period President Vieira kept the initiative. He controlled the pace of the transition and refused to discuss with the opposition a mutually-agreeable timetable. Until the date of the elections was announced, very late in the day, the opposition parties could not be sure how to pace their campaign. Finally, President Vieira was able to use his newly-acquired status as a presidential candidate standing above the fray to reject demands for detailed discussions with the opposition on the holding of both the legislative and presidential elections. All in all, he played his cards superbly well, not surprisingly given that he was a consummate politician of over twenty years standing.

His task was made infinitely easier by the defects of the opposition, most of whom had no political experience. Except for the RGB/MB,[69] the opposition parties were little more than vehicles for the ambition of individual politicians. With little to separate them in terms of ideas, policies and programmes, and a dearth of organisation to sustain a campaign other than in the main cities, these parties found it difficult to stake the specific ground on which they were going to contest the elections. Since ethnic and regionalist parties had been explicitly prohibited by law, none of the opposition parties could campaign openly on separatist issues, even if some of them obviously had identifiable regional support. As in many other African countries, then, there was a mushrooming of political parties with no particular constituency and little to distinguish them.

As in other African countries too, the opposition was singularly inept in its campaigning strategy. Unable to form stable coalitions, to focus on a few significant campaigning issues and to pool their resources, they dissipated their efforts in urban rallies and slanging matches. Short of funds and of the required means of transport, largely bereft of campaigning skills, they failed to address the concerns of the bulk of the population in the countryside. The realisation that they must collaborate more closely in order to vanquish the PAIGC came too late in the day to undo the damage created by the image of opposition parties seemingly more concerned with undermining their competitors than attacking the ruling party.

In Africa the party in power has immense advantages against the opposition when it comes to multiparty elections, if only because it controls the state and all its resources, including coercion. It is up to the opposition to find ways of undermining the legitimacy of the regime. In Guinea-Bissau, the ruling PAIGC was agile in its use of state resources and clever in its political campaign. While the opposition bickered frustratingly in the cities, the PAIGC was out in force in the majority rural areas, making its peace with the formerly politically incorrect local chiefs (or *régulos*) and negotiating support against future benefits. There was too a sprinkling of fear sown by the ubiquitous security police who made plain their hounding of the opposition. In such conditions, it does not seem far-fetched to suggest

[69] And to some extent the Frente da Luta pela Independência Nacional da Guiné (FLING), a party going back to the fifties but which, after independence, had dwindled in importance.

that it was an eminently rational decision for many rural dwellers to vote for the devil they knew, much as they might have resented his excesses.

What is interesting about the case of Guinea-Bissau is how closely it mirrors the experience of other comparable African countries. Where there is little organised opposition inside the country; where opposition parties emerge only after the transition has been announced and then largely as the instruments of ambitious politicians seeking power; where the opposition fails to unite and coordinate its platform and campaign; where it is unable properly to articulate the grievances and demands of the majority rural population; where the ruling party manages to retain control over all aspects of the transition including the timetable; where it takes the trouble to run a serious campaign (as opposed simply to bully the voters); where such are the conditions it is highly probable that the ruling party will emerge the victor. Kenya or Cameroon are good cases in point but it is a pattern that has been found repeatedly across the continent since the early nineties.

What conclusions, finally, can one draw about Angola and Mozambique? Their evolution is interesting because it allows comparison between two countries having suffered prolonged civil war and where, when the transition occurred, the ruling parties faced their former enemy as the main opposition party. Interesting too because, despite the assumptions of many, the governments in place won the elections. Of course, what is important in Angola and Mozambique is that the elections were not merely the result of outside pressure to move to multiparty politics but the outcome of long and complex negotiations to bring civil wars to an end.

The previous section explained how important the weight of history was in accounting for why the process failed in Angola and succeeded in Mozambique. UNITA and RENAMO have been politically different. The former, whatever it may be as a political and military organisation, is above all Savimbi's instrument to gain power in Angola. For thirty years he has pursued the same goal relentlessly and will now not likely be deflected from it. Savimbi is no democrat and he agreed to the elections only because he was absolutely certain that he would emerge the victor. In other words, he was only willing to play the game of multiparty elections because at the time it seemed the most economical way of gaining power. And, indeed, even neutral observers were confident that UNITA would win, such was the magnitude of discontent at the failures and abuses of the MPLA government. It can, therefore, be argued, and argued plausibly, that in Angola Savimbi managed to snatch defeat from the jaws of victory. His campaign was not only poor but he managed to frighten away many who might otherwise have voted for UNITA. The MPLA, on the other hand, conducted a clever and sleek professional campaign, making full use of foreign consultants.

RENAMO, for its part, was originally the handmaiden of the Rhodesian and South African destabilisation engineers. It evolved primarily as a military organisation bent on wrecking FRELIMO's hold on Mozambique. Over the years it developed a most minimal administration in the areas which it controlled. It was only when South African foreign and domestic policy changed, however, and very largely under pressure from Pretoria, that RENAMO made the transition to a formal political organisation and prepared to negotiate with the FRELIMO government. FRELIMO was above all concerned to end the civil war. It never considered RENAMO a particularly dangerous political opponent once the conflict was over. Under pressure, the FRELIMO regime conceded the principle of multiparty elections and prepared itself accordingly. Like the MPLA in this respect it entered the electoral battle determined to run a professional and effective campaign.

During the period leading to the elections, RENAMO revealed itself as a serious political machine, prepared to fight tooth and nail to gain respectability and the financial means for its campaign. Dhlakama is no Savimbi. A shrewd political operator, he knew that RENAMO would not beat FRELIMO and, more importantly, he knew that he would not defeat Joaquim Chissano in the presidential contest. He saw the elections as a means of negotiating the best possible 'deal' for himself and his party. This made him a realist, an ideal candidate for the rough and tumble of electoral politics and a clever negotiator of political and financial benefits. And in this he may be said to have succeeded quite well, for few believed after the peace accord was signed that Dhlakama would carve out for himself and his party such a comfortable niche. Nor had many anticipated that RENAMO would attain the level of electoral support which in the end they did achieve in the 1994 and 1999 elections.

Paradoxically, then, given that RENAMO started life purely as a terrorist organisation, the transformation of the party into a political machine augurs rather well for the survival of peace and multiparty politics in Mozambique. Of course, all depends on FRELIMO's attitude in the years to come. If the old practices of single-party rule make it unprofitable for RENAMO to continue to be a 'mere' opposition party, then disorder could resume. Although it is fair to say that the longer peace lasts, the less likely it is that RENAMO will resort to violence (especially without outside support). The situation in Mozambique is now similar to that of many other African countries where multiparty elections have taken place and where the ruling party has managed to stay in place. The future of all these countries depends on the ways in which the move to multiparty politics brings about meaningful political change and, especially, on what role the opposition can fulfil.

As for Angola, the situation remains tragically unresolved. So long as the peace accord does not result in the disarming of UNITA, the demobilisation of the bulk of the MPLA forces and the integration of the former enemies into common structures, war will continue. Here too there is a paradox: the elections have given the MPLA renewed (electoral) legitimacy at a time when many believed that they would be swept from power. In turn, this electoral legitimacy has given the regime a fresh mandate for continuing the war. This makes for a very unstable situation. Although elections have taken place in Angola, there has not been in the country the process of compromise and reconciliation which alone can make the electoral process meaningful. Peace and democracy are a long way off.

To return now to the question raised at the outset, what is the prospect for democracy on the continent? Much as it is to be desired that the transition to multiparty politics leads to greater democratisation, an analysis of the experience of the five Lusophone countries should induce caution. Throughout this section the focus has been on multiparty politics rather than democracy precisely because they are not synonymous. Nor is it clear that the conditions in black Africa—as against those in Cape Verde, for example—are such as to make multiparty democracy in its European or American variant a tenable prospect. This should not be surprising to us unless we choose to forget the very obvious historical fact that nowhere in the world has democracy emerged and survived without a sufficiently strong and productive economic basis to sustain such a political system.

Nevertheless, it could still be argued that a transition to multiparty politics, whether it ushers in democracy or not, is in itself positive. As concerns Lusophone Africa, it can readily be seen that such a move was clearly more beneficial in some countries than in others; and that even in those countries where it was successful, such benefits as have accrued could easily be reversed. Where the move to multiparty politics can help to bring peace, to open up the political system, to allow free expression, free competition of ideas, criticisms of the regime, and above all force greater political accountability on the government in place, then such transition is to be applauded—regardless of whether the regime is voted out or not.

However, there are cases in Africa where elections other than in strictly controlled terms (by which is meant, for example, the exclusion of ethnic or regionalist parties), might be deleterious. Indeed, there are instances where it could be argued that multiparty politics have made the situation worse, as in Kenya or Cameroon, not because of the theoretically admirable principles of political democracy but because of the dirty and messy business which such competition can induce in practice. Nor, and it has to be said, is a multiparty political system one in which the ordinary citizens of a country are necessarily better off than they would be otherwise, as is amply illustrated by the case of Nigeria during the last civilian regime.

In the end, therefore, the danger is that an excessive focus on the so-called transition to democracy, or even on multiparty politics, will be at the expense of the analysis of what is really happening in Africa today. It may be preferable to focus on political accountability, a much broader concept which makes it possible to try to assess the extent to which power is legitimate in different political settings.[70]

[70]As I do in Chabal, *Power in Africa*, op. cit.

Part II
COUNTRY STUDIES

4

ANGOLA

David Birmingham

LIBERATION IN THE SEVENTIES

The night of 10 November 1975 was an eventful one in the city of Luanda. The guns of Mobutu's Zaire army, helped by the cadres of the Frente Nacional para a Libertação de Angola (FNLA), pounded the northern suburbs of the capital as the citizens of Angola prepared to celebrate an uncertain 'freedom'. A hundred miles to the south Cuban guns, partly staffed by the militants of the Movimento Popular de Libertação de Angola (MPLA), held at bay two *Blitzkrieg* columns of a South African expeditionary force. A third political party, the União para a Independência Total de Angola (UNITA), struggled to seek allies, white and black, domestic and foreign, which might give its soldiers and politicians the edge over their rivals. Meanwhile, off-shore, Portugal's last proconsul in Africa embarked on a gunboat under cover of darkness. At midnight he sailed away declaring that 'sovereignty' had been transferred to 'all of the peoples of Angola'. The heirs to the colonial legacy included not only black members of the three political movements but also a significant number of white immigrants who had helped to build an Angola of private finance and colonial service.

The battle for Luanda is documented by several different sources that dovetail in an unusually satisfying manner.[1] Marina Rey Cabrera edited accounts of the Cuban participation in the Angolan wars, complete with battle plans and diagrams, written by senior officers in the Cuban expeditionary army. John Stockwell published a first-hand history of the American involvement in the war, giving details of the type and quantity of weapons that he supplied to the Central Intelligence Agency's prospective client armies. Ryszard Kapuscinski wrote a vivid description of the battle fronts, and more especially of their wider human context, for his Polish news agency as he hitchhiked his way around the country by road and by

---

[1]Details about these sources will be found in the bibliography.

air in the last days before independence. Franz-Wilhelm Heimer analysed
the significance of the events in detail. And Christine Messiant wrote a
two-volume PhD thesis on the sociological history of the competing leaders
of Angola's militarised society. But the contest for Luanda, fought on
Angola's independence day, was only one of many battles to take place
during the wars of liberation. To understand their significance it is necessary
to step back, perhaps as far as that day in 1969 when António Salazar,
Europe's most durable dictator, finally died after having ruled Portugal
and its colonies with an iron fist for no fewer than forty years.

When Salazar was struck down by a cerebral stroke, and power was
transferred to Marcello Caetano, a former minister of colonial affairs, the
Angolan colonial war of the 1960s had reached stalemate. For some it
was a rather prosperous state of affairs and the country now contained
about 300,000 Portuguese expatriates whose standard of living was in
many cases higher than that of their brethren in Portugal. These migrants
and settlers also enjoyed a lifestyle which was less restricted than that
practised in the archaic social environment of their European homeland
and more akin to that of the Portuguese communities in the Americas.
The Portuguese in Angola associated with an increasingly large number
of urbanised black Angolans who, though poor by the standards of their
white neighbours, nevertheless enjoyed a comparative prosperity when
contrasted to that of their kith and kin in the colonial countryside. Prosperity
was based in part on a policy of industrialisation. In the city and the
provincial towns manufacturers employed some 200,000 people, black
and white, to produce import substitution goods for their own needs and
even to supply the market demands of their neighbours, especially those
in the crumbling Congo republic of Zaire. Foreign investment in Angola
had traditionally been concentrated on the transcontinental Benguela railway
in the south, on the De Beers monitored diamond mines in the north, and
on a few old plantations (some of them Belgian-owned) in the centre.

Once the colonial war had begun, and tax revenue was needed to equip
a large expeditionary army from Europe, controls on foreign investment
were relaxed. After 1963 Portugal allowed the entry into Angola's cities
of European and American management methods and industrial patents.
More strikingly still, American oil companies decided that Angola was
sufficiently stable (or at least controllable) to permit them to start pumping
petroleum from the oilfields which they had discovered off-shore. Salazar
was alleged to have complained, with some justification, that the oil industry
would bring an end to the closed empire of docile black peasants which
his nationalistic, almost fascist, fervour had cherished. In fact, however,
the violent end to empire had its seeds in the failures of old colonial

agriculture, rather than in the successes of modern industry. The anti-colonial war was triggered off by the very peasants whom Salazar had idealised for their malleability and whose powerlessness he had been able to exploit.

The brutality of colonial-style agricultural exploitation was felt in three different ways and in three different zones in Angola. In the south, on the plateau that was later to become the primary zone of conflict when the Russian-American 'Cold War' began to be fought out by proxy in the 1980s, the grievances of local black farmers were based on trade, transport and credit. Black producers primarily grew maize, leaving more lucrative crops such as sunflowers to white farmers who received preferential treatment from the colonial administration. Maize was not a crop that yielded a great margin of profit and what profit accrued went not to the black grower but to the white bush trader who supplied the farmer with his seed. Petty immigrant traders also supplied the credit with which farmers could buy domestic necessities. At the end of the season the shopkeeper bought the maize crop at punitively diminished prices and then took a generous helping of interest on the credit loans he had made. Black growers had no vehicles in which to carry their crops direct to the railhead or to the town and had no alternative income with which to pay off usurious debts to white crop speculators. When farmers could not pay a debt they were required to deliver a family member to their creditor as a 'contract worker', whom the truckers could then carry off to work in colonial zones where labour was scarce. Such hostages must have felt rather like the indentured workers whom the Portuguese, in a form of neo-slavery, had shipped in large numbers in the early years of the twentieth century to the cocoa plantations of the islands of São Tomé e Príncipe. One of the highland kingdoms, Bailundu, was a particularly oppressed zone of labour extraction throughout the twentieth century. Until 1900 it had been the most prosperous and proud of Angola's merchant kingdoms, a fierce rival to a dozen neighbouring highland states of the Ovimbundu people, but in 1902 Bailundu had been devastated in a ferocious war of colonial conquest. Free men now became migrant workers and the vernacular label adopted for a contract worker by the Portuguese was a 'Bailundu', a name commonly used for any migrant from the highland kingdoms. It was perhaps not entirely surprising that one of the redoubts held by Jonas Savimbi and his UNITA guerrillas during the civil wars of the 1990s was the historic town of Bailundu, with its long tradition of resistance to the armed politicians of Luanda city.

If maize was the symbol of oppression in the southern highlands, cotton was the source of misery, poverty and despair in the central lowlands of Angola. The profit margins on cotton were even lower than those on maize and instead of growing it for a meagre cash incentive, or for a supply of goods on credit, peasants produced cotton by compulsory administrative order. In 1945 lowland district officers had complained to the Portuguese government that their Mbundu peasant subjects were starving because they could not grow food crops for their children when all their labour time and their field systems were being devoted to colonial cotton. These presumptuous protesting officials were put in their place by the Lisbon dictatorship and Salazar himself, supported by Caetano, thundered that 'idle' black subjects must be taught the discipline of hard work. No reform of the cotton regime was attempted again and in 1961 the starvation became so acute that rebellion broke out. The warehouses in which cotton seed was waiting to be distributed to the helpless farmers were burnt down and Salazar had to rush in the army, and even his embryonic air force, to bomb the region back into submission. The Mbundu victims, like most peasants, would probably have settled for a quiet life had they been given minimally adequate conditions in which to grow their subsistence food and to sell their cotton crop for cash but instead they were traumatised into a more radical stance. Some of them became militant MPLA guerrillas whom Agostinho Neto mobilised to save Luanda from capture by Zaire or South Africa on the night of 10 November 1975.

The third agricultural zone to become involved in the politics of decolonisation was the north, where real wealth was at stake. The lion's share of Angola's export revenue before independence came from coffee and the annual crop of 200,000 tonnes was the fourth largest in the world. But coffee, like cotton and maize, created deep political scars in the body politic of the colony, which affected the wars of liberation in the 1970s, the wars of intervention in the 1980s, and even the civil wars in the 1990s. The profitability of coffee in the last twenty colonial years brought an influx of white immigrants to the north where they gradually rose from being petty traders and truckers to being prosperous planters on land that they had expropriated from the old local farming community. Upstanding black landowners, many of them elders of the Baptist church, were reduced to the status of day labourers, working alongside 'Bailundu' conscripts on fields which had previously been their own estates. The frustrations were naturally deep and, when the colonial tinder caught fire in 1961, the Bakongo of the north killed not only a thousand whites who had seized their land but also many black migrant workers who had been trucked in from the southern highlands as coffee pickers compelled to work for the settler-planters. The virulence of rivalry between different colonial peoples with different experiences of exploitation was profoundly rational and economic and had no roots in ethnic history since neither the highland kingdoms of the Ovimbundu nor the northern principalities of the coffee-growing Bakongo had experienced any interaction with one another except through the colonial nexus. The bitterness ran so deep that although the diverse peoples of the north, and the many peoples of the south, both became deeply hostile to the Mbundu of central Angola and to their powerful cousins in the city of Luanda, north and south were never able to collaborate effectively in a grand political strategy. Zaire and South Africa would both dearly have liked the Ovimbundu and the Bakongo to work not only with their own invading forces but also with each other as they desperately endeavoured to deny the MPLA and its Mbundu foot soldiers the legitimacy of holding the city throughout the night of 10 November 1975.

The path which had led from the military stalemate of 1969 to the battle for Luanda in 1975 was a tortuous one, in which the political initiative passed from the farmers in the fields to the citizens in the towns. The war for the liberation in Angola was fought not only between the coloniser and the colonised but also between three different factions of urban subject peoples, each with its own range of supporters, weapons and ideological visions. Until 1974, or even into 1975, the Portuguese government, the Portuguese army and the Portuguese settlers were able to hold the ring. In the north the administration changed its original tactics and instead of repression adopted a policy of conciliation towards the black elite and allowed them a limited return to independent coffee growing with marketing and transport in the hands of protected cooperatives managed by local members of the Baptist church. Although even limited new initiatives such as this were resented by white profiteers, they were seen by the Portuguese military establishment as creating reliable allies, wedded to market principles and therefore unlikely to be seduced by any violent nationalistic aspirations advocated by Marxist or Maoist politicians in exile.

In contrast to this northern experiment in winning hearts and minds, the last years of colonialism in the south were quite different. The growth of Afrikaner-style white farming and ranching by Portuguese settlers was protected in the highlands by a policy of repression. Prison-style villages of the type that had been used by a settler regime in Rhodesia, and borrowed from American military practice in Vietnam, were built in the highlands and peasants were herded in at night so that they could not provide food supplies and intelligence to any guerrilla nationalists who might try to travel through the countryside by night. The resulting fragmentation and isolation of Ovimbundu farming communities meant that the mobilisation of anti-colonial opinion in the south was effectively postponed until the fall of the Portuguese dictatorship in April 1974. In the meantime, while the north was seduced, and the south was repressed, the colonial towns remained relatively quiet. Those who had escaped from the countryside to gain a foothold on the colonial ladder of education and opportunity did little to endanger their economic good fortune or their promotion prospects. It was therefore among Angola's exiles, rather than among the urban intelligentsia or proletariat, that the politics of the future were debated. And it was not in Angola that the Portuguese lost their colonial war, but in Guinea and Mozambique.

When the dictatorship collapsed in Lisbon on 25 April 1974 the Angolan exiles were in disarray. Not only was there no unity between the leaders of the northern, southern and central traditions of protest, there was also no unity within each of those traditions. In the north many, if not most, exiles had put their efforts into becoming economically integrated into their country of exile, Zaire, the former Belgian Congo. In many ways this was not difficult. The city of Léopoldville, restored to the old name Kinshasa, had been the urban metropolis which had attracted ambitious young Angolans ever since the beginning of the colonial century. Latter-day refugees, even the tens of thousands who flooded across the border after the coffee-estate massacres of 1961, were able to find succour among people from their own family, their own clan, their own village, their own tradition. People on both sides of the border spoke mutually intelligible dialects of Kikongo and some had an historic loyalty to the ancient kingdom of Kongo, although a century of Portuguese military interference, and of claims to autonomy by the provincial nobility, had seriously weakened royal legitimacy.

As the Baptist mission had been active on both sides of the border ever since the 1870s many exiles were able to find a spiritual home in the chapels of western Zaire. They also obtained education in the mission schools and medical treatment in the mission hospitals. In this world of modernising initiatives and of economic survival the Angolans could not, as foreigners, gain access to the lucrative opportunities of state employment but they profited from their contacts and helped Zairean politicians to run their private business operations. A few of the exiles tried to establish political organisations that would, in the fullness of time, make a bid for political power and a return to Angola. One party, which after several changes of name, identity and ideology became the FNLA, received recognition and support from China, from the Organisation of African Unity (OAU), from the United States, from South Africa and above all from its hosts in Zaire.

In the south political mobilisation was even more difficult than among the northern exiles in Zaire. The ethnic fragmentation of the highland kingdoms, the rival traditions of mission education, the isolation of workers on white farms where they had no access to fellow Angolans with similar grievances, the herding of peasants into security villages by the colonial army, the sparsity of population on the great open plateaux, all of these militated against any kind of political cohesion. As in the rest of Africa middle-class student exiles were to become some of the most prominent of Angola's political leaders but the south had far fewer intellectuals than other regions and virtually no urban tradition of cultural sophistication, literary learning and cosmopolitan travel.

A few southern exiles attempted to join the northern FNLA bandwagon in Kinshasa, but they soon felt despised and instead of their haughty Ovimbundu pedigrees being recognised they were marginalised like country bumpkins. By 1964 the southerners had virtually broken their ties with the elitist Bakongo and within two years had created a liberation movement of their own: UNITA. They eventually gained an exile base in the newly-independent Zambia. Their leader, an ambitious young man of boundless confidence, used every possible network to create a united southern political movement. His association with the Congregationalist churches that had been installed on the plateau by Swiss and American missionaries enabled him to use old-boy networks from the Protestant schools to mobilise support. He also had good contacts with the Benguela railway on which his father had been employed and a group of people linked to each other through service on the railway was able to use the telegraph to maintain subversive communication. Last but not least, Jonas Savimbi was one of the few Ovimbundu who did know his way around the diplomatic circuit—he had been a student in Portugal as well as in Switzerland, though his attempt to study medicine had proved abortive. Instead he had taken courses in politics at the university of Lausanne and called himself 'Doctor'—in the way this honorific title is used in Portugal to denote all graduates. As Dr Savimbi he moved to the United States to further his political ambition, but for all his personal drive and cosmopolitan experience, he was unable, on his return to Africa, to build either an effective political movement or a competent guerrilla army. By the early 1970s he had entered into secret negotiations with officers in the Portuguese army over the possibility of obtaining a neocolonial settlement of the liberation stalemate. He naturally sought a powerful personal role for himself despite his as yet minimal grassroots support in the country.

If the politicians of the north and the south were in deep trouble during the prolonged military stalemate of Caetano's colonial war, the politicians of the centre, linked to the MPLA, were in even greater disarray. Their search for an exile base from which they could effectively operate was constantly frustrated. Zaire, although it tolerated the low-key presence of the FNLA in Kinshasa, was closely tied to Portugal and to the Portuguese colonial economy and had little interest in harbouring a movement of Marxist exiles who might inflame radical rebels in provincial Zaire or drive away Portuguese expatriates in urban Zaire. The MPLA was expelled from Zaire and tried to operate from Congo Brazzaville. The only Portuguese territory they could attack from bases on the north side of the Congo river, however, was the small Cabinda enclave—which it was relatively easy for Portugal to defend, particularly when it became a lucrative region from which the Gulf Oil ocean rigs were serviced. A third haven was eventually found in Zambia, but the host country was not willing to allow any guerrillas to attack the Benguela railway which carried Zambian copper to the Atlantic. This was a problem since, from a freedom fighter's point of view, no other target in the east was of sufficient strategic significance to affect Portugal's hold on Angola. The MPLA movement had to retreat even further from its Angolan homeland and settle in Tanzania, a thousand miles down a trail of thick mud and dust along which it had to haul all its ammunition and weaponry.

So hopeless had the MPLA logistical situation become by the early 1970s that the leadership began to fall apart, with violent rivalry breaking out along ethnic, ideological and class lines. Two rebellious factions split from the party. The 'eastern rebellion' took some of the leadership, along with militants and guerrillas who had been recruited in the highlands, out of the camps in the eastern savannah and eventually into alliance with UNITA, the party of the south. The 'active rebellion' of some of the more intellectual members of the Angolan elite despaired of making any progress under the command of Agostinho Neto and adopted its own breakaway ideological agenda. The Soviet Union, weary of this factionalism among its erstwhile protégés, suspended accreditation and logistical support. However, the situation was unexpectedly transformed when the 'fascist' capital of the Portuguese empire was seized by revolutionaries in April 1974. The 'active rebellion', though not the 'eastern rebellion', scrambled to rejoin the MPLA's 'presidential tendency' and the party leadership sought ways of entering the Angolan heartland and gaining a political foothold in the city of Luanda. The Soviet Union, meanwhile, reversed its decision to abandon Angola and hastily arranged for weapons to be supplied, advisers to be trained, and Cuban troops to be put on stand by for any vicarious intervention that might seem appropriate.

This Soviet volte-face did not immediately win Moscow a privileged place in Angolan politics or calm the power struggles between the faction-ridden exiles returning from the barren eastern marches of the country. The political denouement was complicated by the release from prison of MPLA militants who had spent the war in a Portuguese concentration camp in the country's remote south-western desert. The 'prison graduates', led by José van Dunem, were suspicious of the returning exiles with their conscript guerrillas and preferred to ally themselves to Nito Alves, the young commander of the independent MPLA military region which had held out against the Portuguese in the forested Dembos hills north of Luanda. These internal political leaders adopted ultra-radical stances that were informed by the Maoism of the Portuguese revolutionary left rather than the orthodox Marxist-Leninism of the Soviet Union's protégés returning home from Tanzania. A *modus vivendi* was eventually achieved, however. The young black radicals were adopted by the old pragmatic Creoles and Nito Alves himself was included in a diplomatic mission which visited Moscow and sealed the renewed Soviet alliance.

While the MPLA had been so deeply divided the most plausible postcolonial settlement had seemed to be a coalition between the Bakongo elite, the white settlers and the southern Protestants loyal to Savimbi—an alliance from which most of the MPLA factions would have been excluded. In fact, the ultimate outcome of the power struggle which followed the Lisbon coup d'état was the opposite scenario. The MPLA regrouped its forces, remobilised its foreign allies, and won the battle for Luanda. The three other political tendencies—northerners, settlers and southerners—disintegrated and their foreign supporters fled to Zaire, Portugal and South Africa.

The war which brought the MPLA to power in 1975 and 1976 was known to the victors as the second war of independence. Although its high point had been the battle for Luanda, the war had actually begun four months before independence day, on 9 July 1975. In a week of violence the MPLA troops, brought in from the guerrilla camps in the remote east and the havens of exile abroad, were supported by irregular militias mobilised by the local party leadership which had been organising activist cells of 'people's power' in Luanda city. Within days the four-way power-sharing executive that had been established as an interim government in January 1975 had been broken and the armies and politicians of both the northern FNLA and the southern UNITA had been driven out of the city, leaving the MPLA and the Portuguese in control. The initial MPLA offensive did not make much impact on territory north of the city, which was occupied by FNLA units backed by Zairean troops, but towards the south the MPLA advanced successfully against UNITA, whose leaders had to decide rapidly whether to sue for peace and form a political alliance with the MPLA or rejoin their uncomfortable former allies in the FNLA. Savimbi's initial inclination, as a one time admirer of Mao Zedong, was to accept the advice of radical Portuguese soldiers and join forces with the MPLA. He soon realised, however, that neither South Africa nor the United States was likely to tolerate the advent of a 'Maoist' or 'Marxist' regime in independent Angola. Instead, Savimbi hoped that an alliance with the unreconciled MPLA fighting men of the 'eastern rebellion'—led by a fellow southerner called Daniel Chipenda—would give a UNITA alliance with the FNLA significant military purchase. His calculation failed, however, and in September 1975 it was the MPLA rather than UNITA which dominated the south of Angola.

The revived challenge to the MPLA's prospect of gaining total power came first from the north. American policy, governed at the time by Henry Kissinger in covert association with the secret services, hoped to install a friendly regime in Luanda and put its faith in the northern FNLA. The methods adopted were deeply flawed, however, and an incompetent band of multinational mercenaries was soon worsted, leaving the United States angry and embarrassed. Worse was to follow when it emerged that American oil executives had been keeping their own options open by paying petroleum royalties to an interim MPLA administration which the American government had been attempting to overthrow by violent means. After the American discomfiture in the north it was in the south that a more dramatic foreign intervention occurred. South Africa first sent in advisers to counsel UNITA on ways of outwitting the MPLA, then supplied combat troops, and finally drove in a squadron of armoured cars. With such powerful backing UNITA was able to make the highland city of Huambo, once known as Nova Lisboa, into a capital city and a focus for a rival declaration of independence to the one being prepared for November 1975 in Luanda.

While covert South African troops were being flown into Angola, taking care to mask their identity to avoid a world outcry at the sight of Afrikaner soldiers spreading apartheid, the MPLA equally discreetly received its first contingent of 500 Cuban military instructors in order to stiffen its resistance against the resurgent south. Military instructors from the Caribbean proved quite insufficient, however, to stop what became a full-scale South African invasion when the 'Zulu Column' of armoured vehicles sent up the Angolan coast road captured the port of Lobito and the western end of the Benguela railway. In retaliation Cuban commandos were able to dynamite bridges on the roads between Lobito and Luanda and so prevent further lightning progress by South Africa along the seashore. A second South African column, code-named Foxbat, took an inland route and drove much deeper into Angola. It was only ordered to halt when it reached the northern edge of the highland, poised to advance on Luanda. Fear of discovery by the world media, and the attendant risk of exciting hostile international publicity, deterred South Africa from closing in on the capital and testing the MPLA's

Cuban allies on the city's southern front. The key encounter in the battle for Luanda, therefore, pitted Cuban artillery against Zairean infantry on the northern edge of the city. In the meantime UNITA, with powerful foreign cover supplied by 6,000 South African troops and with FNLA support, declared itself to be the ruling party of a secessionist south, the 'Democratic' Republic of Angola with a highland capital in Huambo. In Luanda the MPLA called the country the 'Popular' Republic of Angola.

After celebrating independence day on 11 November 1975, the MPLA returned to the attack. Within weeks the Cuban soldiers who had been flown in during the last days of colonial rule were reinforced by a seaborne expeditionary army which outnumbered the South African invading force. The Cuban contingent soon rose to 10,000 men equipped with heavy long-range guns and armoured personnel carriers. The MPLA recovery of the provinces began with an attack on the north where the United States covertly but ineffectually tried to maintain its support to the FNLA and the borrowed regiments from the Zairean army. This American support could be neither extensive nor public since, in the months following the loss of Vietnam in April 1975, the US Congress was reluctant to approve any new foreign adventure. The US government had been forced to use stealth in building up armed clients capable of supporting its preferred political options. A dozen small rented planes flew consignments of weapons to the raw recruits of both the FNLA and UNITA but the attempt to stiffen the United States' allies proved to be a humiliating fiasco, which further tarnished its sullied post-Vietnam reputation.

Worse was to follow when news of the South African invasion of Angola broke on the world scene. Such was the profound horror with which the West viewed the racial policies which South Africa practised at home that attitudes towards Angola and to the 'war of intervention' changed throughout Africa and beyond. Sympathy for the Huambo 'democratic' regime rapidly dwindled and toleration of the Luanda 'popular' government grew even among members of the OAU who were traditionally suspicious of Soviet adventurism in Africa. By January 1976, the MPLA forces had effectively recovered the north and were strong enough to attack the south. The alliance between FNLA and UNITA began to unravel in factional disputes. The South African expeditionary army, dismayed at the military incompetence, the administrative waywardness and the black racism of its UNITA allies, decided to cut its losses. As South Africa drew back into Namibia, both UNITA and the FNLA collapsed. The MPLA took over the whole of the country. Only roving bands of dissidents continued to operate in remote districts of the south-east. US intelligence estimated that its covert contribution of 30 million dollars to the arming of the FNLA and UNITA had been dwarfed by a Russian grant of 400 million dollars, spent on arming the MPLA and its Cuban allies. The South Africans had spent 130 million dollars on their cross-border campaign by the time they pulled out in a glare of unwelcome publicity. But the biggest loser had been Zaire whose large and well-funded army had proved to be a mere paper tiger.

No sooner had the war of intervention ended than the new government had to put all its scarce political skills and energies into building the future. The MPLA inherited colonial legacies which were deeply entrenched and Angolan society was found to be as complex as any in Africa. Creating a viable civil society for the nation as a whole would be difficult. One of the most influential sections of Angolan society at the time of independence were the 'old' Creoles of Luanda. This three-hundred-year-old community of black, Portuguese-speaking, Roman Catholics consisted of a close-knit set of families, some of whose ancestors had been accustomed to making marriage alliances with foreign merchants since the seventeenth century.[2] By the twentieth century this assimilated middle class, now primarily black rather than brown, had lost some of the status which had made it influential earlier. The eclipse of the Creoles had largely been the work of white immigrants, a class of carpet baggers who aspired to take away from the old black elite both their employment and their social status. From being colonels of militia and hostesses of society balls the Creoles had declined to become a proud but impoverished 'lumpen aristocracy' living on the fringes of an upstart colonial society. Creoles who tried to defend their historic status against the white parvenu immigrants by legal or political action were exiled to hardship posts in the conquered provinces of eastern Angola, 'the end of the world' when compared to their chic homes in the city. Some persecuted Creoles fled into exile in Portugal to evade the aggression of the new 'rednecks' who had come to seek their fortune in Africa, and it was in Lisbon that some members of this Creole upper middle class began to make subversive contact with radical politicians in the underground opposition to Salazar's dictatorship. It was they who took a leading role in bringing Angolan radicals together under the aegis of the OAU and in forming the original nucleus of the MPLA in 1960.

In the last phase of colonial rule the old Angolan Creoles were challenged not only by white immigrants by also by a new class of young men who had been assimilated into colonial society over the course of the twentieth century. These 'new *assimilados*' still belonged to African society, and still

---

[2]The early history of the old Creoles is convincingly portrayed in the classic historical novel written by Angola's leading novelist, under the nom de plume of Pepetela, *A Gloriosa Família. O Tempo dos Flamengos* (Lisbon: Dom Quixote, 1998, 2nd edn).

spoke Kimbundu in their leisure time, but they had been absorbed into the lower ranks of the colonial establishment by being educated to speak and write in Portuguese. Unlike the old Creoles, whose fortunes had declined during the twentieth century, the new *assimilados* were a rising black class with ambitious expectations which often caused them to be seen to reach above their allotted station. They became disdainful of their country 'cousins' and resentful of the haughty Creoles but their fiercest competitors were another rising new colonial class, the brown *mestiço* sons and daughters of white settlers and black common-law marriage partners. These new 'mulattos' could not aspire to the Luso-African status of the old Creoles but they considered themselves superior to any new *assimilado* who did not have a white parent to give them status, sponsor their education, or find them suitable employment in business or the civil service.

After independence, the colonial niceties of race, pedigree, language, education and ambition were to haunt the MPLA as it struggled to create a stable ruling establishment in the capital city. Despite their differences, however, all of the assimilated factions of colonial society, new and old, black and brown, had a significant advantage in terms of opportunity when compared to the throngs of job seekers who flocked to the city from the largely illiterate rural hinterland. The educated minority also had a political edge over the people of the interior—whether in the south, the centre or the north—when it came to bargaining over the future of Angola. Language was power in postcolonial African politics and it was the *assimilados* who spoke Portuguese, the language of command.

Once the MPLA had secured its hold on the country, disputes within the ruling circle over the nature of the new nation were many. Was Angola to be a radical country with an ideology of egalitarianism which broke with the traditions of class, race and privilege that had been so prominent in the colonial period? Or had the struggle for survival been so disruptive of the elite's way of life that continuity needed to be tightly clasped and old institutions tenaciously maintained. The party also asked itself whether the new leadership was to be the one which had spoken to the world from exile in Brazzaville and Dar es Salaam, or was power to be placed in the hands of those Angolans who had lived in Luanda during the long night of the colonial occupation? Was authority to be in the hands of political theorists or pragmatic administrators, and would power go to the civilian committee men or the military, who held the guns? Equally controversial was the question of whether the senior military men would be those who had fought the colonial forces to a standstill on the remote savannah frontier or the proud pioneers who had maintained the flag of liberation in forest fastness outside the city of Luanda. Rarely had the political heirs in any

African colony been more factionally divided than those who took up the reins of power in Angola. The responsibilities facing the inexperienced cadres who had clung to the city during the noisy night of 10 November 1975 were awesome.

The MPLA soon discovered that coming to terms with the management of a city, a bureaucracy, an economy and a country was a greater challenge than driving out their regional enemies with the help of a disciplined Cuban military force. In the long term it was political, economic and administrative mismanagement which brought systematic instability to postcolonial Angola. Although half of the Cubans in the country were deployed in rebuilding a civilian infrastructure, the city and the country were profoundly disrupted by the flight of ninety per cent of the white public service personnel. Disorder regularly opened up opportunities for rivals to seek power and brought a return of intrusive foreign armies both from the Zairean north and from the South African south.

The mismanagement of government was caused both by inexperience and by fatal rifts in the ideological positions of the members of the ruling party. Whereas most other colonial heirs, particularly in Francophone Africa but to a lesser extent also in Anglophone Africa, inherited an entrenched legal framework, a functioning civil service, an internationally recognised currency and an integrated army, in Angola the abrupt departure of most of Portugal's soldiers, bankers, administrators and lawyers left few functioning institutions which could be adapted to the new political circumstances. But the failure of the MPLA to pick up the colonial mantle and create a recognisably normal postcolonial, or neocolonial, state was not exclusively due to a shortage of experienced personnel. Their difficulties were compounded by resurgent military insecurity in the far north where an irritating separatist movement aspired to gain independence for the enclave of Cabinda, cut off from the Angolan mainland by the Congo river and by a finger of Zaire's territory. Zaire would naturally have liked to annex this territory, then the source of most of Angola's petroleum, and therefore gave discreet support to any troublemakers whom it could find to sponsor.

The result of the military insecurity in Cabinda was far-reaching. Instead of reducing the size of the Cuban expeditionary force after the South Africans had withdrawn, the MPLA was forced to maintain, and pay for, a continued Cuban presence strong enough to protect the Cabinda oil installations. These oil wells were operated by the Texan firm of Gulf Oil and, paradoxically, it was out of the oil royalties that Cuban military salaries were paid. Since the United States was at odds with Cuba over its revolutionary propaganda in the Caribbean and Latin America, and also with Angola over its friendship with the Soviet Union, Washington was somewhat dismayed that Texas was sponsoring 'Moscow's Gurkhas' to protect its oil assets in Africa. Rather more serious than Washington's coolness was the fact that insecurity in Cabinda prevented the Angolan government from concentrating on the creation of a stable political system and repairing the damage done to the national economy by the interventionist phase of the war of liberation.

While security in the oil fields was distracting the government from the task of national reconstruction, another irritating legacy of the liberation wars began to fester in the south. The leader of UNITA, Jonas Savimbi, revived his challenge to the regime by accusing it of being in the pocket of foreigners. He alleged that the MPLA government was not only staffed by whites but was excessively parochial in its ethnic preference for Mbundu citizens. Savimbi's xenophobic, racist and ethnic rhetoric culminated in a strident proposal for the creation of a 'black republic' of Angola to replace the one which allegedly favoured old Creoles, mixed race *assimilados* and white immigrants. By playing the race card, and thereby opening a whole box of repressed colonial neuroses, the UNITA leader was lighting the fuse of a powder trail which had long and painful consequences for any possible postcolonial reconciliation and reconstruction. Savimbi, who had once been sponsored by China, also tried momentarily to play the 'socialist' card. He gambled that this was a direction which Africa would favour and he tried to prove that the MPLA were not the 'true' socialists of Angola. These strategies did not succeed, however, since the race theme did not play well with potential UNITA supporters in Washington or Lisbon and the socialist one did not gain UNITA any credit with Pretoria or Kinshasa. Savimbi had to modify his stand on both scores in his search for international backing. In the meantime, however, the MPLA once more had to postpone the demobilisation of its army in order to keep a wary eye on the disaffected south where Savimbi's voice was heard most clearly.

While the Luanda government was putting scarce political and military energies into resolving issues of regional security, it was seriously neglecting its own constituency in the city of Luanda where it expected its core support to be solid. Thus it was that while the infant government was distracted by distant provincial horizons, it suddenly found that the ground had been dramatically cut from under its feet in its own urban backyard. In May 1977 an attempted coup d'état came perilously close to overthrowing the government of Agostinho Neto and resulted in the death of several senior members of his cabinet. In the city, the expectation that independence would bring rich rewards to young black people had led to constant disappointment through no less than two years of austerity. Suddenly the frustration of those who had won little from independence, and who were intensely jealous of the cosmopolitan elite which had inherited the colonial trappings of power and the visible symbols of prosperity, exploded in violent despair.

The political thinker behind the attempted coup was Nito Alves, the black military leader from the Luanda forest. Although he was subsequently accused of being a racist who had incited the black masses of the slums to rise up against the lighter-skinned cadres in the popular movement, he was in fact more concerned with high-minded ideals than with race-based jealousies. One of his ideological sparring partners was a radical woman philosopher originally from Portuguese India, Cita Vales, and one of his political role models was Enver Hoxha, the Stalinist dictator of Albania. Nito Alves' authority stemmed from having been a self-reliant military commander who had held out for more than a decade against colonial military patrols, regularly ambushing the roads from the city to the north and threatening the heavily-fenced plantation houses on the coffee estates. His guerrilla heroism won him the right to political office, but it did not make him a member of the inner circle and Nito Alves was neither well known, nor particularly trusted, by the cosmopolitan leaders who had spent the liberation war travelling in exile and who expected to be the unchallenged masters of their country on their return.

As the fruits of freedom eluded the populace, the marginalised militants turned from the politics of compromise to the mobilisation of ordinary people. In the poor quarters of Luanda Nito Alves organised study groups in which to debate the ideal of independence, the belief in equality, and the strategy for finding employment after the departure of the 200,000 whites who had fled the country in 1975. At first Agostinho Neto and his party leaders had applauded the mobilisation of street power among 'their people'. 'Peasants' and 'workers' had always been the heroes of the MPLA's armed struggle—although the peasant credentials of the leadership were conspicuously thin and their understanding of the aspirations of workers was naïve. Once the foreign invaders had been driven out in 1976, the MPLA relaxed and failed to perceive the danger signals emanating from the townships on its doorstep. While members of the central committee shared out the spoils of affluence, helping themselves to the villas and sailing yachts left behind by the fleeing white community, people in the street were having difficulty finding enough to eat.

As power and wealth corrupted the victors, the poor began to realise that their own aspirations required a different agenda. Out in Sambizanga, on the edge of the asphalt city, it was the local football club that became the venue for illicit political debate. Football had been the circus which Salazar, like Mussolini before him, had offered his people to quench their otherwise dangerous political thirst and football was accepted by the new nationalists as an appropriate focus for patriotism. In Sambizanga, however, the passion for the sport did not obliterate the desire for social justice or assuage the anger of the people when an incompetent regime was unable to make good a lack of food. So serious did shortages become that the government sent troops into the slums to search out 'hoarders' who could be blamed for withholding stocks of flour from 'the people'. Incensed football supporters met to plot subversion.

When the revolution of 1977 broke, inspired by Nito Alves' study groups, it was actually led by a faction of the army, which included José van Dunem and the 'prison graduates', which had had its ear close to the ground. It confidently expected to receive mass support from the city *musseques*, or slums. The radicals who launched the uprising against the MPLA stalwarts assumed that their popular credentials would win them approval from the Soviet Union. When the crunch of an attempted coup came, the Soviets were apparently slow to decide whether to support Agostinho Neto, the elderly old Creole, or Nito Alves, the vigorous young militant. It was apparently the Cubans who made the decision to back the old guard. Cuban troops moved with alacrity, seized the Luanda radio station, broadcast the news that the putsch had failed, and briskly set about making sure that Agostinho Neto and his surviving cabinet colleagues retained power. Coup leaders were caught and indiscriminately killed; their radical sympathisers were terrified into submission.

The reprisals which the rattled government subsequently took against anyone who might have been involved in the uprising were so savage that Angola was set on a downward path of spiralling violence far outstripping either the cruelties of the colonial war or the brutalities of the war of intervention. From 1977 fear stalked the land and guns outweighed ideals in determining the path to the future. Far from disbanding the much-hated secret police, a Portuguese legacy initially built on the Gestapo model, the survivors of the May coup used political security forces to repress any independence of thought that might inflame the aspirations of the urban population. The bloodstained crisis of 1977 led to fundamental changes in the country's management and from aspiring to be a mass movement seeking support throughout the city, the ruling MPLA turned to becoming a self-selected elite party mendaciously calling itself 'the workers' vanguard'.

At the same time that the government was adopting its new dictatorial mode at home, it was also bringing to a conclusion the last phase of the wars of liberation on the frontiers. The ending of the war between Angola and Zaire in 1978 was made possible by the resolution of an acrimonious Belgian colonial legacy which had long affected the security of both countries. Angola discovered that it could hold Zaire to ransom through the presence on its side of the border of rebel troops from the wealthy copper province of Katanga, or Shaba, in southern Zaire. These troops, known as the Katanga *gendarmerie*, had been refugees in Portuguese Angola ever since they had been driven from their homeland by a United Nations multinational army, following the failed Katanga rebellion in 1963. They had allegedly been used by the Portuguese to hunt down nationalist guerrillas in the colonial war and as such they could not expect to receive generous treatment from a newly-independent nationalist government in Luanda. They therefore sought ways of returning to Zaire and recapturing political power in their old province of Shaba.

Angola was quite willing to be rid of its armed Katanga refugees and was delighted at the prospect that they might weaken the central Zaire government of Mobutu, which had done so much to hinder a peaceful transition to independence in Angola. The first attack on Shaba by the *gendarmerie* was launched in 1977 and caused the Zairean army to crumble, since the Lunda people of the copper province welcomed the invaders as liberators. Western investors in the copper mines were appalled, however, at the concept of 'liberation' from the safe rule of their chosen dictator, General Mobutu. France hastily recruited a Third World army in Morocco and flew it to Shaba to drive out the cross-border invaders from Angola. Such neocolonial interference was only a temporary deterrent, however, and in 1978 the *gendarmerie* invaded again. Once more Mobutu's defence force were worsted. This time the United States was forced to intervene and fly in an even heavier assortment of regiments borrowed from regimes sympathetic to the West. The copper mines were rescued, again.

After facing two potentially lethal attacks Mobutu recognised that it would be in his best interest to negotiate a longer term peace with Angola. Zaire agreed to withdraw any support for anti-government rebels associated with the FNLA who might threaten the stability of the Luanda government from their bases around Kinshasa. Mobutu thereby gave up for the time being any hope either of capturing the Cabinda oil wells or of helping to install in Luanda a government which would be friendly to his own brand of rampant capitalism, in which private participation in business and industry by politicians was strongly favoured. Zaire also hoped that peace with Angola might enable it to reopen the direct railway line from the Zaire copper and cobalt mines to the Atlantic harbour at Lobito, thus greatly facilitating the traditional export of heavy minerals.

Mobutu's peace proposals were accepted by the now ailing Agostinho Neto and Angola moved the Katanga *gendarmerie* back from Shaba, keeping it on standby for any future operations that might serve the government's strategic needs. The peace of 1978 made it possible for several tens of thousands of Angolans to leave their adopted homes in western Zaire and return to their ancestral homes in northern Angola. Their defeated military and political leaders slipped into the shadows of an unpublicised exile from which they only emerged fourteen years later when, after the end of the Cold War, the United Nations was able to bring temporary stability to Angola and organise a multiparty election for which all the surviving old guard politicians came home. Long before that, however, the 'old man' of Angolan politics, Agostinho Neto, was struck down with cancer. In 1979 he died in a Moscow hospital.

SURVIVAL IN THE EIGHTIES

The Angolan wars of liberation ended with the death of Agostinho Neto. Already, however, a new conflict was brewing up, which was once again both a civil and an international war. The key problem in understanding Angola's postcolonial history is the question of why it was that after the protracted and bloodstained birth pangs of the liberation struggle the country failed to settle down and tackle the conventional problems of economic and social development which were the normal legacy of colonialism. The causes of the new wars of the 1980s were many. The role of the Soviet Union in Africa during its last ten years of existence is one factor that needs to be taken into consideration and it may be significant that Angola's second president, José Eduardo dos Santos, was an engineer in the petroleum industry who had been trained in Russia. Another long-distance factor that might be deemed important is the role of the United States which elected a president, Ronald Reagan, who adopted a virulently hawkish agenda during the Cold War confrontations of the 1980s. In the conflict between the United States and Russia one of the irritants was the political agenda of Cuba, which was anxious to build an international reputation of its own and, in the name of Third World freedom, provided extensive civilian and military support to the much-battered MPLA government of Angola.

At a more regional African level, the peace deal with Zaire opened the way for the return to Angola of tens of thousands of old Bakongo exiles. Making political and economic space for these returnees sometimes put strains on the fragile postcolonial government which was only slowly recovering from the virulent purges that had followed the attempted coup d'état of 1977. Meanwhile, on Angola's southern front, South Africa was still smarting from the humiliation of having been defeated in Angola in March 1976. Moreover, it was deeply threatened by political unrest within its own territory when, three months later, the students of Soweto rose up in rebellion, partly fired with enthusiasm by the liberation from white rule which Angola had achieved. The same stirrings of revolution began to mobilise the liberation forces which launched an armed struggle against South Africa in order to win independence for Namibia, using Angola as a training ground for its guerrillas and as a haven for its asylum seekers. Finally, but most pertinently, the last unfinished agenda which brought pervasive grief to the peoples of Angola was the inability of the new government led by Eduardo dos Santos to satisfy the legitimate aspirations of the southern elite of Angola's highland cities who had not been dealt an equitable hand in the settlements of the late 1970s and who remained isolated and aggrieved in their south-eastern guerrilla camps on the remote edge of the old Portuguese colonial world.

It was during the 1980s, beginning with the northern peace secured in Zaire in 1978 and culminating in a southern peace agreed with South Africa in 1991, that Angola experimented with many political, diplomatic and economic survival strategies as the tide of war rose and fell in tandem with the politics of the Cold War—taking on a new intensity with the inauguration of Reagan as president of the United States in 1981 and diminishing with the gradual collapse of Gorbachev's Soviet Union after the breaching of the Berlin Wall in 1989. Beneath the high drama of world politics, daily life in Angola was sustained by the efforts of landless exiles who returned home to engage in petty trade in the city and of working women who persisted in planting local food crops in the suburbs and in the countryside. Meanwhile, the ruling elite earned money from the export of oil and, following international ideological shifts, moved from a Soviet style command management in the early 1980s to an American style free-market in the late 1980s. All the while the South African ministry of defence perfected a policy of destabilisation directed against Angola, which was largely unchanged by the peace initiatives of the mid-1980s. Cuba persisted at the same time in raising the level of its military support for Angola undeterred by the government's shift from nominal socialism to theoretical capitalism. Amidst all the changes the great survivor of the political opposition, Jonas Savimbi, constantly trimmed his sails to the prevailing wind and armed his guerrillas on the proceeds of diamonds dug from Angola's inland river beds.

The ending in 1978 of the old liberation war between Angola and Zaire brought about one of the most fundamental changes to postcolonial Angola in the form of a mass migration of exiles who returned from their havens in the former Belgian Congo to their ancestral homes in the former Portuguese sphere of influence in the old Kongo kingdom. The men and women who came back from Kinshasa, accompanied by a new generation of northern Angolans who had been born in western Zaire, had to work hard to find niches of opportunity. Some settled in the villages of the north and took up farming but life was hard: the plantation industry had collapsed, the white bush traders had gone, and a meagre level of subsistence could only be supplemented by smuggling consumer goods across the border from Zaire in exchange for occasional bags of coffee beans or bunches of cooking bananas and sweet potatoes. Such austerity had little appeal to returnees accustomed to a much higher standard of living and many moved on from the villages to seek their fortune in the yet unknown city of Luanda.

The transition was by no means easy when power and status in Luanda depended on a firm grasp of Portuguese. The returning exiles, educated in Kinshasa, spoke French and were treated as foreigners by the proud and clannish people of Luanda just as they had been treated as foreigners while living on the 'Belgian' side of the border. In the Belgian Congo, and in the successor state of Zaire, immigrants and refugees had no access to state employment and therefore became expert at carving an economic space in the private sector. They worked for the Portuguese who formed the poor white sector of Kinshasa business, acting as butchers' boys in the white-owned slaughter houses, becoming touts for taxi drivers and sometimes graduating to be drivers themselves. Petty trade was their mainstay, hawking shirts through the streets, minding barrows of produce from the countryside, staffing market stalls in the African quarters where they sold everything from plastic sandals to kerosene-fuelled refrigerators. The Kinshasa Angolans gained a business sense which few Africans possessed in Luanda, where much of the petty trade had been in the hands of the Portuguese and where Europeans had acted as cobblers, mechanics, chauffeurs, hairdressers and bar hostesses in downtown Luanda.

The returnees who came 'home' were not merely the children of the northerners who had fled from the vigilante massacres visited on northern Angola in 1961. They were also the grandchildren of black commercial entrepreneurs and artisans from Angola who had served the Belgians over three generations. They arrived in Angola with blue-collar skills which the local white-collar Creoles and *assimilados* did not possess. But they arrived as strangers, with no old family networks to protect them, and so clung to each other thereby generating envy and suspicion among the natives of Luanda. These local black and brown citizens gradually came to recognise, however, that although they knew the working of public-sector employment, they did not understand the commercial sector which had been in the hands of the departed whites. It was in that sector that the returnees identified their opportunities and made themselves indispensable, though not popular, as the city's new trading community. They had the drive commonly possessed by migrants with no access to land ownership, family property, or salaried jobs awarded to local people through the old-boy network, and they therefore survived by entry into the risk-taking crafts and trades. Officially the MPLA looked askance at the rapid, almost rampant, rise of the private enterprises which the northerners established. In practice, however, the scarce skills in business provided one of the most important survival strategies for urban dwellers, whose needs could not be satisfied through the poorly-supplied and inadequately-staffed official agencies. 'Parallel markets' run by 'Zairota' returnees sprang up everywhere and soon even the most hardline ideologues of the MPLA found they were compelled to join the ranks of the free-market customers.

The wildly-uncontrolled market of postcolonial Angola had many interesting effects on post-war survival strategies. One feature was the relationship between the state sector, in the hands of the ruling party, and the private sector, managed by the northern returnees. State employees, Portuguese-speaking Angolans with government-sponsored jobs, received coupons which enabled them to buy a range of authorised goods in state-owned supermarkets at controlled prices. These government-issued rations, including good quality imported whisky, could be sold off at deregulated prices on the parallel market in exchange for all the goods which the planned economy could not supply—ranging from a fresh chicken to a spare part for a Mercedes car. In the process of exchanging coupon goods for black-market goods, money virtually ceased to be recognised and it was barter that became the recognised medium of exchange. The six-pack of lager in aluminium cans became the nominal, and often the physical, measure of exchange, serving as a bulky pseudo-currency. To buy an expensive item on the parallel market, one that cost more than a headload of beer cans, it was necessary to rent a pickup truck to deliver the negotiated price in hard produce.

The free-market barter system in Angola was far from being whimsical and the pseudo-currency values were underpinned by the export price of oil. Prices on the black market shadowed the international price of oil accurately and speedily. Currency, where used, also had a sensitive free-market value which rose and fell like an economic barometer. For large payments, as in the buying and selling of urban real estate, the informal sector sometimes measured values in uncut diamonds, illicitly traded by the matchboxful. The 'alternative' economy created by the Zaire returnees, who had abandoned the political agenda of the FNLA and had become the economic partners of the MPLA, may have been unorthodox but it was certainly not unsubtle; and the scale of its operations was gigantic.

While returned exiles established a private commercial sector which enabled urban Angolans to survive the uncertainties of independence, it was working women who bore the burden of the struggle for survival in the countryside. Young men were constantly liable to be conscripted or kidnapped to serve in Angola's rival armies and it was therefore women, children and old men who were left to fend for themselves, inventing ever more imaginative survival strategies based on small-scale farming and petty barter. The survival of village economies in rural Angola was made enormously difficult by the almost continuous war of destabilisation which gripped the country in the 1980s. Military planners on either side were not averse to starving rural populations in order to drive them out of enemy territory where their farm produce could be captured to sustain the opposing army. One way of manipulating civilian populations was by laying minefields around farm land and water sources. Women going out into the fields, or children going down to the stream, were liable to have their legs blown off. It was even suggested that the strategy was designed to maim rather than to kill, to cripple the opposing society with the cost of feeding and caring for mine victims rather than to eliminate women and children by sudden death.

Although counting unmapped minefields is difficult, it has been roughly estimated that nine million mines were laid in Angola to deny farmers or their families access to farm land. Such a number of mines made Angola's killing fields comparable to those of Cambodia. The plight of the largely female victims was publicised to the world by Princess Diana, to the dismay of a British government which had hitherto sold anti-civilian weapons of every variety almost indiscriminately. The princess visited the minefields, spoke to women in rehabilitation centres and cuddled innocent children fitted with wooden limbs. But however intensively each side in the conflict tried to curb the survival strategies of its opponents, the initiative of village women did not die. In the savagely brutalised regions of the Kwanza valley, the MPLA's home territory and a prime target of UNITA's, women remained defiantly self-sufficient. When well-meaning aid workers tried to establish marketing cooperatives, they declined the proposal, saying that any formally-constituted organisation would fall prey to the politics of men. Men, it was widely believed, would consume the profits of any cooperative by converting the produce into alcohol and tobacco. Women alone could ensure that the fruits of farming reached the mouths of children.

Even though subsistence was the key to rural survival, some market strategies were put in place. On the farm lands south of the Kwanza, for instance, growers were able to take their maize to market by adapting children's scooters to carry bags that were heavier than any woman could carry on her head. The design, and the wooden materials, were entirely local while the frequently-needed repairs required no outside technology.

As on the push-bike trails of wartime Vietnam, women peasants could carry tonnes of farm food over long distances to add a tiny market sector of opportunity to their subsistence survival strategies. When each spasm of war subsided, male-owned trucks returned to the rural districts to buy 'surplus' food in exchange for manufactured city goods that could be used for consumption or for barter. Some of the owner-drivers of bush lorries were erstwhile Portuguese settlers who returned to their former stamping grounds and to their traditional trading pursuits. Neither the self-help scooters nor the old colonial lorries were ever adequate, however, to feed the inland towns, let alone the huge encampments of displaced populations. To fend off hunger in the provincial towns a web of air bridges had to be built by NGOs which flew in food to prevent the rival armies from starving the urban centres held by their enemies. But still the women struggled to achieve self-sufficiency. Down on the coast, displaced women from the highlands showed the utmost ingenuity in creating market gardens in old white suburbs and growing onions and cabbages in former playgrounds. They also dug up the central reservations of roads to plant maize and they used water from the standpipes in the shanty slums to irrigate tomatoes, thus eking a precarious living during the endless round of escalating wars.

One of the economic enclaves in which women gained both wealth and prestige in Luanda was fishmongering. The fishing boats were traditionally owned by coastal men and crewed by immigrant workers from the highlands, some of them Bailundu migrant workers. The selling of the fish had traditionally been the preserve of Luanda women, though in the late-colonial period white entrepreneurs had encroached on their domain and diverted the considerable wealth generated by the industry into the male sector of the economy. When whites fled from Angola at the prospect of a turbulent independence, black women recovered part of their niche in the fish market and the most successful of them became entrepreneurs. They celebrated their wealth as queens of the Luanda carnival, the epitome of prestige among true natives. Rich female fishmongers ostentatiously decked their granddaughters out in the finest costumes of the carnival dance brigades. Even in the years of the most acute wartime austerity women wholesalers were able to order textiles from Europe, America and Asia for competitive carnival display. So prestigious were the carnival queens that the men of the ruling MPLA appropriated the festival for their own political purposes and used it each year to celebrate their victory over South Africa in March 1976. Among the dance companies it was almost always one of the fishing guilds which won the supreme prize, while their farming opponents were cast into a shadow of despair which they and their menfolk drowned in palm wine, cane brandy and alcoholic oblivion.

Under colonialism working-class women, white as well as black, had been seriously exploited and downtrodden. Middle-class colonial women, on the other hand, predominantly but not exclusively white, had gained freedoms in Angola that went beyond those normally available to them in authoritarian Portugal. This tradition of emancipated opportunity carried through into the years of independence and women sympathetic to the MPLA were able to hold such relatively prestigious posts as that of university rector or national librarian. Even UNITA had a woman as one of its economic advisers. In the government, tokenism led to the appointment of some women as junior ministers though none played a role in the running of the oil sector or the management of the army. The party's organisation for women appeared to put women on a pedestal while effectively removing them from any real access to power. High-profile women were more likely to play a role in the dynastic politics of the Luanda families than in any real power struggles, and women with authority were commonly deemed to be an offence to African male pride, as the United Nations discovered to its cost when it appointed a female peace broker to serve in Angola. Margaret Anstee, for all her astute diplomatic activity, found that her Nigerian military commander was barely able to address a civil word to her, so offended had he been at the idea of a woman with power. Jonas Savimbi was even more outraged, describing her in his wireless tirades as little better than a whore. President dos Santos, meanwhile, prided himself on displaying an official wife who belonged to the greatest of the Creole dynasties.

Although women who farmed the land were the heroic survivors of the war years in rural Angola, they were also some of the most abused victims of the male armies which endlessly trampled across the countryside throughout the 1980s. Attitudes to women both in the MPLA war of liberation and in the UNITA war of destabilisation are portrayed in two of Angola's prominent war novels: Pepetela's *Mayombe* and Sousa Jamba's *Patriots*[3] —in both of which frustrated conscripts fantasise about the supply of beautiful women whom their superior officers guard for their own enjoyment. One of the most painful legacies of Portuguese colonialism was the attitude to gender of a ruling class of male immigrants which coopted sexual services from its conquered female victims.

The colonial war of the 1960s did nothing to protect Angolan women from similar predatory experiences and the sexual violations which colonial conscripts inflicted on Angola was seen by the regime's propagandists as evidence of racial toleration rather than of inhuman white arrogance— one bombastic officer even proclaiming the hope that each white conscript

---

[3]Full reference is given in the bibliography, under Angolan literature.

would impregnate half a dozen African women and so pursue the objective of implanting colonial culture by means of rape. The long-term consequences were dire on two scores. On the military field the armies of the 1980s adopted the same predatory attitude to women as the colonisers, but did so in a new health climate in which the HIV virus began to spread uncontrollably through the war zones. At the political level the legacy of colonial fornication brought intensified racial prejudice to a new postcolonial generation as the children of white fathers, whether legitimate or not, saw themselves as superior to other Angolans while the children of black fathers could be roused to a bitter jealousy towards their *mestiço* kin. True blackness became a badge that some politicians, including Savimbi, used to proclaim their superiority over the 'bastard' children of the Portuguese empire who held sway in Luanda.

The economic well-being of the sophisticated elite which ruled Angola after the end of the liberation wars of the 1970s was enhanced throughout the 1980s by the growing supply of crude petroleum. The oil revenue cushioning Luanda from the austerity which the collapse of the colonial economy had inflicted on the countryside was also the economic fuel which made the war particularly ferocious. In Angola, as in other oil-producing African countries such as Nigeria, which had also been wracked, by a postcolonial civil war, those who held the oil wells were unwilling to share their bounty with those who did not. The history of the oil industry had begun to tell on Angola in the last ten years of colonial rule, but after the fall of Portugal petroleum became the most important, indeed almost the only, source of export revenue. Unlike the formerly dominant agricultural economy, the oil industry was not an important source of employment in salaried jobs or in ancillary labouring work. Gulf Oil, renamed Chevron, serviced its Cabinda wells with American crews who came and went via the French oil ports in Gabon, thus avoiding the effects of Angolan violence but leaving little positive mark on society other than the monthly payments to the government. These royalties grew during the 1980s as the great Atlantic oilfield extended south of the Congo river through the shallow waters of mainland Angola. When political conditions seemed right, new oil companies risked their venture capital in exploring blocks of concessions which stretched as far south as Luanda. These companies even began to build a few on-shore facilities on the south bank of the estuary, not far from the stone pillar erected in 1483 by an early explorer who wished to claim the territory for the Portuguese crown.

It can, and perhaps should, be argued that it was oil which kept the several Angolan civil wars running for twenty-five years. The city politicians were able to cream off the profits and the oil companies were able to pump the petroleum from off-shore platforms unconcerned by the ebb and flow of traumatised refugees inland. As the oil was sold, the war continued. The politicians of the south refused to accept political or military defeat so long as the power brokers of the city were unwilling to share the oil spoils and recycle the national wealth in countrywide reconstruction. Centralisation of power was continually reinforced by oil revenues. Politicians who used oil royalties to buy ever more sophisticated weapons of war not only maintained the military advantage but also made substantial personal gains from bonuses and backhanders. The most corrupt of the. politicians saw no personal advantage in ending the bloodshed, so long as they could close their hearts to the suffering in the provinces and rake in their bounty.

In the city the government was able to purchase superficial stability by offering a minimum level of material comfort, and a basic supply of imported food, to the million displaced people who crowded into the peri-urban shanty-towns. The political class was kept on its toes by a constant game of musical chairs in which access to the benefits of office and oil wealth could be granted or withdrawn at the stroke of the presidential pen. The more tightly the owners of the oil held on to their assets, the more open to Western corruption their political system became. This corruption was fed and encouraged by every foreign interest, European as well as American. Expatriate businessmen and foreign politicians offered all conceivable types of illicit inducements in order to bypass any form of local consultation or any method of democratic accountability. Without any national auditing of the oil revenues, the anger felt in the deprived provinces of Angola was all too understandable. But the same Western interests who corrupted the city to get their oil on the best possible terms were the ones who were arming the rebellious provinces and stoking the war of destabilisation.

In 1985 there was a hiccup in the oil-fuelled war. It had less to do with the politics of Cold War interventionism than with the need for the Angolan government to rethink its policies in the light of a drop in the international price of petroleum. Until that time the government had more or less adopted Soviet-style models of economic planning, though few if any of the leaders had much grasp of either the theory or the practice of Marxist-Leninism. Since 1979, when OPEC had negotiated a huge rise in the price of crude oil, Angola had been partially cushioned against any incompetence in its industrial planning system. The earnings from the colonial processing industries of the 1960s that had been nationalised, or confiscated, or simply abandoned by colonists fleeing the uncertainties of war, had been squandered in the first ten years of independence. By 1985 industrial production, and employment in manufacturing, were down by two-thirds to little more than thirty per cent of the production levels achieved in the last full year of colonial management.

In 1980, an MPLA plenary congress had already recognised the problem but sought to put the blame for economic malfunction on individual speculation and administrative incompetence rather than on the theories adopted for the government's economic system. Party members railed against embezzlement, illegal trading, inflation, unbridled corruption, widespread unemployment, the burden of the foreign debt, economic suffocation, the failure of education, the failure of health services to fight against both endemic and epidemic disease, against a state which had become parasitic, but all to little avail. When the next party congress was called, in 1985, the crisis could no longer be blamed on individual failures, and new ideological attitudes began to be expressed in the hope of finding survival strategies at a time of falling national income.

Faced with a drop in oil revenue, and with the failure of the import substitution industries that had been inherited from Portugal to act as the seedbed for industrial growth and the training of a new generation of skilled work people, the MPLA had to turn its attention to ideological re-orientation and to administrative reform. The crisis had bitten deep into the heart of the central system and into the welfare of the urban population which lived within sight of the affluent villas of the ruling elite and who had hitherto been partially cushioned from the deprivations that affected the invisible, war-torn rural areas. Economic decline had led to a serious brain drain. After the departure of white technocrats, bureaucrats, and entrepreneurs in 1975, there had been a steady, but cumulatively crippling, haemorrhage of black middle-class Angolans who left the country to seek job security and professional earnings abroad—whether in the more stable parts of the African continent or in Europe and North America. Trained and educated nationals who remained behind to work with the expatriates who were trying to keep industrial production and government services functioning were constantly handicapped by shortages of imported raw materials, by an absence of spare parts for machines, and by frequent interruptions in the flow of water and electricity when storage dams and power stations were sabotaged by guerrilla commandos.

The circular question of whether the war caused the economic decline or whether the economic decline was the cause of war could no longer be answered by blaming 'brigands', 'saboteurs' and 'opportunists' sponsored by the Cold War protagonists. From 1985 a policy of 'economic purification' was slowly embarked upon, leading to the introduction of at least some market principles and incentives. The mythical idea that Angola could plan for the development of heavy industry on a Stalinist model was dropped but any notion that light industry might be a viable form of economic diversification stumbled on the complete absence of a skilled workforce able to turn local raw material, and notably wood, into finished products. Equally difficult was the idea of reopening agriculture to the commercial sector. Civil servants and politicians had no concept of what risk-taking meant in the field of agrarian production and occasionally assumed, as the planners of Eastern Europe had once believed, that workers could simply be directed into agriculture.

When reform of the economic production processes proved impossible, the government embarked on a scheme for the purging of corruption, partly encouraged by Cuban advisers who had become sickened by the levels of corruption and incompetence that stymied their efforts to bring Angola out of its chaos. Gradually the beer can system of barter was replaced by a twin currency arrangement with the local bank notes being used for soft currency transactions and American dollars employed by the privileged elite for hard currency purchases. Cracking down on the old black market in uncut diamonds led to a degree of judicial ferocity in punishing those who were captured but could not call on adequately powerful political friends for protection. One senior Cuban commander, who was implicated in the corruption was taken home and shot for economic sabotage after allegedly being caught trafficking in diamonds, ivory and ebony carvings in exchange for hard currency or hard drugs, though his crime might have been political ambition as much as financial malpractice. The adoption of market values and of freely-traded currencies may have facilitated the lives of those with access to valuable assets, but they put new consumer pressures on the ever larger communities of displaced persons who lived around the city of Luanda. The economic reform programme also did nothing to satisfy the aspirations of the southern business class which continued to be excluded from the new opportunities and so remained loyal to UNITA and to its leader, Jonas Savimbi.

While northerners had moved into Luanda and become the merchant class, facilitating the wartime survival of an urban population living under a dysfunctional Marxist government, southerners looked abroad to the United States and South Africa for their survival strategies. In so doing their objective was to destabilise the MPLA government and seize the assets of the urban-based economy. While women struggled to support their wartime households, Angola's men were conscripted by ever more extensive armies and forcibly compelled to fight each other, attacking and defending the country's politically significant urban centres and the core oil economy. Whether the war was largely fuelled by the frustrated ambitions of the

UNITA leaders or whether they were simply puppets who opened up Angola as one of the more convenient Asian, African and Latin American playgrounds on which the superpowers acted out their wars by proxy, remains an intractable question. But without the Cold War, UNITA would probably not have survived, and southerners, like northerners, would have found a way to jump on to the central bandwagon.

What made Angola peculiarly different from the Cold War confrontations being fought in Nicaragua or Afghanistan was the presence on its southern border of the apartheid republic of South Africa, one of the most controversial of the pariah nations of the 1980s. The commitment of Angola, supported by Cuba, to freeing South Africa from the racial supremacy of its Afrikaans-speaking government, and the opposing commitment of South Africa to ridding central Africa of a regime friendly to the 'evil empire' of the Soviet Union, gave the war of the 1980s an ideological edge which went beyond a domestic struggle for wealth and power of the type that was to be witnessed in Angola during the civil wars of the 1990s. Although the Angolan war of the 1980s was fought against the back drop of the last decade of Soviet imperialism, and the last decade of South African racial exclusiveness, the determination to continue the war was in part a domestic calculation on the part of the holders of wealth in Luanda, and their northern commercial acolytes, against the modernisers of the south who had been left out in the wilderness.

Since the key to Savimbi's survival from 1979, the year of the death of Agostinho Neto, to 1991, the year of the Bicesse peace accord, was his alliance with the United States, an assessment of American policy before, during and after the Reagan presidency is necessary for an understanding Angola's postcolonial history. The US intervention in the wars of liberation had been ineffectual, and reluctance to be publicly involved in foreign wars led the United States Congress to outlaw, through the 1976 'Clark Amendment', any sending of American weapons to the warring parties in Angola. Although the Carter administration, which took office in 1977, had a relatively liberal attitude in African affairs, and condemned South Africa for its repressive policies, it nevertheless remained a participant in the Cold War and was willing indirectly to support third parties such as Morocco who were prepared to destabilise Angola and disrupt Soviet policy in Africa. Savimbi was permitted discreetly to visit Washington for talks with rightwing foreign policy experts such as Kissinger. The Carter administration, facing a general election, would not have been sorry to see the Russian-backed government in Angola fail. At the same time, corporate America remained keen to do business with Angola, selling aircraft, electronic equipment, computer and oil-drilling technology.

During his first term Reagan was unable to persuade Congress to repeal the Clark Amendment and US business, notably the oil industry, thought that it would be harmful to its commercial interests to demonstrate hostility to the Angolan government. Covertly, however, Reagan fuelled the Angolan sector of the Cold War and vetoed attempts by the United Nations to restrain South Africa's ever more frequent incursions. Although South Africa's attacks were nominally in pursuit of Namibian guerrillas fighting for the independence of their country, in practice many of the targets were Angolan army installations. Even more directly and illegally, the first Reagan administration used third parties to arm Savimbi's southern guerrillas with weapons coming, not directly from the US, but from Belgium, Switzerland, Israel and other American client states—with the funding issuing from Saudi Arabia, the Gulf states and other Western trading partners. To facilitate the delivery of UNITA weapons, a covertly-managed Central Intelligence Agency charter firm won the air supply contract for Angola's government diamond mines. Legitimate supplies of mining equipment were thus carried in conjunction with illegitimate supplies of weapons delivered to opposition units camped out beyond the diamond mines.

Although euphemistically described by the United States as a low-intensity conflict, the pressure of war on Angola eventually became such that in February 1984 the government felt compelled to seek an accord with Savimbi's South African allies which should have ended the hostilities. Savimbi himself, for whom victory, not peace, was the objective, immediately vitiated the South African deal and pounced on Luanda's largest hydroelectric plant with a terrorist attack. The Lusaka Accord between Angola and South Africa, like the Nkomati Accord signed a few months later between Mozambique and South Africa, was soon a dead letter. It had, however, given a temporary breathing space to President Botha who gained an invitation to visit Europe and attempted to sell his country to the West as an honest broker in the Cold War.

In November 1984 Reagan won his second term as American president. He rapidly stepped up his support for Savimbi's campaign to defeat the MPLA and gain power for his southern coterie. With the slogan 'Africa has a right to be free', Reagan was able to get the Clark Amendment repealed and the supply of war materials to Angola was put on a legal, though still unpublicised, footing. Savimbi was presented to the American public not as a 'freedom fighter' but as a champion of 'democracy' and in January 1986 he was invited to the White House. Thereafter UNITA fought its way out of the empty plains of the southeast and back into the populated highlands, where it could pressurise conscripts into joining its fighting force. Civilian deaths rose to hundreds of thousands as 'soft targets' were captured, defended and then recaptured by the opposing sides. In 1987, the war escalated into a conflict over hard targets, most notably the old Portuguese military bases of Cuito Cuanavale on the MPLA side of the battle line and of Mavinga on the UNITA side. The battle lasted for months and the cost in both men and materials escalated, the Cuban force reaching 50,000 men and the war debt to Moscow a billion dollars.

Eventually, however, it was South Africa that was forced to call a halt to the hostilities after the loss of irreplaceable French Mirage jets and the death of many white conscripts, whose funerals could not be hidden by censorship from South Africa's white voting public. South Africa had borne the brunt of the effort to support Savimbi and topple dos Santos ever since its return to Angola in the years following its expulsion in 1976. The justification for returning remained the defence of Namibia, the ex-German colony which South Africa had conquered in 1918 but still held in 1980 despite international resolutions that determined that the United Nations, and not South Africa, was the rightful custodian of Namibian sovereignty. South Africa feared that irregular companies of exiled nationalist freedom fighters would attack its occupying army across the Cunene river. The guerrillas had set up their camps in Angola when attempts to get Western international opinion to support the Namibian freedom struggle, and condemn the illegitimate occupation by South Africa, had failed. Even the Labour government of Britain was unwilling to jeopardise the colonial stability of Namibia at a time when oil prices were high and the industrial world was becoming dependent on alternative nuclear energy for which Namibian uranium was one of the preferred fuels.

South Africa had an economic as well as a strategic agenda in Angola: it aspired to establish neocolonial domination over a neighbour which, during the Portuguese colonial war, had been a valued ally. In order to restore 'harmonious' relations with Angola, South Africa decided to 'destabilise' the government in the hope that when it fell it would be replaced by one that was more amenable to the economic needs of its giant industrial neighbour. One of those was the search for a supply of crude oil that would not be cut off by the economic sanctions imposed by suppliers hostile to apartheid—a search made more urgent after 1979 by the fall of the pro-Western Shah of Iran who had traditionally supplied South Africa's oil refineries. Another economic objective of South Africa's northern outreach was to widen the market for South African exports, both of agricultural foodstuffs and of manufactured consumer goods, at a time when western boycotts were threatening its traditional export markets while its African markets, particularly in Zaire and Zimbabwe, were still too small to make up for the limited purchasing power of its own internal black consumers. South Africa's financial speculators and investors once again hoped that Angola might be opened to new mineral opportunities, including a search for copper mines.

Economic aspirations, however, were probably less important to South Africa than the need to maintain good relations with Reagan's United States. So long as there was a Soviet presence in Angola, South Africa could claim that it was a Western bulwark against Soviet global expansion and Russian 'neocolonialism' in Africa. So long as Angola hosted an expeditionary army from Cuba, South Africa could play effectively on American fears of Cuban ideas of freedom being exported beyond the shores of the beleaguered island, which American governments had so long and so fiercely demonised. By playing up the danger of Soviet influence in central Angola, and by allowing its army to be used to hold down the Cuban force in southern Angola, South Africa safeguarded itself from American interference in its domestic political agenda of segregation and repression. Whenever a Washington lobby, whether white or black, demanded sanctions against South Africa, in order to hasten the advent of African freedom and democracy, Pretoria only had to point to the Russian 'menace' for the appeal to be brushed aside and the alliance between the United States and South Africa to be reaffirmed.

The changes which came to Angola in the late 1980s were brought about by a whole series of mutations in geopolitical relations. At the economic level, the falling price of world energy meant that uranium was no longer such a precious asset. The western members of the United Nations no longer felt the need to defend South Africa's occupation of Namibia and risk incurring the ire of liberal or black members of their electorates. At a strategic level, the South African army found that it no longer had the military capacity to invade Angola and capture its southern military bases. Defeat at the battle of Cuito Cuanavale, coming as it did at the end of the Cold War, had repercussions for both South Africa and Angola. Namibia won its independence and so the issue of guerrilla camps on Angolan territory ceased to be relevant. The South African army lost its prestige at home and its key supporter, President Botha, fell from office, opening the way to a new era of reform and eventually of democracy. The Cuban army agreed to withdraw from Angola and could do so with its head held high after its success against the previously-invincible South African army. In the United States, the hardline regime of Ronald Reagan gave way to the slightly less doctrinaire one of George Bush, the old spymaster who had withdrawn the CIA from Angola in 1976. The Soviet Union disbanded its empire in Europe and surrendered most of its interests in Africa.

The plethora of changes that affected Africa at the end of the 1980s brought real hope that without foreign irritants and interventions peace might at last be a possible option for Angola. The end of the Reagan era, the winding down of the Soviet Union and the implementation of a peace treaty between South Africa and Cuba, still did not bring peace, however, and the domestic causes of the Angolan conflict still held sway, even after the Cold War had ended. In June 1989 Mobutu, anxious to win favour with Washington, tried to broker a local peace deal and invited dos Santos and Savimbi to his great palace at Gbadolite—where the war leader from the highlands and the war leader from the city were tricked into meeting for the first time and frigidly shook hands. Seven days later Savimbi's commandos destroyed the Luanda electricity supply and dos Santos's army re-launched its attack on Mavinga, gateway to the rutted bush trails which led to Savimbi's remote frontier encampment at Jamba. The United States felt compelled to re-enter the war with an airlift of weapons to save Savimbi from being ejected by Soviet-equipped forces. Yet, in March 1990, the United States and Russia, meeting face to face at the Namibia independence ceremony in Windhoek, negotiated their own peace terms for the war in the Angolan theatre. A year later, in May 1991, the Angolans themselves finally signed a ceasefire at Bicesse in Portugal. The peace, orchestrated by Portugal with help from the superpowers, was to be monitored by the United Nations, which sent Margaret Anstee to supervise Angola's first-ever democratic election. Down in the Luanda slums the 1991 accord was gratefully known as Margaret's peace.

POWER IN THE NINETIES

When Angola came out of the Cold War in 1991 it was a different country from the one that had emerged from the colonial war. In 1974, the major export had been coffee, efficiently carried by lorry on asphalted highways built for strategic purposes. In 1991, one of the exports which exceeded coffee was scrap metal, quarried from the half a million tonnes of non-ferrous junk attached to the thousands of military and civilian vehicles which had been blown up along Angola's ruined roads during the years of bitter conflict. The graveyard of military vehicles was matched by the graveyard of human victims. Those who had died of hunger, wounds, disease or gunshots were buried and uncounted, but those who survived—maimed, crippled, displaced and unemployed—were all too visible to the agencies which supplied them with basic meals and artificial limbs. The war of destabilisation, begun on the southern plain in the early 1980s, had spread through the highlands and lowlands until it reached the northern frontier. Only the larger urban enclaves of the highlands, and the cities strung along the Atlantic shore, escaped the day-to-day fighting of war. But even the cities had not been spared the rigorous consequences of war, as hundreds of thousands of war victims emerged from the countryside to seek refuge from the trauma which had engulfed all of rural Angola.

It would be too simplistic to say that a southern army had moved through the countryside destroying everything in its path in order that Angola's peasants would be terrified into accepting the rule of Savimbi's UNITA. Much of the success of the southern army had been due to widespread rural disaffection with the MPLA government and the civil war had therefore gone in tandem with the Cold War and the war of destabilisation. The difficulty the MPLA had in gaining and holding the capital city had meant that rural Angola had been neglected. One of the causes of the great uprising of 1977 had been the suggestion that unemployed urban youths should be dispatched to the country as work brigades to pick the unharvested coffee crop. The youths were alarmed at the prospect. Their dignity depended on being sophisticated urbanites who, despite their minimal amount of schooling, had a taste for sharp dressing. To be sent to a countryside full of yokels and wild animals, not to mention magicians and poisonous snakes, would have been a terrifying experience. But the disdain for the countryside was not only a characteristic of school dropouts. It was also the attitude of salaried workers in the city, who contemptuously described the people of the countryside as the 'Bantu', vernacular-speaking rustics quite unlike themselves with their smooth Portuguese manners. The antagonism between the town and the countryside had paved the way for the war of the 1980s to spread like bush fire from neglected province to neglected province. Regional distrust remained a dreadful burden as the nation sought a sustainable peace for the 1990s.

Burdensome though the legacies of war may have been, the eighteen months from May 1991 to September 1992 was the most spectacular period of optimism and freedom that Angola had ever witnessed. Savimbi and his entourage of generals moved down from the highlands and set up their opulent residential quarters in the Miramar district of Luanda, overlooking the palm-fringed bay. Thousands of highland refugees in the coastal cities loaded their meagre possessions on to their heads and set off for the interior to rediscover their villages and seek out their surviving relatives. International observers poured into the country to marvel at the peace process, at the new economic opportunities, at the adoption by Africa of a democratic procedure to settle differences. The political parties hired public relations firms to run sophisticated election campaigns on television, and the political leaders drew large crowds of cheering supporters to their rallies in the country's town squares.

The UN representative, Margaret Anstee, flew everywhere in decrepit aircraft, parsimoniously funded by the United States and courageously flown by intrepid Russians. She endeavoured to harmonise the two partisan armies that were to be partly demobilised and partly integrated into a single national force. However, the euphoria of peace made supervised demobilisation virtually impossible. The government conscripts vanished into civilian society while the opposition ones were hidden away in provincial redoubts in case the 'leader' should require their services later. The most obsolete of UNITA weapons were handed over to teams of international inspectors but its sophisticated military equipment was cached away in arms dumps strategically chosen around the provinces by Savimbi himself. On the government side a new security force, dressed in a sinister black costume, was armed and trained for action against civilians, should circumstances lead to urban guerrilla warfare after the election. While people danced in the streets and vowed that war should never return, the pragmatic power-brokers on both sides made contingency plans for just such a scenario.

When, after a year of blissful peace, Angola finally went to the polls to elect a parliament and a new president the voters divided cleanly and clearly between the town and the countryside. The towns had more or less survived the war of destabilisation on the basis of imported food paid for with oil revenue and supplemented by NGOs, international aid agencies from across the world. The countryside had done much less well, suffering a sharp loss of earning capacity following the collapse of the colonial infrastructure and the total failure of the Soviet-style economy to create any rural network which could purchase produce from the farmers or distribute to them essential commodities such as soap, salt and cooking oil.

On 12 September, the countryside voted for the opposition, for Savimbi and for change, while the towns voted for the government, for preferential economic treatment and for armed protection from the hungry raiders out in the rural areas. Some modification of the voting pattern was affected by historic or ethnic loyalties, but the UNITA leaders were greatly dismayed to find that a number of urban Ovimbundu in both highland towns and coastal cities had failed to support them in their election bid and had adopted the national urban strategy of voting for the MPLA. Even more dismaying to Savimbi was the betrayal of the United States which, to all intents and purposes, had promised him that if he stopped the war and went to the polls he would undoubtedly win the election. When Savimbi failed to win, by a clear margin of two to one in the parliamentary election and by a decisive if not absolute majority vote for dos Santos in the presidential election, he immediately went back to war. Western-style democracy had no consolation prize for coming second in its first-past-the-post, winner-takes-all, system of voting.

The civil war which broke out in Angola on 12 November was quite different from the colonial war of 1961, from the interventionist war of 1975, and from the destabilisation war of the 1980s. All three of those earlier conflicts had been fought in the countryside and had only indirectly affected the towns. The war of 1992 concerned the cities themselves. The defeated opposition could do its electoral sums as effectively as any United Nations observer and recognised that it was in the urban heartland that it had lost its electoral bid for power. UNITA therefore set out to destroy those cities. It also set out to destroy a government which had proved itself totally unwilling to make any concessions to its opponents by offering a significant post-war redistribution of the economic spoils. The civil war of 1992 initially broke out in Luanda itself, triggered by UNITA's intransigent rejection of the election result but launched and pursued with vigour by the government. Within days the city had been violently cleansed of politicians unwilling to abandon Savimbi's cause. Worse still, the urban militias were given licence to settle old scores by attacking townspeople who were thought to have voted for UNITA. Savimbi refused any compromise solutions, recognising that the presidential system, so attractive to him when he thought he could win, gave all power to the president rather than to the prime minister's cabinet or to the elected parliament. He calculated that his only hope of gaining the power which he had craved almost pathologically since his student days in Switzerland was to seize it through the barrel of a gun.

The post-1992 conflict brought even heavier weapons to Angola than the ones used in previous wars and the big towns of the interior—Huambo, Kuito, Malange—were severely damaged while their populations almost starved. Savimbi no longer had support from South Africa but he did have access to relatively cheap second-hand weapons bought, ironically enough, from the countries of the former Soviet empire. He discovered in particular that the huge republic of Ukraine, with fifty million people struggling to make a living, was willing to sell redundant military equipment and had an air fleet with the capacity to fly weapons, ammunition and fuel oil to makeshift airstrips hidden in the orchard savannah of eastern Angola. Payment for the new UNITA arsenal came from the digging of diamonds extracted from rivers of the interior and flown out through cloak-and-dagger channels to Antwerp, the capital of the diamond-cutting world. In the expensive business of modern war, fought with technologically-sophisticated weapons requiring imported ammunition, UNITA recognised that its diamond wealth was puny when compared to the much greater oil wealth of the Angolan government. In 1993, UNITA attacked the on-shore oil installations at the mouth of the Congo river, either to deprive the MPLA of revenue or to capture an oil supply of its own. The oil port of Soyo temporarily fell into opposition hands but ruptured storage tanks only caused massive pollution while the oil platforms on the ocean horizon were never at risk from military activity. By 1994, Savimbi was forced to recognise that his early military successes had exhausted his resources and could bring no immediate political victory. For long-term survival he needed to seek a truce on the best terms he could extract.

Ending the civil war proved a particularly intractable diplomatic challenge. Margaret Anstee, having orchestrated the election with aplomb, negotiated valiantly to win the peace as well, but it was not until late in 1994 that a new United Nations peacemaker, Alioune Beye, eventually secured an agreement in Lusaka. The accord generated none of the euphoria that had accompanied the peace signed at Bicesse in 1991. Savimbi showed his contempt for the unpalatable necessity of suspending hostilities by staying away from the signing ceremony. He had no desire to come face-to-face with dos Santos who had now outwitted him both in an election, which had been patently free and fair, and in prolonged siege warfare, which had given him control of the highland cities which Savimbi deemed to be his birthright. Savimbi retired to the small highland town of Bailundu to plot future political or military developments. Dos Santos set about consolidating his personal power by both political and financial means. Savimbi evaded all forms of peace monitoring by the United Nations and refused to demobilise under the terms of the Lusaka Protocol. Dos Santos basked in the international acclaim of being a peacemaker who now enjoyed almost unlimited western support for his government. But war remained on the horizon and each rival side tried to provoke the other into being the first to break the Lusaka ceasefire and incur international opprobrium for returning Angola to civil strife. In the highlands the cold hostility, neither war nor peace, lasted for four years. Meanwhile, down on the coast, civil society had been changing.

The end of the Cold War, and the signing of the 1991 peace at Bicesse in Portugal, had brought important changes to the status and role of religion in Angola. For fifteen years after independence the state, and its nominally Marxist-Leninist government, had ignored the churches. Members of the Luanda political elite who had remained affiliated to religious congregations had used great discretion, almost secrecy, when attending services. Even the Methodist church, in which several eminent leaders including Agostinho

Neto himself had been nurtured, received only minimal official toleration. In the 1990s the government moved away from its hostility and an attitude of toleration gradually gave way to an actual wooing of the churches by the presidency. Although ninety per cent of Angolans now belonged to a church, the political influence of the congregations remained weak and the churches proved incapable of preventing further outbreaks of war. No church actively advocated war, but none was openly willing to condemn the concept of 'peace through victory' and church members were trapped by the loss of liberty and human rights which scarred Angolan society throughout the 1990s.

The largest and most united was the Catholic church which, although it had been historically split between foreign missionaries who stood up for black colonial subjects, and Portuguese bishops who were closely linked to the white colonial state, was nevertheless firmly structured around a single authoritative voice which depended on legitimation by Rome. The Protestant congregations, although riven by contrasts of ideology, pastoral tradition and ethnicity, might have expected to benefit from a folk memory of Catholics as supporters of empire and Protestants as the anti-imperialists who had given succour to the liberation movements. Any such legacy of sympathy between nationalists and Protestants was eroded after independence by growing government conservatism; and the old colonial tradition of treating the Catholic hierarchy as the natural ally of government was revived at the end of the Cold War. The Luanda elite, attempting to re-build the country's traditions of power and subordination, approved of the Catholic church's authoritarian hierarchy. Traditional Protestants, and the old independent Kimbanguist and Tokoist churches, were left fragmented on the margins of society. It was a new Pentecostal religious fervour which sprung up to provide a spiritual home for the victims of war who crowded once more into the coastal cities after the abortive peace of 1991.

Once the pan-national Catholic church had overcome the stigma of being a reactionary legacy of the colonial era, its influence began to grow and it became an attractive symbol of power for those who wanted to be associated with the elite. Catholics also began to match Protestants in the dispensing of charity to the dispossessed and in listening to the demands of the voiceless, thus usurping the role of the Methodists' heroic status as defenders of the oppressed—and who were now perceived by some to have been the traditional partners of an uncaring MPLA government. The standing of the Methodists was further diminished when the government presumed on Methodist loyalty and gave them fewer state resources with which to alleviate poverty than it gave to the Catholic church, whose endorsement it now solicited in the game of power politics. As the government wooing of the churches progressed, Christians were openly welcomed into membership of the once-atheist ruling party, and dos Santos appointed church leaders to his privy council. But coopting church leaders into the establishment weakened rather than strengthened the congregations. In Angola no peace and justice commissions were set up, no truth and reconciliation was attempted, no rehabilitation of social relations between former enemies took place and the state remained in full control of daily life.

Members of the churches who wanted their lives to be independent of the politics of clientelism found that they could not subsist without compromise. Non-smoking and teetotal Protestants, who had been morally outraged by the government issue of rations of alcohol and tobacco, could not refuse to receive their allocation since it was only by selling perquisites on the parallel market for a hundred times their posted price that state-sector employees could realise the value of their salary substitute and buy the real necessities of life. The impotence of dependency reached down through the ranks of society and turned everyone into a vassal of the MPLA. While church members were becoming dependent on the party, the party began using the church as a symbol of its own power and prestige. Eduardo dos Santos, the Soviet-trained technocrat, chose to have his son baptised as a Catholic and invited the Pope himself to celebrate mass for the millions in a Luanda football stadium. During the war-torn 1990s, this cohabitation between church and state handicapped the efforts of the churches to find a means of satisfying the intense popular desire for peace. It was not until the middle of 2000 that the churches finally cooperated, regardless of the wrath of dos Santos and his government, and brought the people out on to the streets of the capital to demonstrate for peace. An inter-church congress on the rights and wrongs of entering into dialogue with the 'enemy', rather than allow the war to drag on without end, had finally broken the silence of fear and launched an open public debate about Angola's future.

One political initiative designed to prevent a renewed outbreak of war occurred in 1997. As part of the search for a policy which would defuse the anger of the opposition and minimise the danger of a return to war the president created a 'government of national unity'. In it a limited number of posts were offered to those in the southern elite who were willing to leave the highlands and join the ruling circle in Luanda. Some seventy UNITA members who had been elected to parliament in September 1992 moved to the comforts of the city and took their seats in the legislative chamber while seven of their leaders became ministers and vice-ministers in a cabinet whose padded payroll also included sixty MPLA members. This low-key concession to power sharing with the opposition was silently undermined, however, by the continuing rise of presidential authority.

One of the most potent effects of the failure of the 1992 United Nations election and of the catastrophic war which had followed, was the decision by President dos Santos to concentrate more power in his own hands. From being a single-party state with a disaffected opposition thinly scattered in the provinces and abroad, Angola became a presidential state in which power emanated from the palace. Dos Santos, like Louis XIV, built his palace on the outskirts of the restless city, safely removed from the fickle mob, and it was there that political decisions began to bypass government ministries, party cells and state bureaucracies. Angola was no longer a 'people's republic' and the president's huge well-fortified presidential complex, known as the Futungo, ostentatiously resembled the extravagant luxury of Mobutu in Zaire rather than the austere highland hideouts in which Savimbi dodged from night to night to avoid capture or assassination by his many personal foes and political enemies. But for all the gilding on his cage, dos Santos was almost as much a prisoner as Savimbi and, after 1992, he virtually ceased to travel around the country. Even when he visited his own capital city he did so with a heavily-armed guard. The caged president orchestrated a personality cult leading to extravagant adulation which constantly emphasised the image of the man of peace, in shining contrast to Savimbi, the warmonger. The presidential court even suggested that dos Santos, who had been at war with his own people for twenty years, be nominated for the Nobel Peace Prize!

In 1998 the presidential personality cult reached a climax during a week-long birthday party for dos Santos. He ceremonially visited the restoration work on the seventeenth century chapel of Our Lady of Muxima, launched a regatta and a parachuting competition, awarded new costumes to paramount chiefs, unveiled a commemorative postage stamp and opened an exhibition on 'protecting the sea and its riches'—thereby showing his concern for ecology and the environment while many of his human subjects went on starving. The horrific medical plight to which the country had been reduced gave the president an opportunity to visit favoured hospitals bearing gifts and seeking loyalty, call on a leper colony and a camp for displaced children, and express solidarity with those who campaigned against polio or sustained the victims of AIDS. An American-style fund-raising dinner was devoted to the rehabilitation of the victims of land mines which his government had probably done as much as Savimbi's opposition to scatter over the country. Amidst the hopeless despair which presaged an imminent return to war, the week-long festivities ended with gymnastics, sporting competitions, the cutting of a birthday cake and the award of a Brazilian honorary degree to the president.

The bread-and-circus fantasies were an attempt to overcome rising popular disaffection and an increasing fear of police surveillance. As the president became all powerful even the Luanda elders of the MPLA found themselves marginalised—as was demonstrated when a prime minister from the prestigious van Dunem Creole family was humiliatingly made to carry the blame for government unpopularity. But while the people on the street saw the junketing and partying as an extravagant display of scandal and corruption in high places, the establishment in the bureaucracies saw hero-worship as the necessary gateway to power and status on the fringes of the court. As money poured into the presidency without let or hindrance, the politics of clientelism became ever more pronounced and success depended on largesse.

The development of the untamed market economy in Angola had serious consequences for the middle class. The purchasing power of state salaries dwindled with rampant inflation and bureaucrats, like the displaced poor of the shanties, were driven to live by their wits. Economic insecurity led to corruption, violence and crime, touching the lives of all sectors of society. As in many other parts of Africa, public servants had no choice but to spend their time and energy working in the private sector while retaining their formal jobs in the public sector to ensure for themselves structural positions and state privileges rather than monetary or material reward. As public services withered away only those who offered bribe money, preferably in dollars, could obtain the necessary medicines or documents to survive. Under these circumstances clientelism became at least as necessary as it had been under the Soviet-style economic system but the *nomenklatura*, the privileged elite, had to find new ways of obtaining patrons—since the bourgeois cost of living was comparable to that in Tokyo and yet salaries ranged from an utterly derisory $ 200 to a merely inadequate $ 2,000 per month. Members of parliament, police officers, senior civil servants and army commanders all came to depend on the president in person and he had a pocket deep enough to reward those whom he favoured with an annual 'Christmas bonus' of $ 25,000, the equivalent to ten years' salary for an ordinary government employee.

The sweetening of those on whom the regime depended was matched by the crushing of those who might dissent. During the year 1998, as the expectation that a new civil war would break out became a certainty, the presidential office increased the range of organisations which became dependent on its bounty and were therefore trapped into silent complicity. Benefactions were used both to minimise grassroot protest from the hungry slums which feared a return to war and to manipulate the factionalism which kept the traditional cadres of the MPLA in disputatious disarray. One of the small institutionalised steps on the road to totalitarian presidentialism in Angola had been the creation in 1996 of the Eduardo dos Santos Foundation. The Foundation was designed to implement a widespread policy of privatising the assets of the state so that they could be used to consolidate the power of the president rather than meet any of the more objectively assessed political needs of the nation. The ideology was far from new but in Angola, however, the process was masked by rather more opaque layers of secrecy and cloaked in even more dubious forms of legality than in other countries.

Privatisation policies were politically motivated and designed to prevent the overthrow of the government either by democratic vote, in the 'north', or by mob restlessness in the 'south'. In Angola, the president's patrimonial Foundation refined the politics of patronage by a further concentration of power in the Futungo palace. The funds of the Foundation derived from a presidential 'tax' which mirrored the state taxes levied on international trading firms, petroleum prospectors, construction companies, banking corporations as well as on the smaller domestic businesses. Having creamed off a top slice of the nation's assets, the presidential Foundation went into competition with the state to provide services that had ceased to be available through official channels but which now became privately accessible to the president's clients. A private presidential university was set up to compete with the underfunded national university named after Agostinho Neto—which subsequently lost both foreign finance and foreign personnel. Even greater 'finesse' was shown in the case of a home for abandoned children at Cacuaco for which the Foundation gained public credit with a small subsidy while the core funding was siphoned out of the city council budget. Some of the largesse reached the provinces, but the presidential bounty was predominantly spent in the capital city, the political base with the greatest capacity to make or unmake presidents in the event of revolution.

Manipulating power by wielding carrots and sticks to the elite was rather easier than winning support among the urban masses, for whom poverty was the perceived consequence of the widespread corruption at the highest levels. It became necessary to generate 'spontaneous' outburst of popular enthusiasm for the president. The *sans-culottes* of Sambizanga— the black quarter in which the president had been born but where Nito Alves had mounted his 1977 challenge to the government of Agostinho Neto— were persuaded to come down into the asphalt town and demonstrate their loyalty to the president. The 'spontaneity' had been so well prepared that the chanting crowds wore specially prepared T-shirts bearing pictures of 'their' president. The mobilisation of the dispossessed rapidly grew more sour, however, when the crowds were permitted to search out approved public enemies against whom to vent their rage over their shabby poverty.

The first permitted target was an ethnic one and the demonstrators chanted anti-Ovimbundu slogans as they intimidated anyone who had come down from the highland and might have UNITA sympathies. In order to separate out the faithful from the faithless it was suggested in parliament that identity cards should be issued naming the 'tribe' of each bearer but this calamitous recipe for urban warfare was not followed up. By 1996 the orchestrated politics of violence were extended to include xenophobia and crowds were permitted to attack anyone who might be branded as 'foreign'. A government campaign against aliens was given the chilling codename 'Cancer Two' and the search for enemies was directed not only at Africans, particularly 'Zaireans', but also at the communities of Lebanese and other Asian businessmen whom the population saw as exploiters and whom the president's men now wished to supplant in the lucrative import-export sector of wholesale trade.

While corruption was being orchestrated by politicians down in the city, the highlands were getting ready for war. By the end of 1996 it was estimated that Savimbi's war chest had grown to two billion US dollars and that he had recently been able to buy another 45 tonnes of weapons flown in from Bulgaria to the two mile long airstrip which UNITA conscripts had built near Bailundu. At this time no fewer than 20,000 of Angola's government troops were being tied down in Cabinda where three armed secessionist movements were threatening the security of the oil wells. Each movement had the potential to secure active support from Angola's northern neighbours, Congo Brazzaville and Zaire, either of which would gladly have conquered Cabinda. On 17 May 1997, this foreign situation suddenly altered when Mobutu's dictatorship collapsed in Zaire and a new military dictator, with a shadowy past in the Lumumba era, took control of Kinshasa and entered into an alliance with the dos Santos government in Luanda. As a result of Laurent Kabila's success in Zaire, now restored to the old name of Congo, some 10,000 of Savimbi's troops, who had been sheltered by Mobutu in preparation for a new Angolan civil war, were temporarily stranded and some had to seek refuge in Congo Brazzaville.

Within weeks of the Kinshasa revolution a similar revolution broke out in Brazzaville followed by four months of a peculiarly savage civil war in which 10,000 people were killed. To ensure an outcome that did not threaten its own security, Angola sent an army into Congo Brazzaville from Cabinda to protect the oil port of Pointe Noire and to enable former President Sassou-Nguesso, with the tacit connivance of oil interests in both France and the United States, to overthrow the elected government. In Brazzaville the logistics of civil war took on new dimensions as Croatian mercenaries fought on one side and Uzbekistan supplied transport planes to the other. The turbulence in Kinshasa and Brazzaville disrupted UNITA's war preparation but during 1998 Savimbi retrieved his scattered units, some highly-trained members of Mobutu's fleeing presidential guard, and mobilised a force of 15,000 combat-ready men and 10,000 auxiliary conscripts. He also recruited some of the genocidal Rwanda militants who were hiding in Congo Kinshasa, some orphaned military companies which had lost out in the war in Brazzaville, and some Serbian mercenaries. He had meanwhile also commissioned Morocco to train a new officer corps for UNITA in order to replace those generals who had been seduced into moving to Luanda by reputedly being offered three million US dollars a head to set up a renegade UNITA party in the city.

The dos Santos government prepared for war as actively as did UNITA in the months which followed the apparently accidental death of the United Nations peacekeeper, Alioune Beye, on 18 June 1998. Thirty battalions were deployed around the country and an air force equipped with Brazilian jets fighters was put on standby at Catumbela airbase ready to bomb the highlands. Spanish counter-insurgency specialists retrained 25,000 commandos and special police units who might be needed to repress civilian unrest once the war was launched. The politicians hoped definitively and quickly to drive UNITA's forces out of the country and across the border into Zambia. The generals aspired to capture the Kwango valley where the most plentiful alluvial diamonds were to be found.

In the last weeks of 1998 dos Santos's army was persuaded that any further delay in attacking UNITA would be strategically foolish. The government was right in thinking that Savimbi was arming heavily but it was too late to strike the winning blow and government forces, inappropriately armed and inadequately trained, were fiercely repulsed when they tried to take the highlands. During the first half of 1999 UNITA held the military advantage and even its reluctant recruits, kidnapped from nominally 'friendly' Ovimbundu territory, fought for their lives, terrified by their officers' threats that if they lost the war the *mestiços* of the city would pack them off as despised farm labour to the forests of the lowlands.

The new civil war of 1998 was the most cruel yet seen in Angola and UNITA adopted a policy of starving the cities, notably Malange and Kuito, by refusing to allow humanitarian food supplies to be flown in by the international agencies. It hoped either that the Angolan government would be forced by world opinion to stop a war that was killing civilians, or that the civilians on the coast would rise up in revolt as new waves of displaced persons descended on them from the shattered highland towns. But the world, fascinated by the potential wealth of Angola's oil wells, did not force the government back to the negotiating table and the civilians did not risk any public protest when their streets were patrolled by black-clad security police.

The depraved conflict between a corrupt government mesmerised by wealth and an inhuman opposition obsessed by power carried on throughout 1999 and into 2000. In successful engagements UNITA captured some government weapons, but a shortage of fuel caused it serious logistical difficulties. One solution to the fuel crisis was to buy diesel covertly from the enemy camp. Personal relations across the divide between the two warring elites were much closer than ethnic or ideological enmity. Successive peace negotiations had accustomed the rival delegations to making deals while drinking together in expensive night clubs staffed by the seductive hostesses of Abidjan or Lusaka. But for UNITA to buy fuel on a black market run by enemy officers required a large supply of fresh diamonds. In the late 1990s, during the second civil war, it was loosely estimated that UNITA may have controlled as many as 100,000 men and women who were forced to dig the cold alluvial mud of the Kwango river for increasingly meagre returns on ever smaller gems.

Although Angola's diamonds only earned about one-tenth of the seven billion US dollars a year derived from oil, a significant proportion of them fell into UNITA hands and bypassed official channels licensed by De Beers. Diamond revenues enabled UNITA to continue its military operations after Cold War funding was cut off. With diamond money as an inducement, UNITA leaders were able to win support from French client regimes in Burkina Faso, Togo and Côte d'Ivoire, all of which provided them with travel documents and unauthorised sales papers for diamonds. By the year 2000 so much blood money had become involved in the sale of Angola's diamonds that the United Nations attempted to impose penalties on nations which facilitated the diamonds-for-weapons trade. At the same time, De Beers feared that if it did not stop the diamond cutters and polishers from buying bargain-price diamonds from war zones the world might mount a humanitarian campaign against diamond jewellery similar to the one which animal rights activists had used to make the wearing of furs socially unacceptable in Western society.

Despite all the protests, guns were still flown into highland Angola under cover of darkness, carried by mercenary planes using unsupervised airstrips in countries which were rewarded for closing their eyes. The crisis in diamond sales from Angola only became acute when it was realised that the government supply of 'legitimate' diamonds, dug from a deep-level kimberlite mine, was being enhanced by 'conflict diamonds', which freewheeling generals were buying from their cash-strapped opponents and legitimising with forged certificates of provenance. President dos Santos, whose daughter held a diamond dealing licence, had to act to make sure that Angolan diamond documents were above any suspicion of forgery—which might have closed down the industry on both sides of the war zone. As oil prices fell temporarily to ten dollars a barrel, the government was almost as anxious as UNITA to protect diamond export revenues. Although the MPLA had written off four billion of its eleven billion dollars of old war debts it had been forced to buy hugely expensive new weapons with which to conduct the war of 1998 just at the time when oil prices were dropping. When oil prices recovered the military tide turned. UNITA lost its highland headquarters in Bailundu and the fighting was once more concentrated in the dry, empty, plains on the borders of Zambia through which Savimbi moved in his mobile command caravan visiting his shifting guerrilla camps.

With ever-increasing oil prices the international scramble to obtain a stake in the Angolan petroleum industry reached gold-rush proportions. The giant exploration companies, those of Britain and France to the fore, calculated that the North Sea and Alaskan fields would run out of viable new reserves in the new century and that it was in the ultra-deep concessions off Angola's Atlantic coast that the best prospects lay. Although the technology had not yet been perfected to drill oil from a seabed two miles deep—with underwater stations serviced by automated submarines and with flexible extraction pipes attached to surface platforms out in the ocean—the companies were nonetheless willing to make down payments of $ 300 million for the right to explore each concession block in Angola's deep waters. In the early months of the new millennium Luanda's 'jungle capitalism', to use Tony Hodges' felicitous phrase, was once more awash with money.

The benefits, however, did not trickle down to the people. For them, school teachers continued to be outnumbered by soldiers in a ratio of two-and-a-half to one, while the elite spent one-fifth of the national education budget to educate its children abroad. Voices of complaint, including that of the editor of the one significant independent newspaper in Luanda, were silenced, apparently by MPLA death squads—much as journalists had previously been murdered in Huambo by UNITA. In the countryside, UNITA's 'totalitarian savagery' continued unabated with the kidnapping of all available children for military duty and the burning of dissidents after accusations of witchcraft. While the slaughter went on in the highlands, members of Savimbi's own family sheltered in a haven of exile controversially afforded to them by the president of Togo. In Luanda, oil continued to be the fuel which inflamed civil war as it had been since the dawn of independence on 11 November 1975.

By the year 2000 Angola had come full circle in the 31 years since the death of Salazar. The civil wars of the 1990s, like the colonial wars of the 1960s, had reached a stalemate. The lives of many people were disrupted but no solution to the military confrontation between the central government and the guerrillas on the periphery seemed in sight. The economy had changed from a dependence on the unpredictable price of coffee to a dependence on the equally-fluctuating price of petroleum. In neither case was the industrial sector of production significantly able to cushion the country against the uncertainties of the world market. Politics in 2000 was as unresponsive to public opinion as it had been in 1969, though the dictator who balanced the powers of the several factions of the property-owning class was now a member of the home-grown Luso-African elite of Luanda rather than of Portugal's imperially-oriented *haute bourgeoisie*.

Now, as then, the army kept an eye on political decision making and a finger in the economic pie. Senior officers in the colonial army of the 1960s built their wealth on a black market underpinned by coffee exports and on currency speculation—from which they invested in real estate in Lisbon. In the national army of the 1990s, officers dominated the now privatised trade in diamonds and invested their wealth in the Luanda housing market, earning large fortunes as landlords to the foreign employees of oil companies, diplomatic missions and international aid agencies. Wealth was as sharply polarised in as it had been in late-colonial times but the city slums had grown from half a million established members of the *musseque* families to two million displaced transients camped on the Luanda coastal plain. The colonial class of 300,000 privileged and semi-privileged expatriates had been replaced by a similar number of black Portuguese-speaking Angolans who retained many of the old colonial attitudes of social and moral superiority and who worshipped in the same Catholic churches that had sustained Salazar's brand of authoritarianism. On the streets the Angolan press of the 1990s was as circumscribed in its news and opinions as the censored fascist press of the 1960s had been and Angolan citizens who held political views were as wary of the political police as colonial subjects had been when trying to evade Salazar's secret agents. Freedom of opinion and of opportunity, which had been stifled in the days of empire, proved virtually incapable of resuscitation in the era of liberation.

5

MOZAMBIQUE

Malyn Newitt

INTRODUCTION

Mozambique has seldom been out of the news since it achieved its independence in 1975. At different times it has been in the vanguard of progressive reformist African states, it has hit the world headlines with drought and flood disasters and it has experienced a civil war which has given the world the first clear example of what happens when a modern state disintegrates. It was, moreover, a civil war which provided horrific incidents of systematically orchestrated terror while defying contemporary analysis by being largely free of ideology or competition for power between well-defined and easily-understood groups.

This chapter will examine a number of highly controversial issues which have marked Mozambique since independence and which have meant that the experiences of this country have often commanded centre stage in academic and political debate. Among the questions that have divided commentators are: the inheritance of the colonial period and of the war of independence; the problems caused by Portugal's rapid and unplanned transfer of power; the economic and social consequences of the policies of the Frente da Libertação de Moçambique (FRELIMO) in the immediate post-independence period; the internal and external causes of destabilisation and civil war; the character and evolution of RENAMO and the explanations for political violence in Mozambique; the consequences of the disintegration of the state; the peace process and the nature of international intervention in Mozambique's affairs; and whether the post-war reconstruction of Mozambique after 1994 should be seen as a model for the success of the IMF and World Bank policies or whether it is an example of the undermining of the effective independence of states that follow the IMF line.

THE COLONIAL INHERITANCE AND THE WAR OF INDEPENDENCE

To understand what happened to Mozambique after independence certain key factors relating to the country's geography and to its socio-economic development during the colonial era have to be described.[1] Mozambique stretches along nearly eighteen hundred kilometres of the coast of eastern Africa but the Portuguese never built a communications system linking the south with the north and effective contact only existed between the coastal cities which communicated with each other by sea and later by air. The isolation of the various regions from each other was accentuated by the location of the capital city in the extreme south in a spit of land that is virtually an enclave in South Africa and in most respects belongs to the communications system and economic structure of that country.

Mozambique is crossed horizontally by rivers that flow from the central African highlands creating natural corridors of settlement and penetration all of which lead from the sea inland to the plateau. The country is thus divided into horizontally-stratified regions which throughout its history have repeatedly formed the matrix within which different political regimes have competed. The Zambesi valley with its flood plain and wide escarpment of low veldt, reaching fifty miles either side of the river, has acted like an inward extension of the sea, allowing the cultures and commerce of the Indian Ocean coast to penetrate 400 kilometres inland while helping to perpetuate cultural divisions between the matrilineal peoples to the north of the river and the patrilineal peoples to the south.

The ethnic history of Mozambique is complex. At the level of what David Beach called 'the little society', upwards of twenty different languages are spoken and society is organised in numerous small lineage-based chieftaincies.[2] Since 1500 various groups have established their overrule in large areas of the country—Swahili sheiks on the coasts and islands as well as on the lower reaches of the river valleys, Maravi chiefs over much of the northern interior, the cattle-owning Shona-Karanga over the region between the Zambesi and the Sabi, Afro-Portuguese warlords in the Zambesi valley, and the militarised chieftaincies of the Landins and the Nguni dominating the south. Some of these political systems lasted a long time but they never modified the basic structures of the 'little society' and could be blown away by disasters such as drought and famine or by the invasion of better-organised militarised groups from outside.

---

[1]For the history of Mozambique see Aurélio Rocha, Carlos Serra and David Hedges, *História de Moçambique*, 3 vols (Maputo: Cadernos Tempo, 1983); Malyn Newitt, *A History of Mozambique* (London: Hurst & Co., 1995).

[2]David Beach, *The Shona and Zimbabwe, 900–1850* (London: Heinemann, 1980), p. 89.

In the immediate precolonial period dating from the middle of the nineteenth century the country was dominated by three powerful and expanding cultural and political systems; the Islamic expansion north of the Zambesi carried by the Yao and the coastal Swahili and underpinned by the slave trade; the movement of the Afro-Portuguese out of the Zambesi valley in search of slaves, ivory and land; and the conquest of much of the area south of the Zambesi by the Gaza state bringing with it an overlay of Nguni military, cattle-owning culture. Although these established a kind of cultural hegemony that appeared to divide the country roughly into three zones, there were always underlying survivals of past regimes and older cultures which made Mozambique a palimpsest, resisting simple description.

The colonial regime established by the Portuguese, while reflecting to some extent the tripartite division of the country, caused further fragmentation. Two charter companies, the Niassa Company and the Mozambique Company, ruled the areas north of the Lurio and between the Sabi and the Zambesi in largely autonomous manner until 1929 and 1941 respectively. A central area corresponding roughly with the Zambesi valley and the region controlled by the Afro-Portuguese since the seventeenth century was divided between plantation companies which were also largely autonomous. Finally, three areas (inland of Mozambique Island, Tete and Barue, and the whole region south of the Sabi) were placed under direct government control and were open for labour recruitment by Mozambican and British economic concerns alike.

The colonial economy of Mozambique was based on tropical staples which were produced either by plantation companies for whom peasants had to labour in order to pay off their tax obligation, or by peasant farmers working their own lands who had to sell their produce to the companies. Under this regime Mozambique became a major exporter of copra, sugar, tea, cotton, rice and cashew. At the same time a pattern of labour migration had developed. Although the pole of attraction was the Rand mines which were allowed to recruit directly in Mozambique south of the Sabi, clandestine migrants from the north often made their way south in stages, working on Rhodesian farms or as semi-servile labour in Nyasaland on the way. Labour migrants came from all regions of Mozambique but for obvious reasons were most common in the border areas and all the neighbouring countries had large communities made up of people of Mozambican origin.

Mozambique also provided transport services and port facilities for its neighbours. Railways were built to link Rhodesia and Nyasaland to the port of Beira and the Rand to Delagoa Bay (Lourenço Marques). Later a line was built to link independent Malawi (formerly Nyasaland) to the port of Nacala in the north. The lines, and the roads and pipelines that were built alongside them, tended to etch the horizontal divisions of the country more deeply, so that the various regions of Mozambique became more closely linked with their neighbours than with other parts of Mozambique. Most white settlement took place in and around the coastal cities and it was here that the modern sector of the Mozambican economy developed. Railway and port installations gave rise to service workshops and a range of skilled occupations. To these were added tourism which became important after the Second World War, and secondary industry and market gardening designed to supply the city populations with items for consumption. Heavy industry was limited to the hydroelectric systems built on the upper reaches of the main rivers and the oil refinery in Lourenço Marques. The modern sector of the economy was supported by an educational structure only in the cities and it was in and around Lourenço Marques, and to a lesser extent Beira, that an educated class of Africans emerged, many of them owing their schooling opportunities to the Protestant Swiss missions that were established in the south. Although early in the century African and *mestiço* intellectuals had established their own associations and newspapers, after 1930 these were all tightly controlled by the government, as were workers' associations. Similar restrictions were applied to the white population which began to grow rapidly as a result of government-sponsored immigration in the 1950s. For them as for the Africans and *mestiços* independent political organisation and freedom of expression within the country was impossible. The country was ruled by a centralised authoritarian bureaucracy with a strong tradition of economic planning but with little devolution of power to local authorities and low levels of participation by the population in the processes of government.

Portuguese colonial rule is often held to have been responsible for leaving Mozambique uniformly backward and underdeveloped. However, in many respects Mozambique received a favourable economic legacy from its colonial rulers. Compared with many African countries, Mozambique in 1975 had a relatively diversified economy with strong potential for exports and for earning foreign exchange. It inherited a well-developed system of hydroelectric power and had a range of secondary consumer industries. Although the level of literacy and skills among the peasants and plantation workers was very low, Mozambique did have a substantial and growing urban bourgeoisie and a class of African and white small landowners who were increasing in prosperity. Structurally the economy of Mozambique was closely integrated with that of its immediate neighbours and was able to benefit from the provision of services as well as from inward flows of investment.

The war of independence which began in 1964 was not really concluded by the peace signed between FRELIMO and Portugal in September 1974 but merged with the outbreak of civil strife to create a continuous history of political violence and social breakdown which was to last until 1992.[3]

Until 1964 Mozambique had been remarkably peaceful. Apart from arrests of individual dissidents carried out by the PIDE (the Portuguese secret police) and the much publicised massacre of demonstrators at Mueda in June 1960, there had been relatively little to record in the way of strikes, riots or rural insurrection since before the Second World War. The Portuguese colonial state had functioned with reasonable efficiency, its activities shaped by the economic development plans, the first of which had been drawn up in 1937, and which covered the post-war period from 1953 to 1967. The rising tide of African nationalism had little initial impact inside Mozambique but did affect Tanzania, Zambia and Malawi where Mozambican migrant workers formed embryo political movements in the late 1950s. In 1962 these movements were hastily brought together in Dar es Salaam under the auspices of Julius Nyerere to form a single party called FRELIMO.

For the first five years of its existence FRELIMO was torn by increasingly bitter internal quarrels. Although these feuds were later described in ideological terms which reflected the political perceptions of the Cold War era, at the time they were fuelled by a variety of factors ranging from the ethnic hostility between the northern Makonde and the 'southerners', to personal rivalries which resulted in successive bids to lead the movement by Nkavandame, Mondlane, Simango and Machel, and to disagreements over the strategy and tactics to be adopted in the struggle with Portugal. The internal feuding led to outbreaks of violence in Dar es Salaam and to the assassination of Eduardo Mondlane in 1969. During this period the nationalist military campaign was largely confined to the extreme north and to the shore of Lake Nyasa areas and FRELIMO made no impact in the coastal cities and lowlands or the Zambesi valley where the vast majority of the people lived. Nor, surprisingly in view of the fact that the leadership came from the south, did the party appear to make much headway in the region south of the Sabi whence the majority of the Rand's migrant workers were drawn.

After 1969 the party put its feuding behind it at the price of expelling many of its earlier supporters. From that time FRELIMO, in marked contrast to the MPLA in Angola, remained united and remarkably cohesive

---

[3]The best general account of the war is undoubtedly T.H. Henriksen *Revolution and Counterrevolution: Mozambique's War of Independence 1964–1974* (Westport CT: Greenwood, 1983).

first under the leadership of Samora Machel and then, after his death in 1986, under Joaquim Chissano, with exceptionally few public quarrels, internal struggles for power or breakaway groups. After 1969 its leadership and much of its effective membership was drawn from the southern part of the country, and more specifically from the capital and the old Gaza province.

Although after 1969 FRELIMO's military operations at last began to have some effect inside Mozambique, the most successful of its activities was on the diplomatic front where it secured for itself international recognition as the sole legitimate nationalist movement. This ensured that there would be no challenge to its credentials from the international community nor any repetition of the debilitating struggle for international recognition which took place between the MPLA and FLNA in Angola. After 1969 FRELIMO succeeded in penetrating the Tete province and forced Portugal to concentrate its efforts on protecting the Cabora Bassa dam. To counter this guerrilla campaign the Portuguese adopted a number of strategies which had considerable bearing on the post-independence developments in the country. Population was concentrated in large fortified villages (*aldeamentos*) both for defensive purposes and to enable education and health services to be delivered effectively. The backing of traditional chiefs and religious organisations was sought, a particular effort being put into cultivating support among the Muslim brotherhoods of the northern regions.[4] Finally special forces (Grupos Especiais, the Grupos Especiais Paraquedistas and *Flechas*) were raised from among the African population for combat missions, their numbers rising to 30,000, half the total of the Portuguese armed forces, by 1974.[5] However, only in the final phases of the war, and far too late to make any difference to the outcome, was any attempt made to develop political support among educated Africans in the cities.

These measures, while proving unsuccessful in bringing the war to an end, helped to create an environment hostile to the pretensions of FRELIMO. In the euphoria which accompanied its victory, FRELIMO believed it could ignore those groups that had been closely associated with the colonial regime and failed to take into account the strong latent opposition that existed to its assumption of power.

[4]E.A. Alpers, 'Islam in the service of colonialism? Portuguese strategy during the armed liberation struggle in Mozambique', *Lusotopie* (1999), pp. 165–84.

[5]Norrie McQueen, *The Decolonization of Portuguese Africa* (Harlow: Longman, 1997), p. 125.

DECOLONISATION AND THE TRANSFER OF POWER[6]

The military revolt in Lisbon on 25 April 1974 was followed by six months of political confusion as power was contested between president Spínola and his followers on the one hand, and the radical army officers of the MFA and their left-wing political associates on the other. Although both factions were committed to a political solution to the wars in Africa, Spínola wanted to see a lengthy transitional period followed by elections which would decide the future of the territories, while the officers of the MFA were more concerned with responding to the immediate and overwhelming demand of the armies in Africa to cease fighting and to come home.

In the immediate aftermath of the revolution FRELIMO refused to accept a ceasefire since at that time there was no formal commitment by Spínola or his associates to independence for the colonies. The Portuguese army, however, was unwilling to continue military operations and operated a unilateral truce, retreating to its barracks and armed camps. This enabled FRELIMO rapidly to spread its activities, virtually unopposed, into Manica and Sofala, and beyond into the coastal provinces where until that time it had never operated nor even had an organised presence. Not until 7 September, six months after the revolution in Lisbon, was a formal agreement reached between the combatants to bring the state of war to an end.

During this period the Portuguese authorities remained deeply divided over their decolonisation policy. Spínola, and the governor-general he first appointed, David Texeira, tried at first to use the fact that Portugal still had a firm control of the cities and the most populous areas to create space for the formation of 'moderate' political movements which might challenge the initiative held by FRELIMO. Frantic politicking took place financed, among others, by Jorge Jardim but the Grupo Unido de Moçambique (GUMO), the only credible 'moderate' party, disintegrated and no alternative Mozambican leadership was able to emerge in such a short space of time. Spínola's efforts were, meanwhile, being undermined by the Portuguese army which by July 1974 had begun openly to fraternise with the 'enemy', and by democrats among the local white population who took control of the media and openly worked for FRELIMO.[7] Spínola's efforts were also sabotaged by MFA officers from Lisbon who began secret

[6]The best accounts of the decolonisation process are K. Maxwell, *The Making of Portuguese Democracy* (Cambridge University Press, 1995); Norrie McQueen, op. cit.; Margaret Hall and Tom Young, *Confronting Leviathan: Mozambique since Independence* (London: Hurst & Co., 1997).

[7]McQueen, op. cit.

negotiations with FRELIMO behind his back. In these circumstances it was easy for Machel and his negotiators to play different factions among the Portuguese off against each other and to hold out for all FRELIMO's demands to be met.

These demands became clear as the summer progressed. FRELIMO wanted a complete, immediate and unconditional transfer of power without any prior elections. FRELIMO's fear was that if there was any delay, such as would be caused by the organisation of elections, opposition movements would have time to form and, if adequately financed, might even win. It was aware that, although it claimed to represent all the Mozambican people and derived its legitimacy from its armed struggle against the Portuguese, it had in fact no organised presence in most of the country and had already experienced opposition among the largest single ethnic-linguistic group, the Makua speaking people of the north. Moreover, as the original splits within FRELIMO had indicated, the programme of the party's radical leadership by no means commanded universal support.

The fear that Spínola and his allies might somehow cheat FRELIMO of power and install a conservative neocolonial regime, exactly echoed the fears of most of the officers of the MFA in Lisbon, who cared little one way or the other for the fate of Africa and certainly had no ideas about how to manage decolonisation. Many were also worried that Spínola was intending to introduce a right-wing presidential-style constitution in Portugal which would remove any opportunities for radical social reform. In reality, however, Spínola's position had been steadily weakening since July when his second nominee as governor-general of Mozambique, Soares de Mello, had been forced ignominiously to resign.[8] The negotiations with FRELIMO which were held in Dar es Salaam in August 1974 were conducted on the Portuguese side by Melo Antunes, a known FRELIMO sympathiser, and the final capitulation to FRELIMO in the Lusaka talks in September occurred only days before Spínola himself was forced to resign the presidency. Spínola has usually been written off as having pursued a wholly chimerical vision of a Portuguese Federation or Community which would somehow allow the Portuguese African empire, and with it white domination, to survive. Whether this was or was not Spínola's long-term objective, his views about decolonisation—that FRELIMO should reconstitute itself solely as a political party and that there should be a two or three year transitional period followed by elections, was probably wise if not very practicable in the circumstances.

[8]Ibid., p. 136.

Although the Lusaka Agreement gave FRELIMO the unconditional transfer of power it sought, the movement was to suffer from the fact that its power had not been legitimated in an election. The people of Mozambique were never asked about, and never freely gave their approval to, the transfer and FRELIMO began its rule very much as a revolutionary movement that had seized power, not a democratic movement that ruled by popular consent. Eventually in 1994, after fifteen years of civil war, FRELIMO was forced to legitimate its rule in an election as it should have done in 1975. It is significant also that in 1994, unlike 1975, the international community put pressure on the successful guerrilla movement, RENAMO on that occasion, to declare a ceasefire, to demobilise and to turn itself into a political party before seeking a mandate at the ballot box.

The Lusaka Agreement which was signed on 7 September 1974 established a transitional government that was to last for nine months and was to prepare Mozambique for independence. A Portuguese high commissioner was to preside over a government whose ministers consisted of six FRELIMO and three Portuguese nominees. FRELIMO was to nominate the prime minister and selected Joaquim Chissano, while Samora Machel remained abroad as president-in-waiting until independence day itself. The agreement left a wide range of questions unsettled: state debt, private property, the position of government employees and the colonial army, the future constitution and numerous related matters.

Once established, the transitional government worked on the details of the transfer, looking at questions of debt and disentangling the economic affairs of the two states, but it lacked authority. Perhaps its most remarkable achievement was the de-militarisation of the country. Although many members of the black units that had fought for the Portuguese fled to Rhodesia where they were soon to continue the armed struggle, metropolitan Portuguese forces were withdrawn from the outlying areas and concentrated in the cities before being repatriated. The process went smoothly and there was widespread co-operation between them and FRELIMO—which was to prove crucial to the future of the new state when shortly after the signing of the Lusaka Agreement right-wing elements in the capital tried to stage a coup, seizing the radio station and going on the rampage in the black townships. Portuguese military units promptly put down the rising and restored order.[9]

However, the transitional government was unable to formulate policy of any kind and the uncertainty caused by the situation in Lourenço Marques

---

[9]For the transitional government see Hall and Young, op. cit., chap. 2.

as well as by the continuing political instability in Lisbon, where divisions within the MFA were assuming alarming proportions, led to the wholesale flight of the settler population. FRELIMO did nothing to try to reassure the white population and the early moves that were taken to nationalise health, education and rented housing made the situation worse. Whether FRELIMO wanted to see the white settlers leave as soon as possible to prevent any further coup attempts, or whether it was paralysed by the absence of Machel from taking any effective stabilising action, is difficult to establish, but the result was the flight of most of the skilled administrative, professional class and a large part of the skilled workforce. As the whites fled, many of them taking the road to South Africa or Rhodesia, moveable assets were stolen and in many cases plant and installations were wrecked.[10]

Although the Portuguese ended the war in Mozambique and withdrew in a reasonably orderly manner, handing over power to a political leadership of proven experience and ability, the legacy of the decolonisation process was not a happy one. The concern of both FRELIMO and the MFA to transfer power as rapidly as possible left too many dangerous loose ends. The black Mozambican units of the colonial army were neither demilitarised nor integrated into civil society. No measures were taken to retain white skilled workers, managers or administrators. No constitution had been agreed. There was no guarantee of private property or financial obligations. The position of those who had served the colonial regime was left unsettled. There was no guarantee of civil rights or of political pluralism. The economy of the country was not supported with negotiated loans, trade agreements or aid packages. Relations with neighbours were not settled in any way, and FRELIMO itself was allowed to take over power without any formal process of legitimation. Although not as disastrous as the decolonisation of Angola, the transfer of power in Mozambique contained all the seeds of future trouble. When independence day arrived in June 1975 FRELIMO found itself in command of a ship of state that, if not exactly on the rocks, was lurching rudderless in very rough waters.

THE ATTEMPT AT RADICAL RECONSTRUCTION

The FRELIMO leadership had gained its political experience in exile and in the context of the struggle for independence, and as a consequence had little first-hand knowledge of conditions in Mozambique. Its members

---

[10]A. Rita-Ferreira, *Moçambique post-25 de Abril. Causas do Exodo da População de Origem Europeia e Asiática*, reprinted from *Moçambique. Cultura e História de um País* (Coimbra: Instituto de Antropologia, 1988).

had been closely linked with the leaders of the other revolutionary movements, all of whom had been under the political and intellectual spell of Amílcar Cabral, the leader of PAIGC until his murder in 1973. Cabral had emphasised the need for the newly-independent states to break free from the social and economic patterns of colonialism and to establish their regimes on a different socio-economic model. By the early 1970s the failure of the first generation of independent African leaders to bring about significant change was becoming apparent and this failure was compounded by the global consequences of the 1973 Middle East war which were to lead to a collapse in the price of African raw materials and decades of economic depression.

FRELIMO believed that to be truly independent Mozambique had to break away from its economic subjection to South Africa, Rhodesia and Portugal. This objective was supported by current thinking among other Third World countries and among the grouping of 'non-aligned' states that at the time was particularly influential. It was made all the easier to adopt as the abandonment of industries, offices and property by the retreating Portuguese made it necessary for the state to assume as a matter of urgency a wide range of economic and social functions. FRELIMO's rapid move towards nationalisation and central economic planning was, therefore, both the preferred option of a leadership with a global vision and a necessity forced on it by the threatened collapse of the government and the economy.[11]

Although the FRELIMO leadership had a clearer idea than most of the elite of postcolonial Africa about what needed to be done to transform the colonial inheritance, the state in Mozambique was nevertheless to collapse more swiftly and more completely than in any other former colony. The irony that an apparently able and farsighted leadership which inherited power without any discernible rival, should lead its country so rapidly to disaster, has led to intense controversy. Yet, all commentators accept at least the outline of what went wrong. The FRELIMO leadership attempted a radical reconstruction of Mozambique's society and economy at a time when, as a result partly of natural disasters and partly of the chaos of the decolonisation process, the machinery of government and the economic infrastructure of the country were on the verge of collapse, and when southern Africa itself was about to sail into the eye of the geopolitical storm which marked the final phase of the Cold War.

During the struggle against Portugal FRELIMO had insisted that the war was being fought against the colonial system and not against the Portuguese people or even against the white settlers. This stance was in

---

[11]Mark Simpson, 'Foreign and domestic factors in the transformation of FRELIMO', *Journal of Modern African Studies*, vol. 31 (1993), pp. 309–37.

keeping with the traditional tenets of African nationalism and, like the earlier generation of African leaders, Machel and his associates saw themselves as building a new nation-state which would not recognise differences of ethnicity or race. As Machel put it, 'we killed the tribe to give birth to the nation'.[12] Where FRELIMO's approach departed from traditional African nationalism was in the wide definition it gave to colonialism, which was seen not just as the alien rule of a foreign power but encompassed all the internal social and economic structures which had been utilised by the colonial rulers and which had in one way or another sustained the system. These included traditional chiefs (*régulos*) and heads of families, and religious organisations as well as plantation companies and industrial complexes controlled by Portuguese or multinational companies. The Portuguese colonial government in Mozambique had created a modern economic sector round the coastal cities which was served by a skilled and educated class of professionals. The rest of the country had been systematically excluded from this modern sector. Traditional society based on the customary utilisation of land, had not been disrupted, as it had in South Africa, by expulsion from the land and had been left virtually untouched by western literacy and education. This society was still dominated by heads of families and chiefs who operated within a framework of customary law. All of these groups now found themselves treated as agents of colonialism.

FRELIMO was determined that modernisation should now be extended beyond the cities and should be brought to the rural areas. Its programme involved the provision of education, health and basic services but also the reform of customary law, the establishment of equality for women, and a revision of the judicial process, all of which, in its eyes, required the elimination of the influence of traditional chiefs and religious institutions and their replacement by FRELIMO nominated officials. FRELIMO's contempt for the traditions and practices of rural society and its desire to bring literate 'book' education to Mozambicans at all costs is astonishing in a party which had claimed to represent the interests of the peasantry. It was to lead to fatal acts of misjudgement in social and economic planning.[13]

FRELIMO's drive for modernisation began with the organisation of a literacy campaign and an attempt to make primary education universally accessible. In spite of a lack of infrastructure, this campaign was vigorously and successfully pursued. In the six years from 1975 to 1981, after which

[12]Hans Abrahamsson and Anders Nilsson, *Mozambique: The Troubled Transition* (London: Zed, 1995), p. 85.
[13]For FRELIMO's ideas on modernisation see Hall and Young, op. cit., pp. 81–8.

civil war engulfed the country and development programmes effectively ceased, the illiteracy rate dropped from 95 per cent to 75 per cent and primary school enrolments doubled to 1.4 million.[14] A parallel campaign aimed to bring health services to rural areas so that either a clinic or a regional hospital would be within reach of the whole population. The government placed its emphasis on preventative medicine and an immunisation campaign against smallpox, tetanus and measles is estimated to have reached 90 per cent of the population. The government claimed that it had increased health expenditure per head of the population from $ 1.70 in 1975 to $ 5.60 in 1982 but, to a greater extent than the literacy campaign, health ran into difficulties because of the scattered nature of the rural population and the lack of trained medical personnel.[15] These campaigns were not dissimilar to those carried out after independence by other African states. They were seen as necessary measures to meet the expectations of the population that the end of colonial rule would bring immediate and tangible benefits, and they were essential also to give meaning to the concept of modernisation. However, universal free education and health services are very costly and the problem of making satisfactory provision for these measures, and for others planned by the government, drove FRELIMO rapidly along the path of 'villagisation'—soon to prove one of the most controversial of its policies.

FRELIMO had been born and nurtured in Nyerere's Tanzania where the Ujamaa village system had been introduced. The FRELIMO leaders were greatly attracted to the idea of concentrating the rural population into large villages or rural townships where economic activity could be collectivised, services could be provided, and new political and adminis-trative structures could be introduced so that the people would become detached from the dominant influence of traditional chiefs and lineage heads. Such a policy was similar in many respects to the policy of building strategic villages (*aldeamentos*) which the Portuguese had begun to imple-ment in certain areas before the war and had then adopted as a measure to counter guerrilla infiltration. In fact many of FRELIMO's new villages were based on the former Portuguese *aldeamentos*—in the Tete province as many as 47 per cent of them having their origin in this way.[16] As the

[14]Allen Isaacman, *Mozambique: From Colonialism to Revolution 1900–1982* (Boulder CO: Westview, 1983), p. 139.

[15]Gillian Walt and Angela Melamed, *Mozambique: Towards a People's Health Service* (London: Zed, 1983), p. 144; Isaacman op. cit., p. 139.

[16]João Paulo Borges Coelho, 'State resettlement policies in postcolonial rural Mozambique: the impact of the communal village programme on Tete province, 1977–1982', *Journal of Southern African Studies*, vol. 24, no. 1 (1998), pp. 61–91.

'villagisation' policy was pushed ahead, it was accompanied by measures to promote the independence of women. Polygamy was discouraged and women were given protection in law and encouraged to participate in the new political structures that were being put into place.

The new political structures which were to replace government by colonial administrators were designed to achieve a high degree of central control. They had their roots in the period of the war when such centralised control was of paramount necessity. During the negotiations with the Portuguese leading to independence FRELIMO had rejected any idea of regional autonomy or political pluralism, asserting that the party was the sole representative of the Mozambican people. However, it was only at the Third Party Congress in 1977 that FRELIMO formally opted for a Marxist-Leninist philosophy and organisation. The constitution which was then adopted provided for a tiered structure of national, provincial, district and local assemblies, each level electing representatives to sit in the one above. Only candidates nominated by FRELIMO could stand for election and whole categories of people, including former members of the colonial police and civil service, those with private incomes, members of churches, traditional chiefs and polygamists, were excluded from being candidates. They were also removed from the party which was reconstituted after 1977 as a 'vanguard' party with a restricted membership. The 226 members of the popular assembly, the nation's parliament, were all nominated by FRELIMO.[17] In addition the party created youth, women's and workers' organisations (Organisação de Juventude Moçambicana or OJM, Organisação de Mulheres Moçambicanas or OMM, and so-called production councils) so that major representative pressure groups were also party controlled. The party dominated the political process at every level and to all intents and purposes the party and the state were seen, by those inside and outside Mozambique alike, to be identical.

Such political structures in theory gave the government the means to carry out a radical programme, but they were less effective in realising the other purposes of political parties, to listen, consult and persuade. In this respect the very thoroughness of FRELIMO's centralising political reforms was to contribute directly to its rapid undoing. In its early days FRELIMO was widely seen as a disciplined party with clear ideas and enlightened and modernising policies. Replacing traditional law and social practices with modern structures and ideas underpinned by legal, educational and health reforms was a programme which many development experts

[17]Barry Munslow (ed.), *Africa: Problems in the Transition to Socialism* (London: Zed, 1986) p. 127; Isaacman, op. cit., p. 130.

would have welcomed as an essential pre-requisite for economic progress. What, however, was not immediately apparent was the failure of FRELIMO to win popular support for its policies and the party's increasing recourse to repression as a means of achieving its objectives.

FRELIMO had appreciated the need to establish an effective presence throughout the country at the earliest possible opportunity, not only because it had never been able to organise branches in most of the country prior to independence, but also because the threatened collapse of the economy and the government following the flight of the Portuguese required emergency measures. The immediate steps taken by the regime were intended to establish *poder popular* (people's power) and included the setting up of 'dynamising groups' (*grupos dinamizadores* or GDs)—ad hoc bands of party enthusiasts, mostly young and inexperienced, who were sent into factories, offices and businesses to try to improve production and generally stimulate activity along the lines of government policy. The GDs were an effective way of establishing an immediate presence for the party and the government throughout the country but became a problem as they were largely untrained and unaccountable. Soon FRELIMO was having to find ways to draw the teeth of the more active GDs and to replace them with regular professional cadres. If in the early days the GDs served a useful purpose in asserting the authority of the government and the party, they also began the process of alienation as many people found their interventions offensive and disruptive.[18]

At the same time FRELIMO had been rounding up known opponents of the regime, large numbers of whom were interned and some, like Nkavandame and Simeão, were reported to have been summarily executed.[19] More serious for the regime was the way in which the modernisation programme alienated increasingly large groups within society. Owners of property and businesses, officials of the previous regime and traditional chiefs, all of whom had been identified as enemies of the new order, were soon joined by lineage heads and a broader and vaguer constituency of males who found the regime's policy towards women subversive of the social order and 'villagisation' profoundly disruptive of traditional practices over the allocation and utilisation of land and the ownership of cattle.[20] The Catholic church and its adherents were another

---

[18]For the GDs see Munslow (ed.), op. cit., p. 119; Isaacman, op. cit., pp. 116–21; Hall and Young, op. cit., pp. 51–6.

[19]Africa Watch reported quoted in Hall and Young, op. cit., p. 48.

[20]JoAnn McGregor, 'Violence and social change in a border economy: war in the Maputo hinterland 1984–92', *Journal of Southern African Studies*, vol. 24, no. 1 (1998), pp. 44–5.

major group deliberately targeted by the regime. After the party congress of 1977 measures were taken to take over church property, put an end to public religious festivals and remove the influence of the church from education and marriage. Similar hostility was shown by the party to Islam, while traditional medicine and religious practices were denounced as contrary to the ideals of modernisation.

Although Mozambique had never been noted for strong ethnic rivalries, it was not surprising that the hostility to the changes introduced by FRELIMO should, in the absence of any legal means of expression, begin to assume a regional and ethnic character. FRELIMO's early association with the Makonde had made the Makua peoples of the north, traditional rivals of the Makonde, very suspicious of the party and had led to the failure of early attempts to establish FRELIMO branches there. It is perhaps also significant that Joana Simeão, who was a Makua, had been one of the most prominent opponents of FRELIMO in 1974. After independence Makonde influence declined and the party was increasingly dominated by southerners and non-Africans—partly because Maputo was located in the far south and a high proportion of educated Mozambicans was to be found in and around the capital where educational facilities had for long been available, and partly because the flight of the Portuguese had made FRELIMO highly dependent on foreign *cooperantes* (volunteers) from friendly countries and on the Goanese and Portuguese radicals who had joined FRELIMO at the time of the revolution.

None of this growing hostility would have mattered if the regime had had the capacity to mobilise support, and if it had been able to meet the aspirations of the peasantry who constituted 80 per cent of the population. However, the new institutions of *poder popular*—the party cells, GDs, production councils, assemblies etc.—caused a great deal of confusion and, far from arousing enthusiasm had led within a short time to complete apathy.[21] Moreover, in the five years after independence the economy of Mozambique and the standard of living of the rural population failed to show any significant progress, and in many respects deteriorated from the level at the time of independence.

RADICAL ECONOMIC REFORM

Unlike many African countries which achieved independence already locked into what was virtually a monoculture, Mozambique in 1975 had a diversified and relatively-developed economy. At independence the country produced

[21]Munslow (ed.), op. cit., pp. 130–2.

cotton, sugar, tea and cashew as major export crops. Cotton and cashew, along with a variety of other crops like copra and rice, were grown by individual peasants while tea and sugar were produced by plantation companies. Near the cities and in the Manica highlands a commercial farming sector had developed to provide food for the urban population—the most controversial part of which were the *colonatos*, where subsidised small farms, most of them owned by white Portuguese, were irrigated by the Limpopo dam. A wide range of consumer industries had grown up in Lourenço Marques and Beira, some of them manufacturing for export to neighbouring African countries. A small mining sector in which coal was the most important item was dwarfed by the importance of the service sector. Railways, ports and pipelines turned Lourenço Marques, Beira, and increasingly Nacala also, into major African ports. The service sector also included tourism which was a major earner of foreign exchange. Finally the economy, both at the micro-level of the peasant family farm and at the macro-level of foreign exchange earning capacity, was heavily dependent on the remittances of migrant workers, many of whom were recruited under specially negotiated conditions by the Rand mines but who also included farm workers in Rhodesia, miners on the Copper Belt and emigrant workers in both Tanzania and Malawi. Mozambique's position was favourable when compared to many African countries in the range and diversity of economic activity, its ability to earn foreign exchange and the level of its industrial output. Its problems lay in poorly-developed internal communications and markets as well as in the low level of skills in its workforce.

In common with many Third World countries in the 1970s Mozambique aspired to achieve a level of economic autonomy which would save it from a neocolonial relationship with the former colonial power and from becoming merely peripheral to the major capitalist economies. Development economists of a more left-wing persuasion were convinced that 'development in one country' could be achieved. They emphasised the need for locally-generated capital to be employed first and foremost to meet the needs of an internal market. To achieve this a command economy had to be created with foreign exchange centrally controlled, planned national investment and surpluses extracted from one sector of the economy to provide the capital to develop the other sectors. One of the ironies about newly-independent Mozambique was that its situation closely resembled that which had faced Portugal itself in the 1930s. Salazar, like Machel, had also determined to rescue his country from its dependence on foreign capital and to create an integrated domestic economy which generated its own capital for investment and satisfied a large part of its own market needs. Mozambique and Portugal have not been alone in seeking economic autarky and every country that has taken this road has found that the only domestic source from which capital can be extracted is the peasant economy, with the result that forms of forced labour and peasant coercion have marked the drive for economic development in communist and socialist countries as well as in fascist Portugal and Spain.

The economic strategy followed by the Mozambican government after independence has been much analysed as it has been seen as a test case of what happens if a small and underdeveloped economy tries to 'go it alone' in the modern world. Some observers see the Mozambique case as vindicating the idea of planned socialist development while others are equally sure that the evidence points to catastrophic failure. Mozambique inherited from the Portuguese the machinery, and it must be said a certain appetite, for central economic planning. The plans that were drawn up were based on the nationalisation of most Portuguese businesses—plantations, factories and even retail outlets as well as the power and transport infrastructure, which was for the most part already under state control. The government would control foreign exchange, would prioritise the way it was spent, and would plan state investment. Funds for investment were expected to come from profits earned by the nationalised economy, foreign exchange earned from the provision of services and, it was assumed, foreign aid.

The National Economic Plan, which took shape in 1978, gave pride of place to social improvement in education and health. After these, investment was to be channelled in roughly equal amounts to the industrial sector and to state farms. Industry was seen as the 'modern' sector which would ultimately bring dynamic development to the country and free it from its dependence on imports from the industrialised world. However, a major role was also accorded to the state farms which were formed out of the abandoned *colonatos*—by far the biggest of which was the Complexo Agro-industrial do Limpopo (CAIL) on the Limpopo. State farms such as CAIL were to provide technologically-intensive agriculture which would not only help to make the country self-sufficient in food but would combine production with processing, distribution and training.[22]

Various explicit assumptions underpinned this strategy. The first was that Mozambique would continue to earn foreign exchange through the provision of services. The second was that the peasant sector would continue

[22]There are numerous studies of the Mozambique economy under FRELIMO. For example, Marc Wuyts, 'Money, planning and rural transformation in Mozambique', *Journal of Development Studies*, 22 (1985), pp. 180–227; Philip Raikes, 'Food policy and production in Mozambique since independence', *Review of African Political Economy*, 29 (1984), pp. 95–107; Abrahamsson and Nilsson, op. cit.

to produce not only subsistence crops for its own support and for the payment of taxes but export crops to sustain the country's earnings of foreign exchange. The third was that foreign aid would be available from friendly governments both in the form of expertise and capital investment. Finally, there were a number of unspoken assumptions necessary for the success of this strategy: that nature would refrain from dealing Mozambique a hand of drought, flood or famine, and that the country would remain at peace with its neighbours. After independence Mozambique experienced barely five years of relative stability before the whole state began to collapse and during this period most of the assumptions that underpinned the economic strategy proved to be ill-founded.

The industrial sector had been crippled by the flight of the Portuguese and by widespread destruction or theft of plant. FRELIMO struggled to replace the Portuguese from its own scarce resources of skilled personnel, frequently having to resort to using GDs in place of a non-existent management. As a result, industrial production fell from 48 billion meticais (1980 prices) in 1973 to 34 billion in 1981 and a mere 15 billion in 1985.[23] The state farms in contrast appeared a modest success and the giant CAIL complex, which was within easy reach of the capital, became a showpiece of the regime. Output from the state farm sector remained steady and began to grow in a modest way so that by 1981 agricultural production had almost regained independence levels. However, by 1981 it was becoming clear that the growth in production was being achieved at huge and ultimately unsustainable cost. Seventy per cent of all agricultural investment was being thrown into the state farms and mechanisation on a vast scale was taking place. However, there was no skilled workforce to handle or maintain the machinery and productivity remained very low. Moreover the state farms had themselves become a major grievance for the local population which had hoped to be able to take over the abandoned Portuguese farms.[24] FRELIMO was seen simply to be assuming the role of the colonial state and CAIL became a symbol of a hostile and unsympathetic regime which cared little for the interests of the peasantry.

Meanwhile the assumptions about the continuing productivity of the peasant or family farm sector had also proved false. In part this was not the fault of the government. The years immediately after independence saw climatic instability, which had already ravaged parts of Africa further

[23] Abrahamsson and Nilsson, op. cit., p. 54.

[24] Kenneth Hermele, *Land Struggles and Social Differentiation in Southern Mozambique: A Case Study of Cokwe, Limpopo 1950–1987* (Uppsala: Nordiska Afrikainstitutet 1988, Research Report no. 82).

north, strike Mozambique. Drought affected most of the south in 1978
cutting crop yields, causing famine and creating the need to import food.
Two years later the lower reaches of the rivers that flowed through
southern Mozambique burst their banks and caused widespread flooding
and further losses of peasant crops. By 1983 Mozambique was in urgent
need of emergency food aid. However, while the blows dealt by nature
were unpredictable and unavoidable, deliberate government policy was
also undermining the peasant sector.

The Portuguese had abandoned compulsory crop growing and forced
labour early in the 1960s and the peasant farming economy had been
sustained largely through market forces. Peasants produced surpluses
which were exchanged for consumer goods in local stores, while migrant
workers had begun to invest savings in ploughs, tractors and other modest
improvements to family farms. After independence government restrictions
on foreign exchange began to limit the supply of consumer goods to rural
stores and the peasantry responded by cutting production. Moreover
'villagisation' was causing disruption as well as resentment, while virtually
no government investment was being allocated to the family farm sector
and very little to the cooperatives. Given that most Portuguese-owned
plantations had ceased production, the marketing of export crops fell
drastically. By 1981 much of rural Mozambique was earning its living, as
it had in colonial times, through extra-legal transactions—cross-border
trade, blackmarket dealings and clandestine labour migration—or had
largely reverted to a primitive barter economy.[25] To compound this problem
Mozambique began to experience the mass migration of peasants to the
cities. Already by 1980 there were severe problems in feeding the urban
population and plans were implemented forcibly to remove the urban
unemployed back to the land.

These mounting difficulties should not obscure the fact that the
government was prepared to respond positively to what was happening
and that there were signs of improvement in the general economic situation
by the early 1980s. However as FRELIMO grappled with these problems
its economic strategy was being fatally undermined by the political
instability that was beginning to engulf the whole southern African region.

Under the Portuguese Mozambique had earned large amounts of foreign
exchange from the ports and railways that served South and central Africa,

---

[25]Anna Wardmam, 'The co-operative movement in Cokwe', *Journal of Southern African
Studies*, vol. 11 (1985), pp. 295–304; Wuyts, op. cit.; Abrahamsson and Nilsson, op. cit., p. 80;
McGregor, op. cit., pp. 39–40; S. Kruks and B. Wisner 'The state, the party and the female
peasantry', *Journal of Southern African Studies*, vol. 11 (1984), pp. 105–27.

from tourism and from the remittances of migrant workers. Immediately after independence, and more particularly at the 1977 Party Congress, FRELIMO declared itself a supporter of black majority rule in southern Africa and said that it would implement sanctions against Rhodesia, which had been technically in rebellion against Britain since November 1965. In 1976, before the 1977 Congress, the border with Rhodesia was closed and camps for 10,000 ZANU guerrillas were formed inside Mozambique. These policies had the immediate effect of reducing the use of the railway and port of Beira. The oil pipeline closed down and tourism from Rhodesia ceased.

The situation vis-à-vis South Africa also began to deteriorate though not as fast. Soon after independence South Africa declared its willingness to work with the newly-independent state and offered technical aid for the port and railway of Lourenço Marques, while continuing to buy electricity from Cabora Bassa.[26] However, in 1976 the Rand mines started to change their labour recruitment policies to make more use of domestic labour. No fresh contracts were issued to foreign workers and the numbers of Mozambican miners fell rapidly from around 100,000 to just 30,000. This meant a great reduction in state revenue for the Mozambique government as well as a loss of income for peasant families. At the same time other policies adopted by FRELIMO drastically effected the tourist industry. FRELIMO had seen the existence of the capital's sex industry as one of the worst aspects of colonial corruption. After independence large numbers of prostitutes were rounded up for re-education, bars were closed and the free operation of the sex industry stopped. With it ceased a lot of profitable, if morally undesirable, tourism.

There remained the possibility of foreign aid. During the independence struggle FRELIMO had received considerable support from Non-Aligned and Eastern Bloc countries as well as from some Western countries like Sweden and the Netherlands. It believed that its friends would continue to provide sufficient aid to enable the country to escape the clutches of the US-dominated World Bank and IMF, which were just beginning to flex their muscles in Africa. The confidence of FRELIMO was shown by the strong stand that it took in international affairs, not only declaring itself a Marxist-Leninist state but adopting 'non-alignment' and making firm declarations of support for majority rule in South Africa, Namibia and Rhodesia. The stance that FRELIMO adopted in foreign affairs was in keeping with the ideals of the Non-Aligned movement itself and appeared

[26]M. Azevedo, 'A sober commitment to liberation? Mozambique and South Africa 1974–1979', *African Affairs*, vol. 79 (1980).

to align Mozambique with a substantial bloc of countries in the UN and throughout the world, but it served to alienate its immediate neighbours, Rhodesia and South Africa, as well as the US and its allies, which began to look on Mozambique as another domino that had fallen to communism.[27]

In 1977 the Soviet president had visited Maputo and a treaty of friendship had been signed but although some aid arrived from Eastern Bloc countries and from Cuba, mostly in the form of advisers and skilled personnel, Mozambique's application to join Comecon was turned down in 1981 and the country soon found itself without strong flows of aid or international credit. Borrowing under these circumstances was expensive and unpredictable. Balance of payments problems mounted along with foreign debt while food aid from the UN failed to cover immediate emergency needs.

FRELIMO AS A GOVERNING PARTY

In its early days FRELIMO had been a deeply-divided party with strong factions at war over the leadership, military tactics and the long-term political direction of the movement. The first president, Eduardo Mondlane, is reported to have been assassinated by a rival faction and a number of important figures broke away and even attempted to form competing movements.[28] However, from these early splits FRELIMO emerged in 1969 under the leadership of Samora Machel as a remarkably cohesive party. Most of the leading group came from the south and included intellectuals and poets, whites, *mestiços*, and even some Goanese. Although disagreements occasionally surfaced and minor adjustments were made to the ministerial team, the inner core of FRELIMO's leadership remained united and largely unchanged for twenty-five years after independence—an extraordinary example of political longevity given the disasters which overtook its policies and the chaos into which the country was soon to be plunged.

After 1977 FRELIMO saw itself as a 'vanguard' party leading the people but without mass membership. As one commentator has put it, 'FRELIMO came to depend on a numerically weak but relatively privileged urban proletariat, a burgeoning state bureaucracy, and an external network centred on Moscow.'[29] Ironically Mozambique, which was one

---

[27]Particularly after FRELIMO expelled a number of US diplomats in 1981 alleging that they were spies.

[28]Alex Vines, *Renamo: Terrorism in Mozambique* (London: James Currey, 1991).

[29]Simpson, op. cit., p. 323.

of the earliest African states to undergo total collapse, was also one which attached a lot of importance to Western notions of good governance—where patrimonial politics was not strongly in evidence and where corruption was heavily discouraged. Although the party did not allow any formal political organisation to challenge its supremacy, it was openly and almost ostentatiously self-critical. Machel would frequently devote his long speeches to identifying errors in party policy and shortfalls in meeting targets. His chosen reforming device were the 'campaigns', targeted to increase production, eradicate corruption or improve efficiency, while he himself was immensely energetic and dedicated to the ideals for which FRELIMO stood.[30] Behind Machel's Marxist rhetoric was a politician very similar to the first generation of African nationalist leaders for whom the ideals of the anti-colonial struggle and of non-tribal, non-racial nationalism were a real motivating force, in marked contrast to the military dictators and corrupt politicians who were soon to succeed them and who were protected by the superpowers during the Cold War.

Yet in retrospect it is easy to see shortcomings in FRELIMO's approach to politics. Machel's style of exhortation, his appeals for self-sacrifice and hard work might succeed in war time and might be relevant in facing emergencies but were unattractive as daily fare. The party was deliberately exclusive and its policies alienated large sections of the population. It appeared to be heavily dependent on expatriate advisers—again not necessarily a defect in itself as home-grown expertise in many fields was lacking—but these advisers were often strongly-committed politically and gave the impression of treating Mozambique as some kind of political experiment for which they would not have to take long-term responsibility. Under their encouragement there is no doubt that FRELIMO came to overestimate its capacity to plan an economic transformation of the country and to achieve major social engineering. With the flight of the Portuguese settlers Mozambique was short of skilled personnel in every sector of society and simply lacked the expertise and the professional cadres to carry out ambitious central planning. Inheriting the intensely bureaucratic administration of the Portuguese, government soon became a byword for delay and official obstruction which even Machel's efficiency campaigns could do little to remedy.

In one area in particular FRELIMO's excessive confidence in its own policies proved disastrous. The leadership appeared to believe that it could support the African nationalist cause in Rhodesia and South Africa with no serious consequences to itself and, when the security situation in the

[30]Barry Munslow (ed.), *Samora Machel: An African Revolutionary* (London: Zed, 1985).

country began to deteriorate, it refused to accept that it was itself in any way responsible for what was happening. When the reality of what was occurring in the countryside away from the capital eventually became clear, the leaders of FRELIMO reacted with the naive astonishment of those who have come to believe their own rhetoric.

THE INTERNAL AND EXTERNAL CAUSES OF DESTABILISATION AND
CIVIL WAR

Southern Africa and the Cold War

Prior to the Portuguese revolution of 1974 southern Africa had formed a bloc of white-ruled 'settler' states, closely if informally allied to the United States. The collapse of Portuguese colonial rule brought Marxist regimes to Angola and Mozambique and direct Cuban and Russian intervention in support of the MPLA. South Africa for its part launched an invasion of Angola in the autumn of 1975. However, the election of Jimmy Carter in the United States meant that the US government was reasonably friendly to the aspirations of black nationalism, while the South African prime minister, John Vorster, was prepared to pursue a peaceful diplomatic campaign in Africa to try to get recognition for the policy of creating Bantustans, which came to maturity with the granting of 'independence' to the Transkei in 1976, and for the ideas of a South African led 'constellation of states' in southern and central Africa which would include the former High Commission territories, Malawi and, it was hoped, Mozambique.[31]

In this tense but still not threatening atmosphere Machel felt free to take an independent line in support of the black majority rule parties in Rhodesia and South Africa. The ANC was allowed to operate in Mozambique and FRELIMO lent active support to ZANU forces in their campaigns against the Smith regime in Rhodesia. It can be seen now that FRELIMO experienced a sort of honeymoon period—a few years of relative peace and stability before the consequences of its policies began to turn into a major threat to the survival of the state. To try to decouple Mozambique's economy from that of its neighbours may be seen to have been at best quixotic and at worst ruinous and misguided, but to provide at the same time support for the nationalist movements at war with their white minority regimes was to court disaster.

Rhodesia, threatened on three sides since Mozambique had become independent, decided to take the war to its neighbours—a strategy that

---

[31]For the international context in which FRELIMO operated and its effect on the party see Simpson, op. cit., pp. 309–37.

the Portuguese had scarcely ever adopted during ten years of warfare—and Rhodesian forces began to launch strikes at targets inside Mozambique. The rapid collapse of the Portuguese military effort in 1974, together with the wartime propaganda in which FRELIMO had exaggerated its military successes, had given the regime and its supporters a wholly false sense of its military capability. Faced with the mobile, well-armed and professional Rhodesian forces FRELIMO was able to offer little resistance. The Rhodesians, however, did not have the manpower to mount a sustained military campaign in Mozambique let alone an occupation, so they resorted to a tactic that previously the Portuguese had used with some success. They raised and armed a force of black Mozambican exiles.

The rise of RENAMO

Colonel Ken Flower, the head of Rhodesian military intelligence, who was later to take the credit for inventing the Mozambique National Resistance (MNR), said that his task had been made easier by the fact that elements of the black troops recruited by the Portuguese had taken refuge across the border in Rhodesia, while white Portuguese who had fled the country provided intelligence and probably also financial support. The MNR was founded in 1975 and began to broadcast to Mozambique through its station named 'Voice of Free Africa'. By 1978 it was acting in support of the Rhodesians in raids and sabotage deep within Mozambique.[32] At first FRELIMO took the line that MNR was simply a unit of the Rhodesian forces and that its military activity would cease once the Rhodesian problem had been resolved. MNR was not seen as having any independent role and was certainly not considered to represent any serious opposition to the regime within the country.

Before 1980 this assessment of MNR was close to the mark though better intelligence about the movement might have raised a few doubts. It appears that in the early days much of the MNR leadership, and probably the rank and file as well, came from the Ndau group of Shona speakers who lived along the borders of Rhodesia, primarily in the Manica and Sofala and Tete provinces. Those who knew the history of the region would have been aware that the Shona had a long tradition of guerrilla-style resistance, strongly supported by their spirit mediums, against Afro-Portuguese warlords, Ndebele and Gaza *impis*, Rhodesian settlers in the 1895–6 rebellion, and against the Portuguese colonial authorities in a succession of wars between 1880 and 1917. The nineteenth century wars of the Ndau

---

[32]For the origin of RENAMO see Vines, op. cit.

with the Gaza were particularly relevant as the FRELIMO regime was led largely by people from the south and Ndau-led opposition to the 'southerners' evoked memories of resistance to Mzila and Gungunhana a hundred years earlier. Nevertheless the MNR campaign should not be seen as primarily an ethnic conflict of the kind that was tearing Angola apart. It was at the outset a movement raised and largely directed by Rhodesian intelligence.

With the accession of Zimbabwe to independence in 1980 the regional situation seemed to have changed wholly in Mozambique's favour. Machel had given strong support to Mugabe, who emerged the victor in the Zimbabwe elections, and it was anticipated that the railway, the port of Beira and the oil pipeline would all soon be re-opened. The same year the Southern Africa Development Coordination Conference (SADCC) was formed, an organisation linking the central African states, including Mozambique, and designed to co-ordinate economic development and to stimulate investment. However, despite these favourable factors, the situation within Mozambique continued to deteriorate until the state itself was faced with collapse.

As the painful process of peace was being negotiated in Zimbabwe, Mozambique was devastated by severe floods and the economy continued to stagnate. Moreover the first flush of optimism following independence was wearing off as the problems which face all bureaucracies—corruption, delay and incompetence—were taking their toll. A weakened Mozambique now had to face developments far more threatening than the limited war with Rhodesia. In 1978 Vorster had been replaced by Botha as prime minister of South Africa, while 1980 saw the election of Reagan as president of the USA. Botha's accession to power marked the ascendancy of the South African military and with it a re-orientation of the Republic's policy away from conciliation and coexistence. A 'total strategy' was now adopted aimed at intimidating neighbouring states into withdrawing support from the ANC.

Like the white Rhodesians before them, the South African military saw in MNR, which now became more widely known as RENAMO (Resistência Nacional Moçambicana), the perfect instrument of its policy. During the period of the scramble for Africa in the nineteenth century, Europeans had found it comparatively easy to exploit African rivalries and to enlist Africans to fight on Europe's behalf. South Africa now sought to repeat these tactics in the context of the late-twentieth century, exploiting regional and ethnic rivalries and playing on the desire of leading Africans excluded from office to gain power and to use it for immediate gain for themselves and their followers.

Before the handover of power in Zimbabwe, the South African military arranged the airlift of RENAMO forces to South Africa. Once retrained and re-equipped, they were to take on a new and more active role in the struggle for southern Africa. RENAMO meanwhile had itself undergone some changes. The death in 1978 of its first leader, Andre Mtsangaissa, had led to a power struggle from which Afonso Dhlakama, the son of a Ndau chief, had emerged victorious. In the new phase of its existence not only was RENAMO drilled in a more brutal and destructive form of warfare but it started to look for allies outside Africa. Offices were opened to represent RENAMO interests in Germany, Britain, the United States and, of course, Portugal, and it sought a role for itself in Cold War politics alongside other non-communist insurrectionary movements like the Nicaraguan Contras.[33]

RENAMO's attacks inside Mozambique were now aimed specifically at cutting the communication systems, a policy designed to lead to the rapid fragmentation of the country and to crippling the newly-formed SADCC, whose only hope of economic independence from South Africa had been to develop the railways and ports of Mozambique instead of having to rely on those of South Africa. During the period 1980–3 RENAMO carried out a concerted campaign of destruction against roads and railways, industrial installations and government schools, offices and health centres. The operations were supported by the South African army and were mounted from temporary bases, the most important of which were located in Gorongosa in Manica province. RENAMO's attacks clearly served the identifiable interests of the South African military when they cut the communications systems linking central Africa to the Mozambican ports, but the attacks on government institutions and personnel, on FRELIMO party officials and on foreign *cooperantes*, served another agenda.

The aim here seems to have been to destroy utterly not only FRELIMO's social development programmes but the whole credibility of FRELIMO as an effective government. Where FRELIMO had placed all its emphasis on the need to modernise, RENAMO, without any rhetoric except that of the gun and the machete, seemed to be pursuing an anti-modernisation war, a vendetta against every aspect of modernity. Moreover, where guerrilla movements, like FRELIMO itself in the 1960s, had conventionally sought to base themselves among the peasantry and to survive by hiding among the rural population, RENAMO waged a particularly horrific war on the rural population itself, carrying out exemplary massacres and mutilations and recruiting child soldiers who were forced to kill villagers and even members of their own families as part of an initiation process.

As these methods of barbarism emerged during the period when South

---

[33]Vines, op. cit.

African control of RENAMO was most direct, it must be assumed that this was part of the counter-insurgency strategy devised by the South African security services. Unfortunately these methods were to spread rapidly in Africa's fast disintegrating state and security systems and in the following decades west African fighters in far off Liberia and Sierra Leone were to show themselves assiduous pupils of RENAMO's methods.

The disintegration of the Mozambican state and the Nkomati Accord

A glance at statistics for 1981 shows Mozambique enjoying a modest but encouraging economic growth. In fact these figures, reflecting the outcome of developments over the previous years, disguised what was really happening in the country at that time, as throughout Mozambique the faltering FRELIMO programme rapidly collapsed. Outside the towns government largely ceased to function, communications were cut, services broke down and marketing and distribution became impossible. People began to flee from RENAMO attacks, crossing the borders into neighbouring countries or taking refuge in the cities and towns of the coast. Agricultural and industrial production slumped and the Zambesi plantations in particular were effectively closed down. At the same time the depredations of the RENAMO fighters were made far worse by the widespread flooding, which was then followed by famine. Often in the past outbreaks of banditry and the breakdown of civil order within African chieftaincies had occurred as a result of drought and famine. So many people lived on the margins of existence that bad years would push many of them into the position where the only means of survival was to prey on others. In many respects the phenomenon of RENAMO becomes more easily understood when it is seen in this historical context.[34]

As the FRELIMO state disintegrated, the leadership sought ways out of the dilemma in which it found itself. It tried to cope with the security problem by a reform of the military. Old FRELIMO fighters and generals were retired and, with British aid, an attempt was made to train the armed forces. However, these were ill-equipped and, although they occasionally had some successes against fixed targets like the RENAMO headquarters in Gorongosa, they could never match the fast-moving RENAMO forces which were provided by the South Africans with modern communications equipment. Moreover they had difficulty supplying their units in the bush and areas reclaimed from RENAMO often had to be rapidly abandoned again.

[34]Newitt, op. cit., pp. 574–7.

FRELIMO also, somewhat reluctantly, began to overhaul its policies. In the Fourth Party Congress held in 1983, significant economic reform was announced, reform which recognised in particular the need to redirect the fast evaporating investment funds from the state farms to rural cooperatives and family farms, and to concentrate industrial production on consumer goods.[35] Discussions were also opened with the churches to try to heal the rift that had occurred after 1977. None of these measures, however, had much immediate impact on the spread of banditry and civil strife and FRELIMO stuck firmly to its public position that RENAMO was a group of bandits financed and organised by South Africa, with no internal support, and that its successes were in no way the result of FRELIMO's own policies.

FRELIMO also began urgently to seek help overseas. Missions went to the major western capitals to press for diplomatic as well as military and financial assistance. Part of FRELIMO's task now was to decouple itself from the Eastern Bloc and to persuade Western governments that it was not a militant Marxist state and that it was open to foreign investment. This initiative was vigorously pursued because of the urgent need for emergency food aid. By 1983 the country was having to import 30 per cent of its basic food requirements, while the sharply rising cost of oil and the decline in agricultural exports pushed the government into a disastrous, if apparently unavoidable, policy of borrowing.[36] In 1984 Mozambique applied to join the IMF and became a member of the group of states covered by the Lomé Convention. It also negotiated the first rescheduling of its debts, which amounted to about $ 2.4 billion. Another move by FRELIMO was to seek practical military assistance from the SADCC countries. Zimbabwe gave the most effective response, sending troops to try to protect the road and rail corridor to Beira.

The Reagan and Thatcher administrations were not unsympathetic to Mozambique's plight and saw in the Mozambican situation a way of using local conflict to further Reagan's favourite concept of 'constructive engagement'—bringing about controlled change in the region along lines favourable to Western interests. At the urging of the USA Machel began talks directly with South Africa in 1983. The result of these negotiations bore fruit in the Nkomati Accord, which was signed on 16 March 1984. According to the terms of this agreement, South Africa and Mozambique each agreed to stop giving military support to rebel movements which were attacking the other. At the time the Accord was variously interpreted either

[35]Abrahamsson and Nilsson, op. cit.
[36]Ibid., pp. 103–6.

as a humiliating surrender by FRELIMO of its proud post-independence stance against South Africa, or as a piece of subtle diplomacy whereby the FRELIMO regime gained recognition and even modest support from its arch foe. FRELIMO hoped that the Nkomati Accord would put an end to the South African support of RENAMO and that without this support the movement would wither away. It even allowed the South Africans to draw up an agreement, the Pretoria Declaration, which would have established a ceasefire. This premature attempt at peace rapidly broke down, however, as RENAMO insisted that elections for a new government should be part of any deal.

South Africa's motives in signing the Nkomati Accord remain obscure and it is not clear if it ever intended to carry out either the spirit or the letter of the agreement. Most commentators accept that the overthrow of the FRELIMO government had never been a South African objective and that the limited recognition that the Accord gave to FRELIMO did not represent any significant change of policy. It also seems clear that the South Africans had sought a deal which might enable the power supplies from Cabora Bassa to be restored and South African exports to the region to pick up again. If this was the case, it is difficult to explain why the South African military continued to supply RENAMO and did nothing significant to limit its activities. The enigma of South African policy at the time of Nkomati is explicable only on the assumption that there were deep disagreements between the diplomatic and military factions within the South African government—the former still looking for a measure of détente and pursuing the old ideal of the 'constellation of states' while the latter was intent on campaigns of destabilisation to weaken its opponents.[37]

AFTER NKOMATI

The five years that followed Nkomati saw the strange and complex history of Mozambique evolve in new directions. Nkomati acted as a shake to the Mozambican kaleidoscope which rearranged the pattern without radically altering the components of the situation in which the country found itself.

After Nkomati the diplomatic initiative began to pass to FRELIMO, which had a tradition of good diplomatic contacts. Indeed much of the international network of support that had helped sustain it in its struggle with the Portuguese was still intact. FRELIMO had proved helpful to Britain in the Lancaster House negotiations leading to Zimbabwe's

---

[37]A perceptive contemporary account of South African policy is R.M. Price, 'Pretoria's southern African strategy', *African Affairs*, vol. 83 (1984).

independence and it was to play a similar minor but useful role in brokering talks in Angola and Namibia.[38] FRELIMO sought to portray the war in Mozambique as a conflict between a humane and progressive government against the darkest forces of banditry and barbarism, cynically manipulated by South Africa. This campaign was immeasurably strengthened when in 1988 an inquiry by the State Department in Washington headed by Robert Gersony upheld many of the official assertions about RENAMO terrorism. It is widely accepted that the Gersony report once and for all prevented any official US endorsement of RENAMO as a bona fide anti-communist movement.[39]

RENAMO also began to mount a diplomatic offensive. After Nkomati South Africa began to withdraw from direct control of RENAMO and the rebel forces now had to operate increasingly from bases within Mozambique. As a consequence they moved part of their operations north of the Zambesi where they could make use of bases in Malawi and profit by the undoubted hostility that had always existed between FRELIMO and the population of the central and northern provinces. RENAMO now became less a group of bandits and started to interact in significant ways with the local population. It was after Nkomati, for example, that RENAMO began to recruit civilians to provide the movement with some administrative capacity.[40]

RENAMO's conservative backers in Europe and America had tried to portray the terrorist forces as a political movement respectable enough to meet the, admittedly unexacting, standards of the extreme right. Its diplomatic presence in Western capitals was orchestrated from Lisbon by Evo Fernandes (until his murder in 1988) who successfully recruited support from the Christian right in the USA, from Christian sects operating in South Africa and from right-wing circles in Germany, Kenya, Britain and Portugal. Apart from a shared doctrinal anti-communism these groups were linked to Portuguese and South African business and probably had their eyes on rich pickings should RENAMO ever come to power.[41]

Given that forming a RENAMO government was not part of the agenda of the South African military, it was essential for RENAMO, if it wished

[38]Joanne Michi Ebata, 'The Transition from War to Peace: Politics, Political Space and the Peace Process Industry in Mozambique 1992–1995' (PhD thesis, London: London School of Economics, 1999), p. 142.

[39]Robert Gersony, *Summary of Mozambican Refugee Accounts of Principally Conflict-Related Experience in Mozambique*, (Washington DC: Bureau for Refugee Programmes, 1988).

[40]Carrie Manning, 'Constructing opposition in Mozambique: RENAMO as a political party', *Journal of Southern African Studies*, vol. 24, no. 1 (1998), pp. 161–89.

[41]Vines, op. cit. An example of pro-RENAMO propaganda is Jorge Correia, *RENAMO. Resistência Nacional Moçambicana* (Lisbon: Forum Moçambicano, 1989).

to succeed in ousting FRELIMO, that it transform itself into a political party which could gain world-wide recognition. Dhlakama was persuaded to set up a national council which is supposed to have met for the first time in 1987 in order to endorse a political programme. This process was dismissed by many at the time as a farce and was discredited the following year by the appalling revelations of the Gersony Report. However, in the light of what happened in the 1990s it is worth looking at the political programme that did eventually emerge with official RENAMO endorsement. This programme, while talking in general terms about freeing the country, ending Marxist tyranny and introducing multiparty democracy, stressed the need to restore traditional authorities and freedom of religion. The last two points suggest strongly that RENAMO was retreating from its policy of terror and was now seriously trying to establish a constituency among the Mozambican population.

While FRELIMO and RENAMO were both trying to build up diplomatic support abroad, regional conditions for a peace settlement were gradually coming into existence. In 1986 Gorbachev's accession to power had been followed by a declaration that the Soviets had no formal interest in southern Africa. This opened the way for effective peace negotiations in Angola while the departure of Reagan from the political scene in 1988 made the task of negotiating a southern African settlement far easier. Possible solutions to Mozambique's problems were now being sought in a regional context and became tied to the settlements in Namibia, Angola and South Africa itself.

FRELIMO meanwhile still sought a military victory. To achieve this it tried to mobilise effective military support from its neighbours, Zimbabwe and Tanzania, to put pressure on President Hastings Banda to expel RENAMO from Malawi, and to close its supply bases in that country. A number of regional summits were held and it was when returning from one of these in 1986 that Machel's plane, piloted by Russians, apparently flew into South African air space and crashed into the mountains, killing the president.

Machel's death may possibly have been engineered by the South African military but if this assassination was designed to destabilise Mozambique still further, it signally failed to do so.[42] The leadership passed smoothly to Joaquim Chissano. There was no power struggle and once again FRELIMO demonstrated its extraordinary cohesion and its ability to maintain a united front. Chissano was dedicated to the path of change which had been

[42]For the theory that Machel was assassinated see *Samora: Why He Died* (Maputo: Mozambique News Agency, 1986).

initiated under Machel and his accession made little difference to the direction of Mozambican policy.

The pressure put on Malawi did however help to change the course of the civil war, though hardly in the direction that Machel had hoped.[43] After the 1986 summit RENAMO found itself effectively expelled from its bases both in South Africa and Malawi, and although it continued to receive supplies from South Africa, some of them airlifted from the Comoros Islands where the South African military mission sustained President Ahmed Abdullah in power, the RENAMO forces had to base themselves within the country. From being highly mobile, hit-and-run military units, RENAMO now had to try to control territory and population on a long term basis. It was this more than any other factor that forced the rebel movement to look for allies against FRELIMO in the countryside.

FRELIMO had always portrayed RENAMO as ruthless bandits who preyed on the population. This description of the enemy had the effect of denying RENAMO any legitimacy while at the same time absolving the government of all blame for the rapidly-deteriorating situation. However, research carried out in northern Mozambique by the French anthropologist Christian Geffray in 1983–4 provided evidence that RENAMO was being actively supported by sections of the population alienated by FRELIMO's 'villagisation' programme. Geffray pointed to the confused pattern of local rivalries and vendettas that underlay the larger conflict between FRELIMO and RENAMO. His views were challenged, not least because of the localised nature of the research, but his work had forced observers to look more closely at RENAMO and its activities.[44]

It is now clear that the need to base its activities within the country forced RENAMO commanders to develop alliances with local chiefs, with religious groups and spirit cults and with sections of traditional peasant society that were eventually to give it a firm constituency as a political party. RENAMO's espousal of the cause of persecuted religions struck a chord with elements of the Christian right in the USA and South Africa which began to portray RENAMO fighters as soldiers of the gospel who went into battle with bibles in their hands. As the debate gathered momentum over whether RENAMO had significant support within Mozambique, other explanations were offered for the movement's evident success. It was claimed that RENAMO had a particular appeal for groups who felt

[43]David Hedges, 'Notes on Malawi-Mozambique relations', *Journal of Southern African Studies*, vol. 15 (1989), pp. 617–44.
[44]Christian Geffray, *La Cause des Armes au Mozambique. Anthropologie d'une Guerre Civile* (Paris: Karthala, 1990).

disadvantaged and disempowered by FRELIMO's rule—in particular the unemployed youth and the less-educated.[45] Others saw the conflict as being fought along classic fault lines of urban versus rural society or the coast against the hinterland. Although the RENAMO commanders never abandoned their methods of terror, like the colonial rulers before them they found it easy to divide local communities which were isolated and fragmented in the countryside or had been alienated by FRELIMO policies and had neither the desire nor the leadership to resist. RENAMO commanders would contact and seek to win over chiefs or lineage heads who had grievances against the FRELIMO administration or who had suffered during the process of villagisation. RENAMO was even joined by some people who had received education up to secondary level. What, however, emerged most clearly after peace was eventually established was that Mozambique was divided very much along regional lines, with FRELIMO commanding overwhelming support in the south and RENAMO receiving strong backing in the central provinces north and south of the Zambesi.

At first, however, RENAMO's position within the country rested on the mobilisation of forced labour, the exactions of food from the local population and the kidnapping of women and children. Their armed camps took on the character of the old *aringas* (fortified stockades) which had been established by the *chicunda* (slave) soldiers of the Afro-Portuguese and Swahili warlords of the late-nineteenth century. At that time armed bands would establish a stronghold, levy food and labour on the local population which they dominated by a mixture of strategic alliances and terror, and gradually build up their strength through kidnapping children and incorporating them into their forces and seizing women from the local populations. These time-honoured processes of state formation in Mozambique were now revived to enable RENAMO to turn large areas of the country into their fiefdom.

After 1986 RENAMO began to control considerable areas of land in Manica and Sofala as well as in Zambesia and Nampula provinces to the north. By the end of the decade the FRELIMO government was only able to exercise authority in the major coastal towns and in one or two garrisoned

---

[45]In particular see the articles of K.B. Wilson—for example, 'Cults of violence and counter-violence in Mozambique', *Journal of Southern African Studies*, vol. 18, no. 3 (1992), pp. 527–82. Also Abrahamsson and Nilsson, op. cit., pp. 88–92, where an attempt is made to establish a socio-economic profile of RENAMO supporters. For child soldiers see Carol Thompson, 'Beyond civil society: child soldiers as citizens in Mozambique', *Review of African Political Economy*, vol. 80 (1999), pp. 191–206.

towns inland, while its communications were maintained largely by air. As a government it had ceased to function outside the capital, which somehow remained an oasis of relative calm surrounded by banditry and devastation. Even the road and rail links with South Africa, barely fifty miles away, were insecure. The second city, Beira, was largely a ruin, its economic life had ceased and refugees and squatters inhabited the empty buildings. Crowded refugee camps huddled in the relative safety of the other coastal towns. Some areas of the countryside were nominally under government control but fields could only be tilled under guard during the day time and villages were abandoned at night when their inhabitants would trek long distances to the shelter of the towns. Most government services could no longer be provided at all, revenue could not be collected and the army could not be paid on a regular basis. Reluctant conscripts, in some respects worse armed than their RENAMO opponents, began themselves to act as bandits extorting food from the peasantry they were supposed to be guarding and engaging in illegal trading.[46]

Unable to mount effective military action against RENAMO the government began to encourage the emergence of local peasant militias and one of these briefly achieved unexpected success. The Naparama were a peasant militia raised and led by António, a 'traditional' leader of considerable charisma. António claimed to endow his followers with immunity from injury and death by RENAMO and the movement grew rapidly in strength. It registered many localised victories, clearing whole districts of a RENAMO presence and allowing peasants to return to their land. There was some irony in the fact that one of the most effective actions against RENAMO turned out to be a recourse to the very traditional beliefs and culture that FRELIMO had set out to eradicate. However, the Naparama movement stalled in 1991 when António was killed fighting RENAMO forces.

THE END OF THE CIVIL WAR

The making of the General Peace Agreement

Mozambique had shocked the world with the horrific nature of the violence unleashed by RENAMO and by the extent of the collapse of the state, but during the 1990s it was to experience a dramatic reversal in its fortunes

---

[46]A remarkable account of the survival strategies of ordinary Mozambicans during this time is C. Nordstrom, *A Different Kind of War Story* (Philadelphia PA: University of Pennsylvania Press, 1997).

which no one had even hoped for, let alone predicted. By 1992 a fully-fledged peace agreement had been signed leading to multiparty elections in 1994 and a relatively smooth transition to peace, and by the end of the decade Mozambique was experiencing the most rapid economic growth of any country in Africa. What factors led to this extraordinary change in the country's fortunes?

For nearly a decade FRELIMO had refused any suggestion that it should talk to RENAMO, still officially described as a group of bandits manipulated by South Africa. Talks, it was held, would confer some legitimacy upon RENAMO and would give it a status as a political movement that it did not deserve. However, with the failure of the Nkomati Accord to yield any tangible results and with the war spreading into the northern regions of the country, FRELIMO authorised renewed contacts with the enemy. For a long time these achieved nothing as RENAMO was not willing to recognise FRELIMO as the legitimate government of Mozambique any more than FRELIMO was willing to recognise RENAMO as a legitimate political movement. However in the late 1980s the situation began rapidly to change. The end of the Cold War heralded by Gorbachev's accession to power in the USSR saw supplies of oil and arms from the Eastern Bloc countries to the Mozambique government begin to dry up, making the prospect of a military victory increasingly remote, while economic collapse was making the government ever more reliant on foreign loans to survive. Motivated principally by a strong instinct for survival, the FRELIMO leadership took the decision to dismantle the structures of a one-party Marxist state and to undermine RENAMO's newly-adopted democratic platform by a radical change to the constitution. At the Fifth Party Congress held in 1989 the claim to be a Marxist-Leninist state was formally abandoned and a wide-ranging constitutional reform was announced, introducing a multiparty democracy underpinned with the full panoply of individual human rights. By the end of the decade little was left of FRELIMO's former mission of socialist reconstruction.[47]

The Bicesse Agreement, 31 May 1991, had suggested that a solution to the conflicts in Angola and Namibia could be achieved. When de Klerk became South Africa's prime minister in 1990, he began to rein in the South African military. The main support for RENAMO's military capability was thus removed. In the same year Namibia became independent and peace talks in Angola led to the withdrawal of Cuban forces, a ceasefire and the setting of a date for multiparty elections. However, if these developments were all creating an environment which pushed FRELIMO and RENAMO

---

[47]For the context of this radical change of direction see Simpson, op. cit., pp. 309–37.

reluctantly towards peace, the decisive factor was probably the crippling drought which in 1990 began to affect an already-devastated land. The famine which followed brought both FRELIMO and RENAMO to the point of exhaustion, so that neither side was able to continue the armed struggle. RENAMO was now under as much pressure as FRELIMO to make peace since the withdrawal of South African support left it with few options apart from the continuation of a low-level guerrilla campaign conducted with dwindling resources.

If internal conditions in Mozambique and the changing political environment in southern Africa go part of the way towards explaining the moves towards peace, a significant role was also played by outside actors. After the abortive peace negotiations that had followed the Nkomati Accord in 1984, secret contacts were maintained between RENAMO and FRELIMO mostly through third parties, in which Jaime Gonçalves, the Archbishop of Beira, played a significant role. By 1988 pressure for more talks was coming from the USA, Kenya, and Zimbabwe which was anxious to end its military commitment in Mozambique. An attempt by African diplomats to broker peace led to a meeting in Nairobi where both sides put forward proposals. However, talks planned to be held in Blantyre in June 1990 collapsed when Dhlakama failed to make an appearance.[48]

At this stage FRELIMO approached the Vatican and the Italian government to help the peace proposals forward and the Vatican suggested making use of the services of the Italian lay brotherhood of Sant'Egidio as brokers. The peace talks which followed dragged on from July 1990 to the final signing of a General Peace Agreement in Rome in October 1992. These negotiations took an inordinately long time as RENAMO realised that in Rome it had an equality of status with FRELIMO that it did not enjoy in Mozambique itself, and it sought to get as much advantage as possible from the peace protocols. It challenged, for example, the right of the Mozambique government to legislate while the negotiations were underway. However, RENAMO was not just looking for equality of status, it was desperately worried that after a ceasefire it would be at the mercy of the FRELIMO government which it felt could renege on any agreement. In the final stages of the negotiations RENAMO tried to hold out for some form of power-sharing arrangement in the run up to elections. FRELIMO for its part was anxious to be recognised as the legitimate government and to keep the peace process as far as possible in African, or even Mozambican, hands. Although it was happy to make use of Italian mediation it tried to delay any involvement by the UN in the monitoring of the final peace settlement.

[48]Ebata, op. cit., p. 146.

The General Peace Agreement that was eventually signed on 4 October 1992 made provision in outline for multiparty elections, demobilisation and the formation of a new national army, and for RENAMO to retain a security role in the areas it controlled—although the government had the formal right to establish civil administration there. In many respects the Agreement was sketchy and left much detail unresolved, even after more than two years of negotiation. Its formal terms incorporated extensive compromises by both sides—though in the end both sides obtained what for them had been the most important issues at stake. FRELIMO gained formal recognition as the legitimate government of Mozambique and RENAMO formal recognition as a legitimate political party. At the time of the signing of the Agreement there was some scepticism over whether it would succeed. In spite of meetings between the two leaders, there had been no real reconciliation and many felt that this was not an African peace arrived at through negotiation and adjustment by the African parties to the conflict. Although not exactly imposed by outsiders, it was a peace whose terms had been worked out by third parties and which above all represented the interests of UN and Western diplomacy. Moreover, the lack of detail over the implementation meant that the UN would assume a much greater role in Mozambique in the two years leading up to the elections than had ever been anticipated. It was a fragile peace and all participants were aware that a similar process in Angola had come rapidly unstuck.

That, in the end, the peace settlement in Mozambique held was the result of three factors. First, and clearly most important, Mozambique was destitute and neither side had the capacity to continue to fight a war. Second, Dhlakama lacked the charisma and international standing of Savimbi and showed himself ready to accept a well-rewarded role as peacemaker and politician. Third, the UN decided to pour resources of men, money and material into Mozambique to prevent the peace process coming unstuck— in marked contrast to the minimalist role it had assumed in Angola.[49]

Foreign intervention and the success of the General Peace Agreement

When peaceful elections were eventually held in Mozambique in October 1994 the result was heralded as an outstanding success for the UN's peacekeeping operation, indeed almost the only notable success it had to

---

[49]The making and implementation of the peace agreement has been studied in depth by Ebata, op. cit.; and Cameron Hume, *Ending Mozambique's War: The Role of Mediation and Good Offices*, (Washington DC: United States Institute of Peace Press, 1994).

show. However, not everyone agreed with this analysis and the peace process as well as the reconstruction that followed posed a number of questions, which had world-wide implications, about the extent to which a state that has undergone complete disintegration can regain any real independence. The peace process, successful as it was in many respects, was nevertheless flawed and Mozambique might easily have returned to war as had happened in Angola.

In Angola a peace agreement had been signed in 1990, a small UN observer corps had been appointed and elections had been held in September 1992 before proper demobilisation of the armed forces had taken place. The result of the elections, which took place just as Mozambique signed the General Peace Agreement, led to a rapid renewal of the war. The events in Angola were running a year or so ahead of those in Mozambique and all the participants in the Mozambique peace process were able to observe what was happening in Angola and to learn from it. Running parallel was the settlement in South Africa which also began its peace process in 1990 and, like Mozambique, reached the stage of free elections in 1994. It was feared that failure in Mozambique might derail the peace process in South Africa which was seen by the international community as far more important. Exceptional efforts were therefore made to see that the transition in Mozambique was a success.

When the General Peace Agreement was signed the UN had no mandate for operations in Mozambique and had not organised its mission. Although an Italian, Aldo Ajello, was appointed UN commissioner within days, a budget for the UN operation was only agreed in March 1993 and his appointment was not confirmed till April 1993. The UN, advised by Ajello, decided to abandon the idea of a limited role as in Angola, and to mount a major peace-keeping operation. In the event it organised a force of 7,000 soldiers (ONUMOZ, the United Nations Organization for Mozambique) with an immense back up of technical and administrative personnel. This confirmed the worst fears of FRELIMO who found that the UN was effectively establishing a parallel government in the country, securing access to RENAMO-held areas still barred to the government and, through its technical unit, delivering food, consumer goods and even laying on services in many parts of the country.[50]

Demobilisation of the rival armies and de-militarisation of the country was seen as the key to success, just as the inability to secure this had been the key to failure in Angola. UN troops began to arrive in February 1993 and the last Zimbabwean and Malawian soldiers had left by July.

[50]Ibid., pp. 176–7.

Demobilisation eventually began in January 1994 and was completed by September. In Angola this process had never been effective as both sides had held back arms and significant parts of their forces. In Mozambique the process was given impetus by the soldiers themselves on both sides, who staged mutinies and demanded that demobilisation be speeded up so that they could receive the generous pay off that the UN had arranged for them. In the end 90,000 troops were demobilised along with 95,000 dependants and a small new army of 12,000 was established.[51]

While the demobilisation process stuttered and stalled, arrangements were being made for the full incorporation of RENAMO into the political system. A UN administered trust fund, which eventually grew to $ 18 million, was set up for RENAMO in May 1993 and Dhlakama visited Maputo for the first time in August. RENAMO was now able to establish itself in the capital taking one more step on the way to transforming itself into a political party in preparation for the elections due to be held in October 1994. Although the electoral commission that oversaw the registration of voters was an all-Mozambican affair, the actual election itself was overseen by the UN which poured 3,000 observers into the country and mounted an operation costing $ 64.5 million, 95 per cent of which was paid for by external donors. The election monitors had at their disposal 300 vehicles, 6 aircraft and 26 helicopters.[52] In the run up to the election an intensive information campaign had been organised using nine local languages as well as Portuguese.

The USA, backed by other Western ambassadors, tried hard to influence the result, putting pressure on FRELIMO to accept the idea of a government of national unity following the elections and urging the population to give a strong vote to RENAMO. In the event, voting was a peaceful process and the result proved decisive, if in some respects rather surprising. In the direct ballot for president Chissano polled 53.3 per cent of the vote and Dhlakama 33.7 per cent. This overall majority for Chissano left Dhlakama little ground to challenge the result. The elections for the new assembly however were much closer. FRELIMO won 44.3 per cent and gained 129 seats while RENAMO polled 37.8 per cent and gained 112 seats. The União Democrática (UD) coalition which gained 9 seats got 5.1 per cent of the total votes. FRELIMO won overall in Maputo City, Maputo Province, Gaza and Inhambane in the south and Niassa and Cabo Delgado

---

[51]Richard Synge, *Mozambique: UN Peacekeeping in Action 1992–94* (Washington DC: United States Institute of Peace Press, 1997), p. 16.

[52]Ebata, op. cit., p. 262.

in the extreme north. RENAMO won in Sofala, Manica, Tete, Zambesia and Nampula, the populous centre of the country dominated by the Ndau and Makua speaking people.[53]

The strength of RENAMO's vote and the fact that FRELIMO only secured a victory in six of the eleven provinces surprised many observers who could not understand how so many voters could support a party whose name was still inextricably linked to the appalling atrocities committed against the civilian population. However, on closer examination the result was not so surprising. RENAMO had been consciously engaged on a policy of building support in the country since 1986, and more energetically since the peace process had begun. By 1994 it was able to attract educated and even professional people who thought that membership of RENAMO offered a 'fast track' to personal advancement—an appeal that was especially strong in the central regions of the country where people of all ethnic backgrounds had resented the dominance of southerners in the FRELIMO government.[54] At the time of the election RENAMO still controlled about 25 per cent of the country and government administration had not been fully re-established. Emergency food and other forms of aid had been delivered by outside agencies but this largesse had appeared to arrive with the consent of RENAMO not the government. The FRELIMO government seemed to many to be a powerless abstraction which had no direct bearing on their lives. In addition to this the Catholic church as well as foreign governments had all urged a strong vote for RENAMO as the only way of guaranteeing peace. And it was peace, rather than FRELIMO or RENAMO, for which the electorate was really voting. All the evidence suggests that votes were cast in whatever way seemed to promise peace rather than a return to violence. Votes went to RENAMO in areas where it was visibly the stronger and to FRELIMO in areas where the government was seen to be effective.

The greatest fear in the international community was that Dhlakama would follow the example of Savimbi, reject the election results and return to war. There were signs that he thought of doing this. On the eve of the election he tried to declare a boycott and after the election was over he queried the result. However, he was subjected to intense international pressure and his party were allowed generous financial support to prepare for the elections. Eventually, with reluctance, he did so.[55]

---

[53]Synge, op. cit., p. 139.
[54]Carrie Manning, op. cit., pp. 174–5, 188.
[55]Synge, op. cit., pp. 130–3.

From the time of the signing of the General Peace Accord to the declaration of the election results two years later, Mozambique had been effectively ruled by the UN. Most of the important functions of government, ranging from demobilisation and disarmament to the resettlement of refugees and soldiers and the administration of emergency aid, had all been carried out by UN agencies or by NGOs. Huge sums of money and thousands of personnel had been poured into Mozambique and the UN had set up a parallel government which largely pushed the Mozambican authorities to the side lines. The UN was much criticised for having cajoled the.rival parties as opposed to working with them to bring about reconciliation, and for having swamped Mozambique with an expensive and wasteful UN administration that would inevitably leave a vacuum when it withdrew. Ajello was accused of having acted exactly like an old-style colonial governor while the Supervisory Commission which oversaw the whole process 'evolved into ... a local Security Council where the parties were expected to account before a UN chairman surrounded by a Council of Ambassadors'.[56]

On the other hand, those involved in the peace process knew the depth of the hatred and distrust between FRELIMO and RENAMO and suspected that, left to themselves, there would not have been the will to carry through the precariously-negotiated peace agreement. The only hope lay in creating a momentum that could not be stopped and in throwing money at any problem that threatened to stand in the way of peace. In the end this approach was vindicated and was strongly, if silently, backed by the people of Mozambique—the 1.7 million refugees who streamed back to their villages, three-quarters of them without any form of assistance, and the soldiers who insisted on their own rapid demobilisation and were reintegrated into their communities with traditional cleansing ceremonies.[57] And, for once, natural forces aided rather than hindered the cause of peace, the plentiful rains in 1992 ensuring an annual 400 per cent increase in food production .

Although the UN began to dismantle its operation soon after the elections, it left behind a government whose legitimacy was now universally recognised in Africa and in the rest of the world, and one which had attracted a large amount of international goodwill. FRELIMO was in some ways back to where it had been in 1975, inheriting a war-torn country crying out for peace and reconstruction. It now had the opportunity to make a fresh start.

[56]Ebata, op. cit., p. 246. Ebata is particularly critical of the whole UN operation.
[57]Ibid., pp. 225–7, 238.

MOZAMBIQUE UNDER THE YOKE OF THE IMF

Between 1990 and 1994 the international community and the UN had devoted a great deal of attention to Mozambique, with the result that the war had been ended and the refugees had returned home. Huge sums had been invested in development projects and a series of donor agreements had led to the restructuring of Mozambique's debt and the provision for future funding needs. However, as Richard Synge observed,

... at the end of the process, Mozambique had increased rather than shaken off its dependence on international financial and humanitarian assistance, and the voices of ordinary Mozambicans were in danger of being drowned out by the agendas of international development agencies.[58]

Was this a fair assessment of the price that Mozambique had to pay for peace?

Having narrowly won the elections in 1994 FRELIMO was faced with the immense task of knitting together a fragmented society, implementing fresh social and economic programmes and making the new political and administrative machinery work smoothly. Moreover, FRELIMO found it had much less freedom of manoeuvre and flexibility in the development of its policies than it had in 1975.

The six years between the elections and the end of the century saw profound economic changes brought about by the wholesale adoption of the free-market measures prescribed by the World Bank and the IMF. However, the experience of these years raised fundamental questions about both the long- and short-term consequences of the IMF/World Bank prescriptions. Among the most important of these were the extent to which structural adjustment undermined the responsibility and independence of the government; whether the government had the capacity to create the infrastructure for further development while having to service debt and limit public expenditure; and whether free-market economies and liberal democratic structures lead inexorably to rampant corruption and the destruction of the idea of public service.

The changes in economic policy had been planned long before the peace process began. It is perhaps more helpful to see the peace process as arising out of the change in political and economic direction rather than the shift in economic direction coming as a result of peace. The structural adjustment programme agreed with the World Bank and the IMF in 1986 had been

[58]Synge, op. cit., pp. 165–6.

incorporated into the Programa de Reabilitação Económica (PRE) which began to be implemented in 1987. This involved the removal of price controls and the freeing of the market in food, the privatisation of state enterprises, devaluation of the currency, and the drawing up of a new code to encourage inward investment. It also entailed heavy cuts in public expenditure which had made it difficult for the government to find the funds to play a significant role in reconstruction during the 1992–4 period.

In the period up to 1994 the benefits of this policy were slow to reveal themselves. While the urban poor of Mozambique saw their living standards decline sharply, agricultural production, particularly in the peasant sector, was slow to recover. After the good rains of 1993 the situation began to improve, though the rise in prices paid for peasant produce was more than offset in most cases by the rising cost of consumer goods following the devaluation.[59] Industrial production continued to decline as antiquated plants were no longer able to compete with modern industries elsewhere. Imports continued at a very high level, amounting to seven times the value of exports. Inflation also remained very high over this period, seldom sinking below 40 per cent per annum.

If the IMF/World Bank prescriptions were proving a mixed blessing, the arrival of the UN in 1992 acted like a massive blood transfusion for the Mozambique economy. Employment increased and GDP was artificially swollen by the expenditure of the UN and the NGOs which poured into the country after the signing of the peace agreement. One unforeseen consequence of this period was the heavy distortion of some sectors of the economy caused by the UN presence. Wages and salaries in UN and NGO service were high and could not be matched by the government, while the high levels of expenditure created demands within the market for goods and services that would not easily be sustained after the UN left. Once the elections were over the UN began to scale down its presence although the level of NGO activity remained high and foreign aid was to constitute more than 50 per cent of GDP for the rest of the century.

After 1994 the government discarded the reluctance with which it had treated foreign intervention during the peace process and began to commit itself to the measures demanded by the IMF as the only way of securing economic progress. Although Chissano made it clear in speeches that the long-term objectives of the government in the field of education, health and welfare had not been abandoned, new planning priorities and the need to service the huge foreign debt meant that education and health slipped

[59]Graham Harrison, 'Marketing legitimacy in rural Mozambique', *Journal of Modern African Studies*, vol. 38, no. 4 (1998), pp. 569–91.

down the list of government priorities. Chissano defined the new priorities as 'creating the conditions for the expansion of the private sector, particularly the informal agricultural sector'.[60] The Reform and Economic Development Plan (1997) set as its priorities the 'overhaul of the outdated commercial code, removal of administrative barriers to investment and private sector growth and reform of the public sector'.[61] It is difficult to imagine a greater reversal in policy between these statements and the priorities which the government had set itself in 1977.

During the five years after the election the government sought to bring about an economic transformation of the country. The foundation of the Mozambican 'miracle' was to be a classic formula of low inflation and strong currency. Some success was achieved as inflation steadily fell from 54 per cent in 1995 to 1.4 per cent in 1998, while the metical appreciated against all currencies including the dollar over the same period.[62] Increased direct foreign investment was expected to be the reward for financial prudence. Foreign investment had been deregulated in 1993 and a promotion agency entitled the Centro de Promoção de Investimentos (CPI) had been created. By 1997, $ 346.2 million had been invested in 449 projects, the lead being taken by Portugal and South Africa, the two countries from whose economic clutches Mozambique had at one time aspired to free itself.[63] Chissano justified this, declaring in 1998 that the government wanted 'a dynamic and responsible private sector, that would work together with the government, trades unions and the rest of civil society'.[64] To achieve adequate inflows of foreign investment the CPI pressed the government to create Industrial Free Zones around Beira, Maputo and Nacala and along the 'corridors' leading to these ports. In this way the historical geography of the region once again became a determinant of policy as it had been in colonial times.[65] In addition, a special investment regime was created for the Zambesi valley where all capital and intermediate goods would be exempt from import duties and from sales and consumption taxes and all investments from corporation tax for three years.[66]

Since 1987 the government had gradually been implementing another

[60]Economist Intelligence Unit (EIU), *Country Profile: Mozambique,1998–9* (London: Economist Intelligence Unit, 1999).

[61]Ibid.

[62]Official statistics show inflation falling as follows: 1995: 54%; 1996: 16.3%; 1997: 5.8%; 1998: 1.4% (Jan-April), *Africa Research Bulletin* (ARB), May-June 1998.

[63]EIU, op. cit.

[64]*Mozambique File* no. 267, October 1998.

[65]EIU, op. cit.

[66]*Mozambique File* no. 267, October 1998.

strand of the PRE: deregulation and privatisation. The removal of subsidies on consumer items and the freeing of the retail market had begun before the peace was signed. In 1993 foreign investment was deregulated; in 1997 state banks were sold off and a new land law allowed foreign companies to acquire land rights; in 1998 the state secretariat for cashew was abolished and a stock market was created as part of a strategy to mobilise savings; and in 1999 VAT was introduced.[67] Meanwhile 700 state owned enterprises, including 40 large companies, were privatised in a process described by *The Economist* as 'one of the most rapid and successful privatisation programmes in sub-Saharan Africa'.[68]

Foreign debt meanwhile dominated much of the discussion between Mozambique and the donor community. Mozambique had begun talks to reschedule its debts in the early 1980s but the agreements reached at the time had achieved little except to delay payments, while unpaid charges accumulated to form new debt. By 1994 Mozambique's debt stood at $ 7.3 billion. The Mozambique government pressed for a cancellation of all its debt, hoping that its cooperation with the World Bank and the IMF would earn it credit with those institutions. It was assisted by a sustained international campaign which focussed on debt relief as the most urgent form of aid for sub-Saharan Africa. In the event Mozambique was one of the principal countries whose indebtedness was dealt with under the Heavily Indebted Poor Countries (HIPC) Initiative in 1998, though the result was hardly what the government had been pressing for. In return for the cancellation of $ 1.4 billion of debt Mozambique had to repay annually the equivalent of 20 per cent of export earnings. In practice this meant that, as a result of these negotiations, debt service payments would actually rise.[69]

Industry, including the processing of raw materials, had been one of the most dynamic sectors of the colonial economy in its final days. In 1973 Mozambique ranked sixth in the whole of Africa for value added in the industrial sector. However, manufacturing was the slowest part of the economy to respond to the liberalisation measures taken after 1987 until 1995 when output rose by an average of 11.1 per cent each year.[70] The most important developments in this sector were the construction in 1998 of a major aluminium plant and the discovery of substantial natural gas reserves north east of Maputo by the South African company SASOL in the same year.

[67]*ARB* June-July 1998.
[68]EIU, op. cit., p. 17.
[69]*ARB* March-April 1998.
[70]EIU, op. cit.

As a result of these wide-ranging economic changes Mozambique's economy, as measured by GDP, showed some spectacular rates of growth prompting some talk of Mozambique not just as an 'economic miracle' but as a potential 'African tiger'. GDP grew 6.2 per cent in 1996, 7.9 per cent in 1997 and an impressive 9.4 per cent in 1998. However, not everyone was euphoric about what was happening and the apparent success story told by the large annual rates of growth were criticised as being illusory and for disguising the emergence of major social and political problems. The FRELIMO Central Committee criticised

... current company legislation [as] far too permissive. Large numbers of foreigners use local figureheads or legal loopholes when setting up Company Head Offices. Many companies are formed simply to get access to international finance or to escape income tax at home.[71]

And there was concern that labour laws and environmental controls were being flouted by foreign-owned companies which continued to press for an ever more 'liberal' environment in which to operate.

Meanwhile large numbers of Mozambicans were being pushed into the informal economy of smuggling, illicit trading and corruption. In 1998 *The Economist* estimated that the informal economy was so large that GDP was being underestimated by as much as 70 per cent.[72] An alarmingly high proportion of GDP was also still being accounted for by aid, giving rise to doubts about whether the expansion of the economy was based on any real growth of productive capacity. Moreover, after five years of this 'economic miracle' the people of Mozambique still remained, officially, the poorest in the world.

Political consequences of the peace process

At the Party Congress in 1989 FRELIMO had announced comprehensive constitutional changes designed to cut the political ground from underneath RENAMO by introducing the liberal democratic changes that it had been demanding. These constitutional revisions were duly brought forward in December 1990: political parties were to be allowed, the separation of powers was decreed, the president was to be elected by direct suffrage, ownership of private property was to be permitted and FRELIMO's control of trades unions and other organisations was removed.[73] These measures

---

[71]*Indian Ocean Newsletter*, January 1999.
[72]EIU, op. cit.
[73]Simpson, op. cit., pp. 331, 334.

certainly had the effect of pre-empting RENAMO but by not allowing its rival any part in these decisions FRELIMO failed to integrate the rebels into the constitutional process. In the event RENAMO accepted these changes though at one time their exclusion had threatened to sabotage the peace negotiations. One noticeable result of the separation of the party from the government was that party members were free to enter business and to establish companies in a way that had not been allowed before. That, and the opportunities provided by the huge flows of UN and aid funds, led to a rapidly growing corruption within the police and the administration, a problem from which Mozambique had been relatively free before 1990.[74]

After the 1994 elections FRELIMO faced growing popular discontent due to the conditions of poverty in which people lived, the low salaries paid to professionals and the declining public services. Chissano expressed FRELIMO's irritation with the opposition which he accused of being 'destructive'. 'I think', he said, 'opposition should at least try to come up with their own programmes if they oppose ours.'[75] Aware that a remote bureaucratic government might well find itself alienated from the population, as had happened in the early years after independence, FRELIMO announced some constitutional changes in 1997 which would give a certain measure of local autonomy to municipalities. Even so the government feared that RENAMO would profit electorally from the discontent, the scale of which was forcefully brought home in the local elections in 1998 when the electorate stayed away and turnout was a mere 15 per cent.

Nervousness existed not only in the FRELIMO government but in the international donor community which had invested so much of its prestige in securing a stable outcome to the Mozambican civil war. There was anxiety also about the coming elections for the legislature and for the office of president which were due to be held in 1999. As the Mozambique government could not afford to mount an election as elaborate as that of 1994, there were fears that a flawed process might give an excuse for disillusioned members of RENAMO to go back to the bush. In the end the USA agreed that it would fund the elections and once again an international observer corps was deployed to monitor the voting.

The elections were held in December 1999 with a turn out of 68.09 per cent. Although RENAMO unsuccessfully challenged a number of the results, the outcome was similar to that of 1994 though it showed a marked closing of the gap between RENAMO and FRELIMO. Chissano once

---

[74]EIU, op. cit.; *ARB* June-July 1998—$ 47.6m supposedly spent on renewing cashew trees had disappeared.

[75]*Peace and Reconstruction. Interview with President Joaquim Alberto Chissano* (Harare: SARDC, 1997. Occasional Paper), p. 5.

again gained an absolute majority but with a vote of 52.29 per cent against Dhlakama's 47.71 per cent. Dhlakama had increased his share of the poll significantly from 33.7 per cent in 1994. In the elections for the national assembly, RENAMO emerged victorious in six provinces with FRELIMO winning in five. In 1994 FRELIMO had come first in Niassa which in 1999 narrowly supported RENAMO. FRELIMO won 133 seats with 48.54 per cent of the vote while RENAMO won 118 seats with 38.81 per cent. FRELIMO had managed to increase its share of the vote but only at the expense of minor parties.[76]

Joaquim Chissano had survived a potential electoral upset but the elections showed that, since 1994, FRELIMO had made little progress in the central areas of the country while RENAMO had survived as a political party and had not withered away during five years of peace which had left it in the political wilderness.

International orientations

During the peace process, and particularly during 1992–4, Mozambique had been virtually a protectorate of the United Nations. Once the elections were over and the UN began to withdraw FRELIMO had to find a position for itself in an international order that had changed in many fundamental ways. Mandela and the ANC had emerged victorious from the elections in South Africa and the new order in southern Africa promised a wholly new level of cooperation between the states of the region. This took the form of a reorganisation of the old SADCC and, in 1995, of a move to bring Mozambique into the Commonwealth.

The proposal that Mozambique should join the Commonwealth took most of the members of that body by surprise but, strongly backed by the southern African states, it was voted a member at the Auckland meeting in 1995. This move to join what had always been a 'club' of Anglophone nations was justified on the grounds that Mozambique had cooperated closely with Commonwealth policies against Rhodesia and apartheid South Africa and had suffered considerably as a result. In 1987 a special Commonwealth fund had been created to compensate Mozambique for its losses. Those who knew their history could also point out that until 1930 Mozambique had virtually been a British colony, with its northern and central regions ruled by British-controlled charter and plantation companies. Chissano believed that joining the Commonwealth would bring a wide range of benefits in the form of regional cooperation but saw it also as a

[76]Details of the election results on http://www.mozambique.mz/governo/eleicoes/finais.htm.

firm commitment by Mozambique to the liberal democratic path of political development.

Mozambique's accession to Commonwealth membership greatly alarmed Portugal which saw one of the eight ships in the worldwide Lusophone fleet sailing away to join the Anglophones. It was certainly this shock which stimulated the diplomatic initiatives which resulted in 1996 in the creation of the Comissão dos Paises de Língua Oficial Portuguesa (CPLP) of which Mozambique was a founder-member.

The floods of 2000: a defining moment

In late February 2000, with the new government only a few weeks in office, Mozambique was hit by the worst floods in living memory. Cyclone 'Eline' hit the coast of Mozambique on 21–22 February and, overnight on 25 February, the lower reaches of all the rivers from the Incomati to the Buzi broke their banks inundating vast areas of land. The scale of the disaster was such that the number of displaced persons (at one stage numbering 700,000) and the need for emergency aid almost threw Mozambique back into the situation it had been in before the end of the civil war.

However, as the disaster worsened, the television crews of the world were on hand and the dramatic rescue operations carried out by helicopters which appeared on prime-time television led to a massive international relief operation The government for its part was faced with a vast organisational task in managing the relief effort, the distribution of aid and the resettlement of refugees. The floods caused widespread damage. Seven hundred people lost their lives and in Gaza province alone 200,000 head of cattle perished while hundreds of thousands of people were displaced. Moreover there were many wholly unforeseen side effects like the dislodging of buried land mines by the floods. The net effect was to revive the flow of relief aid at a time when donors were beginning to tire of supporting Mozambique's economy. The Mozambique government received an additional $ 350m in aid, while £ 22m was privately donated to charities by the British public alone. A widely-held view was summed up in *The Times'* headline 'Mozambique must not be allowed to sink'. Mozambique had become the model for a country trying to recover from civil war and to establish democratic institutions, and therefore deserved special treatment from the international community.[77]

[77]For a preliminary assessment of the impact of the flood see Linus C. Okere, 'British press reporting of the Mozambique floods: the Baby Rosita factor', paper presented to an international conference 'Mozambique in the Commonwealth: urban and environmental realities after the flooding', Institute of Commonwealth Studies, London, October 2000.

The great flood of February 2000 highlighted in a dramatic way many of the themes that had marked Mozambique's twenty-five years of independence. The flood itself was an overwhelming external catastrophe, which Mozambicans themselves could not control, and which literally swamped the country's painstaking plans for development. Once more Mozambique was placed at the mercy of the aid donors while the tentative steps taken towards greater self-sufficiency were wiped out. The urgent need for relief and the medium-term problems of resettlement brought administrative challenges which stretched the capabilities of the government to breaking point. Once again FRELIMO had been caught unprepared by the magnitude of the challenge it faced, though with some skill the party leadership used the catastrophe to do what it had always done best, to win friends and influence people in the international community. The devastated country won the sympathy and concern of the world.

Yet experienced Mozambique watchers had a distinct impression of *déjà vu*. The repetitive cycles of Mozambique's history were encapsulated in this paradigm of disaster and chaos followed by international relief and tentative recovery. This cycle was confirmed by Chissano himself who, in a television interview during the flood crisis, renewed his call for a cancellation of Mozambique's foreign debt, so that Mozambique could raise fresh loans. In this way even the wisest and most experienced of leaders, who in so many ways personified independent Mozambique, found himself bound to the wheel of history.

6

GUINEA-BISSAU

Joshua Forrest

Guinea-Bissau's independence in 1974 was celebrated with unusual acclaim throughout Africa and other parts of the world because of two main factors. First, it signified the culmination of the militarily successful eleven-year anti-colonial struggle waged by the Partido Africano da Independência da Guiné e Cabo Verde (PAIGC).[1] Secondly, Amílcar Cabral, who had led and steered the movement, had placed Guinea-Bissau 'on the international map' through his articulate expression of the legitimacy of the country's nationalist struggle in the face of Portuguese colonial exploitation.[2] The achievement of independent power augmented the international visibility of the PAIGC and of Guinea-Bissau (despite Cabral's own assassination the previous year). At the same time, the popular trust generated by the PAIGC during the course of the lengthy nationalist struggle and the party's pragmatic success in organising and directing that struggle produced considerable domestic confidence in the ability of the new ruling party successfully to manage the country's political and economic affairs.

Nonetheless, as will be shown, throughout the period 1974 to 2000, the PAIGC would not prove capable of achieving its goals in political system-building or economic development. I do not explain this as a problem intrinsic to that political party but rather in terms of three broader phenomena that have characterised postcolonial Guinea-Bissau as they have other similar sub-Saharan African polities: (1) economic policy choices that were of direct benefit to state elites (despite noteworthy tactical shifts) and which deepened the country's economic weakness; (2) the effect of enduring and formidable

---

[1]For an analysis of Guinea-Bissau's liberation struggle see Mustafah Dhada, *Warriors at Work: How Guinea was Really Set Free* (Niwot CO: University of Colorado Press, 1993).

[2]See Patrick Chabal, *Amílcar Cabral: Revolutionary Leadership and Peoples' War* (Cambridge University Press, 1983); for Cabral's own writings and speeches see Amílcar Cabral, *Unity and Struggle* (London: Heinemann, 1980); *Revolution in Guinea* (New York: Monthly Review Press, 1970); *Return to the Source* (London: Monthly Review Press, 1973).

social, political and economic legacies from the colonial and precolonial periods; and (3) the increasingly personalistic and factionalised nature of politics, reflecting the informalisation of political power.[3]

In the first place, then, it is crucial to recognise that the country's continuing economic malaise was in part the consequence of the policy decisions of the post-independence political elites, both during the Luiz Cabral regime (1974–80) and under President Nino Vieira's autocracy (1980–99). These decisions reflected a growing reliance on external rather than domestic bases of economic activity; the failure to offer sufficiently fair trading opportunities to the majority of the country's producers; and the decision to allow certain politically-connected elites to benefit most fully from the economic changes that did occur. The increasing external economic dependence coincided with a preference for inappropriate mechanised technologies which represented a repetition of policy errors committed by the colonial state. Meanwhile, the economic free trade 'opening' of the late eighties and early nineties was managed in a way that largely benefited state-connected big traders. Overall, these policy choices ended up widening the growing rift between the majority of Guineans and the government thus adding to the growing level of popular discontent with the PAIGC leadership.

The second factor refers to 'objective' colonial and precolonial era legacies, which included an infrastructurally underdeveloped state, strongly-entrenched indigenous local-level power structures, and inter-ethnic social and economic practices. Although during the colonial period, annual taxation drives and forced labour provoked enormous hardships, the colonial state in Guinea was largely unsuccessful in introducing a system of appointed, pliant chieftainships. Ordinary peasants were often able to consolidate village-level political institutional practices that originated in the precolonial era— including collective leadership (in some parts of the country) and the political empowerment of locally-selected religious societies (in others).[4] Thus, while the colonial state held power at the national level, indigenous power structures at the local level remained at variance with the political preferences of the colonial state and acted as a *de facto* brake on the state's policy capacity (apart from once-a-year taxation drives and forced labour campaigns).

As a result, post-independence Guinea-Bissau would inherit a state infrastructure that hardly extended outside Bissau and was unable to

---

[3]Patrick Chabal and Jean-Pascal Daloz, *Africa Works: Disorder as Political Instrument* (Bloomington IN: Indiana University Press, 1999).

[4]These points are more fully detailed in my forthcoming study of Guinea-Bissau's colonial state-society relations.

execute its policies effectively. The newly-installed PAIGC leadership pursued an economic policy focused on the coordination of industrial and agricultural development, but the government lacked the administrative capacity to implement this successfully so that by the early eighties, the development drive had ground to a halt.[5] Meanwhile, in the countryside, where some 85 per cent of the population live, the localisation of power meant that people were able to reconsolidate community-level political institutions. At the same time, they pursued production and inter-ethnic marketing activities that reflected precolonial trade strategies and networks, which had endured through the colonial epoch.

It is important to appreciate the 'objective' infrastructural conditions with which the new leadership was confronted. These included a relatively insulated and underdeveloped state bureaucracy, a predominantly agricultural economy whose main cash crops were traded on 'informal' (unregulated) markets,[6] and a principally rural population that was able to strengthen its own political institutions at the local level through a process I call localisation. These defining characteristics of the Guinean polity would, in fact, help to shape the country's political and economic evolution through the postcolonial period 1974–2000.

The third factor accounting for Guinea-Bissau's lack of development was the growing 'informalisation' of politics, through which rules and institutions become less important than informally-crafted personal power networks within the state.[7] Mustafah Dhada argues that this process actually began in Guinea-Bissau during the armed struggle, in that Amílcar Cabral's charismatic, personalised leadership, and not simply the organisational skills of the PAIGC, accounts for the success of the national liberation struggle.[8] Although this is partially true, it is also important to emphasise that the choices made by peasants to support the PAIGC during the nationalist campaign reflected a certain grassroots independence and a determination to secure local autonomy that went beyond Cabral's personal qualities.

[5]Rosemary E. Galli and Jocelyn Jones, *Guinea-Bissau: Politics, Economics and Society* (London: Frances Pinter, 1987); Joshua B. Forrest, *Guinea-Bissau: Power, Conflict and Renewal in a West African Nation* (Boulder CO: Westview Press, 1992).

[6]Formal markets are either government-run or are private markets whose dealings are recorded for tax purposes; informal market trading takes place outside the orbit of officially known or acknowledged transactions. See Gracia Clark (ed.), *Traders Versus the State: Anthropological Approaches to Unofficial Economies* (Boulder CO: Westview Press, 1988); M. Estelle Smith (ed.), *Perspectives on the Informal Economy* (Lanham MD: University Press of America, 1990); Janet MacGaffey, *The Real Economy of Zaire* (Philadelphia PA: University of Pennsylvania Press, 1991).

[7]Chabal and Daloz, op. cit., pp. 1–2, 6–7.

[8]Dhada, op. cit.

Thus, I argue that it was more the case that 'personalism' became the defining motif of Guinea-Bissau's politics after independence, when the PAIGC had secured state power. The problem here, as throughout sub-Saharan Africa, in a context in which national states were defined by an absence of well-institutionalised bureaucracies and by unfamiliarity with a rules-based political culture, was that certain individuals and their factions came to dominate national political life. Thus, beginning gradually with the Luiz Cabral regime, and then to an intensified degree during Nino Vieira's presidency, the Guinean polity would be characterised by personalism and the efflorescence of factional discord within the urban-centered state bureaucracy.

In the following sections I pursue these points more fully, making clear how economic policy errors, enduring historical legacies, and the informal-isation of power in large part account for Guinea-Bissau's developmental problems.

ECONOMIC REFORM

I begin with a discussion of the issues and policy choices related to eco-nomic development. During the first six years of independence, the PAIGC government appeared to some extent to be guided by the general ideo-logical concerns of a rudimentary form of African socialism (although that term was not used). By this I mean that the economy was to be run by state officials responsible for managing markets and trading points, for overseeing the purchase of peasant-grown agricultural products, and estab-lishing prices for items of domestic consumption. Thus, the 'formal' economy was officially nationalised and run through Armazéns do Povo, or People's Stores, a chain of approximately 120 merchandise outlets and SOCOMIN (Sociedade Comercial-Industrial), a government import-export agency that sought to provide Guineans with a fair exchange of their agri-cultural products for imported goods. However, over time, due to low crop purchase prices, these outlet stores proved unable to offer the required diversity of products at affordable prices, and they were increasingly plagued by shortages of desired goods and by corrupt practices, such as profiteering by managers in the late seventies and early eighties.[9]

Moreover, the national government sought to promote industrial devel-opment, most notably through its support of the giant Cuméré production plant—devoted principally to rice hulling and groundnut oil production. However, this effort faltered as a result of a lack of trained personnel and

---

[9]Forrest, op. cit., pp. 87–9; Galli and Jones, op. cit., pp. 114–20.

the inadequate supply of primary products to assure a profitable return, illustrating thereby the mismatch between the plant's size and the country's productive capacity. The endeavour significantly increased the government's deficit.[10] The disappointing results of this major project virtually ended the potential for the synergetic, coordinated relationship between Guinea-Bissau's agricultural and proto-industrial sectors sought by the country's development planners.

At the same time, the state became increasingly dependent on foreign aid and on international development projects, but most of these were inadequately linked to local production systems and had little chance of success. A large part of the problem was the fact that government decision-makers were overly ambitious with development technology and too dismissive of existing production methods. For example, it was decided to use tractors and various modern mechanical devices to replace manual labour and local inputs in the construction of riverine dams with a view to creating new, or restoring older, ricefields. However, just as during the colonial period, multiple coordination and technical errors produced poor results—for instance, canal locks were either not installed or did not function properly. As a result of these and other factors, half the 'modern' mini-dams and dikes actually had a negative impact on rice production, another 25 per cent were not functioning at all, and only 25 per cent were working effectively.[11]

If the overly technical approach to development projects led to disappointing results, the outcome of the government's macro-level agricultural policy based on consumer food support and low producer crop prices proved similarly unsatisfactory. Indeed, by the early eighties, peasants were selling so little grain to the government that barely 2,000 tonnes were available from the People's Stores in urban areas.[12] The relative paralysis of trade involving state agencies during the late seventies and early eighties was countered by the expansion of informal cash-exchange and barter-based markets. This, in combination with the shrinkage of the formal trading sector, led the government to embark on privatisation reforms in 1984. However, from the outset, instead of grappling directly with on-farm problems and engaging in direct dialogue with the country's own traders, the government decided to work ever more closely with international advisers and lenders—thus, the initial privatisation reforms

---

[10]Galli and Jones, op. cit., p. 119.

[11]Rui Ribeiro, 'Barragens em bolanhas de agua salgada' in *SORONDA. Revista de Estudos Guineenses*, no. 4 (July 1987), pp. 38–57.

[12]*Nô Pintcha* [Bissau], 15 March 1986.

were bolstered by a standby IMF facility beginning in 1984. By 1987, on the advice of the IMF and the World Bank, the state initiated structural adjustment programmes (SAPs) that included the encouragement of private enterprise, currency devaluations, reduction of government spending, cuts in food subsidies and the raising of producer prices, especially of cashew nuts and palm kernels.[13] The government of Guinea-Bissau received a total of $ 31.2 million from the IMF in the period 1987–90 as an incentive to proceed with the reforms.[14]

These reforms had a mixed impact. The number of private firms did expand, and cash crops, mostly cashew and palm kernel, exported through state-monitored transportation routes increased by more than 50 per cent during this period.[15] In addition, cashew trees were cultivated in many parts of the country and cashew nuts became the country's primary export crop.[16] Furthermore, some women traders found ways of taking advantage of the freer trade climate to accumulate personal savings from selling both food and cash crops. Mancanhe and Balanta women augmented their income considerably through the sale of cashew nuts and cashew products (juice and wine), while also raising fruit and vegetable crops and selling them in open-air markets near Bolama and Bissau. As a result, the income of the women traders grew and was often invested in local economic 'societies', independent gender- and age-based mutual aid associations that used cash savings for both personal needs and for ceremonial purposes (such as funerals).[17] In some cases the increase in cash crop earnings by women also provided those involved with a somewhat larger degree of economic independence from traditional male elders at the village level.

However, the SAP reforms and the new privatisation policy also produced more problematic, if unforeseen, consequences. The expanded import-export trade generated a moderate proliferation of *pontas*, plantation-style trading-farms approved by the state, which rose from around 800 in 1989 to 1,200 by 1998.[18] Some of these *pontas* had originally been

[13]Forrest, op. cit., p. 89; Galli and Jones, op. cit., pp. 114–17.

[14]Forrest, op. cit., p. 91.

[15]Ibid., p. 90.

[16]'Guinea-Bissau on the reform path', *Africa Research Bulletin: Economic, Financial and Technical Services*, vol. 35, no. 1 (16 Jan.–15 Feb. 1998), p. 13320.

[17]Philip J. Havik, 'Female entrepreneurship in a changing environment: gender, kinship and trade in the Guinea-Bissau region' in Carl Risseuw and Kamala Ganesh (eds), *Negotiation and Space: A Gendered Analysis of Changing Kin and Security Networks in South Asia and sub-Saharan Africa* (London: Sage Publications, 1998).

[18]Rosemary Galli, 'Liberalisation is not enough: structural adjustment and peasants in Guinea-Bissau', *Review of African Political Economy*, no. 49 (winter 1990), pp. 52–68, and for the 1998 figure see *Africa Research Bulletin*, op. cit.

established during the nineteenth century as peanut-growing farms but had declined toward the end of that century due to the spread of indigenous warfare. They were then re-established to a limited degree after being encouraged by the colonial state in the period 1920–50, before being largely abandoned during the independence struggle in the sixties and seventies.[19] The expansion of these *pontas* during the late eighties and nineties reflected the postcolonial state's turn toward privatisation, with the owners, the *ponteiros*, becoming the key beneficiaries of medium- and long-term loans associated with the structural adjustment programme. The problem was that the majority of these *ponteiros* were high-ranking government officials who were not commercial farmers and who did not, therefore, have the ability or commitment to turn their new *pontas* into productive enterprises. As a result, few hectares of land were actually devoted to commercial farming, despite the fact that these *ponteiros* did receive favourable loans as part of this process of agricultural privatisation.[20]

Thus, the *ponteiros* and a number of private women traders were the greatest beneficiaries of the SAP reforms. However, the situation of the majority of food consumers did not markedly improve, as the instability of the national currency (peso) was marked by repeated devaluations, and the price of bread and rice (the basic food staples) continued to rise. Moreover, while the central government and the World Bank made available a small amount of credit to the *ponteiros*, they would not provide agricultural credit to the country's smallholders—the vast majority of Guinea-Bissau's farmers who produced most of the food on which the population depended.[21] The lack of credit support to small farmers and the inefficiency of the *pontas* also meant that the privatisation reforms would fail to stimulate a rise in the production of groundnuts, Guinea-Bissau's second most important cash crop, while producer price increases failed to offset the currency devaluations.

In regard to cashew, the primary export crop, government provided favourable cash or barter exchanges (usually two kilos of rice for one kilo of nuts) when world prices were high in the late eighties and early nineties but this rate of return declined as of 1991.[22] Cashew production peaked in 1992–3 at 30,000 tonnes (when the world prices were still reasonably good)[23]

[19]Joye Bowman, *Ominous Transition: Commerce and Colonial Expansion in the Senegambia and in Guinea, 1857–1919* (Aldershot: Avebury, 1997); Galli and Jones, op. cit., pp. 42–4.

[20]Galli, op. cit., pp. 63–4.

[21]Galli, op. cit., pp. 64–5.

[22]'Guinea-Bissau on the reform path', op. cit.; Galli, op. cit., p. 61.

[23]'Country surveys: Guinea-Bissau' in *Africa Today* (London: Africa Books Ltd, 1996, 3rd edn), p. 845.

but declined thereafter, which is why many traders stopped benefiting from selling cashew to export-oriented merchants and instead focused on local activities such as turning cashew into juice or wine and selling this locally.

On reflection, the slight expansion of the formal sector spurred by the reforms, while helping some traders for a limited time, did not, for the most part, benefit the preponderance of ordinary producers or consumers. However, it was the case, as it had been for many decades (and centuries), that most of the peasantry had access to alternative trading venues. Rural and urban 'informal' barter exchanges made it possible for people to obtain food (particularly rice) in many parts of the country. Despite the aforementioned benefits accruing to some women traders, the vast majority of women in fact traded locally in conventional ways on the informal markets that dominated, and continue to dominate, the rural sector.[24] Within many villages, barter exchanges involving cattle, cow products, handicraft artifacts and agricultural produce (vegetables and grains) continued to sustain most people. Meanwhile, imported goods (for example, clothing, radio, batteries and bicycles) were brought in from Senegal or from Guinea-Conakry by long-distance trade specialists known as *djulas*.[25] These *djula* traders continued to ply the rural market circuits selling their finished goods for CFA francs or bartering them for cash-value products produced by Guinea-Bissau's villagers such as peanut, dye, rice and artisanal goods.[26]

The combination of local informal market trade and long-distance unregulated commerce meant that most Guineans engaged in alternative marketing practices that represented the major portion of their exchanges. The SAP reforms had served to generate a modest amount of free trade activity but most benefits were enjoyed by a tiny group of traders, especially the *ponteiros*, as their connections to state agencies helped to ensure that they would receive most of the SAP-related favourable credit rates. What was occurring, in fact, was a growing division between predominantly export-oriented, state-connected, private traders and the vast majority of rural producers and unregulated traders who developed and expanded their independently-controlled exchange systems. Although a small section of women traders did profit from the freer trading climate, the government's policy-making priority of developing international links with the IMF and the World Bank (rather than focusing on internal rural-urban links and

[24]Havik, op. cit., p. 216.

[25]Forrest, op. cit., p. 93; Galli and Jones, op. cit., p. 114.

[26]Lars Rudebeck, 'The effects of structural adjustment in Kandjadja, Guinea-Bissau' in *Review of African Political Economy*, no. 49 (winter 1990), pp. 34–49.

rural development) had failed to produce a meaningful improvement in production, marketing or consumer choice for most people.

Moreover, by the nineties, the government's increasing dependency on external fiscal support coincided with a growing internal problem of corruption at various levels of the bureaucracy. Serious problems emerged regarding receipts and spending records on the part of various ministries, leading international lenders to lose confidence in the reliability of national accounts. At the same time, persistent arrears in the payment of the country's debt servicing convinced the IMF to halt its provision of financial payments to Guinea-Bissau in the period 1990–4. Nonetheless, the basic policy of external dependency remained unchanged, as the government pursued a wide variety of alternative external sources (mostly bilateral loans) and succeeded in obtaining development pledges totalling $ 357 million during a special donor Round Table held in Geneva in December 1994.[27] This, along with promises of government belt-tightening, of improvement in internal financial oversight procedures, and the decision to continue the policy of privatisation, convinced the IMF to restore credits to the government in January 1995.

Meanwhile, the Vieira regime's growing reliance on external sources was further diversified through the intensification of ties with France and with Francophone west Africa, especially Senegal, with a view toward incorporation into France's west African economic zone. By the mid-nineties, Vieira had attended several Franco-African summits and begun to consider exchanging the Guinean peso for the CFA franc. By 1997, this relationship had in fact progressed to Guinea-Bissau's formal integration into the CFA zone. The country adopted the CFA franc as its official currency in January 1997 and the peso was abandoned in July of that year.[28]

Overall, then, in regard to economic policy, the high-level machinations of the national government had generated an ever-widening gulf between, on the one hand, the leadership and state-linked traders and *ponteiros* and, on the other, the overwhelming majority of ordinary Guineans. Although a small number of ordinary traders did profit from the domestic freeing of trade activities and from easier access to officially sanctioned international market outlets, it was largely state employees or those with direct connections to them who benefited (legally or otherwise) from IMF funding and the World Bank loans. Most Guineans continued to make ends meet through

[27]'Country surveys: Guinea-Bissau', op. cit., p. 844.

[28]'Guinea-Bissau on the reform path', op. cit. However, there were problems with the currency transition, including the inability of thousands of farmers to exchange their pesos for francs before the July deadline. 'Guinea-Bissau,' *New Africa Yearbook 1999/2000* (London: IC Publications, 2000), p. 231.

informal local and long-distance markets. In this regard, the SAP reforms exacerbated the resource differential between elites and ordinary people, while bolstering the resources of those in power. At the same time, the ruling regime appeared to shift progressively into 'foreign' orbits (IMF, franc zone), underlining its ever more apparent disregard for the broader impact of its decisions on the general population.

THE LOCALISATION OF RURAL POLITICS

Similarly, the state leadership paid little attention to the fortification of a national administrative framework that would improve the quality of communication with, and feedback from, the grassroots level of ordinary villagers. Instead, as I make clear in the following section, ministry and party officials remained preoccupied by various national political crises and factional disputes. What is important to underline here is the fact that the system of regional and community-based administration—the village committees (*comités de tabanca*)—that had been established at independence became increasingly detached from central state power. In a process of augmenting localisation, these committees were for the most part either marginalised from rural politics or staffed by traditional village leaders who had no link to the national government.

It should be emphasised that this process was consistent with the broader political preferences of villagers—many of whom had fought against colonial rule, among other reasons, to ensure that central state power would not interfere with their daily lives. This commitment to local-level autonomy explains why they had so enthusiastically supported the PAIGC-led national liberation war. After independence, having achieved this success, they were more interested in reconsolidating local control than in ensuring the functioning of the newly-formed village committees.

Thus, a variety of localised peasant social and political structures with roots in the precolonial period, and that had never been fully 'captured' by the colonial state, now re-emerged with particular vigour. Political loyalties, social networks and local resources became more clearly organised around village-controlled rather than state-controlled power bases. As I make clear below, formerly defunct kingships were re-established and consolidated in a number of Mandjack areas; idiosyncratic social movements arose, including the Ki-Yang-Yang youth 'cult' among many Balanta; and there was a widespread expansion of 'spirit societies' controlled by locally selected religious-political leaders who had no link to the state. All these traditions hark back to ancient, community-based sources of political power and of social organisation.

I am not arguing here that Guinean peasants now opposed the PAIGC, but rather that they were more interested in reclaiming their relative political autonomy. They were able to do so in part because of the preoccupation of state leaders with growing factionalism within the party and because the state lacked the infrastructural resources and the personnel to enforce a more thoroughgoing bureaucratic control over rural political life. As a result, a *de facto* localisation of political power occurred throughout the countryside.

For example, in the village of Maque (Oio region), those who had been ascribed power according to historically-defined patterns ignored the village committees and continued to make primary local policy decisions.[29] In the mixed Mandinka-Balanta village of Kandjadja (also in Oio region), the village committee, purportedly a state agency, in fact consisted primarily of individuals from traditionally powerful families who continued to exert their authority in ways that were consistent with those families' preferences.[30] In the Balanta village of Infandre (Mansoa region), the village committee was ignored in favour of a grouping of male elders known as *pam* which continued to wield political and economic power.[31] In the principally Mandjack villages of Caboi and Caió (Cacheu region), social, economic and political power was exercised by religious leaders rather than by village committee members.[32]

More generally, in the predominantly Balanta villages of Tombali and Catio regions, different types of decision-making responsibilities were assigned to specific age-group units, with selected elders, known as *fan bodja*, accorded the right to determine how land tracts were utilised.[33] In these regions, the government's village committees were largely accepted but they did not displace the traditional, age-group based system of local political power.[34] Indeed, village control over local decision-making and disregard of colonial state-appointed officials had been a defining motif of rural political life among the Balanta until the seventies,[35] during which

[29]Hans Schoenmakers, 'Old men and new state structures in Guinea-Bissau' in *Journal of Legal Pluralism*, nos 25 and 26 (1987), pp. 117, 131–2.

[30]Lars Rudebeck, op. cit., p. 43.

[31]Schoenmakers, op. cit., pp. 132–3.

[32]Eve Lakshmi Crowley, 'Contracts with the Spirits: Religion, Asylum, and Ethnic Identity in the Cacheu Region of Guinea-Bissau' (PhD thesis, New Haven CT: Yale University, 1990), pp. 244–5.

[33]Walter Hawthorne, 'The Interior Past of an Acephalous Society: Institutional Change Among the Balanta of Guinea-Bissau, *c.*1400–*c.*1900' (PhD thesis, Stanford CA: Stanford University, 1998), p. 61; Diana Lima Handem, Nature et Fonctionnement du Pouvoir Chez les Balanta Brassa (Thesis, Paris: Ecole des Hautes Etudes en Sciences Sociales, Centre d'Etudes Africaines, 1985), p. 71.

[34]Forrest, op. cit., p. 52.

[35]Hawthorne, op. cit.; Handem, op. cit.

time they ignored colonial chiefs. This relative autonomy had in fact served as a mobilisational springboard for many Balanta fighters during the national liberation struggle. After independence, political power in Balanta areas continued to be wielded by locally-approved ruling groups (decision-making tending to take place collectively) rather than by state officials.

Moreover, by the eighties, enough social space had been created to make possible the emergence of a new social movement, known as Ki-Yang-Yang, forged by some young Balanta women who embraced many aspects of 'traditional' Balanta culture but rejected that which allocated power to male elders. By emphasising women's social and economic independence, the movement encouraged women's own resource accumulation and personal choice of marriage partners while promoting the destruction of ancestors' shrines.[36] It also countered the traditional practice among Balanta male youths of proving their virility through acts of violence or cattle theft.[37] The movement embraced modern aspects of social life such as formal schooling while condemning the use of alcohol. Overall, it represented defiance against traditional male power and 'backward' practices; but it also fully embraced a Balanta identity, which it sought to reform.

At the same time, it should be understood that Ki-Yang-Yang emerged in a socio-historical context that reflected a long history of women's secret societies among the Balanta,[38] as well as an ancient tradition among Balanta youth of temporarily defying their elders in order to assert their personal independence.[39] In this respect, Ki-Yang-Yang was both a modern and a distinctly Balanta movement. However, it declined precipitously in the nineties (with participant youth apparently running out of rebellious steam),[40] and did not, in the end, displace the *fan bodja* and other elder male authority groups or the many age-group-based power structures that continue to orient village life in Tombali and Catio regions. Ultimately, the relative weakness of the village committees, the continued importance of the age-groups, and the ability of social movements such as Ki-Yang-Yang to emerge, all reflected the extent to which rural local power in the postcolonial period has been determined through community-based structures rather than through state-directed mechanisms.

This was made particularly clear in Cacheu region where there occurred the expansion of ancient spirit societies and the revival of popular, community-based kingships. Here it is important to note that through the

[36]Philip J. Havik, op. cit., p. 216.
[37]Carlos Cardoso, 'Ki-Yang-Yang: uma nova religião dos Balantas?' in *Soronda: Revista de Estudos Guineenses*, no. 10 (July 1990), pp. 3–15.
[38]Havik, op. cit., p. 217.
[39]Hawthorne, op. cit.; Handem, op. cit.
[40]Havik, op. cit.

course of the colonial period, many Mandjack villagers in Cacheu had rejected the authority of those traditional chiefs who had been deemed to be linked to the collaborationist, pro-colonial, Basserel kingdom.[41] As a result, by the time of independence, the Basserel king wielded no meaningful influence while most Cacheu region communities were effectively autonomous. In many cases individual chiefs were chosen who represented a new generation unconnected to state power and who were determined to defend village autonomy.

At the same time, in a process that occurred throughout the colonial period and intensified after independence, many Cacheu region communities came to be ruled by spiritual groupings that were formed on the basis of territorial affiliation, profession, age-group membership, or common devotion to a particular spirit form.[42] Through these spirit societies, people chose local political leaders, participated in frequent collective meetings, made crucial decisions regarding interpersonal relations as well as resource accumulation, and invested their savings in ways that reinforced their devotion to and inclusion within those spirit societies. Here it is also important to emphasise that spirit society leaders enabled people of non-Mandjack origin to join these societies and to rise to prominent roles within them. As a result, many migrants from Papel, Mancanhe, Balanta, Mandinka, and other ethnic group origins did in fact join these spiritual groupings, which became ethnically mixed, thereby building on a lengthy historical tradition of inter-ethnic mingling in Guinea that dates from the early precolonial period.[43]

These forms of local power consolidation were not perturbed by the advent of postcolonial state-building, as the aforementioned village committees generally were not respected (or had not been created in the first place) in most of Cacheu region. Moreover, by the late eighties, people decided to take advantage of their *de facto* local level autonomy to devise an entirely new, often spontaneously created form of self-rule: popular kingships. These kingships emerged in local communities as a kind of political movement among ordinary people who either reconstructed older monarchical forms in 'modern', i.e., popularly chosen, form or simply 'invented' monarchies that did not previously exist.[44] Most of the new

---

[41]Edward Eric Gable, 'Modern Manjaco: the Ethos of Power in a West African Society' (PhD thesis, Charlottesville VA: University of Virginia, 1990).

[42]See Crowley, op. cit.; Gable, op. cit.

[43]George E. Brooks, *Landlords and Strangers: Ecology, Society, and Trade in Western Africa, 1000–1630* (Boulder CO: Westview Press, 1993).

[44]On the subject of popular kingships see Clara Carvalho, 'Ritos de Poder e a Recriaçao da Tradição. Os Régulos Manjaco da Guiné-Bissau' (PhD thesis, Lisbon: Instituto Superior de Ciências do Trabalho e da Empresa, Lisbon, 1998).

popular kingships were established between 1987 and 1993; for example, several kingships were reconstituted in Caió district, on the isle of Jeta and on the isle of Pecixe. Whether created or reconstructed, the kingships did not replace spiritual societies and individual chieftainships but rather were added on to them—serving essentially as unifying cultural representations of social integration that provided people with a reinvigorated sense of community and of social and political identity.

What was the reaction of the national government to these popularised kingships in Cacheu region? Although the state had outlawed traditional kingships shortly after independence, by the early nineties the marginalisation of official state structures from community life meant that alternative realms of authority were the sole sources of legitimate political leadership at the local level. Thus, in 1992, the central government officially rendered legal the restoration of local kingships—and then immediately sought to incorporate them into a fledgling, paper-thin, national administrative system through the appointment of selected kings and chiefs to formal posts such as 'sector president'. However, these new kings did not seek to involve the state in local affairs, nor did they aid the government in carrying out national policies, but rather served largely to protect their local communities from external intervention. Thus, the kingships were restricted principally to local political actors who above all affirmed the political autonomy of their respective communities, not through any form of active resistance—interactions with state authorities were respectful—but simply by not serving as state actors. Ultimately, they represented a mechanism through which local power was revitalised and the state was, in effect, forced to retreat from community-level political and social decision-making. This localisation of power, inherited from the precolonial and colonial periods and expanded in the post-independence period, functioned as a *de facto* barrier to the state's penetrative reach and dramatically illustrated the limits of the government's national policy capacity.

POLITICAL INFORMALISATION, AUTOCRACY, AND MULTIPARTYISM

If the national state wielded little direct control over rural communities— while centuries-old social institutions exerted powerful influence—it was also true that, at the higher reaches of central state power, political incoherence and discord set back internal bureaucracy-building. Indeed, in an institutional context defined by a fragile state and the absence of attention to formal rules, internal factionalism and the informalisation of power undermined the emergence of an effective national political system and the development of constructive linkages between state and population. Like other sub-Saharan African regimes, the political unity that had been forged within the nationalist party degenerated after independence, manifesting itself in the advent of sectional (personalistic and factional) power struggles. The postcolonial presidents of Guinea-Bissau remained in power in so far as they were able to strengthen their respective power networks and incorporate into those networks supporters from the bureaucracy and the armed forces.

In a process that began with President Luiz Cabral and intensified under President Nino Vieira, sectionalism was revealed in, *inter alia*, the preparation of coups d'état, the repression of opponents to the regime (both real and imagined), and a breakdown of inter-ethnic unity (among leaders) which led to a politics of ethnic exclusivism.[45] As noted before, the peoples of Guinea-Bissau had historically displayed a large measure of inter-ethnic cooperation in respect of the formation of political alliances, trade, social relations and military affairs, during the precolonial and colonial periods, as well as during the anti-colonial nationalist war.[46] However, the breakdown of political unity at the level of the national leadership (though not at the popular, community level) after independence brought about a degree of tension among a number of senior officials. During the late seventies, discord over various practical issues (such as the coordination of the Bissau and Praia bureaucracies) as well as over development policy issues, led to tension between the Cape Verdean and Guinean wings of the PAIGC. This discord appeared to assume special importance due to the lingering impact of colonially-induced antagonisms along with more objective social and cultural differences. Cape Verdeans in Guinea-Bissau, most of whom had been brought in by the Portuguese to Guinea-Bissau over the past century to perform low-level administrative functions, are of *mestiço* background and were often perceived to have originally obtained special privileges under colonial rule, including education, training, and access to government jobs.[47] The fact that Cape Verdeans had been classified as *civilizados*, which accorded them a social status of near equivalence to the Portuguese, accentuated their separation from the *indigena* African masses and helped set the stage for postcolonial conflict.

As tensions developed during the late seventies, some Guinean PAIGC members in Bissau became wary of the high proportion of people of Cape Verdean origin in the Bissau-based government and played up their history

[45]Galli and Jones, op. cit., pp. 92–9; Forrest, op. cit., pp. 55–8; and Joshua B. Forrest, 'Guinea-Bissau since independence: a decade of domestic power struggles', *The Journal of Modern African Studies*, 25, 1 (1987), pp. 95–116.

[46]Forrest, work-in-progress.

[47]Galli and Jones, op. cit., pp. 31–2, 93, 99.

of social advantages. Luiz Cabral's inability to grapple effectively with this issue contributed substantially to growing popular discontent, particularly in Bissau. The PAIGC lacked a strong, popular leader of Amílcar Cabral's stature to overcome this growing tension. He had been the main driving force of bi-nationalist unity between the two countries, and now there was no high-level party cadre who was able to stall the rise of anti-Cape Verdean sentiment. In 1980, resentment against Cape Verdeans in the PAIGC was exacerbated when the party began to formulate national constitutional proposals which specified that Cape Verde's president should be Cape Verdean while introducing no restriction for Guinea-Bissau's president— a clear signal of potential continued Cape Verdean control in Bissau. Taking advantage of immediate hardships caused by severe rice shortages in the capital city, João Bernardo (Nino) Vieira, the prime minister and military commander, organised support groups with the armed forces and successfully carried out a virtually bloodless coup d'état.[48] This move would produce an end to the relationship between Guinea-Bissau and Cape Verde, while also resulting in the ousting of many Guineans of Cape Verdean origin from top positions within the Bissau regime.

As a result of these measures, and because of his reputation as the country's most famous war veteran (due to his accomplishments as a military commander during the liberation struggle), President Nino Vieira's regime enjoyed at first very strong popular support. However, the illegal seizure of power delegitimised the notion of a formal, institutional power transfer among a number of other government leaders and military men and fuelled their ambitions, as had occurred throughout sub-Saharan Africa since independence.[49] This exacerbated internal schisms within the Bissau government and intensified its organisational fragmentation through the eighties. Actual or purported coup attempts were allegedly carried out by Vice-President (at the time) Vitor Saúde Maria (1983) and the head of the armed services, General Paulo Correia (1985).[50]

All such attempts failed. Maria escaped to Portugal while Correia, not as fortunate, was executed along with six others in 1986. It was widely believed that ethnic affiliation was a factor, as Correia, a Balanta, had a large following among the mostly Balanta armed forces. President Vieira, who is Papel, may thus have sought to forestall the potential build-up of a pro-Correia Balanta military faction by getting rid of him. The fact that

[48]Forrest, *Guinea-Bissau*, pp. 56–8; Galli and Jones, op. cit., p. 99.

[49]Robert H. Jackson and Carl G. Rosberg, *Personal Rule in Black Africa* (Berkeley CA: University of California Press, 1982).

[50]Forrest, *Guinea-Bissau*, pp. 58–62.

the highly-respected government general prosecutor, Viriato Pã (a prominent lawyer of Balanta backround), was also executed suggests the extent of Vieira's concern (or paranoia) over an ethnically-inspired backlash.[51]

Overall, these events added to the level of internal dysfunction plaguing the Guinea-Bissau state, while continuing political tensions convinced the president to instruct his security forces to implement a more thorough oversight of government officials. The Vieira regime assumed an increasingly authoritarian character, which would intensify through the nineties, despite the advent of multiparty elections (as discussed below). Two mass graves were found in September and October 1999—one near Bissau, with 14 bodies of people believed killed during the mid-nineties, and the other near Mansoa, containing 22 bodies, apparently of accused coup plotters executed in 1986.[52] The impact of the discovery of these mass graves in Bissau was to augment the level of popular hostility against the PAIGC in general and Vieira in particular.

By the early nineties, the Vieira-controlled state, facing real and perceived internal challenges, largely out of contact with the population, and ever more economically reliant on international largesse, decided to adopt a formal democratic political framework, which had become a condition of further IMF/World Bank funding. Thus, the advent of multiparty democracy and the emergence of new political parties in 1991, marked the end of the one-party state and the beginning of multiparty competition. I will suggest here that, while multipartyism channelled a wellspring of discontent against the Vieira regime, it also exacerbated the level of political infighting and did not produce a stable acceptance of rules-based alternation of political power.

As discussions over the timing of forthcoming national elections proceeded, an alliance of new parties, the Democratic Forum, fearing electoral manipulation by the Vieira regime, pressed for the establishment of a national multiparty electoral commission to oversee the forthcoming elections. The commission was set up in 1992, but disputes over procedural issues regarding the legislative and presidential ballots led to repeated postponements.[53] In addition, a purported coup attempt in March 1993 led to the arrest of 50 soldiers, which thrust the country back into a state of

---

[51]Beyond the six 1986 executions, 52 purported supporters of Correia, most of whom were Balanta, received long prison terms.

[52]LUSA [Portugese news agency] report, 9 October 1999; José Pedro Castanheira, 'A última batalha', *Revista/Expresso* [Lisbon, report from Bissau], 22 May 1999.

[53]Tony Hodges, 'Guinea-Bissau' in *New Africa Yearbook 1999/2000* (London: IC Publications, 1999), p. 227.

political instability, and resulted in the elections being delayed until July 1994.

The PAIGC became the majority party within the national popular assembly by winning 62 seats (out of 102), while the Movement-Bafatá, headed by Domingos Fernandes Gomes, assumed the position of the main opposition with 19 seats. The remaining seats were apportioned among the Social Renovation Party (PRS), with 12 seats; the Union for Change (UM), with 6 seats; and the Liberation Front for the National Independence of Guinea (FLING), with 1 seat.[54]

In the presidential election, held in August 1994, João Bernardo Vieira was unable to win outright on the first ballot, so a second round was held in which he, with 1,599,930 votes and 52.02 per cent of the share of the vote, edged out Kumba Yalla, who had 1,147,518 ballots and 47.98 per cent of the vote.[55] In the campaign leading up to this contest, the incumbent sought to play the ethnic card to the fullest extent, repeatedly warning the population not to allow a Balanta to gain presidential power and implying that Kumba Yalla, who is Balanta, would rule on a narrow ethnic basis. Nonetheless, with nearly half of the ballots, Yalla proved that he had gained support from a cross-section of ethnic groups, as had Vieira.[56] Thus, people did not vote along narrow ethnic lines, the results instead reflecting a lengthy history of inter-ethnic cooperation in Guinea-Bissau. Vieira won for a variety of reasons, including an intense propaganda drive on his part, the benefits of the stature and visibility of his position as president, and the fact that the multiple political divisions among the opposition in the parliamentary balloting left many unsure about displacing Vieira from the presidency.[57] At the same time, some Guineans were convinced, although this could not be proved, that the president had found a way of distorting the polling process and had not in fact won 52 per cent of the vote.

Overall, the advent of multipartyism meant at best a minor step forward with regard to the establishment of a popularly legitimate democratisation process. While the election process itself represented a popular channel for political participation, the extensive political manoeuvrings and instability in the two years that preceded the voting (including an apparent

---

[54]'Country surveys: Guinea-Bissau', op. cit., p. 843.

[55]*Elections Today: News from the International Foundation for Electoral Systems*, vol. 5, no. 1 (December 1994), p. 27.

[56]The Balanta represent 32 per cent of the population—the largest single ethnic group—and not all voted for him.

[57]Gérald Gaillard, 'Guinée-Bissau. Un pas douloureux vers la démocratie' in *Afrique Contemporaine*, no. 191 (Jul.-Sept. 1999), p. 54.

coup attempt), as well as the president's heavy-handed 'campaigning' (which many interpreted as a not-so-veiled threat to vote for the PAIGC) cast doubt on the commitment of the participants to rules-based electoral proceedings. Moreover, as before, the Vieira regime ended up remaining in full control of the government and the PAIGC became the majority party in parliament, so that many Guineans were left with the sense that, somehow, Vieira had found a way to remain in full command of the state and that the multipartyism meant little in terms of who held the reins of national power.

Vieira himself seemed to handle poorly the criticisms of his regime voiced by opposition party members. He unleashed harsh attacks on his opponents and many politicians felt that his government continued to suppress key activists behind the scenes. Indeed, despite the elections, Vieira's behaviour would increasingly parallel that of other west African autocrats. He was protected by personally-appointed special guards, he sent police to watch over or threaten opponents, and he isolated himself ever more fully from the public and from members of his own party. In this respect, it appears that multipartyism in the early nineties contributed to the informalisation of power and to the exacerbation, rather than the easing, of autocratic rule. It helped to diversify the field of politics and provided for a greater number of organisational and personal challengers to the president without ever producing evidence of a broader commitment to pluralistic political values or to a rules-based political order. Moreover, the president and his loyalists reacted to the multiplication of politicians by hardening the autocratic aspects of the regime. At the same time, the fiscal crisis of the Guinean state, caused by inefficient accounting, corruption, and repeated funding misallocations, left the government unable to pay civil servants' salaries.[58] Government workers reacted by engaging in a series of strikes, which added to the sense of political unrest, contributed to the near-paralysis of many ministries, and augmented the growing popular dismay with Vieira's administration.

In 1997, President Vieira sought to deflect criticism by replacing his prime minister, Saturnino da Costa, with a popular war veteran, Carlos Correia.[59] However, internal PAIGC discord regarding Vieira's autocratic methods and other issues produced schisms in the party throughout 1997. By early 1998, that discontent came to be shared by a number of top military officers, and Vieira, as he had done in the past, sought to preclude the potential for a coup attempt by singling out for dismissal one of his presumed would-be coup-plotters—this time the military chief of staff, Ansumane

[58]Tony Hodges, op. cit., p. 228.
[59]Ibid.

Mané. However, as is made clear in the section below, Vieira overplayed his hand, since the armed forces had become sufficiently alienated from the president and the general population had tired of misrule. Many villagers, for example, did not believe that Vieira (or the ruling party) had won the elections cleanly, and were convinced that his continuing hold on power had become a type of autocracy that could eventually threaten their own local autonomy. The fact that most soldiers, who hail from rural backgrounds, are closely attuned to popular opinion added to a political climate that would prove unfavourable to the president.

POPULAR WAR

As the national regime became ever-more distant from the peasantry, it also became alienated from Vieira's own original power base, the military. Moreover, by 1998, demonstrating the extent to which he had enclosed himself in a political shell, Vieira became increasingly suspicious of his chief of staff, Mané, with whom he had previously shared a long-term political bond (Mané had engineered the 1980 coup that had placed Vieira in power) and personal friendship (Vieira's mother referred to Mané as her son).[60] In January 1998, Vieira suspended Mané on suspicion of gun-running, a charge that, even if not altogether false, was more politically than legally motivated. While Mané was later found innocent by a parliamentary committee, it is probable that army personnel loyal to him were involved in selling arms to Casamance separatists who were engaged in an armed rebellion struggle against the Dakar regime.[61] However, many soldiers and officers loyal to Vieira were also involved in the lucrative underground gun trade.[62] The problem here was that the Senegalese government was convinced that Ansumane Mané was the principal force behind arms sales to the Casamance separatists.[63] This was not the case and Vieira knew this, but the president, who had spent the previous years courting Senegalese (and Francophone) support, felt the need to demonstrate to Dakar his public

[60]Gaillard, op. cit., p. 46.
[61]Reuters report, Richard Waddington, 8 June 1998; *Africa Research Bulletin*, vol. 35, no. 2 (1–28 Feb. 1998), p. 12995; Gaillard, op. cit., p. 51. For more details on the Casamance secession struggle and links with Guinea-Bissau see Gaillard, op. cit., and Linda J. Beck, 'Sovereignty in Africa: from colonial inheritance to ethnic entitlement? The case of the Casamance secessionist movement', paper presented at the American Political Science Association meeting, September 1999.
[62]Gaillard, op. cit., p. 51; *Africa Research Bulletin*, vol. 35, no. 2 (1–28 Feb. 1998), p. 12995, and vol. 35, no. 8 (1–31 August 1998), p. 13226.
[63]Gaillard, op. cit., p. 51; Beck, op. cit.

condemnation of the Casamance separatists. Vieira thus played up Dakar's charges and continued to foster suspicion regarding Mané in the months following the January suspension. By June 1998, the president, who feared a coup attempt, decided to remove Mané from the position of military chief of staff.[64]

For the bulk of the armed forces, this was the final blow. It precipitated a widespread military revolt on 7 June that was quickly joined by the vast majority of soldiers. Only the most devout Vieira army loyalists were willing to defend his regime. An estimated 2,000 out of a total of 3,500 Guinean soldiers deserted the president and joined the pro-Mané rebellion.[65] This is why, to save his regime, the president turned to President Diouf of Senegal to plead for military aid. Nearly 3,000 Senegalese troops were sent to Bissau in June 1998 along with several hundred support troops from Guinea-Conakry.[66] This suggested the extent to which Vieira had invested his own political loyalties externally (rather than domestically), and symbolised the final abandonment of his erstwhile popular base.

However, Vieira's reliance on (chiefly) Senegalese military support backfired. The Casamance separatists, who share strong historical links with Guineans (Casamance was part of Portuguese Guinea until 1886), were viewed favorably in much of Guinea-Bissau.[67] The northern rural population in particular, which enjoys deep family, ethnic and trade-based ties to the peoples of the Casamance, did not wish to see the Bissau government become a close ally of a Dakar regime determined to crush the separatist movement.[68] Mané was known to be sympathetic to the Casamance fighters and this increased the level of domestic support for his troops.[69]

However, it must be emphasised that overall popular hostility toward the Vieira regime was the primary motivation of the rebels. The government had manifested in virtually every sphere of public policy-making a profound disregard for the ordinary Guinean and a willingness to extend autocratic rule in order to preserve power. When the war erupted, rebel supporters

---

[64]Gaillard, op. cit., p. 51 in fact suggests that the Senegalese government may have pressured Vieira into dismissing Mané. It was also the case that Guinea-Bissau and Senegal had signed a security agreement in October 1997, reflecting Vieira's support for Dakar's effort to curtail separatist rebels, see *Africa Research Bulletin*, vol. 35, no. 2 (1–28 Feb. 1998), p. 12995.

[65]Associated Press report, Ian Stewart, 25 June 1998.

[66]Gaillard, op. cit., p. 47, and Linda J. Beck, op. cit.

[67]Jorge Heitor, 'Conversações sobre o futuro de Casamansa decorrem na Gâmbia' in *Diário de Notícias*, 21 June 1999.

[68]Gaillard, op. cit., pp. 51–2.

[69]'Guinea-Bissau. Army uprising,' *Africa Research Bulletin* vol. 35 no. 6 (1–30 June 1998), p. 13133.

openly compared their struggle to that of the independence war against the colonialists.[70] The rebels of Guinea-Bissau were, in fact, massively supported by the rural population—as much as 90 per cent according to BBC observers.[71]

Thus, despite the arrival of foreign troops to support the president, fighting continued from May through August 1998. Bissau was effectively divided in half, while the rebels were clearly in control of most of the countryside.[72] Heavy artillery and fierce firefighting continued from 8 June through the first three weeks of July within the city of Bissau and near the airport, just north of the capital. Senegalese troops figured prominently in the Bissau fighting, and were accused by Guineans of wanton looting and abuse of unarmed citizens.[73] Fierce fighting produced a mass exodus of the capital city (whose population totalled 300,000) in late June 1998, leaving it desolate except for the hundreds of bodies of dead soldiers littering the streets.[74]

Meanwhile, the Senegalese strengthened their contingent in Bissau with several hundred additional troops and covertly sent forces to northern Guinea-Bissau from southern Senegal in order to attempt a rear guard action against the pro-Mané fighters.[75] Senegalese troops also pounded the Guinean towns of Ingone and Bula with heavy artillery, both to lend support to Vieira's fight against pro-Mané forces and to attack Casamance separatists who were suspected of having set up bases in those towns.[76] But rural Guineans, acutely aware of Vieira's growing links to Dakar (and by extension to Paris), responded.[77] The massive popular support for the pro-Mané rebels virtually guaranteed both the military failure of the Senegalese quasi-mercenaries and the political demise of the Vieira government. By July 1998, the fighting had extended to key rural towns including Bafatá, Buba, Gabu, Farim, Mansoa and Canchungo.[78] People with access to rifles, including old hunting

[70]Statements from rebels, quoted in ibid.

[71]BBC report by Mark Doyle, Bissau, 7 July 1998.

[72]Associated Press reports by Ian Stewart, 24 June and 13 November 1998; BBC report, 7 July.

[73]BBC report by Mark Doyle, Bissau, 7 July 1998.

[74]Associated Press reports by Barry Hatton and David Guttenfelder, Bissau, 15 and 16 June 1998.

[75]Gaillard, op. cit., pp. 47, 52; 'Guinea-Bissau—Senegal. Array Chief of Staff suspended', *Africa Research Bulletin*, vol. 35, no. 2 (1–28 Feb. 1998), p. 12995.

[76]Associated Press reports, Ian Stewart, 16 and 19 June 1998, and Reuter's report, 18 June 1998.

[77]To cite one example, Guinea-Bissau and Senegal had signed a security agreement in October 1997 reflecting Vieira's support for Dakar's effort to curtail the Casamance separatist rebels. *Africa Research Bulletin*, vol. 35, no. 1 (Jan. 1–31 1998), p. 12958.

[78]Gaillard, op. cit., p. 47; ibid., p. 13189.

single-shots, and veterans of the independence struggle contributed to the rebel effort against Vieira loyalists and their Senegalese allies.[79]

A ceasefire was agreed upon in the last week of July 1998, and in August 1998 a peace accord was signed, but fighting broke out again six weeks later, during the first week of October 1998. Senegal sent 1,000 *diambar* crack troops to reinforce the 3,000 regulars already in Bissau.[80] Nonetheless, by October 1998, pro-Mané troops controlled all the towns outside the capital city.[81]

Various efforts at negotiation took place between November 1998 and January 1999, and temporary agreements were reached, with the Economic Community of West African States (ECOWAS) agreeing to send some troops (from Togo, Benin, Niger, Guinea and Senegal) to oversee the transition to a new government consisting of both rebel generals and Vieira regime officials.[82] However, this government did not prove functional and on 8 May, provoked by the arrival of a Guinea-Conakry warship transporting heavy arms to the Vieira loyalists, the rebels unleashed an all-out assault against the loyalists and their Senegalese support troops.[83] This would represent the final, decisive battle: pro-Mané troops pushed all loyalists (mostly members of the presidential guard) and Senegalese into the heart of Bissau and then out-fought them in the streets.[84] Shortly afterwards, President Vieira fled the country, first to the Gambia then to Portugal. The conquest of Bissau by Mané's fighters forced the surrender (or disappearance into hiding) of all remaining loyalist troops, prompting the departure of all remaining Senegalese allies. The total number of war casualties on both sides during the nearly year-long conflict was about 2,000 Guinean soldiers (loyal and rebel), a minimum of 1,000 Senegalese troops, and approximately 3,000 civilians.[85]

Although the principal impact of this rebel military victory was the popular overthrow of a despised regime, many domestic observers regarded the event as proof that the people of Guinea-Bissau had successfully resisted a Francophone effort at absorbing Guinea-Bissau into its political orbit. The success of the rebels in this regard was symbolised by their capture of a dozen French soldiers who were protecting the French Cultural Centre,

[79]Associated Press report by Ian Stewart, 26 June 1998.
[80]BBC report, 23 October 1998.
[81]Gaillard, op. cit., p. 48; BBC report, 23 October 1998.
[82]Associated Press report, 19 November 1998; Associated Press wire service, 27 December 1998; Africa News Service, Bissau, 15 December 1998.
[83]Gaillard, op. cit., p. 50; *Africa Research Bulletin*, vol. 36, no. 5 (1–31 May 1999), p. 13540.
[84]Castanheira, op. cit.
[85]Personal sources (April, May and June 1999), and Castanheira, op. cit.

and who emerged from the building with hands over their heads carrying white flags.[86] The French Cultural Centre was promptly destroyed.[87]

Within one week of their battle victory in May 1999, pro-Mané generals formed a ruling junta (led by Mané) and assumed full control of the national government.[88] As Mané claimed that he himself was uninterested in a formal political post, the victorious troops chose Malam Bacai Sanha, until then speaker of parliament, as interim president of the country, with Francisco Fadul, a highly-respected adviser to Mané, as prime minister; the junta itself continued to make all major decisions.[89]

The junta held fast to its promise of carrying out post-war national elections, which were held on 28 November 1999 (parliamentary vote and first round presidential ballot) and 16 January 2000 (presidential run-off). In the parliamentary balloting, the PAIGC lost its control of the legislature, with the Partido da Renovação Social (PRS) obtaining 38 seats and becoming the largest party in parliament; the Resistência Guiné Bissau (RGB) party 28 seats, and the PAIGC only 24 seats.[90] In the first round of presidential balloting, contested by twelve candidates, Kumba Yalla, head of the PRS, captured 38.8 per cent of the vote while interim president Malam Bacai Sanha of the PAIGC gained 23.4 per cent.[91] Yalla and Sanha then faced each other in a 16 January 2000 run-off ballot, in which Yalla was elected president of Guinea-Bissau with 72 per cent of the vote—and in doing so won revenge for his 1994 second place finish.[92]

President Yalla, a former PAIGC cadre with a reputation as an intellectual and a charismatic speaker, is intensely popular in many parts of the country, among a wide spectrum of ethnic groups, and not only among his own Balanta people.[93] As president, Yalla appointed a number of officials from other opposition parties—but not from the PAIGC, the party effectively

---

[86]Photograph of captured French commandos outside French Cultural Centre in Bissau in José Pedro Castanheira, op. cit.

[87]Ibid., and Gaillard, op. cit.

[88]Castanheira, op. cit.

[89]Personal information from Philip J. Havik, June 1999; *Africa Research Bulletin*, vol. 36, no. 5 (1–31 May 1999), p. 13541.

[90]Other parties receiving parliamentary seats included the Aliança Democrática (AD), 4 seats; the União para a Mudança (UPM), 3 seats; the Partido Social Democrático (PSD), 3 seats, and the União Nacional para a Democracia e o Progresso (UNDP), 1 seat. *Africa Research Bulletin*, vol. 37, no. 1 (1–31 January 2000), p. 13829; also: Wendy Cue, U.N. Information Officer, *Communication Bulletin*, Bissau, 21 December 1999, based on news reports from the BBC, *Diário de Notícias*, and PANA news service.

[91]Cue, op. cit.

[92]António Soares Lopes, 'Temos de ultrapassar os fantasmas do tribalismo', *Publico* [Lisbon: report from Bissau], 24 January 2000.

[93]*Africa Research Bulletin*, vol. 37, no. 1 (1–31 Jan. 2000), p. 13829.

displaced from power.[94] Several Balanta were nominated to key posts in the new government, including the Minister of the Interior, suggesting that Balanta would no longer be excluded from top posts, as they had been under the presidencies of Nino Vieira (1980–99) and Luiz Cabral (1974–80), while members of other ethnic groups also gained key ministerial posts.

Although it is too early to assess Yalla's regime, it appears likely that Ansumane Mané and other generals who played key roles in the popular war are wielding an influence on the newly-elected regime.[95] Thus, a key factor will be the nature of civil-military relations, especially as President Yalla himself has strong ties to the military: he was the preferred presidential candidate of the junta, and in the eighties had served as adviser to General Paulo Correia (a popular military officer who was executed in 1986 on treason charges).[96] Support for Yalla in 1999 was believed to represent an effort to affirm an historical link between Correia and Yalla, thus bestowing upon Yalla a sort of symbolic inheritance of the social memory of anti-Vieira military activism. For these reasons, it is likely that Yalla will allow the military a behind-the-scenes role in national decision-making.

Meanwhile, ethnic politics seems unlikely to cause political turmoil in the foreseeable future. Yalla's chief opponent for the presidency, Sanha, of Biaffada origin (a very small group) made much of Yalla's Balanta ethnic identity during the presidential campaign, as he sought to inspire concern about the potential Balanta predominance in a Yalla regime. Sanha in fact talked of a Balanta government bent on revenge for the 1986 executions of Correia and other Yalla allies.[97] However, considering that the PSR had pulled in a large number of votes from non-Balanta, this ethnic concern was clearly not broadly shared. Moreover, as Yalla's political party, the PSR, did not obtain a majority, the newly-elected president proceeded to build a relatively broad ruling coalition that included members of other parties and people from a variety of ethnic origins. Yalla, then, seems to be building upon the country's long history of inter-ethnic cooperation.

A more serious political problem facing the new government is whether to carry out a trial-in-absentia of former President Vieira, which is strongly favoured by some veteran military men (who wish to have Vieira brought to justice for ordering executions during his tenure) and by opposition politicians seeking to bring further disgrace on the PAIGC. However, some fear that such a trial would open numerous internal divisions within the

[94]*Africa Research Bulletin*, vol. 37, no. 2 (1–29 Feb. 2000), p. 13860.
[95]Personal sources, Bissau.
[96]Ibid.
[97]Ibid.

new government and would embarrass those who had previously worked with Vieira but later joined the opposition. Thus, it remains an open question as to whether such a trial will take place. If it does not, then the Yalla government will be in a position to focus its attention on the process of post-war reconstruction.

CONCLUSION

If the final quarter of the twentieth century began with the successful conclusion to an anti-colonial war that ushered into power a regime full of promise and potential, the century closed with the resumption of popular warfare intended to oust a government that had fallen wholly out of favour with the general population. To a large extent, this train of events reflected the inheritance of an infrastructurally and bureaucratically weak nation-state and a series of economic policy decisions that indebted the country and were not reflective of its actual production structures and rural marketing networks. At the same time, the state was further weakened through the informalisation of politics, involving increasing factionalism and personalised rule, which deepened the growing alienation of the rural population. Finally, the inheritance of a weak colonial bureaucracy and of precolonial indigenous traditions which included the dominance of local-level political institutions and inter-ethnic cooperation also helped to shape the postcolonial flow of politics.

Initiated by Luiz Cabral and exacerbated by President Nino Vieira, the increasing preoccupation with the reinforcement of narrow power networks loyal to the president produced an ultimately self-destructive pattern of internal repression and externally-oriented economic and political strategies. The attempted policy 'corrections' of the mid-1980s shifted the country toward privatisation and multipartyism, neither of which resolved the underlying political leadership crises or reduced the fundamental disparity between state-connected private traders and the majority of peasant producers, traders and consumers. While some women entrepreneurs did benefit from the domestic free trade climate, the principal beneficiaries of the SAP reforms were *ponteiros* and other already-privileged elites with close links to government leaders. In this respect, structural adjustment functioned largely as a prop to the ruling regime. Meanwhile, most of the population obtained consumer goods and sold agricultural products on informal, inter-ethnic, local and long-distance trading circuits that harked back to precolonial times.

These repeated economic and political crises rendered the state progressively less capable of setting up an effective rural administrative structure, so that political power in the countryside became increasingly localised—meaning that power was in effect distributed among local socio-political authorities that were fundamentally autonomous and divorced from state-controlled agencies. Age-groups, popular monarchies, a women's peasant movement and multi-ethnic spirit societies represented local-level social institutions in which people invested their political and economic resources. Many of these institutions represented precolonial forms of social authority that remained deeply popular, reflecting ancient traditions such as inter-ethnic cooperation in religion and trade that endured through the colonial period and were expanded after independence. On reflection, it is clear that Portuguese colonialism proved relatively fleeting and had not undermined the social foundations of authority in much of the countryside. Rather, the weakly-institutionalised colonial state would be passed on to its postcolonial inheritors and would prove, in the period from 1974 to 2000, incapable of crafting a coherent or nationally-integrated administrative structure.

This localisation of rural power coincided with economic policy choices that further widened the political gap between ordinary Guineans and the government. Here I refer especially to the growing links established between the Guinean state and international political and economic actors. By the late nineties, the increasingly unpopular Vieira regime had elected to become politically reliant upon Senegalese (and French) support while also gravitating toward economic dependency on Francophone aid. This exacerbated its alienation from the predominantly rural population as well as from its erstwhile urban political supporters, while also provoking the ire of the armed forces, who were heavily influenced by their direct connections to the peasantry.

The Vieira government would soon find itself confronted by a massively supported domestic rebel army that would out-fight both Vieira army loyalists and their Senegalese allies in eleven months of conflict, affecting the whole country. To a large extent, this represented a victory by the people of Guinea-Bissau over and against a weak state. It dramatised the limited nature of the organisational and infrastructural potency of the state, which proved unable to stem the tide of rebellion, despite President Vieira's success in obtaining foreign military support. The state's fragility was rooted in a long history of superficial colonial institution-building, and stood in marked contrast to powerful, locally-based social institutions with precolonial roots.

The first year of the new millennium bore witness to a rapid transfer of national power from the victorious rebel generals to a popularly-elected government. As in 1974, so too in 2000, a new government owed its forma-tion to the successful conclusion of a popular war. The recently installed, domestically applauded, regime is faced with multiple challenges affecting the viability of the Guinean polity, including the fact that, as its first year in office began, there was no visible representation of public administration anywhere in the countryside.[98] However, it may be that over the long term, these factors may exert a positive impact, serving to ease state-peasant tension. The lack of a rural state presence may augment the villagers' 'comfort level' with the government, while the continuing influence of the peasant-staffed (erstwhile rebel) army may serve as a popular check on state power.

Nevertheless, it should be recalled that, twenty years earlier, President Vieira had taken power in a context of overwhelming popular support and widespread opposition to the delegitimised regime of Luiz Cabral. Thereafter, however, the Vieira regime, like that of Cabral's, made a series of economic policy errors and became increasingly characterised by the informalisation of political power, which was further accentuated by the advent of multipartyism in the early 1990s. In this respect, a key question regarding the recently-installed Yalla regime will be the extent to which it will be able to avoid·the factionalisation and personalisation of political power that defined the period 1974–2000. This is an especially important issue, given the exacerbation of sectional power struggles following multiparty elections in the early 1990s. At the same time, in the wake of the economic policy errors of the previous regimes, it remains to be seen if the new leadership can focus on managing a modest economic agenda that is in tune with the needs of ordinary producers and traders, and which builds on the country's tradition of inter-ethnic cooperation. Finally, it will be important to observe if the government can demonstrate continuing respect for the local autonomy that prevails in the countryside and is rooted in the community character of precolonial political institutions.

[98]José Pedro Castanheira, op. cit.

7

CAPE VERDE

Elisa Silva Andrade

INTRODUCTION

Before discussing the postcolonial experience of Cape Verde it is useful to remind ourselves of some of the archipelago's characteristics. Located in the sub-Sahelian region, the country is composed of ten islands, of which only nine are inhabited, and five islets, forming a total land mass of 4,033 square km. Situated about 300 miles from the mainland, Cape Verde is divided into two groups: the Windward Islands—Santo Antão (779 square km.), São Vicente (227 square km.), Santa Luzia (35 square km.), São Nicolau (343 square km.), Sal (216 square km.) and Boavista (620 square km.); and the Leeward Islands—Maio (269 square km.), Santiago (991 square km.), Fogo (476 square km.) and Brava (64 square km.). The archipelago is subject to the harsh vagaries of its semi-arid climate, with a dominant dry northeastern wind and an all too short and irregular rainy season from August to October. As a result water shortages are chronic and droughts are very frequent.

It is generally agreed that the islands were discovered by the Portuguese between 1460 and 1462, though it is likely that Africans from the mainland had visited them before but, finding conditions unpropitious, had not settled there permanently. The population is derived from a genetic mix of Europeans (Portuguese, Spaniards and Italians) and Africans from the Guinea Coast, brought in as slaves. Hence, the immense majority of Cape Verdeans are today *mestiços*, with a wide range of skin colours. The physical and climatic constraints of life on the islands have always been harsh for all the inhabitants and the experience they have shared has created a specific culture, which is a unique blend of African and European customs. Above all, the archipelago evolved a common language (Crioulo, a Creole language based on Portuguese but suffused with African expressions) which, despite the differences in pronunciation to be found on the various islands, is understood everywhere and spoken by all social classes.

The Africans who were brought to the archipelago were forcibly removed from their social and cultural environment, and dispersed within the different islands. They lost their kin and ethnic ties. However, despite the repression they endured as slaves (slavery was only officially abolished in 1878), they were able to preserve a number of cultural traditions which today form an important part of the Cape Verdean cultural identity.[1] The feast of the *tabanka*, with its king, its saints and the daughters of the saints, underpins a system of mutual aid—as can commonly be found on the continent. The use of the mortar and pestle, the expertise in weaving and dyeing textiles, the use of certain musical instruments, and the very special adaptation brought to the Catholic faith, are all testimonies of Cape Verde's African heritage.

Portugal brought to the islands not just a system of administration but also dress habits, housing patterns (square rather than circular dwellings), the construction of towns and cities, public buildings, a large number of feasts and festivals, music and folklore and, above all, the Portuguese language. European social and cultural traditions, dominant as they were because of colonial rule, were all adapted and transformed as a small number of Portuguese overlords lived in close proximity with a large number of slaves and *mestiços*. There are, of course, differences between the islands, due in part to the type of population originally settled there as well as to their distinct geography and socio-economic attributes. Overall, however, it can be said that the archipelago is characterised by a relatively homogeneous Creole culture, with widely shared traditions and a common linguistic heritage.

THE POLITICAL CONTEXT OF ECONOMIC AND SOCIAL DEVELOPMENT SINCE INDEPENDENCE

The colonial legacy

After over two centuries of Portuguese colonial domination and over a decade of clandestine nationalist struggle, Cape Verde became independent on 5 July 1975 under the leadership of the Partido Africano da Independência da Guiné e Cabo Verde (PAIGC)—a party created by Amílcar Cabral but whose main terrain of action was in Portuguese Guinea, where it waged an anti-colonial guerrilla war between 1963 and the 25 April 1974 revolution in Portugal. The colonial legacy was not encouraging.

---

[1]For an introduction to Cape Verde's culture and oral literature see Caroline Shaw, 'Oral literature popular culture in Cape Verde and São Tomé e Príncipe' in Patrick Chabal *et al.*, *The Postcolonial Literature of Lusophone Africa* (London: Hurst & Co., 1996).

The archipelago was economically weak, if not destitute. Its agriculture suffered from a severely unequal land distribution, ranging from extensive properties often owned by absentee landlords (as on Santiago) to fragmented holdings (as on Fogo). Production was limited by the fact that the islands had been in drought since 1968 and that erosion had already severely damaged the environmental fabric of the country. Animal husbandry was limited to its simplest expression: only animals that could withstand drought and hunger remained alive. Fishing, potentially important for the country, was sharply divided. The coastal population carried out some small-scale artisanal fishing for subsistence and the internal market. Industrial fishing was the preserve of foreign companies.

The population's subsistence level was extremely low, since productivity was poor and unequal land distribution left many in the countryside without the means to survive. Portugal had invested very little to improve agriculture. Land conservation had been neglected, water-retention schemes were non-existent, and little had been done to restore the islands' sadly depleted vegetation. Added to this, the rate of illiteracy in the rural areas was over 90 per cent and the colonial state had omitted to make efforts to provide professional help in order to improve rural productivity and the diversification of agricultural production. Emigration continued to be the main option for poor, and even well-educated, Cape Verdeans.

The industrial sector was obsolete, limited as it was to a few food-processing plants (fish processing and tinning) for export, the exploitation of salt and pozzolana[2] mines, desalination plants in São Vicente and Sal, as well as naval facilities in Mindelo and the international airport in Sal. The country's infrastructure was minimal since in 1968 there were only 842 kms of roads, most of which unpaved, and very few outside of the main island of Santiago. This obviously did not encourage the industrial or tourist development of the archipelago.[3]

Given the weakness of agricultural and industrial production, these two sectors contributed respectively in 1974 to only 15.9 and 6.4 per cent of GDP. Hence, internal trade depended very heavily on foreign imports and consisted in large measure of food—which made up around a quarter of the country's total imports during the decade which preceded independence.[4]

---

[2]Pozzolana is a type of volcanic ash used for mortar or for cement that sets under water.

[3]The bulk of the information for this section comes from Elisa Silva de Andrade, *Les Îles du Cap Vert. De la 'Découverte' à l'Indépendance Nationale (1460–1975)* (Paris: L'Harmattan, 1996).

[4]The ratio of exports to imports went from 17.9 per cent in 1970 to 7.9 per cent in 1971, 7.3 per cent in 1972, 4.3 per cent in 1973 and 3.3 per cent 1974. See Andrade, op. cit.

The constant decline in agriculture, due in great part to continued drought, was such that in the last few years of colonial rule, half of all public expenditures (54 per cent in 1974) were met by a direct subsidy from Portugal.

The nutritional situation was extremely poor with average intake limited to 1,900 calories and 58 grammes of proteins—whereas estimates of need range around an average of 2,200 calories and 67 grammes of proteins. Health provision was limited, with mortality rates in 1973 at 9.3 per thousand and infant mortality rates at 103.9 per thousand. There were at that time only twelve doctors, two pharmacies, 91 nurses and 96 auxiliary nurses, two hospitals (Praia and Mindelo), five dispensaries and three medical laboratories.[5] Furthermore, provision of drinking water and sanitation was limited. It is estimated that, at independence, only 20 per cent of the population had access to clean drinking water, mostly in the urban centres. Finally, social and sanitary infrastructure was lacking, especially in the rural areas.

The situation in education was not much better. Despite the efforts made by the colonial administration in the few years preceding independence, only around 20 per cent of the school-age population was in primary school.[6] The level of illiteracy only improved marginally during the twentieth century, from 88 per cent in 1900, 83 per cent in 1920 to 75 per cent in 1975.[7] Although that figure was respectable in comparison with many other African countries, it was far below that which Portugal had claimed in the sixties, when Cape Verde was held as a symbol of the success of colonial rule.

The archipelago's main socio-economic problem was (and remains) unemployment, ranging from 60 to 75 per cent of the active population in 1974. Such unemployment left Cape Verdeans in a precarious economic situation. Portugal had failed to tackle the structural nature of the problem, having precious little to help create employment. It only provided emergency food aid when drought made it absolutely necessary, often too late and after famine had set in. At independence, the new regime was compelled to take emergency measures. Only large-scale public works, financed by international food aid (the PAIGC government sold the donated food aid at market prices and used the proceeds to fund development projects) provided employment to those who had no other possibility for earning a living—that is a substantial proportion of the population.

[5]Ibid.
[6]Ibid.
[7]António Mendes Correa, *Ilhas de Cabo Verde. Ultramar Português II* (Lisbon: Agência Geral do Ultramar, 1945), p. 199.

Postcolonial politics

The government of the newly-independent Cape Verde sought immediately to address the main problems facing the country: namely unemployment, education and health. Their approach stressed sustainable human development rather than socialism, the party's official ideology. The instruments they used were the successive government programmes and national plans for development. The main objective of sustainable human development was seen to be the improvement of society as a whole rather than merely the economy. Such an approach required progress in the living and working conditions of the majority, rather than the minority, and had to be based on the reduction of poverty and the eradication of misery on the archipelago. This development policy combined a strong concern for the environment (so precarious in Cape Verde), for economic growth and for the human and social problems affecting the population as whole.

At independence, the newly-installed government set up a general political framework, the Lei de Organização do Estado (Law for State Organisation), which essentially laid down the state's prerogatives and its legal obligations. The political complexion of the one-party state adopted at independence was made explicit in the first constitution, approved by the national assembly in September 1980. Following the break with Guinea-Bissau in 1980, the party called a congress which approved the creation of the Partido Africano da Independência de Cabo Verde (PAICV), whose ideology was unchanged except for the abandonment of the objective of achieving the unity of the two countries.[8] Article 3 stated that the Republic of Cape Verde was 'a national revolutionary democratic state ... dedicated to the abolition of the exploitation of man by man'. Article 4 enshrined the dominance of the ruling party, the (PAICV), as the 'leading political force of society and state'.

Though officially socialist, Cape Verde was in practice governed by what Aristides Lima called 'an administrative and paternalist system of power'— that is essentially a pragmatic state in which the government ruled with the consent of the majority of the population—as expressed in one-party legislative elections. He writes: '... the national revolutionary democracy, as it is understood in the constitution, embodies both a political and social

[8]See *Do PAIGC ao PAICV—Documentos* (April 1981), p. 104. Following the coup d'état in Bissau, where the (Cape Verdean) president, Luiz Cabral, was overthrown by his (Guinean) prime minister, João Bernardo Vieira, the Cape Verdean government dissociated itself from Guinea-Bissau and from their common party, the PAIGC, to form a specifically Cape Verdean party, the PAICV. Henceforth, PAIGC will be used to refer to the party before 1980 and PAICV after that date.

dimension. As a national democracy, it aims to consolidate the nation. As a revolutionary democracy, it seeks to establish a society free of exploitation, especially as the hitherto powerless social strata have now been brought into power'.[9] Until 1990, Cape Verde remained a one-party state.

What is now called the democratic transition, that is the move towards a multiparty political system, was set in motion in the mid- to late eighties— at a time when several African countries were in the process of initiating democratic reforms. The impetus for political change in Cape Verde came from a younger generation of party members, many of whom were technocrats, who had grown impatient with the increasing rigidity of the party and favoured political and economic liberalisation. Nevertheless, the international context was also important. The fall of the Berlin Wall, the collapse of communism in the Soviet Union, as well as the stress on democracy within the donor community, all had an impact. The Franco-African Summit of La Baule (June 1991), linking for the first time, foreign aid with democratisation, was critical for all countries, including Cape Verde, which had links with France.[10]

Although there is some debate as to when the 'transition' began in Cape Verde, it is clear that it was set in motion in the mid-eighties by the third PAICV government when it sought administrative reforms to make possible greater liberalisation of the economy. It was at that time that the government initiated a policy of support to the private sector and created the Unidade de Promoção Industrial, a semi-official institution aimed at offering credit to small private enterprises. The Third Party Congress, held in November 1988, marks the beginning of a systematic reform of the economic system. What it proposed was nothing less than a new strategy of externally-oriented development. What was intended was an integration of the Cape Verdean economy into the world system, making full use of the country's (admittedly limited) comparative advantages. In other words, the government now formally recognised what it had long accepted in practice—that is, that any notion of self-sustaining or self-contained socialism was unworkable.

Although the impetus for the reform was economic, it soon engendered a new political momentum. According to Aristides Lima, the first phase of the transition occurred between 1988 and February 1990, at which time the PAICV's National Council decided, following a survey of public opinion, 'to propose a move towards a multiparty political system'.[11] The second

[9]Aristides Lima, *Reforma Política em Cabo Verde. Do Paternalismo à Modernização do Estado* (Praia: [the author] 1991), p. 9.
[10]Jacques Belotteau and Michel Gaud, 'La marche vers le multipartisme', *Afrique Contemporaine*, no. 158 (1991), p. 53.
[11]Lima, op. cit.

phase extended to the legislative elections in January 1991, in a context in which internal social and political demands became more acute and the international community increasingly favoured political liberalisation.

In May 1990, President Aristides Pereira resigned as secretary general of the PAICV in order to prepare himself for the forthcoming competitive presidential elections—he was replaced by the then prime minister, Pedro Pires. In June and July, legislation was approved to enable multiparty political activities.[12] In September, the national assembly agreed to a new constitutional law which revoked Article 4 of the constitution and institutionalised political pluralism.[13] Finally, in October three further legislative reforms were passed: one to define the legal position of political parties, one to introduce a proportional voting system (à la Hondt), and the last to allow all parties access to public media.[14] It was in this context that the main opposition party, the Movimento para a Democracia (MPD), was established in November 1990.

The 1991 elections brought the transition to an end and institutionalised multiparty politics in Cape Verde. The legislative poll of 13 January 1991 was won by the opposition MPD with 62 per cent of the votes and 56 seats in the national assembly against 32 per cent and 23 seats for the ruling PAICV. The presidential elections of 17 February 1991 delivered an even more emphatic verdict, with the MPD candidate, António Mascarenhas Monteiro, garnering 75 per cent of the votes against the incumbent, Aristides Pereira. In December, the first-ever local elections were held in which the two main parties competed with various independent candidates. The MPD won the majority of municipalities with 58.8 per cent of the votes while the PAIGC obtained 36.2 per cent. The allocation of councils, however, reflected a more diverse political panorama: eight for the MPD; four for the independents; and only two for the PAICV. In the 1999 local elections, the MPD lost one municipality and held seven. The PAICV also took seven, thus showing a clear increase in popular support. The others went to independent candidates, some of whom supported by either one of the two main parties. Although the election results were a deep shock to the PAICV, and indeed the international community,[15] the party and its leaders

[12]Lei no. 74/III/90, de 29 de Junho in *Boletim Oficial* no. 25, 2.ª, Suplemento; Lei no. 81/III/90 de 29 de Julho in *Boletim Oficial* no. 25, 2.º, Suplemento.

[13]In *Boletim Oficial* no. 39, Suplemento.

[14]Lei no. 86/III/90 de 6 de Outubro in *Boletim Oficial*, no. 40, Suplemento; Lei no. 87/III/90 de 13 de Outubro in *Boletim Oficial*, no. 40, Suplemento; Lei no. 90/III/90 de 27 de Outubro in *Boletim Oficial*, no. 43, Suplemento.

[15]Given the comparatively excellent record of the PAICV administration and the improvised nature of the opposition, most observers had counted on the victory of the incumbent party.

were praised for the way in which the vote was held, the swiftness with which they accepted defeat, and the manner in which they eased the transition for their MPD successors. Indeed, for many the Cape Verdean experience was seen as the success story of democratisation in Africa.[16]

In the 1995 legislative elections, the MPD was re-elected with approximately the same percentage of votes whilst the PAICV was unable to increase its share. The Partido da Convergência Democrática (PCD), for its part managed to capture one seat.[17] However, in the December 2000 legislative elections, the MPD was defeated and the PAICV returned to power with a majority of 40 deputies against 30 to the MPD. In the 1996 presidential elections, the incumbent, António Mascarenhas Monteiro, stood unopposed and was re-elected in an election marked, not surprisingly by a very low turnout of 45 per cent. Following the PAICV's victory in the February 2001 elections, its former leader, Pedro Pires, was elected president, thus completing a complete change of power in favour of the PAICV.

Whilst it is easy to understand why the Cape Verdeans should have wanted a political change after fifteen years of single party rule, it is more difficult to understand why the MPD managed to retain power for so long, since its record in office was significantly better than that of its predecessor. Indeed, given the difficulties faced by the PAIGC at independence, it could be argued that the nationalist party's accomplishment were most impressive. Interestingly enough, however, the MPD has now been swept from office after a decade in power, as though the Cape Verdean population had given the government that long to demonstrate that it could carry out its programme of reform. The recent government change must thus be seen both as a vote of no-confidence for the MPD and, perhaps equally importantly, as an indication that there is a desire on the part of the Cape Verdeans to ensure that no political party remains in power too long. In this respect, then, the most recent regime change is confirmation that democratic practices have taken root in the country.

The gains derived from the country's transition have been important. There is now a framework of pluralist political rights, human rights protection and an acceptance of political, cultural and religious diversity which ensures the strengthening of democracy. The holding of the subsequent

---

[16]'L'Archipel de l'espérance', *Jeune Afrique* n.° 1575 (6–12 March 1991), p. 30.

[17]The full results were as follows (1991 figures in brackets). The MPD received: 61 [70.8] per cent of the votes and 50 [56] seats; the PAICV: 29 [29.1] per cent of the votes and 21 [23] seats; the PCD: 6 per cent of the votes and 1 seat. The total number of seats in the national assembly was reduced from 79 in 1991 to 72 in 1995. See Economist Intelligence Unit, Country Profile, 1999–2000, *São Tomé e Príncipe, Guinea-Bissau, Cape Verde*, p. 56.

elections as well as most recent developments have also shown that political pluralism is thriving. Two new political parties have been created by MPD dissidents in the last few years: the PCD and the Partido da Renovação Democrática (PRD).

Development policies

Since the situation at independence was so precarious, the newly-formed PAIGC government was compelled to devote its energy to the most 'rational' management of its less-than-fulsome colonial legacy. Its first priorities were to improve the country's physical and social infrastructure and, above all, to seek to meet the basic needs of the population. This it was able to do due to international aid and an efficient system of administration. From the beginning the government marketed the food and other material assistance received in order to support development projects and avoid the 'dependency syndrome' which had become common in the final years of Portuguese colonial rule.

Government policy was centred in the first place on (1) the development of food, health and education; and (2) the improvement of the natural environment so damaged by land degradation and erosion. Until 1978, emphasis was placed on emergency programmes to repair the harm inflicted by nearly a decade of continuous drought. Funding was devoted to land and water conservation and short-term employment schemes to provide vital income to the poorest and least-qualified sectors of the population, particularly in the rural areas. These emergency measures were successful and the country's slide into poverty was arrested.

The First Development Plan (1982–5) followed on the emergency programmes and continued to prioritise the improvement of the basic living conditions of the population and the development of the essential infrastructure. Resources were to be devoted to rural development, transport, communication, and small-scale industry. The Plan set two major objectives. The first laid emphasis on agrarian reform, literacy, agricultural support, co-operative movements, health education, the improvement of the living environment and the development of small business. The second was to seek the largest possible popular involvement in the priorities thus outlined. The Second Development Plan (1986–90) sought to consolidate the objectives outlined in the First and stressed in particular the achievement of broad economic equilibria; a greater link to the world market, particularly in the areas of fishing, tourism and services; and the reduction in social and regional inequalities, among others, through an appropriate land reform.

The MPD government set out in April 1991 the outline of its programme of government. In the first instance, the new regime introduced reforms in the public sector guided by two key principles: less but better central government, and better as well as more accountable local government. The means taken to achieve these included the transfer of competence to the local level; the transfer of human, material and financial resources to the municipalities so as to enable them to take over these developmental tasks; and the training of local authorities for these enlarged responsibilities. Pursuing some of the measures set in train by the previous regime, the MPD government devolved to the regional-level legislation that impinged on local matters, the administration of locally-collected taxes, the approval of regional development projects, the supervision of public services at the local level, and the possibility of establishing links with foreign cooperation bodies within nationally-agreed parameters.

In the economic sphere, the government formalised its programme in the Third Development Plan (1992–5), which only took effect in 1993 (after the meeting of the donor round table conference in November 1992). The MPD's economic policies centred on the liberalisation of the economy and the reduction of poverty. Here too, the new government followed in the footsteps of the previous one—notwithstanding its ringing declarations to the contrary. It took steps to accelerate the programme of economic liberalisation initiated in 1989 and continued to highlight the importance of reducing underemployment and unemployment. It introduced measures, as we have seen, to further the decentralisation of economic development. It began to privatise public enterprises. It took steps to reduce the budget deficit in relation to GDP. It sought to reduce the budget deficit, stabilise inflation and preserve the external trade balance without jeopardising existing productive investment.

The Third Development Plan also stressed the human aspect of development, emphasising the need to initiate moves to improve health, education, nutrition, and the environment—aiming thereby to reduce poverty and strengthen social justice. Among the more notable policies, it is important to highlight the restructuring and liberalisation of the business sector, the modernisation of the administration, and the greater prominence given to the protection of the environment. The Fourth Development Plan (1997–2000) adopted substantive reforms of the financial system, the judiciary and of parliament, which reinforced the measures already taken to decentralise, privatise and seek to reduce poverty. In this they were consistent with the pledges made by the MPD when it took office in 1991. It is too early to assess whether the Fourth Plan, in many ways the pinnacle of the government's liberalisation ambitions, will have borne the expected fruits.

THE IMPLEMENTATION OF DEVELOPMENT POLICIES

The economy

Despite fundamental structural problems and the absence of natural resources, the Cape Verdean economy experienced high real term growth between 1975 and 1990: 11 per cent in 1976–80; 6 per cent in 1982–5, but falling to 2.5 per cent until 1990. According to Agnelo Sanches, the period 1975–80 privileged the internal market and the public sector. GDP growth was respectable considering the problems the country faced. Inflation was reduced and the external balance remained positive. During the period 1980–88, the economy grew in real terms by an average of 6 per cent a year. This was due to the rapid expansion of the service sector, the high level of public investment in infrastructure and in social welfare (education, health and housing) as well as in productive activities (fishing and transport). Inflation was reduced from 21 per cent in 1983 to 3.5 per cent in 1988. The currency (the Cape Verdean escudo, or CVEsc) was stable. The ratio of debt servicing to exports represented an average of 11 per cent during the period 1986–90.[18]

Nevertheless, economic growth—most of which was generated by the activities of the tertiary sector—did not provide a solid enough basis for the creation of employment. By 1990, unemployment stood at 26 per cent of the active population. Moreover, external debt began to impinge more heavily on the budget deficit. In 1990, the primary sector only contributed 15 per cent to GDP. The secondary sector—essentially light transformation industry, fishing and artisanal production—did not contribute more than 17 per cent to GDP during the eighties. The tertiary sector, for its part, contributed a full two-thirds of GDP. During that period, the CVEsc maintained its parity against the basket of nine reference currencies—this in a context where the average inflation rate did not go beyond 10 per cent.

As concerns public finance, the state's receipts increased by around 12 per cent, ranging from 16 per cent of GDP in 1985 to 15 per cent in 1990. State expenditure, including payment of debt interest, remained at around 15 to 16 per cent of GDP during the same period. With the exception of 1987, the external balance decreased during this period and went into the red in 1989.[19] Nevertheless, Cape Verde pursued a very cautious policy of borrowing from abroad. It is estimated that in 1990, external debt was

[18]Agnelo Sanches, *Cabo Verde: Subsídios para o Estudo da Dimensão Internacional do Desenvolvimento* (Praia: Projecto NLTPS, February 1996), p. 17.

[19]*Criança e Mulher em Cabo Verde. Analíse de Situação* (Praia: UNICEF/ Governo do Cabo Verde, October 1993).

around $ 150 million, or around 40 per cent of GNP of which 95 per cent was composed of long-term lending on concessional rates. Debt service was reduced in 1991 to $ 5 million.[20] Foreign trade has always been, and continues to be, characterised by the limited income generated from exports, the importance of services in export income, and by the very small export–import ratio. Exports consist essentially of fish products and bananas. Service income stems from Sal international airport and the port of Mindelo.

By the late eighties, it had become clear that the government was no longer able to continue to rely on the 'recycling' of foreign aid for purposes of development—meaning here the use of the domestic sale of foreign aid (primarily food) for financing development projects. Among the factors weighing heavily on the economy were an increasing debt service, the poor productivity of a number of public investments, the financial difficulties which a number of public enterprises faced, and the stagnation and/or reduction of public support for development. Nevertheless, the arrival of the MPD government in 1991 did not lead to dramatic changes in the economic profile of the country.

According to IMF sources, GDP growth rose from 3 per cent in 1992 to 5.6 per cent in 1998.[21] This was due especially to the high level of public expenditure, especially in the areas of transport, communications, infrastructure, energy and construction.[22] But such growth had very little impact on the structure of internal production, which continues to be heavily dependent on the tertiary sector—despite the government's attempts to attract foreign investment and to encourage the growth of business in the secondary sector. The basic configuration of the economy has changed very little since the MPD has been in power. The tertiary sector continues to account for about two-thirds of total activity. The secondary sector remains at about 20 per cent, while the primary hovers around 13 per cent. This is a serious problem since the latter continues to employ the largest number by far. Although it contributes around 13 per cent of GDP, this sector continues to absorb around 47 per cent of the full-time active working population—which demonstrates the very limited productivity of agriculture and fishing in Cape Verde. Indeed, during the period 1991–7, the primary sector's contribution to GDP shrank by 3 per cent.

[20]Jacques Richard, Gil Laines, Joel Dine and Bruno Ballet, *L'Aide Française au Cap Vert: 1975–1990* (expert report, Paris: s.n., 1994), p. 32.

[21]*Relatório de Actividades do Governo Referente ao Ano de 1998* (Praia: Governo de Cabo Verde, Gabinete do Primeiro Ministro, s.d.).

[22]Public expenditures rose from 17.5 per cent of GDP in 1991 to 60 per cent in 1995. See *Note Situation. Document de Strategie par Pays, sur les Défis du Développement pour la Période 1991–2001* (Praia: Banque Africaine de Développement, 16–17 November 1998).

Although the secondary sector is also limited, there is evidence of some advances since 1996. This is due in the main to the setting up of a number of businesses funded from private domestic and foreign investment, especially in the area of tax-free industry and production for export. Nevertheless, development in this area is constrained because of the relatively high cost of certain factors of production such as transport and energy. There is also a limit to how much foreign capital is attracted to Cape Verde, since so far it is mostly Portuguese business (often with links to the archipelago) which has been willing to invest.

If the overall growth of GDP has been satisfactory, particularly given the problems faced by the country as a whole, it has not generated sufficient employment. Despite an improvement in the last few years—unemployment stood at 38 per cent of the active population in 1996; it is now estimated at around 26 per cent—the scarcity of jobs undoubtedly remains the most important economic and social problem for Cape Verde. There are also strong regional disparities resulting in much higher unemployment in the islands of Fogo and São Vicente, for example.[23]

At the macro-economic level, the present situation is marked by a significant increase in the deficit of the public sector allied with a serious increase in domestic public debt—which rose from 4 per cent of GDP in 1991 to 45 per cent in 1997, at which time it amounted to $ 186 million.[24] In order to try to eliminate such debt over the next two decades, the government has created a trust fund to be provisioned from the receipts from privatisation ($ 80 million) and bilateral and multilateral international aid ($ 100 million).[25] As of mid-1999, international aid was $ 26 million short of the $ 100 million target.[26] In order to make good the domestic funding of the trust fund, the government had to speed up privatisation after 1998.[27] It was also in January of that year, that Cape Verde signed an agreement with the IMF to introduce a structural adjustment programme (SAP). Between 1994–8, 35 public enterprises had been privatised. In 1999, further key privatisations were made: two commercial banks (the Banco

[23]Instituto do Emprego e Formação Profissional, *Inquérito às Forças de Trabalho 1996— Cabo Verde* (Portugal: Gabinete do Adjunto do Primeiro Ministro, Ed. Ministério para a Qualificação e Emprego, Departamento de Estatística, 1997).

[24]Banque Africaine de Developpement, op. cit.

[25]The main donors are the World Bank, the European Union, Portugal, the African Bank for Development, Switzerland and Austria.

[26]Yves Bourdet, *Cabo Verde. Dando Vida Nova à Política de Reforma, e Depois ...* (Stockholm: ASDI [Swedish International Development Cooperation Agency], 2000) p. 7.

[27]Bourdet, op. cit., p. 17.

Comercial do Atlântico and the Caixa Económica de Cabo Verde); an insurance company (Garantia), a risk-venture company (Promotora), an oil company (ENACOL), the water and electricity company (Electra), a construction business (CVC), a travel agency (Arca Verde) and a maritime enterprise (ANV). The government retained a minority interest in the two banks and in the public service companies.

There is, however, doubt that such privatisations are of benefit to the country or its population. Some question whether the process is economically beneficial in a situation where a number of public enterprises are unlikely to be profitable. It could lead to possible degradation in services later, especially since such public services were privatised without putting in place proper public supervisory bodies to regulate their performance and the cost of such monopolies. Others point to the fact that few Cape Verdeans have access either to the capital or credit to enable them to purchase the privatised firms, thus leaving them to be taken over by foreign interests. As a result, a number of Cape Verdean institutions have been purchased by Portuguese buyers, including a number of state-owned bodies; Portugal's Caixa Geral de Depósitos bought 60 per cent of BCA's shares, 95 per cent of Garantia's and 60 per cent of Promotora's; similarly the Montepio Geral de Portugal, owns 26 per cent of CECV. Such a state of affairs, it is argued, is hardly conducive to healthy competition. The fact that a large proportion of privatised enterprises are in foreign, primarily Portuguese, hands is unlikely to generate future investment in the country since profits are more likely to be exported back to Lisbon. This could be one of the reasons why the apparently healthy economic growth registered in the last few years has not resulted in greater employment in the country.

External debt rose from 34 per cent of GDP in 1995 to 52 per cent in 1999, amounting to $ 292 million. Debt service in that year represented 11 per cent of total export receipts.[28] The trade balance is perennially in deficit since on the whole exports only cover around 5 per cent of imports, and there is very little prospect that this could be improved in the near future. The balance of payments is structurally in deficit (13 per cent of GDP in 1999). However, the balance of services—made up essentially of the income from Sal international airport, tourism and port services—registers a surplus. It is important to stress the continued importance of outside remittances (mostly from migrant workers) and the transfer of capital to the equilibrium of the balance of payments. Inflation, which

[28]*Rapport National du Développement Humain, Cap–Vert 1999* (provisional), (Praia: UNDP, July 1999), p. 20.

stood at 10 per cent in 1990, fell from 9 per cent in 1997 to 4 per cent in 1999, which confirms that there are no strong inflationary pressures in Cape Verde. It remains, however, around 2 per cent higher than the average for the European Union. This is important because Cape Verde has entered into a currency agreement with Portugal which, on the one hand, prevents Praia from resorting to printing money and/or inflation to reduce the ratio of domestic debt to GDP and, on the other, commits the government to respecting the so-called Maastricht criteria—a tough agenda for a country as poor and as devoid of resources as Cape Verde.[29]

Land reform and cooperatives

In its first programme of government, the PAIGC regime set out to increase popular participation and to respond to the needs of the bulk of the population. In particular, it aimed to make greater economic activity possible amongst the more precariously-placed agricultural producers and village dwellers. To this end, it sought to promote the development of cooperatives in the rural areas and to support small-scale business and commercial activities. Accordingly, it devised a programme of land reform, with the objective of granting more secure tenure to those who worked land they did not own. That this was a serious problem on the archipelago was not in doubt: already in the period after independence, a number of small tenant farmers on Santiago and Santo Antão had refused to continue paying rent on their holdings. The majority of farmers worked in very difficult conditions.

As already mentioned, the land tenure situation was precarious, with a small number of large landowners (some of them absentee) and a large number of tenant farmers living in the most uncertain circumstances. In 1982, 39 per cent of farmers (with, at the extremes, 51 per cent on Santiago and 19 per cent in São Nicolau) did not own land and were either tenant farmers or sharecroppers. The rest were small landholders, of whom 50 per cent were also simultaneously tenants and/or sharecroppers. According to 1980 official figures, there were on the six main islands (Santiago, Santo Antão, Fogo, Brava, Boavista and São Nicolau) 5,730 tenants and 25,359 sharecroppers.[30] The government considered that such a situation

[29]These criteria include a ratio of debt to GDP lower than 60 per cent and/or moving towards that target; public deficit lower than 3 per cent of GDP; an inflation rate at most 1.5 per cent higher than the inflation rate of the three countries with the best record.

[30]República de Cabo Verde, *Lei no. 9/II/82 de 26 de Março (Lei das Bases da Reforma Agrária)*, March 1982.

was both inequitous and not conducive to the improvement of living and working conditions in Cape Verde. For this reason, it decided that the land reform should tackle first the issue of land tenure. The programme emphasised the need to better the livelihood of those who lived from farming and to increase agricultural production. The government laid down its two main objectives: (1) to alter the structure of landholding so as to allow all those who live from farming access to land; (2) to establish the technical, financial and economic means that would make possible the growth of agricultural production and ensure that producers were the main beneficiaries of rural improvements.[31]

The plan was to transfer ownership of property that exceeded one hectare of irrigated land or five hectares of dry land to the state. This was to take place through a proper process of expropriation and compensation. The land thus acquired would be devolved for effective production to those farmers who occupied it legally at the time of the transfer.[32] The pace of expropriation was to be dictated by the state's ability to finance compensation. It was made clear that the expropriation of land was only directed at those who did not exploit their land directly and at the absentee landlords. However, for obvious political reasons, the law exempted the land belonging to emigrant workers, even where such land was not exploited directly by them or their family.[33] Finally, a number of additional measures were announced to support rural development: credit, training, and the improvement of infrastructure and distribution of commercialised products.

According to independent reports, however, the programme of land reform, as formulated in the 1982 Lei das Bases da Reforma Agrária (basic law on agrarian reform), did not, as was expected, promote rural development. It generated strong resentment, even among those who were meant to be the direct beneficiaries of the programme. The attempt to put into practice the law's dispositions, as for example the conversion of sharecropping into tenancy, created dissatisfaction among both owners and producers and, more importantly, did not result in the reduction of landownership or in an increase in production.[34] In reality, therefore, the

[31]Intervention by the Minister of Rural Development during the second session of the second legislature, as referenced in the texts issued on the occasion of the 'second national seminar on land reform'.

[32]Ibid.

[33]Article 2, Paragraph b, of the *Lei das Bases da Reforma Agrária*. Given the number of emigrants and their economic importance in terms of the remittances they sent back to Cape Verde, there was no question of the government taking any measure that would alienate this key constituency.

[34]P. Affonso Leme Machado and F. Edeson Teofilo (consultants), *Legislação Agrária*

land reform did not achieve much. It is estimated that in the period 1983–90 only 493 families benefited from the transfer or land—and, on the whole, the land transferred was too small to sustain the total number of the beneficiaries.[35] Machado and Teofilo concluded that the aims of land reform had failed to materialise both because the actual transfer of land was insufficient and because, where it had taken place, the people concerned had simply not had access to the means required to cultivate the land properly. In those conditions reform did not free the producers from the overwhelming constraints that made agriculture so precarious.[36]

Whatever the limits of land reform, however, the government's policy did have an effect on agriculture, even if it did not fundamentally alter the structure of landholding in the country. First, it did link land tenure and production much more explicitly. Second, and according to Machado and Teofilo, rural producers benefited from the large-scale public investment in infrastructure, land reclamation, reafforestation and water-retention schemes financed by the state and international aid. Given the lack of cultivable land on the archipelago, the two consultants make clear, it is simply not possible to provide land to all those who suffer rural unemployment. On the other hand, rural producers are not organised in syndicates or unions so as to enter into collective negotiation with the state. Machado concluded that, whether or not land reform is beneficial to rural development, 'the appropriation of rent by landowners ... is an injustice perpetrated on those who cultivate the land directly and receive no help, either through labour or investment, on the part of the landowner.'[37] In some instances, former landowners were even able to reclaim the land granted to tenants or sharecroppers who had benefited from the ruling given by the former commission on land reform.

As concerns the creation of cooperatives, the PAIGC government created in 1978 the Instituto Nacional de Cooperativas (INC), with the aim of aiding the cooperative movement in the areas of management, training, technical assistance, financial and material support, taxation and legal affairs. In 1979, the national assembly passed the basic law on cooperatives which regulated their operations and set up the Fund for

---

da *República de Cabo Verde. Lei Rural e Estruturas Agrárias* (Rome: FAO—TPC/CVI/2252, 1993).

[35]Ibid., p. 44.

[36]Cláudio Alves Furtado, 'A mulher e as políticas de desenvolvimento rural' in *A Mulher Caboverdiana e o Desenvolvimento*, First Workshop, Instituto da Condição Feminina, January 1993, p. 41.

[37]P. Affonso Leme Machado, *Legislação Agrária da República de Cabo Verde* (Rome: FAO—TCP/CVI/2251, September 1992), p. 22.

Support to Cooperatives (FAC), intended to regulate and distribute funds (particularly foreign aid) through the INC. In the first period, 1975–7, the emphasis was placed on consumer cooperatives, designed to prevent excessive fluctuation in the price of the basic necessities and to regulate supply to the rural areas. Of the 125 (mostly consumer) cooperatives set up during that period, only 25 survived. Nevertheless, by 1980 there were 254 cooperatives (of which 123 were consumer cooperatives), with a total of 19,500 members. Between 1982 and 1984, another 99 were set up and the number of members quadrupled between 1980 and 1984–5. In 1993, there were 183 cooperatives (with 21,446 members), of which 123 were consumer cooperatives (with 19,520 members, of whom 60 per cent were women); 22 producer cooperatives (agriculture and fishing), with 248 members; and 12 savings and credit cooperatives (with 870 members, of whom 56 per cent were women).[38]

Despite the political changes following the 1991 elections, the improvement of the employment situation continued to be a priority for the government. However, with the introduction of more liberal economic policies, and the move towards privatisation, the cooperative sector was now required to operate on a par with the private sector. As a result the INC was abolished in 1997 and the FAC in 1999, removing all external support from the cooperative movement. There are today in the country 250 formally registered cooperatives, of which only 85 are thought to be functioning. More than 50 per cent of consumer cooperatives, so important during the seventies and eighties, have ceased to operate. On the other hand, production cooperatives have gained more importance in the last few years.[39]

In a recent report on rural development, the author concludes that the cooperative movement as organised by the INC had not been properly developed, particularly in agricultural production and fishing.[40] Since then, a large number of other associative organisations have emerged which have been involved in projects implemented by the Ministry of Agriculture, Food and Environment[41]—among which the most significant have been those intended to transform the Frentes de Alta Intensidade de Mão-de-

---

[38]*Plano de Desenvolvimento Cooperativo, 92/92. Diagnóstico, Orientações Estratégicas, Programas* (Praia: Instituto Nacional de Cooperativas, 1993); and *Relatório de Actividades 92* (Praia: Instituto Nacional de Cooperativas, 2 March 1993).

[39]Ibid.

[40]Nieuwkerk, *Projet de Développement de l'Agriculture et de l'Elevage à Assise Communautaire. Île de Santiago, Cap Vert* (Paris: IRAM, 1997).

[41]In particular through the Projecto de Desenvolvimento da Agricultura e Pecuária com Base Comunitária (project for the development of agriculture and fishing on a community basis) which works in three distinct zones: arid, semi-arid, and higher altitude humid zones.

Obra (FAIMO),[42] government employment creation schemes funded from
the proceeds of foreign aid. The new policy favours a new type of
employment contract. In 1997 in Santiago there were 18 such associations
legally registered and 16 working towards that status—each one with 200
to 250 members. A few of these functioned as businesses, with a restricted
number of members, and employing labour on a contractual basis.

Employment

Since underemployment or unemployment has clearly been Cape Verde's
greatest problem ever since the nineteenth century, the government aimed
to take measures to begin to alleviate the problem when it took power in
1975. Among its first aims were to deploy labour used under the FAIMO
scheme to development projects; to employ the unemployed for public work;
and to survey the best ways to generate the kind of economic development
that would further reduce unemployment. During the period 1981–5, the
government used the Plan to consolidate the gains made in the early period,
particularly in the provision of temporary employment and the creation
of permanent jobs within the ambit of newly-developed projects.

Despite these efforts, the fight against unemployment proved very
difficult. Given an average population increase of 2 to 2.5 per cent during
the seventies and eighties, the increase in employment struggled to match
population growth. In 1990, it was estimated that a total of 31,000 were
unemployed, that is 26 per cent of the active population. However, and
much more ominously, unemployment among the young was all too high,
with 70 per cent looking for their first job.[43] In its 1991 report the UNDP
emphasised that unemployment remained the single most important
constraint on development.[44] This was so despite the relative importance
of work related migration, which obviously alleviates the situation, and
continued use of the FAIMO which had managed to provide employment
to around a third of those who were in employment. Young people
represented 40 per cent of all those employed by the FAIMO.[45] The report

[42]This derived from the Portuguese scheme which consisted of providing emergency
food aid in exchange for employment on public works. The FAIMO used aid funding to
provide temporary employment.

[43]These figures do not reveal the full extent of unemployment since women, presumed
to be at home, are not registered within the 'active population'. See *III Plano Nacional de
Desenvolvimento, 1992–1995. I Volume, Relatório Geral.*

[44]*Cooperação e Desenvolvimento* (Praia: UNDP, December 1992).

[45]*III Plano Nacional de Desenvolvimento,* op. cit.

also pointed out that since unemployment was worse among young people and women, it led to urban migration, and to the creation of shanty-towns on the outskirts of the main cities, Praia and Mindelo.

Faced with the dilemma of continued unemployment, the MPD regime opted to privilege the modernisation of the economy and the reduction in regional disparities. The first was based on a greater integration into the world economy with its consequent opening up of the borders and further liberalisation of the economy, aiming to combine greater competitiveness with balanced development. To this end the government sought to encourage the kind of productive investment that would maximise employment, blending labour-intensive schemes with economic growth. The second was grounded in the efforts to decentralise both economic activity and decision-making, particularly in regard to the use of FAIMO at the local level.

Despite the efforts made by successive governments since independence, unemployment remains both structurally high and socially disruptive. There has been insufficient scope for the type of sustained economic development that would provide employment to match population growth. The substantial decrease in emigration to those Western countries (Europe and the United States) where Cape Verdeans had habitually been able to find jobs—reduction due in the main to the fall in demand for such unskilled labour—has further aggravated an already precarious situation.[46] Unemployment remains at a stubborn quarter of the active population (women make up 56 per cent of the unemployed and only 36 per cent of the employed). Young people (men and women) in the age group of 14–24 represent 58 per cent of the unemployed total. Regional variations are also still important, with the three main islands (Santiago, São Vicente and Santo Antão) forming 85 per cent of the unemployed, respectively 54 per cent, 21 per cent and 10 per cent.[47]

In this situation, the government again placed the reduction of unemployment at the heart of its latest plan for national development (1997–2000), within the ambit of its programme for the reduction of poverty. Again, it favoured a 'liberal' solution, stressing the development of the private sector, the increase in direct foreign productive investments and the growth of goods and services. This was only implemented in full in 1999 and it is too early to assess whether the continued reliance on the market will make an inroad into this most intractable structural problem.

[46]*Coopération au Développement, Cap-Vert,* (report, s.l.: UNDP, 1998).
[47]*Análise de Situação: Criança e Mulher em Cabo Verde 1998. Programa de Cooperação 2000–2004* (Praia: UNICEF/Governo de Cabo Verde, January 1999).

Given the limitations of the privatisation programme as it has been implemented so far, it is possible that this too will fail seriously to generate new
employment opportunities.[48]

Education and training

After independence, the PAICV government saw education as a priority
and placed the greatest importance on the development of training. To
this end, it initiated a number of key policies soon after independence,
among which the most significant were: the reform of all curricula and
the preparation of new school textbooks; the widening of the network of
schools; support to students from less-favoured social classes; and
improvement in the training of teachers. The First Development Plan
continued to allocate priority resources to education and sought to improve
the provision of basic primary teaching with the aim of enabling all children
to start their education at age seven, reduce illiteracy, strengthen teacher
training, and improve schools and classrooms.

Total primary school student numbers increased steadily (to 61,000) by
1980. Between 1974 and 1980, the number of teaching rooms went up from
717 to 901; there was also much effort to reduce illiteracy among young
people aged fifteen or under. In the period 1988–92, there was an average
annual increase in the number of basic primary education pupils of 2 per
cent. The total number of primary students went from 52,947 to 56,349.
Further school education—that is, the two years following primary school—
saw a very significant increase during the eighties, rising from 6,760 in
1980 to 13.515 in 1990. During the same period, the overall average increase
in further school students was 8.4 per cent, with a total of 15,833 in 1992.

However, these figures are aggregates and do not reveal the very real
regional and local disparities to be found between and even within the
different islands. For example, as a rule rural areas received much less
satisfactory provision of basic education and as a result far fewer young
people attended school, especially beyond the basic primary level. It is
estimated that the cities of Praia and of Mindelo absorb around 70 per
cent of all teachers.

Nevertheless, the achievements of the first government were considerable
if one considers that fully 89 per cent of the population receive primary

---

[48]For an assessment of the Third Development Plan (1992–5) see Ministério da
Coordenação Económica, *III Mesa Redonda dos Parceiros de Desenvolvimento, Reunião
de Seguimento* (Geneva: s.n., 10 January 1995).

education up to years 5 and 6. 58 per cent received the first part of secondary education and 12 per cent the final part of secondary schooling. During its period of office, the PAICV presided over a reduction in illiteracy from 101,259 in 1975 to 52,672 in 1991.[49]

When it came into power, the MPD government stressed (as had the previous regime) the importance of human development and placed as policy priorities the betterment of social justice, the reduction in poverty, the improvement of health, education and nutrition. At the same time, it emphasised the reduction in the role of the state and the wish to stimulate private initiative. For this reason, it favoured an education that would more easily enable young people to acquire the means of their own economic independence. This entailed a more resolutely professional or vocational approach, making it possible for students to become adaptable to the demands of the modern labour market. It also required a context in which the different levels of education were more firmly interlinked.

Although much had been achieved in the area of professional training since 1982, when the Instituto de Formação e Aperfeiçoamento Profissional Extra-Escolar (IFAP), there was much to be done to stimulate and coordinate the various initiatives taken in this field. The MPD government believed that the lack of middle- and higher-ranking professionals and of properly qualified workers was a serious hindrance to development. As a result it committed itself in its development plan (1992–4) to improve existing provisions, widen access to professional training, and to link much more concretely the education provided with existing or envisaged professional employment in Cape Verde.

The main achievements in this area were the transformation of the basic structure of the education system, the development of new curricula, the production of more didactic material, the improvement of the school network, the stress on adult education, and increasing support to more socially relevant forms of education. The number of children aged 7–18 to receive full-time education increased from 103,700 in 1991 to 119,000 in 1995. Professional education is now supported by the Instituto do Emprego e Formação Profissional (IEFP), the Conselho do Emprego e Formação Profissional (CNEFP) and the Fundo de Promoção do Emprego e Formação (FPEF). Despite these significant changes, however, there remain important constraints on professional education, particularly when it comes to coordinating training with employment possibilities. Finally, the reform of the education system is still in progress and it is thus too early to assess its success.

[49]In *III Plano Nacional de Desenvolvimento, 1992–1995. II Volume, Relatórios Sectoriais.*

Health and social welfare

The first PAIGC government (1975–80) programme gave a high priority to social welfare, stressing particularly the protection of the poor and those who were vulnerable (children, women, the chronically ill). Investment in health was made and free medical treatment was introduced, funded by the state and by foreign aid for health and nutrition. A service for the protection of children and family planning (PMI/PF) was introduced from 1977[50] and was extended to all districts by 1983.[51] By 1990, all pregnant women received pre-natal care, with an average of three visits during pregnancy, and 90 per cent of children were vaccinated.[52] Despite these advances, there was still a shortage of personnel and a lack of integration of the PMI/PF with primary health care. Even with unequal regional coverage, access to health care was in line with the recommendations of the World Health Organisation (WHO)—that is, virtually all the population was within one-and-a-half hour's walk from the nearest health centre.[53]

Mortality rates also improved. Mortality for infants between 1 to 4 years of age reduced from 8.4 per thousand in 1978 to 1.4 per thousand in 1991. To put this achievement in perspective, it is instructive to study the comparative WHO general infant mortality figures for those African countries with the best record: South Africa, 89 per thousand; Kenya, 84; Zimbabwe, 83; Cape Verde, 44; and Mauritius, 33. Overall mortality rate for the country in that year was 6.5 per thousand—with the main cause of death being related to nutritional deficiency.[54] In terms of social welfare, the state's activities were limited, by a lack of fund, to the distribution of food, the granting of subsidies, basic health care and provision for the disabled. In reality, here the government was almost entirely dependent on foreign aid and technical assistance.

[50]*As Mulheres nas Ilhas de Cabo Verde—A Força dos Números* (Praia: UNDP, December 1992).

[51]Birth rate began to decline during that period, except among the 15–19 age group. The average number per children declined from 6.4 to 5.9 between 1980 and 1990.

[52]G. Bouillon, *Evaluation Revue à Mis-Parcours du 2eme Programme FNUAP 1991–1995 au Cap-Vert* (Praia: s.n., June 1993).

[53]There were in 1990: 2 main and 3 regional hospitals, 14 health centres with a full-time doctor; 17 MPI/PF centres, 28 health centres with a full-time nurse, and 50 basic health units with a full-time health worker. See *III Plano Nacional de Desenvolvimento, 1992–1995. II Volume, Relatórios Sectoriais.*

[54]*Analyse de Situation au Regard de la Condition de la Femme et de l'Enfant sous le Rapport des Indices de Pauvreté* (Praia: Gouvernement du CapVert/UNICEF, August 1975); *Analyse de la Situation de l'Enfant et de la Femme en République du Cap-Vert* (Praia: Gouvernement du CapVert /UNICEF, October 1989); *Criança e Mulher em Cabo Verde—Análise de Situação* (Praia: Governo do Cabo Verde/UNICEF, October 1993).

Despite the progress made in the provision of health care and social services to the population since independence, by 1991 mortality rates and the incidence of illness remained high—reflecting here the precarious living conditions of the Cape Verdeans. For this reason, the Third Development Plan (1992–5) set out clear policies to improve the situation further. Among the measures envisaged were the improvement in nutrition, the consolidation of primary health care to the whole population, the strengthening of the management of health delivery, the development of training and the regional adaptation of health care.

The efforts made to train health professional was successful since it enabled Cape Verde virtually to dispense with technical assistance in this area. However, results fell short in respect of the improvement of the health infrastructure, most particularly in the central hospitals, which remained under-provisioned and under-resourced despite consuming (in 1993) three-quarters of the medicine available for the whole country.[55] In order to improve the health budget, a new system of fees was introduced in 1993, restricting free access to health care to those suffering from serious illness, the unemployed, those working for FAIMO, pregnant women and children under two years of age.[56] The latest development plan (1997–2000) recognises the limitations of the health service, particularly for those who are most vulnerable: the poor and ill. It also admits that infectious diseases have been resilient, with recent outbreaks of cholera and even poliomyelitis. AIDS has now appeared and, although still limited, there are fears that it could spread rapidly. Finally, there is recognition that health and development are correlated.[57]

As concerns social welfare, the government, in line with its 'liberal' views, envisages that responsibilities be shared between the public and private sectors. If the state is responsible for the management of a human development policy, it behoves other bodies—such as NGOs, church organisations, private institutions—to bring whatever help they can to improve the delivery of welfare provisions. For its part, the government claims to be committed to the alleviation of unemployment, the protection

[55]The increase in the transfer of acute cases to Portugal reflects these deficiencies. See Ministério da Coordenação Económica, op. cit.

[56]It is well to remember that under the PAICV government, health care had been free but that means-tested payments were introduced by the MPD.

[57]The latest figures available in the development plan are as follows for 1998: 164 doctors, 287 nurses. The ratio of doctors per capita is 1:2,552 and of nurses 1:1,452. There are 2 main central hospitals, 3 regional hospitals, 18 health centres, 21 health stations, 91 basic health units and 5 PMI/PF. See *III Plano Nacional de Desenvolvimento, 1992–1995. II Volume, Relatórios Sectoriais*.

of the environment, and the better integration of the various sectors of society into a self-sustained process of development.[58] To this end, the latest development plan stresses the following social policies: better protection of the most disfavoured; an improvement in the delivery of hospital-based social services; a better integration of national and international (private and public) resources; and a strengthening of the means available at the local level. Whatever the good intentions, however, it is clear that in the present economic situation, the government will find it most difficult to provide sufficient social welfare services. Only an improvement in the employment situation would generate sufficient revenues for such purposes.

The provision of water and of sanitation

The extreme scarcity of rainfall on the archipelago is a major constraint on the provision of water and the improvement of sanitary conditions. Given that at independence only 20 per cent of the population had access to drinkable water—and that mostly in the urban areas—the first government considered the increase in availability a key priority. With the support of UNICEF and the UN Sahel Organisation (UNSO), it undertook, during 1977–81 the development of water and sanitation facilities on the islands of Maio, Boavista, São Vicente and São Nicolau. Despite substantial achievements in the eighties, only 52 per cent of the population had access to safe water in 1991. The situation was far worse in the rural areas (particularly on Santiago, Fogo and Santo Antão, where 85 per cent of the rural population live) where only 34 per cent had such facilities.[59]

Although a number of the objectives set out in the Second Development Plan (1986–90) were in fact achieved, the new MPD government still maintained that more needed to be done in this area. The Third Development Plan (1992–5) laid down ambitious objectives for access to drinkable water which, so far, have only been attained in São Vicente, where 65 per cent of the population is now supplied. The provision of sanitation, on the other hand, remained far too limited—with only Praia and Mindelo benefiting from any sewerage system. Accordingly, the latest plan (1997–2000) aims to extend proper sanitation to the whole country, particularly in Praia where rapid and unregulated urbanisation is causing serious problems. Other urban

---

[58]*Análise de Situação. Criança e Mulher em Cabo Verde* (Praia: Governo do Cabo Verde/ UNICEF, January 1998).

[59]*Análise de Situação. Criança e Mulher em Cabo Verde* (Praria, Governo do Cabe Verde/ UNICEF, 1993).

centres will also receive priority treatment. Finally, there are plans to establish a water-quality control laboratory in every municipality.

Assessment

An appraisal of the quality of sustainable human development in Cape Verde requires a discussion of a certain number of indicators of social well being. There is universal provision of basic health care but the price of medicine is often too high. Infectious diseases, including HIV, are on the increase. There are serious nutritional deficiencies in the country, with shortages of vitamin and calcium intake. In 1994, it was estimated that 6 per cent of the population suffered acute and 15 per cent chronic malnutrition. As we have seen, almost half of the population has no direct access to clean drinking water. There are continuous, and strong, inequalities between the sexes, with women forming the majority of the unemployed and illiterate and suffering frequent violence within the family setting. There is now an increasing number of 'street children' to be found in the cities of Praia, Mindelo and Sal. Prostitution and social delinquency are also on the increase.[60] A 1994 study indicates that 14 per cent of the population can be considered 'very poor' while 30 per cent are 'poor'—60 per cent of the very poor households are headed by an illiterate woman.[61]

The best available information suggests that the situation may well deteriorate for a number of reasons. First, the limits on public spending on health and the emphasis on the role of private medicine, which are now government policy, are going to be problematic in a context where few people can afford to pay for medical care. There are dangers that such policies will lead to growing inequalities in access to health provision and an increase in the rise of infectious diseases.[62] Second, the introduction of the means-tested provision of school meals is bound to affect a large number of children since the criteria are not well-understood or applied. Although there is no reliable data on this issue, it is likely that a relatively substantial number of children only eat a nutritionally-balanced diet through school meals. The reduction of aid in this area from the FAO is in this respect ominous. Finally, the privatisation programme has so far led to the loss of public service employment which has not been made up by the creation of private

[60]*Análise de Situação. Criança e Mulher em Cabo Verde*, 1998, op. cit.

[61]*La Pauvreté au Cap Vert. Évaluation sommaire du Problème et Stratégie en Vue de son Allègement* (Report no. 13126, s.l.: Banque Mondiale, Région Afrique, Département Sahel, Division des Operations-Pays, June 1994).

[62]*Cabo Verde. Relatório Nacional de Desenvolvimento Humano 1999* (s.l.: UNDP, s.d.).

sector jobs, resulting in greater underemployment or unemployment with their attendant social and health problems.[63]

CONCLUSION

The analysis of economic and social development in Cape Verde since independence raises some fundamental questions about the future political directions of the archipelago. Is the current rapid liberalisation of the economy, in a context where there is no substantial class of national entrepreneurs and very little prospect that it will develop rapidly, a viable means of ensuring economic growth and sustainable human development? Indeed, the privatisation programme was seriously criticised by the PAIVC because, in a environment lacking in transparency, there is very strong suspicion that it has engendered corruption and other illegal practices. If such policies increase the number of deprived poor people, with no hope of employment, is there not a risk of social disruption, or even violence? Finally, even if, as appears to be the case, economic growth is picking up, will the structural adjustment programme allow an improvement in the human development of Cape Verdeans and a reduction of poverty and inequality? Clearly, the ruling MPD did not manage in the last elections to convince the population that it is the best party to meet those challenges. The question now is whether the delay in fulfilling some of its most important commitments, especially in respect of unemployment, will conspire to undermine the efforts of the new government.

[63]Ibid.

8

SÃO TOMÉ E PRÍNCIPE

Gerhard Seibert

INTRODUCTION

Historical background

São Tomé e Príncipe is a small and impoverished country of 140,000 inhabitants and a GDP of less than $ 50 million. An analysis of the country's postcolonial period must take into account the characteristics produced by size and insularity. The small island economy has been constrained by a tiny domestic market with diseconomies of scale, geographical isolation causing deficient and expensive transport, and a narrow economic base. Societal features of small countries include the prevalence of face-to-face relations, a particularistic value orientation, a small-town mentality, a lack of privacy and anonymity and a tendency toward personalist politics. To some extent these particularities have hindered the social-economic development and influenced local politics of the archipelago. Equally important is that São Tomé e Príncipe has no ethnic, linguistic or religious divisions. Finally, the country has not been affected by civil war, external destabilisation or recurrent natural disasters.

São Tomé e Príncipe experienced almost 500 years of colonial rule by Portugal. However, despite this continuity, there was a rupture in colonial domination after the decline of the sugar industry in the mid-seventeenth century, when the local Creoles, known as *forros*, came to exercise virtual control over the archipelago. The Portuguese re-colonised the islands in the second half of the nineteenth century introducing new cash crops. Then, large cocoa estates not only dominated the plantation economy, but also shaped the social relations between the white colonists, the native Creoles, and imported African plantation workers. The Portuguese gradually extended the plantations at the expense of the *forros*, whose lands were held by title or customary usufruct, through purchase, fraud and force.

Consequently the *forros* were marginalised and lost their *de facto* political and economic power to the Portuguese.

The *forros*, who are the descendants of Portuguese settlers and the manumitted slaves of the sixteenth century, refused manual fieldwork on the plantations, known as *roças*, since they considered it demeaning and beneath their free status. They became an intermediate group between the whites at the top of the colonial hierarchy and the contract workers at the bottom. In the early twentieth century a few *forro* planters still engaged successfully in cocoa production but, during the interbellum, most remaining Creole planters lost their plantations due to over-consumption and fragmentation by inheritance. While before World War I the Creole elite had derived wealth and status from the ownership of plantations, thereafter they worked predominantly in the lower ranks of the colonial administration. These administrative positions became the main resource base for their kinship-based and clientelist networks. Since then administrative jobs have been highly valued by the *forros*. As a result, a bureaucratic culture has developed, viewing such positions as an available resource base for personal appropriation and redistribution, to the detriment of economic rationality and administrative efficiency.

After the abolition of slavery in 1875, and due to the *forros'* negative attitude towards plantation work, the Portuguese recruited large numbers of contract workers in Angola, Cape Verde and Mozambique in order to satisfy the growing demand for labour. From the beginning of the twentieth century until the 1940s, the indentured workers outnumbered the native islanders. The contract workers lived exclusively in barracks on the plantations, while the *forros* lived in the towns and other dispersed communities. The *forros* maintained an attitude of superiority towards the contract workers and disdained them. In turn, due to their persistent refusal to work on the Portuguese *roças*, the *forros* acquired the reputation of being lazy, idle and arrogant people among the white population that treated them with contempt.

Decolonisation and factional struggles

In February 1953, ambitions by the colonial government to force *forros* to work on the plantations in order to solve the problem of labour shortages provoked a spontaneous insurrection by the Creole population that feared losing their intermediate position within the plantation society. On the orders of Governor Carlos Gorgulho (1945–53) the local police, supported by armed white volunteers and incited by contract workers unleashed a wave of violence against the *forro* population, killing a number of innocent and defenceless people. The atrocities against unarmed *forros*, frequently referred to as the Batepá War, later served to denounce Portuguese colonialism and were used as one of the founding myths of anti-colonial resistance.

The foundation of the Comité de Libertação de São Tomé e Príncipe (CLSTP) by a small group of young Creole exiles in 1960 marked the beginning of the organised political struggle for independence. Miguel Trovoada, at the time a law student in Lisbon, became the leader of the CLSTP. However, the small group of nationalists was divided into two factions, based in Libreville and Accra respectively, which were frequently involved in personal quarrels and largely inactive in the archipelago where the Portuguese maintained full control. Following the military coup in 1966 in Ghana, the CLSTP was expelled from Accra and remained virtually non-existent for several years. Not before July 1972 did nine exiled nationalists meet in Santa Isabel (later renamed Malabo), Equatorial Guinea, and reconstituted the CLSTP as the Movimento de Libertação de São Tomé e Príncipe (MLSTP). Manuel Pinto da Costa, who had just obtained a doctorate in economics in former East Germany, became secretary-general, while the other participants all became members of the political bureau of the MLSTP, which set up its office in Santa Isabel.[1] Its political programme demanded 'total independence', 'the establishment of a republican, democratic, secular, anti-colonial and anti-imperialistic regime', 'an agrarian reform including a better distribution of land', and 'the gradual introduction of a planned economy'.[2]

However, before the military coup of 25 April 1974 in Lisbon, the MLSTP did not carry out any political action in São Tomé e Príncipe. After the creation of the MLSTP, the Portuguese secret police in the archipelago did not report any political activity and formed the impression that the few nationalists present were inactive or disorganised.[3] Only with the revolution in Portugal did the political struggle within the archipelago begin in earnest. In May, a group of moderate Creole civil servants and local Catholic priests founded the Frente Popular Livre (FPL), advocating a federation with Portugal with the prospect of progressive autonomy. Meanwhile the MLSTP

---

[1]The others present were Leonel Mário d'Alva, Deputy Secretary-General; Miguel Trovoada, Secretary of Foreign Affairs; Guadelupe de Ceita, Secretary of Social and Financial Affairs; Carlos Graça, Secretary of Culture and Education; José Fret Lau Chong, Secretary of Propaganda; João Torres, António Oné Pires dos Santos and Alexandrina Barros.

[2]Carlos Benigno da Cruz (ed.), *S. Tomé e Príncipe. Do Colonialismo á Independência* (Lisbon: Morães Editores, 1975), pp. 79–82.

[3]Sub-delegation of the Direcção-Geral de Segurança in São Tomé, Reports 1972–3. Arquivo Nacional Torre de Tombo.

had moved its office to Libreville. As the leadership was poorly prepared and feared that they might be detained when they entered São Tomé from foreign territory, they postponed their arrival in the archipelago. Instead, they instructed the MLSTP's representative in Lisbon, the lawyer Gastão Torres, to return home with the overseas São Tomense students to agitate for total independence and the recognition of the MLSTP as the sole legitimate representative of the Sãotomean people. When Torres and about twenty students, who were politically strongly influenced by the ideas of Pan-Africanism, Black Power, Marxism and Maoism, arrived in June 1974 in São Tomé they set up the Associação Cívica pró-MLSTP in order to support the struggle for independence. At that time the MLSTP, whose leaders had lived abroad for more than ten years, was virtually unknown in the country. The Cívica succeeded in mobilising the plantation workers and the native Creole population alike by organising demonstrations, strikes and boycotts that continued until September. Encouraged by their success the more radical Cívica members, gathered around the political bureau members Gastão Torres and Pedro Umbelina,[4] grew politically more ambitious, which inevitably increased the rivalry with the comparatively moderate MLSTP leadership in Libreville. Meanwhile, following a meeting with the MLSTP in Libreville in August, the FPL, which had enjoyed little popular support, was dissolved.

Despite the absence of bloodshed and armed violence,[5] the turmoil and anti-Portuguese agitation resulted in the departure of virtually all of the white colonists, who numbered about 2,000. Finally, in late September 1974 the Portuguese initiated direct negotiations with the MLSTP in Libreville. In November the two parties signed the Algiers Agreement that regulated the decolonisation process of São Tomé e Príncipe. On December 21, a transitional government led by the MLSTP was installed. Local functionaries replaced the departed Portuguese senior civil servants, although their educational level was largely inadequate for their new positions. In March 1975 a fierce factional struggle over the dissolution of the native troops split the Cívica and the leadership in Libreville. The former, more radical faction, demanded the replacement of the native troops by a police force and a people's militia. Finally, the conflict was decided in favour of the moderates headed by Miguel Trovoada and Pinto da Costa, who

---

[4]They had joined the political bureau of the MLSTP earlier in 1974.

[5]In September 1974, two islanders were killed, one because of a stray bullet and the other in a street accident related to the unrest. The two unfortunate men remained the only victims of the independence struggle.

enjoyed the support of the majority of the population and the Portuguese government. Consequently, they expelled Torres and Umbelina from the party. They left the country together with the militant students, who continued their studies abroad.[6]

A SOCIALIST EXPERIMENT IN A SMALL ISLAND REPUBLIC

Creating state and society

On 12 July 1975, São Tomé e Príncipe gained independence and constitutionally became a one-party state ruled by the MLSTP, which had won the elections for a 16-member constituent assembly five days before.[7] Pinto da Costa became president and headed the government, while Trovoada was appointed prime minister of the new state with a population of 80,000. The MLSTP followed the examples of its sister nationalist parties from the Portuguese-speaking countries and opted to organise state and society according to Soviet-style socialism. The country's first constitution defined that, as revolutionary vanguard, the MLSTP was the leading political force of the nation with a duty to determine the political orientation of the state.[8] The MLSTP never formally adopted the denomination 'Marxist-Leninist', since the party was committed to the so-called socialist 'orientation', a prior stage to socialism conceived by Soviet theorists in the 1960s. However, until 1983, the explicit ultimate political aim was to end the exploitation of man by man through the construction of socialism. The legislative power of the state was vested in a 33-member Assembleia Nacional Popular (ANP), whose members were selected by the MLSTP. In 1980 the regime introduced the election of the delegates of seven district assemblies by a show of hands during mass meetings. In turn, the district delegates chose the representatives to the ANP, which now numbered 51 deputies. In practice the parliament acted as a mere political rubber-stamp, clapping its hands in support of the government and ratifying unanimously its decisions. The district delegates were used to mobilise support for political cam-

[6]To some extent the factional struggles during the decolonisation process also mirrored personal cleavages within the local elite families. In part it was also an inter-generational struggle between the radical students and the elder Libreville faction.

[7]Some 21,000 registered voters elected by secret ballot the 16 deputies out of 52 candidates, almost all of whom had been nominated by the MLSTP. Consequently, the MLSTP candidates gained 90 per cent of the votes.

[8]Constituição Política approved by the political bureau of the MLSTP and the constituent assembly in November 1975.

paigns organised by the regime, for which they in turn were rewarded with favours. Despite the socialist rhetoric there was little real popular involvement in policy decisions or their implementation.

Right after independence the regime consolidated its power according to the socialist blueprint by creating so-called mass organisations and setting up the security apparatus. In 1975, it established the party sections for children, youth and women, respectively the Organização dos Pioneiros (OPSTEP), the Juventude do MLSTP (JMLSTP), and the Organização das Mulheres (OMSTEP). In practice these bodies had considerable organisational shortcomings which limited their ability to reach beyond their leadership structures. Attempts to set up an official trade union were not realised before 1990. Any political organisation and association outside the one-party structure was prohibited. Furthermore, the government fully controlled the few local media: the Rádio Nacional and the paper *Revolução*, founded at independence. Free political debate and a free press were neither desired nor possible. In late 1975, the regime established the Tribunal Especial para Actos Contra-Revolucionários (TEACR) with the objective of finding the true, or presumed, adversaries of the regime. At the same time the newly-created secret service, the Departamento da Segurança Nacional (DNS), was directly subordinated to President Pinto da Costa. The agents of the secret service appeared ubiquitous and brought about an atmosphere of intimidation and fear among the population. In September 1977, the small contingent of native troops was renamed Forças Armadas Revolucionárias de São Tomé e Príncipe (FARSTP). Two years later, conscription was introduced for all males.

The regime joined the IMF and the World Bank as early as 1977 and always maintained foreign relations with the West as part of an official policy of non-alignment. Western countries remained the most important importers of the country's cocoa, the principal export. Nevertheless, there is no doubt that at the time the regime favoured relations with the then socialist countries, which were considered 'natural allies', since their own country was viewed as part of the socialist bloc. In particular, bilateral political and economic ties with the MPLA government in Luanda were strengthened. Angola supplied São Tomé e Príncipe with fuel on concessionary terms at the price of only $ 4 per barrel, at a time when the world market price was $ 20.[9] When the regime felt threatened by an alleged foreign invasion in 1978, Luanda sent some 1,500 soldiers who, though gradually reduced to 500 men, remained in the archipelago until 1991.

[9]*Nova República*, no. 17, 12 August 1992.

Cuba, which provided the Angolan government with military support, also became an important ally of São Tomé e Príncipe. Right after independence the first Sãotomean students and military personnel were sent for education and training to Cuba. When Pinto da Costa visited the Caribbean island in 1978 he assured his hosts that his country was also determined to construct a society without exploiters or the exploited. At that time, there were about 140 Cuban experts in São Tomé e Príncipe, who had established a parallel administration on all decision-making levels. In contrast, the Soviet Union provided mainly military aid and training. Such close co-operation with their socialist allies obliged the MLSTP regime to implement their policies internally. As a consequence of the preferential ties with the socialist countries, relations with neighbouring Gabon and the Western countries deteriorated considerably.

Committed to a socialist ideology, the MLSTP proclaimed the emancipation of women as a political goal and granted equal rights to the plantation workers. Consequently, the plantation communities could interact more freely with the larger Creole society and the colonial boundaries between the different socio-cultural groups became more blurred. Shortly after independence, the government introduced free health care and free compulsory education for all citizens. The elimination of an illiteracy rate of 85 per cent was considered a priority. In the first decade after independence more than 700 students, many of them from modest social backgrounds, were sent abroad for professional training and university education. Cuba, the Soviet Union and other former socialist countries played an important role here too, since they provided by far the greatest number of scholarships. The returnees were given positions within the expanding state apparatus and the state-owned enterprises and they were incorporated into a local elite that gradually became less exclusive. In particular people who were loyal to the party leadership succeeded in climbing up the social ladder. Due to their positions and ties with the holders of political power they gained access to state resources extending thereby existing clientelist relationships. However, the vast majority of the population remained largely outside these distribution networks.

The purge of the radicals in March 1975 had not ended factional struggles within the ruling *forro* elite. Soon after independence old cleavages and personal rivalries, often dating back to the exile years, re-emerged within the MLSTP. It was an intra-elite struggle for power and resources, conducted by intrigues and conspiracies, and accompanied by actual or alleged coup attempts, which in turn served to increase the authoritarian and repressive character of the regime. In early 1977, Health Minister Carlos Graça, who was considered a reactionary, went into exile to Libreville, because he disagreed with the government's economic and foreign policies and feared his detention. In the same year, nine citizens were arrested and accused of having planned to detain Pinto da Costa and his cabinet ministers. The TEACR sentenced them to prison terms ranging from three months to 16 years.[10]

At the beginning of that year, Albertino Neto, the first commander of the FARSTP, and six others were imprisoned and accused of being 'agents of imperialism' and of having planned to kill the president. Neto and three defendants were sentenced to between 22 months and five years imprisonment, while two others were acquitted. Carlos Graça was sentenced in absentia to 24 years of forced labour. Following the detention of Neto, the regime created a paranoid climate claiming that unidentified 'imperialist' ships and planes had attempted to invade the country with the support of internal reactionaries. Pinto da Costa even reported both to the UN Security Council and the OAU that an invasion was imminent. As the 120-strong FARSTP was considered too weak to defend the regime, it sent an urgent request for military support to Luanda, which was immediately approved. Apart from Carlos Graça's presumed coup plans, the failed mercenary invasion of Benin led by Bob Denard, the assassination of Congo's President Marien Ngouabi, and the failed coup attempt of Nito Alves in Luanda, all occurred in early 1977, increasing thereby the regime's fears.[11]

Due to its geographical and political isolation, São Tomé e Príncipe had now been turned into an almost closed society. In August 1979, a population census, which had been perceived by the *forro* population as an attempt to introduce forced labour on the plantations, provoked a two-day popular revolt in São Tomé. The security forces detained some 100 people, many of whom were beaten and tortured. The next month, during a meeting of the MLSTP central committee its members accused Trovoada of connivance in the census riots and of having known of a plan to assassinate Pinto da Costa. During the tumultuous session, Trovoada, who was said to be in favour of a more pragmatic economic policy, was shouted down as an 'enemy of the people' and 'agent of imperialism'. Finally, he was arrested and kept in custody without charge or trial until July 1981, when he was released and went into exile in Paris. The principal cause of Pinto da Costa's rupture with his former intimate friend Trovoada was not so much political disagreement as a straightforward struggle for power.

---

[10]In September 1978, Loreno da Mata, one of these prisoners, was shot dead by a prison guard. He remained the only political prisoner, who was murdered during the authoritarian regime that never became as violent as other similar regimes.

[11]At the time, neighbouring Libreville had a reputation as a base for mercenary operations.

After Trovoada's removal, the regime pursued a more radical course and ruled with an iron hand. Nevertheless, in December 1981, the lack of consumer goods triggered hunger riots on Príncipe, which were accompanied by secessionist demands. Consequently, Pinto da Costa dismissed the defence minister, Daniel Daio, for having failed as security chief. In fact, he considered him a potential threat to his power. In 1982, Daio and three other members resigned from the political bureau of the MLSTP in protest against the radical party line and Pinto da Costa's authoritarian style. Growing popular discontent with the regime had also contributed to conflicts and intrigues within the MLSTP, used by Pinto da Costa to outmanoeuvre his rivals and replace them by members of his family and other persons loyal to him. He now had reached the climax of his personal power. Protection by the secret police and the Angolan troops ensured that his position remained unchallenged. He was simultaneously head of state, party leader, head of government, and army commander.

Only exiled dissidents challenged Pinto da Costa's autocratic rule but this opposition remained divided by personal and political quarrels. In 1981, exiles set up the Frente de Resistência Nacional de São Tomé e Príncipe (FRNSTP), based in Libreville, where it enjoyed the support of President Omar Bongo. The leader of the FRNSTP was Carlos Graça. Although the group had about a hundred armed men, its actions did not go beyond mere political propaganda such as the distribution of pamphlets in São Tomé. Dissidents exiled in Portugal founded the União Democrática e Independente de São Tomé e Príncipe (UDISTP) and the Acção Democrática Nacional de São Tomé e Príncipe (ADNSTP). Despite their fragmentation, the activities of these splinter groups worried the MLSTP government. It repeatedly complained in Lisbon that the exiled opposition could freely agitate. Around that time the former activists of the Cívica, who had finished their courses abroad, had returned home, where they were integrated into the state apparatus. A few of them joined the MLSTP and quickly became government ministers. They later belonged to the core group of young politicians who would promote political change within the party. However, most of them maintained their distance with the MLSTP and kept their dissident views to themselves. For the time being, any free debate or organised opposition was impossible.

Economic policy

Since colonial rule had impeded the access of blacks to higher education, at the time of independence there was a great shortage of trained and experienced personnel to replace the departed whites. The nationals who took over the public administration and the economy were mostly inadequately trained for their tasks. Vacant and newly-created jobs within the bureaucracy and the economy were usually allocated to *forros*, while the majority of the former contract workers remained on the estates. Due to the Creoles' preference for administrative jobs and their disdain for plantation labour, not even the poorest *forros* were willing to work on the plantations.

In its first ambitious programme the MLSTP government announced the diversification of agriculture and the development of fishing and tourism. The land distribution demanded earlier by the MLSTP had been dropped in favour of production in large state-owned units, which now were considered to offer better development prospects than small-scale agriculture. The role of the cocoa estates, which in 1975 employed about half of the labour force and provided almost all the national export earnings, was crucial for the economy. During a mass rally in September 1975 the government nationalised the Portuguese-owned plantations without compensation. The action was defended as a necessary response to the withdrawal of the Portuguese and the virtual absence of local entrepreneurs. The nationalised estates, which in early 1979 were regrouped into 15 so-called Empresas Estatais Agro-Pecuárias, covered 92 per cent of the total land area. The nationalisation allowed the *forro* elite to regain the control of the land, from which the Portuguese had dispossessed their ancestors some hundred years before. By contrast, a land distribution that would also have benefited the plantation workers would have meant a loss of such control.

The internal structure of the estates remained unchanged. The former white personnel on the plantations were replaced by *forros*, who generally lacked agricultural know-how. The majority of the field workers were the former contract workers, who were mostly excluded from administrative jobs in the oversized and inefficient offices of the *empresas*. Owing to the unrest during the decolonisation process, cocoa production dropped by some 50 per cent to 5,000 tonnes in 1975. After 1976 São Tomé e Príncipe benefited from high world cocoa prices. However, prices slumped drastically from 1980. The temporary price boom had helped to disguise the real weakness of the cocoa sector which had been affected by serious deficiencies. Since independence there had been almost no investment on the estates to purchase new machinery, replace old cocoa trees or improve the management. Moreover, the state had failed to introduce new forms of training and incentives for the plantation workers. Consequently, the productivity of the estates dropped from 450 kg/ha of cocoa before independence to 165 kg/ha in 1983. To make things worse the estates cultivated less than half of the land available to them. Consequently, the country's total cocoa output began to decrease gradually and reached only 3,400 tonnes in 1984. The export income fell from $ 27 million in 1979 to only $ 9 million in 1981.[12] Instead of helping to finance the planned diversification of the economy the state-owned plantations had become highly indebted. As a result, the government had to fund public investment with foreign loans, which led to an increasing external debt burden.

After independence, all existing non-agricultural enterprises were nationalised and in 1979 central planning was introduced. In addition, the government created various new companies in trade, transport, construction, energy, fishing, and small industries. While there was a shortage of skilled personnel, the overall workforce of these companies was oversized, reflecting an employment policy that was guided by political dogma and the prevalent clientelistic practices. Appointment to management posts depended more upon patronage or the degree of kinship of the candidate with a minister than upon individual qualification. Nationalisation allowed the ruling elite to monopolise access to land, jobs and other resources through the state in order to maintain political control and attract followers. Most of the new investment was too large, poorly managed, and loss making, further damaging public finance. The companies did not achieve a single target programmed in the various economic plans. Instead, their production costs were higher than the value of their output. Public enterprises were often transformed into instruments of individual appropriation rather than state accumulation since they were harmed by fraudulent practices and theft on the part of their managers and personnel. For example, the two state-owned companies for import and export conceded so-called credits to hundreds of people in cash and kind, which were never repaid. These loans had amounted to $ 23.3 million in 1993 when 48 per cent of the national budget had to be used to finance the interest and repayment of these debts.

It would be short-sighted to attribute economic failure only to the ideological proclivity for a planned economy. The lack of trained cadres, the institutional and organisational shortcomings, the allocation of jobs guided by clientelism and nepotism, fraudulent practices, and an inadequate work ethic due to a history of forced labour also contributed to the poor performance of the economy. An outbreak of the African swine fever in 1979 and a severe drought in 1983 only aggravated economic decline. In the end, the economic crisis forced the MLSTP regime to redefine its foreign policy in search of aid, which the socialist allies could not provide. Notwithstanding the people's disengagement from the party,

[12]*Africa Contemporary Record 1982/83*, p. B406.

the regime's main motive for the political re-orientation initiated around 1984, was sheer economic necessity, rather than popular pressures for change.

Political and economic liberalisation

The regime's shift away from the socialist model was a gradual and peaceful process that lasted about five years. In July 1984 Pinto da Costa admitted publicly for the first time that his regime had taken wrong political decisions due to a lack of experience. Subsequently, he appeased former dissidents and tried to broaden the base of his regime. In early 1988, Carlos Graça, who meanwhile had resigned as president of the FRNSTP, became foreign minister in a new government. His return helped Pinto da Costa to weaken the external opposition, reconcile himself with President Omar Bongo, and give credibility to his political re-orientation abroad. Simultaneously, the regime started a diplomatic offensive towards the West to improve bilateral relations in order to gain economic aid. As was to be expected, the Western countries and multilateral donors rewarded the regime's new foreign policy by promising to finance São Tomé e Príncipe's development plan for 1986–90, including the rehabilitation of the cocoa plantations. In 1986, the first contract with a foreign company for the management of a cocoa estate was signed and subsequently an investment code was introduced to attract foreign private investment.

After having proved its intention to abolish the planned economy, the MLSTP regime signed an agreement to undertake a structural adjustment programme (SAP) with the IMF and the World Bank in 1987. The SAP aimed at devaluing the local currency, reducing the state deficit, rehabilitating the estates by putting them under foreign management contracts, privatising the unprofitable public enterprises, and liberalising the entire economy. Another key element of the programme was the diversification of the economy by developing other cash crops and tourism. However, the SAP still remained reliant on the plantation economy and again cocoa had to generate the surplus for the diversification of the economy. The reform policies resulted in the inflow of foreign funds, which created new opportunities for corruption involving various government members with the complicity of foreign actors. These corruption scandals revealed the openness of local office holders to bribes and made clear the methods of foreign business interests in poor vulnerable countries.

The rapprochement with the West entailed various political and personal conflicts within the government involving competing groups and individuals, who either felt their interests threatened, or, conversely, wanted to capitalise on newly-emerging opportunities to gain power. These struggles within the regime resulted in five cabinet reshuffles between 1985 and 1988, when Pinto da Costa replaced various ministers with a leftist reputation by people associated with neo-liberal positions in order to give credibility to the change. At a party congress in 1985, the MLSTP redefined itself as a broad front of all citizens and dropped the former socialist concepts. During a meeting of the central committee in October 1987, the MLSTP decided to supplement the liberalisation of the economy with political reform, including the direct election of the head of state by secret ballot and the admission of different political currents within the single party. The protagonists of the renovation of the MLSTP were the young ministers who had completed their studies abroad in the early 1980s. They had neither strong links with the founding generation of the MLSTP nor with the so-called orthodox party faction that resisted change.

Apparently dissociated from the political process, in March 1988, the splinter group Frente de Resistência Nacional de São Tomé e Príncipe (FRNSTP-R) led by Afonso dos Santos tried to seize power in an amazingly amateurish seaborne operation. The security forces easily detained the 45 invaders. The following year, dos Santos was sentenced to 22 years imprisonment and his accomplices also received custodial sentences. However, they were all granted amnesty in 1990. In early December 1989, the MLSTP organised a national conference for political liberalisation, the very first in Africa. After vehement discussions, the participants approved the transition to democracy and a free-market economy. The outcome of the conference exceeded all expectations, since the introduction of a multiparty system had not been unequivocally on the agenda of the MLSTP. Pinto da Costa and various ministers had repeatedly rejected liberal democracy as unsuitable for their country. Their aim had not been to change the regime but, on the contrary, to maintain power under shifting political conditions. The collapse of the Soviet Union in the late 1980s and pressures from within and outside the country had accelerated, as well as guided, the whole process of political change.

The democratisation process

In a popular referendum in August 1990, 81 per cent of the 42,000 voters ratified a new democratic constitution drafted by the MLSTP with Portuguese assistance. Based on the semi-presidential Portuguese system, the constitution gave the president executive powers in the areas of defence and foreign policy. At a party congress in October of the same year the MLSTP was reconstituted as the Partido Social Democrata (MLSTP/PSD), claiming to have adopted the ideology of social democracy. Pinto da Costa refrained from contesting for the party leadership since he wanted to run in the presidential elections as the people's candidate. At his behest and with the support of the renovators, Carlos Graça was elected the new secretary-general. The majority of the orthodox faction, who belonged to Pinto da Costa's former inner group, was not re-elected to the new executive committee. In the course of this process the exiled opposition and local opponents of the regime constituted new political parties. In October, returned exiles of the three splinter groups—FRNSTP, UDISTP and ADNSTP formally formed the Coligação Democrática da Oposição (CODO). Following the national conference, a heterogeneous alliance including former Cívica activists who had not compromised themselves with the regime, former ministers ousted by Pinto da Costa, old dissidents, and young professionals had founded the Grupo de Reflexão. In November 1990, the group was transformed into the Partido de Convergência Democrática (PCD-GR), of which the leadership was dominated by the former Cívica leaders, whose political ambitions had remained dormant under the MLSTP regime. Daniel Daio, the former defence minister, became secretary-general of the PCD-GR. In December, Afonso dos Santos, the pardoned leader of the failed invasion, and his supporters founded the Frente Democrata Cristã (FDC), which advocated a future coalition with the MLSTP/PSD. The CODO lacked local followers, since the party had come from abroad and had no charismatic leader, while the FDC had no appreciable local following at all. In contrast, the PCD-GR united by far the largest number of opponents of the regime and benefited most from the euphoria created by the political change.

In São Tomé e Príncipe the democratic transition was carried out by the same people who had dominated local politics since independence. During the entire process the MLSTP succeeded in imposing its rules and its timetable on the opposition. However, in the first democratic multiparty elections, held on 20 January 1991, the PCD-GR gained a landslide victory with 33 seats, while the ruling MLSTP-PSD secured only 21 seats in the 55-member national assembly. The CODO obtained the remaining seat. The MLSTP/PSD was completely stupefied by the defeat, but immediately accepted the outcome. The victory of the opposition was possible because it had largely remained united and it had succeeded in articulating popular demands for change. In contrast, the MLSTP/PSD was worn out and had lost legitimacy after 15 years of dictatorial rule marked by economic decline. Owing to his party's defeat, Pinto da Costa confirmed his decision, already announced the previous November, to withdraw his candidature for the presidential elections. He did not want to risk the humiliation of a defeat at the hands of his arch-rival, Miguel Trovoada, who had enjoyed great popular support since his return from French exile in May 1990. Due to his detention and forced exclusion Trovoada acquired the aura of a 'saviour' who could free the people from mismanagement, misery and autocratic rule. Both the PCD-GR and the CODO supported Trovoada, while the MLSTP/PSD did not present another candidate. On the eve of the presidential elections two of the remaining three competitors also withdrew, robbing Trovoada of the political triumph of a victory in contested elections. Finally, on 3 March, Trovoada, unopposed, was elected president with 82 per cent of the votes—on a turnout of only 60 per cent.

MULTIPARTY DEMOCRACY: THE FIRST TEN YEARS

Free elections and political instability

The first ten years of liberal democracy in São Tomé e Príncipe have been marked by continuous economic decline, widespread corruption and political instability. However, since 1991, human rights have been respected and, although plagued by organisational shortcomings, relatively free and fair legislative and presidential elections have been held regularly. The distribution of money and the mobilisation of patron-client relationships have become recurrent components in the elections, reflecting the influence of local social practices on the formal democratic structure. During elections the sluggish bureaucracy virtually ceases to function at all, since civil servants are either participating in the campaign or are idle awaiting the outcome. Election campaigns have not been based on programmatic issues, rather they have been dominated by mutual accusations of corruption, mismanagement and incompetence. Nevertheless, in São Tomé e Príncipe elections have provided a functioning mechanism to sanction a government for poor performance and the failure to reward its supporters after having·assumed office.

Only the three major parties—the MLSTP/PSD, PCD-GR and Acção Democrática Independente (ADI), established in 1992 by followers of President Trovoada—have enjoyed electoral support. Unlike the other five small parties, they have at least at the top level a working party organisation, they are able to raise funds, and they have a significant membership. All parties owe their existence to the factional struggles and personal strife which occurred within the MLSTP and, consequently, they have been primarily based on personal splits or interest groups rather than on opposing political programmes. As the parties do not represent different class interests either, their social basis is heterogeneous. Party membership is often based on personal bonds such as kinship, friendship, and patronage mirroring the personalistic and largely non-substantive character of local politics. Accordingly, parties do not serve exclusively political purposes. They are frequently considered as channels of patronage by poor people in need and they serve politicians to attract clients. The leadership of all parties has come from the small urban *forro* elite, who work predominantly in the public administration. Owing to the lack of local financing, the parties rely on illegal access to government funds or foreign support, although the law prohibits financing from abroad.

Changes of government through the ballot box have occurred peacefully and according to the constitutional rules. This ability of the parties to compete for power within the democratic structure marks the relative success of liberal democracy in São Tomé e Príncipe. The continuity of the system was threatened when young officers staged a military coup in August 1995. The military, who felt marginalised, neglected and impoverished since the democratic transition, justified the coup attempt on the grounds of widespread corruption, government incompetence and the deplorable state of the army. After one week of negotiations the insurgents returned to the barracks, having been granted a general amnesty, and the constitutional order was restored. The ambiguity of the semi-presidential constitution has been a fertile ground for various conflicts between the head of state and the successive governments of changing coalitions. Tension has also arisen as a result of competition for funds provided by external aid and foreign business interests. Both factors played a major role when President Trovoada dismissed the first PCD-GR government headed by Daniel Daio in April 1992, arguing that the state institutions were not functioning well and that there was no prospect for consensus with the prime minister.

The alliance between Trovoada and the PCD-GR had only existed for tactical reasons. Right after the elections the PCD-GR contested the president's right to control defence and foreign affairs, including the all-important department for cooperation. Conflicts emerged on deals favoured by Trovoada, such as the sale of two estates to French businessmen and the storage of industrial waste by an Italian company. In May 1994, the new PCD-GR prime minister, Costa Alegre, deprived Trovoada of the crucial control of foreign aid by creating a separate secretariat of state for cooperation. In turn, Trovoada undermined government policy by vetoing government decrees creating two credit lines for small entrepreneurs to be administered directly by the prime minister. Trovoada wanted to prevent the PCD-GR from attracting clients and regaining the electoral support lost since its defeat in the 1992 local elections. However, the government circumvented the presidential veto by 'normative despatch'—by which the prime minister can issue an order which, unlike a 'decree', need not be ratified by the president. Consequently, in July 1994, Trovoada dismissed Prime Minister Costa Alegre on grounds of a lack of institutional loyalty in some government actions. However, the principal bone of contention had been the government's refusal to approve the project of an economic free-trade zone submitted by a French company that had close ties with Trovoada.

In January 1996, President Trovoada gained direct influence over government affairs when the ADI participated in a coalition with CODO and the MLSTP/PSD, which had won the early elections in 1994. This government, headed by Armindo Vaz d'Almeida, the deputy secretary-general of the MLSTP/PSD, soon revealed its priorities when, after a few days in office, it ordered 18 brand-new Renault cars for cabinet ministers at a cost which represented twice the government's annual budget for education. The government justified the extra-budgetary acquisition as 'urgent and in the recognised national interest'.[13] In September 1996, Prime Minister Vaz d'Almeida was dismissed by a motion of no-confidence presented by his own party, accusing his government of corruption and mismanagement. He had lost the support of his party since many members felt that they had not been rewarded sufficiently by his government, while the ADI had been disproportionately favoured by the allocation of key ministries. Subsequently, the MLSTP/PSD, now dominated by another faction, formed a coalition government with the PCD-GR. In May 1997, this government rejected Trovoada's unilateral decision to establish diplomatic relations with Taiwan in exchange for $ 30 million in development aid, since it wanted to maintain the long-standing relationship with the People's Republic of China. The political stalemate lasted until October of the same year when the government finally accepted the diplomatic recognition of Taiwan.

Coalitions have frequently been formed against a common adversary, rather than because of genuinely common political objectives. In the course of the process, former political allies have become fierce rivals, while erstwhile adversaries have joined in coalition. The MLSTP/PSD government sworn-in in early 1999 has been the eighth government since 1991. The resulting political instability and the high turnover of office-holders involved have weakened the already slack bureaucracy, which in turn has negatively affected the country's development. The performance of most governments

[13]The World Bank, São Tomé e Príncipe. *Public Finance Review*, September 1997.

has remained far behind the targets set. Likewise the ability of the opposition to present constructive and viable alternatives to government policies has been weak. Despite frequent pious words on the need to combat corruption and bring morality back into public life, the abusive and fraudulent use of public property has continued apace under all administrations. Only since 1998 has the government succeeded in improving the country's economic and fiscal performance, albeit with the support of an IMF staff-monitored programme.

The failures of economic reform and external aid

The World Bank blamed pervasive government control of the economy and foreign financed investments that did not build on the local economy's comparative advantage for the failure of the socialist MLSTP regime. These investments had not led to economic growth but had resulted in an unsustainable foreign debt, which had increased from $ 23 million in 1980 to $ 153 million in 1990. The SAP (1987–96) included a comprehensive economic development programme for São Tomé e Príncipe, which aimed to turn the downward trend of the 1980s into economic growth and a stable macroeconomic policy in the 1990s. Competitive politics and civil rights provided by liberal democracy were expected to play a positive role in the functioning of the free-market and private business. The World Bank forecasts real GDP to grow annually between 3.3 and 4.5 per cent during the 1990s.[14] In fact, due to the poor performance of the economy, average real annual growth in the period 1991–7 did not exceed 1.5 per cent, whereas the population continued to grow by 2.5 per cent per year. Only in 1998 and 1999 did real GDP rise by 2.5 per cent.

The multilateral creditors expected the democratic government to reduce expenditures and increase revenue to reduce the fiscal deficit that had averaged 40 per cent of GDP in the 1980s. However, until 1998 almost none of the public finance targets set by the IMF had been met. Revenue remained below projection while expenditure exceeded the values set in the annual budget. Low revenue was partly due to tax evasion and fiscal fraud, including the excessive exemption of import duties and the under-billing of imports by customs officers in exchange for bribes. Excessive public spending was repeatedly attributed to official foreign travelling. For example, in 1996 the government spent more on trips abroad than on the salaries of the country's 3,600 civil servants.[15] Lack of financial

[14]The World Bank, São Tomé e Príncipe. *Country Economic Memorandum*, June 1993.
[15]The World Bank, São Tomé e Príncipe. *Public Finance Review*, September 1997.

discipline, extra-budgetary spending and irregularities facilitated by the absence of control and auditing as well as the non-application of legal penalties also detracted from a sound execution of the budget.[16] The government financed the fiscal deficits by external funds and central bank credits resulting in a continuous growth of money supply, which in turn led to high inflation rates and a constant devaluation of the local currency. Only because of an IMF staff-monitored programme has the government succeeded in improving fiscal and economic performance since 1998. In that year there was a surplus in the primary budget, the inflation rate had been reduced, and the exchange rate of the local currency had been stabilised. In April 2000, the IMF rewarded the government with the concession of a three-year poverty reduction and growth facility (PRGF) worth $ 9 million.

The structural reform of the financial sector has been comparatively successful, although banking has been seriously affected by fraudulent practices. During the old regime the Banco Nacional de São Tomé e Príncipe (BNSTP) assumed the role of central bank, commercial bank and savings bank. In 1992, the Banco Central de São Tomé e Príncipe (BCSTP) replaced the BNSTP as central bank. Functionaries of the BCSTP repeatedly engaged in illicit practices such as the abuse and embezzlement of foreign funds and private deals with foreign companies on the illegal issue of special coins. The greatest scandal occurred in early 1999 when the governor and the administrator of the BCSTP were dismissed for their involvement in the attempt to sell falsified Sãotomean treasury bonds worth $ 500 million in a Brussels bank.[17] The savings bank, Caixa Nacional de Poupança e Crédito (CNPC), set up in 1993 was completely ruined by internal disorder, financial malpractice, and irregularities. The CNPC's director personally approved credit requests, which according to the rules had to be submitted to the administrative board for decision. Numerous credits were conceded without meeting any financial criteria and their total value even surpassed the fixed maximum credit volume. Although the IMF demanded the closure of the savings bank as early as 1995, it was not before October 1997 that the government liquidated the CNPC, by which time outstanding liabilities had reached some $ 900,000. Many of the debtors were politicians and other prominent people with close links to the government, the CNPC's only shareholder.

The results of agricultural reform have lagged far behind targets set to reduce food imports and to increase agricultural exports. In 1991, agriculture

[16]Missão do Banco Mundial. Aide memoire, 3–17 December 1996.
[17]In October 1999 the two suspects were detained in São Tomé, but in March 2000 they were released, under obscure circumstances, until their trial.

accounted for 23 per cent of GDP, two-thirds of employment and over 95 per cent of exports. The reform of the sector aimed at diversifying and increasing food and cash crop production through the privatisation of the management of state-owned plantations and the development of smallholder agriculture. Initially, the World Bank advocated the rehabilitation of large-scale cocoa production in the short run, arguing that there were no private farmers. In the early 1990s, foreign companies managed five estates, while two plantations were run by local private enterprises. At the time the international cocoa price was more than a third lower than the one forecast by the World Bank for that period. In 1997, the World Bank admitted that the investment of $ 40 million in the rehabilitation of the privately-managed plantations had been a failure. The productivity on these rehabilitated estates had remained far below the forecast. The low yields were partly caused by an insect infestation, the spread of which had been facilitated by the government's poor provision of agricultural services. The failure of the rehabilitation project left the state with huge foreign debts, while the foreign companies earned their management fees financed by multilateral creditors without great entrepreneurial risks. By 1996, the foreign funds invested in agriculture, representing 20 per cent of São Tomé e Príncipe's total external debt, had failed to generate the expected higher export income.[18]

The distribution of former estate land as part of the reform has been one of the most fundamental socio-economic changes in the country's recent history since, for the first time, it gave African immigrants and their descendants the right to own a plot of land. The objective was to transform São Tomé e Príncipe's plantation economy into a new agrarian structure dominated by small- and medium-sized farmers. Between 1993 and 1998, the government allocated a total of 18,000 ha of which 75 per cent went to small farmers and 25 per cent to medium-sized enterprises. The owners of the latter have been politicians, civil servants and traders, who mostly lack agricultural know-how. Despite prescribed procedures, the attribution of the medium-sized farms was largely irregular. The government of Vaz d'Almeida (1996) even distributed these farms during cabinet meetings without any restraint. Furthermore, ministers purchased state property on the estates to be dismantled at artificially low prices.

The land distribution to the smallholders was no less arbitrary and opaque, often favouring former estate administrators and other privileged people. Many of the new smallholders have been constrained by a lack of training, tools and credit, poor access to markets due to inadequate roads

[18]The World Bank, São Tomé e Príncipe. *Public Finance Review*, September 1997.

and deficient transport, and the theft of crops. One objective of the agricultural reform was to increase cocoa output to the pre-independence level of 10,000 tonnes. Actually, cocoa exports dropped to 3,200 tonnes in 1997, below the output of 3,400 tonnes in 1984 that had led to the rehabilitation programme signed with the World Bank. In 1996, cocoa still accounted for 97 per cent of the export of goods. These figures prove the complete failure to increase cocoa production and to diversify agricultural exports. More successful has been the production of meat and food crops such as plantain, taro, tomato and onion, which have increased since the land distribution began.

The small manufacturing sector in São Tomé e Príncipe accounts for only 11 per cent of GDP (1998). The liquidation of the unprofitable state-owned companies and the privatisation of the viable ones, which had been at the heart of the economic reform, was executed slowly and reluctantly and was only concluded in 1998. The new economic strategy was based on private-sector development, while the role of the government was restricted to providing a policy environment conducive to private investment and the necessary infrastructure and institutional support. Small industries, food processing, tropical forest products, fishing and tourism were identified as potential growth sectors. In fact, with the exception of a modest expansion of the tourist industry, so far none of the sectors have actually been developed. The World Bank has blamed the government for failing to create the necessary supportive framework and adequate infrastructure and has identified weak decision-making and poor organisation as the main reasons for mediocre economic management.[19] In May 1997, the government granted a South African company the concession to establish a free-trade zone on Príncipe, but this project has not yet come off the ground either. Significant developments have occurred in the rehabilitation of the road network and in telecommunications. Meanwhile, high expectations have been raised in respect of the exploitation of deep-sea oil deposits discovered in the country's territorial waters. Negotiations with Nigeria on the delimitation of the common maritime border reached a conclusion on 21 February 2001. The two countries signed in Abuja a treaty on the joint exploration of petroleum in the waters where the maritime borders of both countries meet. The agreement with the oil company Mobil on a product-sharing agreement should soon be finalised.

Despite some debt forgiveness and rescheduling, São Tomé e Príncipe did not succeed in achieving the reform aim of reducing its debt burden. On the contrary, from 1990 to 1999 the foreign debt almost doubled from

[19]The World Bank, São Tomé e Príncipe. *Draft Development Strategy Note*, May 1996.

$ 153 million to $ 290 million. The concession of bilateral and multilateral development funds within the framework of the reform programmes has contributed considerably to the unsustainable debt burden. The highly indebted poor countries (HIPC) initiative launched in 1996 has become the only means of relieving São Tomé e Príncipe from its largely non-reschedulable debts. The successful execution of the three-year programme financed by the PRGF is a precondition for future debt reduction as part of the HIPC initiative. While the country has for many years received the world's largest official development assistance per capita, although the absorption and effectiveness of foreign aid have largely been disappointing. Despite large amounts of aid, until recently there has been no real economic growth, while mass poverty has increased in recent years.

The World Bank has attributed the ineffectiveness of foreign aid to a lack of donor co-ordination and the government's poor organisational capacity.[20] However, institutional habits and political behaviour characterised by clientelism, endemic corruption, and the lack of accountability have also contributed to the poor returns on aid. The weak institutions have been affected by an overall slackness, a lack of reliability and poor co-ordination. The latter has been caused by the priority which office-holders have frequently given to the personal competition for funds to the detriment of policy implementation. The inflow of foreign funds has increased and facilitated the opportunities for rent-seeking and corruption with the tacit acceptance of the donors. As a result, a small and relatively rich local elite has emerged that has been sustained largely by external funds. They have used these resources predominantly for private consumption and clientelistic redistribution rather than for productive investment in the economy.

The routine and impunity of corruption

Initially, the first democratically-elected government promised to make a new start by publishing a white book on the mismanagement and corruption of the former regime. However, the document has never appeared, evidently because the PCD-GR government could no longer legitimately denounce the irregularities and abuses of its predecessors since its own members had quickly become involved in the same practices. All parties have as frequently condemned corruption while in the opposition as they have practised it while in power. Given the weakness of the local economy and the country's dependence on development assistance, corruption and other forms of illegal misappropriation thrive largely on external resources. The

[20]Ibid.

direct involvement of foreign actors capitalising on the vulnerability of the country and the receptivity of local office-holders has played an important role as far as corruption is concerned. Apart from corruption within the public administration in general, financial institutions, the privatisation process, the customs service, the use of donor funds, foreign food aid and other forms of foreign assistance have all been susceptible to fraud and graft.

The erosion of real wages by austerity measures and inflation has certainly contributed to the expansion of (at least petty) corruption, since salaries which are no longer linked to the prices of primary necessities have made civil servants more receptive to bribery. While corruption has become part of a survival strategy for many civil servants, it has been a means of enrichment for the political and administrative elite. They frequently regard their public office as a source of private income, from which they try to maximise income. These predatory attitudes are deeply rooted in local institutional habits and are not linked to a particular political party or regime. Although they cannot be equated with illicit activities, local social practices such as kinship-based and clientelist solidarity networks and pressures towards redistributive accumulation have been favourable to fraud.[21] The free-market economy and neo-liberal propaganda have also unintentionally encouraged corruption, since they promote an acquisitive spirit and the accumulation of personal wealth.

Another reason favouring the increasing routinisation of corruption in São Tomé e Príncipe has been the virtual disappearance of control over public funds since independence. The supreme court, which has been charged with auditing all public expenditures since 1991, has not been able to carry out this task due to a lack of financial and human resources. A major reason facilitating corruption has been the *de facto* impunity for offenders, since there is a complete absence of legal sanctions. Since 1975, only one prominent politician has been tried for corruption by the local court (in 1996), and nobody has been sentenced. Parliamentary commissions have inquired into some corruption cases, but this has not resulted in a charge against the culprits, let alone their punishment. The judiciary has been plagued by financial constraints, inadequate means, and a lack of adequately trained judges. Besides, in practice, the judiciary is not impartial, since the judges are frequently subject to intimidation and personal pressures, which is a common feature in the small and impoverished environment of São Tomé

---

[21]On the cultural embeddedness of corruption and similar practices see Jean-Pierre Olivier de Sardan, 'A moral economy of corruption in Africa?', *Journal of Modern African Studies*, vol. 37, no. 1 (1999), pp. 25–52.

e Príncipe. Whenever somebody accused of corruption is threatened by legal action, influential people are mobilised to protect the accused. Within the local elite the imposition of legal sanctions against corrupt individuals is likely to meet with social disapproval, since people tend to avoid the risks involved in a possible open conflict in a small society characterised by face-to-face relations. In the absence of controls and legal sanctions, corruption provides immediate returns without great risks. In contrast, sound business activities usually imply greater inputs, higher risks and a profit often only in the long run. Instead of risking legal sanctions, corrupt office-holders have frequently been promoted to well-paid jobs in local projects and international organisations. While the introduction of democracy has not reduced the prevalence of corruption, freedom of speech and democratic institutions have at least made corruption an issue of public debate and inquiry.

CONCLUSION

Both Soviet-style socialism and western democracy have been imposed on São Tomé e Príncipe's small and insular Creole society, whose culture, language, and economy were shaped during 500 years of Portuguese colonialism. Historically, social life in the archipelago has always been structured along personal networks based on kinship and patron-client ties, while factional struggles for power and wealth have dominated local politics. Since the early twentieth century, employment in public administration has been the main resource base for the maintenance of a local clientelism that has been sustained by scarcity, impoverishment and the absence of functioning and impartial institutions. Institutional habits have developed that treat public functions primarily as a resource base for private appropriation and redistribution, to the detriment of economic rationality and administrative efficiency.

Despite socialist rhetoric, after independence the state, the party and public enterprises became the principal resource for the persistent kinship-based and clientelist networks. The external means that sustained the system came from the socialist allies. In exchange the MLSTP regime supported the socialist countries in international organisations and organised state, society and economy in accordance with their political doctrine. However, the MLSTP lacked the capacity and ability to manage the country's economy. This failure resulted in a severe economic crisis that deprived the regime of the resources necessary to maintain its followers and legitimise its rule. When the socialist allies did not provide sufficient means to sustain the regime, they were substituted by Western donors. The new patrons conditioned their assistance on demands for economic and political reforms, which finally resulted in the introduction of multiparty democracy.

While the formal political system has changed, the holders of power have continued to come from the public administration and operate within the existing bureaucratic and cultural norms. Consequently, the democratic institutions have, to a large extent, combined the privatisation of the state with the persistent kinship-based and clientelist modes of resource distribution. The state apparatus has remained the stronghold of patronage politics, since it employs the important actors and still controls most external and internal resources. Thus, liberal democracy has been unable to transform the weak bureaucracy from a redistribution centre of public funds to private pockets into an efficient administration providing the conditions for economic development. However, no longer constrained by the totalitarian ideology of the former system the clientelist structures have been adapted to a system of regulated competition including the acceptance of electoral defeat.

BIBLIOGRAPHY

compiled by Caroline Shaw

GENERAL WORKS

Birmingham, D., *Frontline Nationalism in Angola and Mozambique* (Oxford: James Currey, 1992).

———, *Portugal and Africa* (New York: St Martin's Press, 1999).

Bloomfield, R. (ed.), *Regional Conflict and U.S. Policy: Angola and Mozambique* (Algonac MI: Reference Publications, 1988).

Campbell, B., *Libération Nationale et Construction du Socialisme en Afrique. Angola, Guinée-Bissau, Mozambique* (Montreal: Éditions Nouvelle Optique, 1977).

Chabal, P., *Political Domination in Africa* (Cambridge University Press, 1986).

———, *Power in Africa* (London: Macmillan, 1992, 1994).

——— and J.-P. Daloz, *Africa Works: Disorder as Political Instrument* (Oxford: James Currey, 1999).

Chan, S. and M. Venâncio, *Portuguese Diplomacy in Southern Africa, 1974–1994* (Braamfontein: South African Institute of International Affairs, 1996).

Crocker, C., *High Noon in Southern Africa: Making Peace in a Rough Neighborhood* (New York: W.W.Norton, 1992).

Davies, R. and M. Ncube, *South African Strategy towards Mozambique in the 'Accord Phase' from March 1984 to September 1985 / Destabilization of Angola and its Implications for Decolonization of Namibia: The Role of South Africa and the USA / USA and South African Militarism: An Instrument against National Liberation, Democracy and Development in Southern Africa* (Lesotho: Institute of Southern African Studies, 1991).

Hanlon, J., *Beggar your Neighbours: Apartheid Power in Southern Africa* (London: Catholic Institute for International Relations in collaboration with James Currey, 1986).

Harding, J., *Small Wars, Small Mercies: Journeys in Africa's Disputed Nations* (Harmondsworth: Penguin, 1993).

Henriksen, T. (ed.), *Communist Powers and sub-Saharan Africa* (Stanford CA: Hoover Institution Press, 1981).

——— and W. Weinstein, *Soviet and Chinese Aid to African Nations* (New York: Praeger, 1980).

Isaacman, A. and D.Wiley (eds), *Southern Africa: Society, Economy, and Liberation* (East Lansing MI: Michigan State University, African Studies Center, and University of Minnesota, Department of Afro-American and African Studies, 1981).

Konczacki, Z., J. Parpart and T. Shaw, *Studies in the Economic History of Southern Africa. Volume 1: The Front-Line States* (London: Frank Cass, 1990).

Kuder, M., *Gemeinschaft der Staaten Portugiesischer Sprache. Ziele, Strukturen und die Sieben Mitgliedsländer, Angola, Brasilien, Guinea-Bissau, Kap Verde, Moçambique, Portugal, São Tomé e Príncipe—Comunidade dos Países de Língua Portuguesa (CPLP)* (Bonn: DASP-Institut für Brasilien-Afrika-Portugal der Deutschen Gesellschaft für die Afrikanischen Staaten Portugiesischer Sprache: Verband Portugiesischer Unternehmen in Deutschland, 1997).

Legum, C., *The Battlefronts of Southern Africa* (New York: Africana, 1988).

Lopes, C. and L. Rudebeck. *The Socialist Ideal in Africa: A Debate* (Uppsala: Nordiska Afrikainstitutet 1988).

Lusotopie, *Transitions Libérales en Afrique Lusophone* (Paris: Karthala, 1995).

McQueen, N., *The Decolonization of Portuguese Africa: Metropolitan Revolution and the Dissolution of Empire* (London: Longman, 1997).

Marchal, R. and C. Messiant, *Les Chemins de la Guerre et de la Paix. Fins de Conflit en Afrique Orientale et Australe* (Paris: Karthala, 1997).

Meyns, P. (ed.), *Demokratie und Strukturreformen im Portugiesieschsprachigen Afrika. Die Suche nach einem Neuanfang* (Freiburg: Arnold Bergstraesser Institut, 1992).

———, *Konflikt und Entwicklung im Südlichen Afrika* (Opladen: Leske und Budrich, 2000).

——— and D. Nabudere (eds), *Democracy and the One-Party State in Africa* (Hamburg: Institut für Afrika-Kunde, 1989).

Minter, W., *Apartheid's Contras. An Inquiry into the Roots of War in Angola and Mozambique* (London: Zed, 1994).

Moíta, L., *Os Congressos da Frelimo, do PAIGC e do MPLA* (Lisbon: Ulmeiro, 1979).

Oyebade, A. and A. Alao (eds), *Africa after the Cold War* (Trenton NJ: Africa World Press, 1998).

Pélissier, R., *Africana. Bibliographies sur l'Afrique Luso-Hispanophone (1800– 1980)* (Orgeval: Pélissier, 1980).

Rudebeck, L., *Conditions of People's Development in post-Colonial Africa* (Uppsala: University of Uppsala, 1990).

———, (ed.), *When Democracy Makes Sense: Studies in the Democratic Potential of Third World Popular Movements* (Uppsala: University of Uppsala, 1992).

——— and T. Negash (eds), *Dimensions of Development with Emphasis on Africa: Proceedings from the Interdisciplinary Conference on Third World Studies, Uppsala, March 1994* (Uppsala: Nordiska Afrikainstitutet, 1995).

——— and O. Törnquist (eds), *Democratization in the Third World: Concrete Cases in Comparative and Theoretical Perspective* (London: Macmillan 1998).

Vines, A., *Angola and Mozambique: The Aftermath of Conflict* (London: Research Institute for the Study of Conflict and Terrorism, 1995).

Zischg, R., *Die Politik der Sowjetunion Gegenüber Angola und Mozambique* (Baden-Baden: Nomos, 1990).

ANGOLA

Adams, I., *The War, its Impact and Economic Transformation in Angola* (Bellville: University of the Western Cape, Centre for Southern African Studies, 1996).

Africano, M. A. *L'UNITA et la 2ème Guerre Civile Angolaise* (Paris: L'Harmattan, 1995).

Akpan, K. and G. Simpkins, *E Depois do Alvor. A Luto pela Autodeterminação em Angola* (Lisbon: Nova Nórdica Editora, 1989).

Anstee, M., *Orphans of the Cold War: The Inside Story of the Collapse of the Angolan Peace Process* (London: Macmillan, 1996).

Bhagavan, M.R., *Angola's Political Economy, 1975–1985* (Uppsala: Scandinavian Institute of African Studies, 1986).

Birmingham, D., *Frontline Nationalism in Angola and Mozambique* (Oxford: James Currey, 1992).

Bittencourt, M., *Dos Jornais às Armas. Trajectórias da Contestacão Angolana* (Lisbon: Vega, 1999).

Black, R., *Angola* (Oxford: Clio Press, 1992 [World Bibliographical Series]).

Bravo, M. (ed.), *Angola. A Transição para a Paz, Reconciliação e Desenvolvimento* (Lisbon: Hugin, 1996).

Bridgland, F., *Jonas Savimbi: A Key to Africa* (Edinburgh: Mainstream, 1986).

———, *The War for Africa: Twelve Months that Transformed a Continent* (Gibraltar: Ashanti, 1990).

Brittain, V., *Death of Dignity: Angola's Civil War* (London: Pluto, 1998).

Broadhead, S., *Historical Dictionary of Angola* (2nd edn) (Metuchen NJ: Scarecrow Press, 1992).

Brönner, G. and O. Jürgen, *Die Angolanische Revolution* (Vienna: Globus, 1976).

Campbell, B., *Libération Nationale et Construction du Socialisme en Afrique. Angola, Guinée-Bissau, Mozambique* (Montreal: Éditions Nouvelle Optique, 1977).

Cabrera, M.R., *La Guerra de Angola* (Havana: Editora Politica, 1989).

Carrasco, C., *Los Cubanos en Angola (1975–1990). Bases para el Estudio de una Guerra Olvidada* (La Paz: Centro de Altos Estudios Internacionales, Universidad Andina, 1996).

Carreira, I., *O Pensamento Estratégico de Agostinho Neto. Contribuição Histórica* (Lisbon: Dom Quixote, 1996).

Carvalho, R.D. de, *Percurso Angolano em Território Kuvale* (Lisbon: Cotovia, 1999).

Ciment, J. *Angola and Mozambique: Postcolonial Wars in Southern Africa* (New York: Facts on File, 1997).

Correia, P., *Descolonização de Angola. A Jóia da Coroa do Império Português* (Lisbon: Editorial Inquérito, 1991).

———, *Angola. Do Alvor a Lusaka* (Lisbon: Hugin, 1996).

Davies, R. and M. Ncube, *South African Strategy towards Mozambique in the 'Accord Phase' from March 1984 to September 1985 / Destabilization of Angola and its Implications for Decolonization of Namibia: The Role of South Africa and the USA / USA and South African Militarism: An Instrument against National Liberation, Democracy and Development in Southern Africa* (Lesotho: Institute of Southern African Studies, 1991).

Dias, J., *Angola: From the Estoril Peace Agreement to the Lusaka Peace Accord, 1991–1994* (Geneva: the author, 1995).

Ebinger, C., *Foreign Intervention in Civil War: The Politics and Diplomacy of the Angolan Conflict* (Boulder CO: Westview Press, 1988).

Ekwe-Ekwe, H., *Conflict and Intervention in Africa: Nigeria, Angola, Zaire* (London: Macmillan, 1990).

Ferreira, M., *A Industria em Tempo de Guerra (Angola, 1975–91)* (Lisbon: Cosmos and Instituto da Defesa Nacional, 1999).

Grohs, G. and G. Czernik, *State and the Church in Angola 1450–1980* (Geneva: Institut Universitaire de Hautes Études Internationales, 1983).

Guimarães, F.A., *The Origins of the Angolan Civil War: Foreign Intervention and Domestic Political Conflict* (London: Macmillan, 1998).

Hare, P., *Angola's Last Best Chance for Peace: An Insider's Account of the Peace Process* (Washington DC: United States Institute of Peace Press, 1998).

Hart, K. and J. Lewis (eds), *Why Angola Matters* (Oxford: James Currey, 1996).

Heimer, F.-W., *Der Entkolonisierungskonflikt in Angola* (Munich: Weltforum-Verlag, 1979).

Heitman, H., *War in Angola: The Final South African Phase* (Gibraltar: Ashanti, 1990).

Henderson, L., *Angola: Five Centuries of Conflict* (Ithaca NY: Cornell University Press, 1979).

Heywood, A., *The Cassinga Event: An Investigation of the Records* (Windhoek: National Archives of Namibia, 1994).

Heywood, L., *Contested Power in Angola, 1840s to the Present* (Rochester NY: University of Rochester Press, 2000).

Hodges, T., *Angola to the 1990's* (London: Economist Intelligence Unit, 1987).

_____, *Angola to 2000: Prospects for Recovery* (London: Economist Intelligence Unit, 1993).

_____, *Angola in 2000* (London: Economist Intelligence Unit, 1996).

_____, *Angola from Afro-Stalinism to Petro-Diamond Capitalism* (Oxford: James Currey, 2001).

James, W. M., *A Political History of the Civil War in Angola: 1974–1990* (New Brunswick NJ: Transaction Publishers, 1991).

Jorge, M., *Pour Comprendre l'Angola. Du Politique à l'Économique* (Paris: Présence Africaine, 1997).

Kahn, O., *Disengagement from Southwest Africa: The Prospects for Peace in Angola and Namibia* (New Brunswick NJ: Transaction Publishers, 1991).

Kalflèche, J.-M., *Jonas Savimbi. Une Autre Voie pour l'Afrique* (Paris: Critérion, 1992).

Kapuscinski, R., *Another Day of Life* (London: Pan, 1987).

Kassembe, D., *Angola. 20 Ans de Guerre Civile. Une Femme Accuse* ... (Paris: L'Harmattan, 1995).

Kaure, A., *Angola: From Socialism to Liberal Reforms* (Harare: SAPES Books, 1999).

Kivouvou, P., *Angola. Vom Königreich Kongo zur Volksrepublik* (Cologne: Pahl-Rugenstein, 1980).

Klinghoffer, A., *The Angolan War: A Study in Soviet Policy in the Third World* (Boulder CO: Westview Press, 1980).

Kuder, M., *Angola. Naturraum, Wirtschaft, Bevölkerung, Kultur, Zeitgeschichte und Entwicklungsperspektiven* (Munich: Weltforum, 1994).

Lecoff, G., *Angola. Independência Envenenada* (Lisbon: Edições Flecha, 1977).

Legum, C. and T. Hodges, *After Angola: The War over Southern Africa* (New York: Africana, 1976).

Loiseau, Y., *Portrait d'un Révolutionnaire en Général. Jonas Savimbi* (Paris: Table Ronde, 1987).

Maier, K., *Angola: Promises and Lies* (London: Serif, 1996).

Marcum, J., *The Angolan Revolution. Volume 1: The Anatomy of an Explosion* (Cambridge MA: MIT Press, 1969).

———, *The Angolan Revolution. Volume 2: Exile Politics and Guerilla Warfare* (Cambridge MA: MIT Press, 1978).

McCormick, S., *The Angolan Economy: Prospects for Growth in a Postwar Environment* (Washington DC: Center for Strategic and International Studies, 1994).

Meier, T., *Die Reagan-Doktrin. Die Feindbilder, die Freundbilder: Afghanistan, Angola, Kambodscha, Nicaragua* (Bern: P. Lang, 1998).

Messiant, C., '1961: l'Angola Coloniale. Histoire et Société; les Prémisses du Mouvement Nationaliste' (Paris: E.H.S.S., Doctorat de 3ème cycle, 1983, 2 vols).

Minter, W., *Operation Timber: Pages from the Savimbi Dossier* (Trenton NJ: Africa World Press, 1988).

———, *Apartheid's Contras: An Inquiry into the Roots of War in Angola and Mozambique* (London: Zed, 1994).

Miranda, F., *Angola. O Futuro é Possível* (Lisbon: Vega, 2000).

Mohanty, S., *Political Development and Ethnic Identity in Africa: A Study of Angola since 1960* (London: Sangam Books, 1992).

Nowlin, D. and R. Stupak, *War as an Instrument of Policy: Past, Present, and Future* (Lanham, MD: University Press of America, 1998).

N'tyamba, J., *Huambo, 56 Dias de Terror e Morte. Testemunho de um Sobrevivente* (Huambo: Jango, 1994).

Pacheco, C., *MPLA: Um Nascimento Polémico (as Falsificações da História)* (Lisbon: Vega, 1997).

Patrício, J., *Angola-EUA. Os Caminhos do Bom-Senso* (Lisbon: Dom Quixote, 1998).

Ptak, H, *Angola, vom Bürgerkrieg zur Neuen Ordnung. Eine Unterrichtung Anlässlich des Waffenstillstandes von Lissabon* (Heidelberg: Klemmerberg-Verlag, 1991).

Queirós, C., *Angola. Outubro de 1992: Um Passo para o Futuro* (Lisbon: Pesquisa, 1995).

Rocha, A. da, *Economia e Sociedade em Angola* (Luanda: Luanda Antena Comercial, 1997).

_____, *Angola, Estabilização, Reformas e Desenvolvimento* (Luanda: Luanda Antena Comercial, 1999).

Rone, J., *Angola: Violations of the Laws of War by Both Sides* (New York: Human Rights Watch, 1989).

Roque, F., *Building the Future in Angola: A Vision for Sustainable Development* (Oeiras: Celta Editora, 1997).

Schubert, B., *Der Krieg und die Kirchen. Angola, 1961–1991* (Lucerne: Editions Exodus, 1997).

Sebastião, A., *Dos Campos de Algodão aos Dias de Hoje* (Luanda: s.n., 1993).

Sogge, D. (ed.), *Sustainable Peace: Angola's Recovery* (Harare: Southern African Research and Documentation Centre, 1992).

Somerville, K., *Angola: Politics, Economics and Society* (London: Frances Pinter, 1986).

Spies, F., *Operasie Savannah. Angola, 1975–1976* (Pretoria: Suid-Afrikaanse Weermag, 1989).

Spikes, D., *Angola and the Politics of Intervention: From Local Bush War to Chronic Crisis in Southern Africa* (Jefferson NC: McFarland, 1993).

Steenkamp, W., *Borderstrike! South Africa into Angola* (Durban: Butterworths, 1983).

Stockwell, J., *In Search of Enemies: A CIA Story* (London: Deutsch, 1978).

Strachan, B., *Angola: The Struggle for Power: the Political, Social and Economic Context, 1980–1993: A Select and Annotated Bibliography* (Johannesburg: South African Institute of International Affairs, 1994).

Sundiata, I., 'Cabinda, the politics of oil in Angola's enclave' in R. Cohen (ed.) *African Islands and Enclaves* (London: Sage, 1983).

Tvedten, I., *Angola: Struggle for Peace and Reconstruction* (London: Westview Press, 1997).

Van der Winden, B. (ed.), *A Family of the Musseque: Survival and Development in Postwar Angola* (London: One World Action, 1996).

Venâncio, M., *The United Nations: Peace and Transition: Lessons from Angola* (Lisbon: IEEI, 1994).

Vicente, S., *Angola e África do Sul* (Luanda: Ensa, 1994).

_____, *A Gestão Política da Economia de Angola* (Luanda: Instituto Nacional do Livro e do Disco, 1995).

_____, *Petróleo. Política, Económica e Estratégia em Angola* (Luanda: Instituto Nacional do Livro e do Disco, 1995).

Vines, A., *One Hand Tied: Angola and the UN* (London: Catholic Institute for International Relations, 1993).

_____, *Angola between War and Peace: Arms Trade and Human Rights Abuses since the Lusaka Protocol* (New York: Human Rights Watch, 1996).

———, *Peace Postponed: Angola since the Lusaka Protocol* (London: Catholic Institute for International Relations, 1998).

———, *Angola Unravels: The Rise and Fall of the Lusaka Peace Process* (New York: Human Rights Watch, 1999).

Windrich, E., *The Cold War Guerilla: Jonas Savimibi, the U.S. Media and the Angolan War* (New York: Greenwood, 1992).

Winslow, P., *Sowing the Dragon's Teeth: Land Mines and the Global Legacy of War* (Boston MA: Beacon Press, 1997).

Wolfers, M. and J. Bergerol, *Angola in the Front Line* (London: Zed, 1983).

Wright, G., *U.S .Policy towards Angola: The Kissinger Years, 1974–76* (Leeds: University of Leeds, African Studies Unit and Department of Politics, 1990).

———, *The Destruction of a Nation: United States' Policy toward Angola since 1945* (London: Pluto Press, 1997).

Selected Angolan literature

Agualusa, J.E., *A Conjura* (Lisbon: Caminho, 1989).

———, *A Feira dos Assombrados* (Lisbon: Vega, 1992).

———, *Estação das Chuvas* (Lisbon: Dom Quixote, 1996).

Barbeitos, A., *Angola, Angolê, Angolema* (Lisbon: Sá da Costa, 1976).

———, *Nzoji (Sonho)* (Lisbon: Sá da Costa, 1979).

———, *Fiapos de Sonho* (Lisbon: Vega, 1992).

Jamba, S., *Patriots* (London: Fourth Estate, 1990).

Lima, M., *Os Anões e os Mendigos* (Porto: Afrontamento, 1984).

Pepetela, *Mayombe* (Lisbon: Edições 70, 1980).

———, *Yaka* (Lisbon: Dom Quixote, 1985).

———, *O Cão e os Caluandas* (Lisbon: Dom Quixote, 1985).

———, *Lueji* (Lisbon: Dom Quixote, 1990).

———, *A Geração da Utopia* (Lisbon: Dom Quixote, 1992).

———, *O Desejo de Kianda* (Lisbon: Dom Quixote, 1995).

———, *Parábola do Cágado Velho* (Lisbon: Dom Quixote, 1996).

———, *A Gloriosa Família* (Lisbon: Dom Quixote, 1998).

Rui, M., *Quem me Dera Ser Onda* (Lisbon: Edições 70, 1982).

———, *Crónica de um Mujimbo* (Luanda: União dos Escritores Angolanos, 1989).

———, *1 Morto and os Vivos* (Lisbon: Cotovia, 1993).

———, *Rioseco* (Lisbon: Cotovia, 1997).

Xitu, U., *Mestre Tamoda e Outros Contos* (Lisbon: Edições 70, 1977).

———, *Manana* (Lisbon: Edições 70, 1978).

Selected literary criticism

Chabal, P. *et al.*, *The Postcolonial Literature of Lusophone Africa* (London: Hurst & Co., 1996).

CAPE VERDE

Andrade, E., *Les Îles du Cap Vert. De la 'Découverte'à l'Indépendance Nationale (1460–1975)* (Paris: L'Harmattan, 1996).

Araújo, C. (ed.), *De Mindelo para Cabo Verde. Convergência para a Solidariedade* (Mindelo: Forum Convergência, 1995).

Bigman, L., *History and Hunger in West Africa: Food Production and Entitlement in Guinea-Bissau and Cape Verde* (Westport CT: Greenwood Press, 1993).

Cabral, N., *Le Moulin et le Pilon. Les Îles du Cap Vert* (Paris: Karthala, 1980).

Cardoso, H., *O Partido Único em Cabo Verde. Um Assalto à Esperança* (Praia: Imprensa Nacional de Cabo Verde, 1993).

Cardoso, R., *Cabo Verde, Opção por uma Política de Paz* (Praia: Instituto Cabo-Verdiano do Livro, 1986).

Carreira, A., *The People of the Cape Verde Islands* (London: Hurst & Co., 1982).

Davidson, B., *No Fist is Big Enough to Hide the Sky* (London: Zed, 1981).

_____, *The Fortunate Isles: A Study in African Transformation* (London: Hutchinson, 1989).

Dumont, R. and M. Mottin, *L'Afrique Étranglée. Zambie, Tanzanie, Sénégal, Côte-d'Ivoire, Guinée-Bissau, Cap-Vert* (Paris: Seuil, 1980).

Foy, C., *Cape Verde: Politics, Economics and Society* (London: Frances Pinter, 1988).

Furtado, C., *A Transformação das Estruturas Agrárias numa Sociedade em Mudança* (Praia: Instituto Caboverdiano do Livro e do Disco, 1993).

Kuder, M., *Die Republik Kap Verde* (Bonn: Deutsche Afrika-Stiftung, 1985).

Langworthy, M. and T. Finan, *Waiting for Rain: Agriculture and Ecological Imbalance in Cape Verde* (Boulder CO: Lynne Rienner, 1997).

Lima, A., *Reforma Política em Cabo Verde. Do Paternalismo à Modernização do Estado* (Praia: the author, 1991).

Lesourd, M., *État et Société aux Îles du Cap-Vert. Alternatives pour un Petit État Insulaire* (Paris: Karthala, 1995).

Lobban, R., *Cape Verde: Crioulo Colony to Independent Nation* (Boulder CO: Westview Press, 1995).

_____ and M. Lopes, *Historical Dictionary of the Republic of Cape Verde* (3rd edn) (Metchuen NJ: Scarecrow Press, 1995).

Martins, O., *Independência* (Praia: Instituto Cabo-Verdiano do Livro, 1983).

Meintel Machado, D., 'Cape Verde, survival without self-sufficiency' in R. Cohen (ed.) *African Islands and Enclaves* (London: Sage, 1983).

Meyns, P., *Blockfreie Aussenpolitik eines Afrikanischen Kleinstaates. Das Beispiel Kap Verde* (Hamburg: Institut für Afrika-Kunde, 1990).

Querido, J., *Cabo Verde. Subsídios para a História da Nossa Luta de Libertação* (Lisbon: Vega, 1989).

Romero, V., *Guinea-Bissau y Cabo Verde. Los 'Afrocomunistas'* (Madrid: Molinos de Agua, 1981).

Sanches, A., *Cabo Verde. Subsídios para o Estudo da Dimensão Internacional do Desenvolvimento* (Praia: Ministério da Coordenação Económica, Direcção Geral do Planeamento Projecto NLTPS, February 1996).

Shaw, C., *Cape Verde* (Oxford, Clio Press, 1991 [World Bibliographical Series]).
Silveira, O., *Contribuição para a Construção da Democracia em Cabo Verde. Intervenções* (Mindelo: Gráfica do Mindelo, 1995).

Selected Cape Verdean literature

Almada, J. (ed.), *Mirabilis de Veias ao Sol. Antologia dos Novíssimos Poetas Caboverdianos* (Lisbon: Caminho, 1991).
Almeida, G., *O Testamento do Sr Napumoceno da Silva Araújo* (Mindelo: Ilhéu, 1989).
———, *O Meu Poeta* (Mindelo: Ilhéu, 1990).
———, *A Ilha Fantástica* (Lisbon: Caminho, 1994).
———, *Os Dois Irmãos* (Lisbon: Caminho, 1995).
———, *Estórias de Dentro de Casa* (Lisbon: Caminho, 1996).
———, *A Família Trago* (Lisbon: Caminho, 1998).
Amarilis, O., *Cais do Sodré té Salamansa* (Coimbra: Centelha, 1974).
———, *Ilhéu dos Pássaros* (Lisbon: Plátano, 1982).
Fortes, C., *Pão e Fonema* (Lisbon: s.n., 1974).
———, *Árvore e Tambor* (Lisbon: Dom Quixote, 1986).
Osório, O., *Clar(a)idade Assombrada* (Praia: Instituto Caboverdiano do Livro, 1987).
Vieira, A., *Cântico Geral* (Lisbon: África, 1981).
———, *O Eleito do Sol* (Praia: Sonacor, 1989).

Selected literary criticism

Chabal, P. *et al.*, *The Postcolonial Literature of Lusophone Africa* (London: Hurst & Co., 1996).

GUINEA-BISSAU

Aaby, P., *The State of Guinea-Bissau: African Socialism or Socialism in Africa* (Uppsala: Nordiska Afrikainstitutet, 1978).
Andrade, M. de, *Amilcar Cabral. Essai de Biographie Politique* (Paris: François Maspero, 1980).
Andreini, J. and M. Lambert, *La Guinée-Bissau. d'Amilcar Cabral à la Reconstruction Nationale* (Paris: Éditions L'Harmattan, 1978).
Augel, J. and C. Cardoso, *Transição Democrática na Guiné-Bissau e outros Ensaios* (Bissau: Instituto Nacional de Estudos e Pesquisa, 1996).
Bigman, L., *History and Hunger in West Africa: Food Production and Entitlement in Guinea-Bissau and Cape Verde* (Westport CT: Greenwood Press, 1993).
Campbell, B., *Libération Nationale et Construction du Socialisme en Afrique. Angola, Guinée-Bissau, Mozambique* (Montreal: Éditions Nouvelle Optique, 1977).
Carvalho, C., 'Ritos de poder e a recriaçao da tradição. Os régulos manjaco da

Guiné-Bissau' (PhD thesis, Lisbon: Instituto Superior de Ciências do Trabalho e da Empresa, 1998).

Chabal, P., *Amílcar Cabral: Revolutionary Leadership and People's War* (Cambridge University Press, 1983).

Chéneau-Loquay, A. and P. Matarasso, *Approche du Développement Durable en Milieu Rural Africain. Les Régions Côtières de Guinée, Guinée-Bissau et Casamance* (Paris: L'Harmattan, 1998).

Davidson, B., *No Fist is Big Enough to Hide the Sky* (London: Zed, 1981).

Davila, J., *Shelter, Poverty and African Revolutionary Socialism: Human Settlements in Guinea-Bissau* (London: International Institute for Environment and Development, Human Settlements Programme, 1987).

Dhada, M., *Warriors at Work: How Guinea was really set free* (Niwot CO: University of Colorado Press, 1993).

Dowbor, L., *Guiné-Bissau. A Busca da Independência Económica* (São Paulo: Brasiliense, 1983).

Dumont, R. and M. Mottin, *L'Afrique Étranglée. Zambie, Tanzanie, Sénégal, Côte-d'Ivoire, Guinée-Bissau, Cap-Vert* (Paris: Seuil, 1980).

Forrest, J. B., *Guinea-Bissau: Power, Conflict and Renewal in a West African Nation* (Boulder CO: Westview, 1992).

Freire. P., *Cartas à Guiné-Bissau. Registros de uma Experiência em Processo* (Guinea-Bissau: Departamento de Edição/Difusão do Livro e do Disco, 1978).

Galli, R., *Guinea-Bissau* (Oxford: Clio Press, 1990 [World Bibliographical Series]).

_____ and J. Jones, *Guinea-Bissau: Politics, Economics and Society* (London: Frances Pinter, 1987).

Gjerstad, O. and C. Sarrazin, *Sowing the First Harvest: National Reconstruction in Guinea-Bissau* (Oakland CA: LSM Information Center, 1978).

Goulet, D., *Looking at Guinea-Bissau: A New Nation's Development Strategy* (Washington DC: Overseas Development Council, 1978).

Handem, D. and F. da Silva (eds), *A Guiné-Bissau a Caminho do Ano 2000. Conferência INEP/CESE* (Bissau: Instituto Nacional de Estudos e Pesquisa, 1989).

Hochet, A., *Paysanneries en Attente. Guinee-Bissau* (Dakar: Enda, 1983).

Imbali, F. (ed.), *Os Efeitos Sócio-Económicos do Programa de Ajustamento Estrutural na Guiné-Bissau. 1: Projecto de Estudo INEP/CESE* (Bissau: Instituto Nacional de Estudos e Pesquisa, 1993).

Kasper, J., *Bissau. Existenzsichernde Strategien in einer Westafrikanischen Stadt* (Bern: Lang, 1994).

Koudawo, F., *Eleições e Lições. Esbofos para uma Análise das Primeiras Eleiçoes Pluralistas na Guiné-Bissau* (Bissau: Ku Si Mon Editora, 1994).

_____ and P.K. Mendy (eds), *Pluralismo Político na Guiné Bissau* (Bissau: Instituto Nacional de Estudos e Pesquisa, 1996).

Kurz, A., *Die Jangue-Jangue in Guinea-Bissau. Eine Moderne Anti-Hexerei-Bewegung? Machtkonflikte im Kontext von Alter, Geschlecht und Reproduktion* (Frankfurt am Main: Verlag für Interkulturelle Kommunikation, 1996).

Lobban, R. and J. Forrest, *Historical Dictionary of the Republic of Guinea-Bissau* (2nd edn) (Metchuen NJ: Scarecrow Press, 1988).

Lopes, C., *Ethnie, État et Rapports de Pouvoir en Guinée-Bissau* (Geneva: Institut Universitaire d'Études du Développement, 1983).

———, *Guinea-Bissau: From Liberation Struggle to Independent Statehood* (London: Zed, 1987).

———, *Para uma Leitura Sociológica da Guiné-Bissau* (Lisbon: Editorial Economia e Socialismo, 1988).

Meier, W., *Problematik Sozialrevolutionärer Regime in der 'Dritten Welt'. Eine Vergleichende Betrachtung der Entwicklungen in Guinea-Bissau (1974–1990) und Nicaragua (1979–1990)* (Marburg: Tectum, 1993).

Monteiro, A. (ed.), *O Programa de Ajustamento Estrutural na Guiné-Bissau. Análise dos Efeitos Sócio-Económicos* (Bissau: Instituto Nacional de Estudos e Pesquisa, 1996).

Oramas Oliva, O., *Amilcar Cabral. Un Précurseur de l'Independance Africaine* (Paris: Indigo et Côte-Femmes, 1998).

Pierson-Mathy, P., *La Naissance de l'État par la Guerre de Libération Nationale. le Cas de la Guinée-Bissau* (Paris: UNESCO, 1980).

Romero, V., *Guinea-Bissau y Cabo Verde. Los 'Afrocomunistas'* (Madrid: Molinos de Agua, 1981).

Rudebeck, L., *Guinea-Bissau: A Study of Political Mobilisation* (Uppsala: Nordiska Afrikainstitutet, 1974).

———, *Guinea-Bissau. Folket, Partiet och Staten: Om den Fredliga Kampen för Utveckling* (Uppsala: Nordiska Afrikainstitutet, 1977).

———, *Problèmes de Pouvoir Populaire et de Développement. Transition Difficile en Guinée-Bissau* (Uppsala: Scandinavian Institute of African Studies, 1982).

———, *Conditions of People's Development in Post-Colonial Africa* (Uppsala: University of Uppsala, 1990).

———, *'Buscar a Felicidade'. Democratização na Guiné-Bissau* (Bissau: Instituto Nacional de Estudos e Pesquisa, 1997).

Schoenmakers, H., *Staatsvorming, Rurale Ontwikkeling and Boeren in Guiné-Bissau* (Leiden: African Studies Centre, 1991).

Silva, A., *A Independência da Guiné-Bissau e a Descolonização Portuguesa. Estudo de História, Direito e Política* (Porto: Edições Afrontamento, 1997).

Urdang, S., *Fighting Two Colonialisms: Women in Guinea-Bissau* (New York: Monthly Review Press, 1979).

MOZAMBIQUE

Abrahamsson, H., *Seizing the Opportunity: Power and Powerlessness in a Changing World Order: The Case of Mozambique* (Gothenburg: Gothenburg University, Department of Peace and Development Research, 1997).

——— and A. Nilsson, *Mozambique: The Troubled Transition: From Socialist Construction to Free Market Capitalism* (London: Zed, 1995).

———, *Ordem Mundial Futura e Governação Nacional em Moçambique. 'Empowerment' e Espaço de Manobra* (s.l.: CEEI-ISRI; Padigru, 1995).

Alden, C., *Mozambique and the Construction of the New African State: From Negotiations to Nation Building* (New York: St Martin's Press, 2001).

Andersson, H., *Mozambique: A War against the People* (London: Macmillan, 1992).

Armon, J., D. Hendrikson and A. Vines (eds), *The Mozambican Peace Process in Perspective* (London: Conciliation Resources in association with Arquivo Historico, 1998).

Azevedo, M., *Historical Dictionary of Mozambique* (Metuchen NJ: Scarecrow Press, 1991).

Baraldi, G., *Mozambico. Quale Indipendenza* (Milan: Ottaviano, 1979).

Berman, E., *Managing Arms in Peace Processes: Mozambique* (Geneva: United Nations Institute for Disarmament Research, 1996).

Birmingham, D., *Frontline Nationalism in Angola and Mozambique* (Oxford: James Currey, 1992).

Bollati, S. and F. Bollati, *Mozambico. Dalla Guerra alla Pace* (Rome: Editalia, 1992).

Bowen, M., *The State against the Peasantry: Rural Struggles in Colonial and Postcolonial Mozambique* (Charlottesville VA: University of Virginia Press, 2000).

Cabrita, J.M., *Mozambique: The Tortuous Road to Democracy* (New York: St Martin's Press, 2000).

Cahen, M., *Mozambique. La Révolution Implosée: Études sur 12 Ans d'Indépendence, 1975–1987* (Paris: L'Harmattan, 1987).

Campbell, B., *Libération Nationale et Construction du Socialisme en Afrique. Angola, Guinée-Bissau, Mozambique* (Montreal: Éditions Nouvelle Optique, 1977).

Chan, S. and M. Venâncio, *War and Peace in Mozambique* (London: Macmillan, 1998).

Chingono, M., *The State, Violence and Development: The Political Economy of War in Mozambique, 1975–1992* (Aldershot: Avebury, 1996).

Christie, I., *Samora Machel: A Biography* (London: Panaf, 1989).

Ciment, J., *Angola and Mozambique: Postcolonial Wars in Southern Africa* (New York: Facts on File, 1997).

Coelho, J. and A. Vines, *Pilot Study on Demobilization and Re-Integration of Ex-Combatants in Mozambique* (Oxford: University of Oxford, Refugee Studies Programme, 1994).

Davies, R. and M. Ncube, *South African Strategy towards Mozambique in the 'Accord Phase' from March 1984 to September 1985 / Destabilization of Angola and its Implications for Decolonization of Namibia: The Role of South Africa and the USA / USA and South African Militarism: An Instrument against National Liberation, Democracy and Development in Southern Africa* (Lesotho: Institute of Southern African Studies, 1991).

Denny, L., D. Ray and J. Torp, *Mozambique—São Tomé e Príncipe: Politics, Economics and Society* (London: Frances Pinter, 1989).

Doig, A. and R. Theobald (eds), *Corruption and Democratisation* (London: Frank Cass, 2000).

Ebata, J.M., 'The Transition from War to Peace: Politics, Political Space and the Peace Process Industry in Mozambique 1992–1995' (PhD thesis, London: London School of Economics, 1999).

Egero, B., *Mozambique: A Dream Undone. The Political Economy of Democracy, 1975–84* (Uppsala: Nordiska Afrikainstitutet, 1987).

———, Moçambique. Os Primeiros Dez Anos de Construção da Democracia (Maputo: Arquivo Histórico de Moçambique, 1992).

Espling, M., Women's Livelihood Strategies in Processes of Change: Cases from Urban Mozambique (Gothenburg: University of Gothenburg, 1999).

Fandrych, S., Konfliktmanagement und—Regelung der Vereinten Nationen in Mosambik (Hamburg: Institut für Afrika-Kunde, 1998).

Finnegan, W., A Complicated War: The Harrowing of Mozambique (Berkeley CA: University of California Press, 1992).

First, R., Black Gold: The Mozambican Miner, Proletarian and Peasant (Brighton: Harvester, 1983). Pictures by Moira Forjaz. Worksongs and interviews recorded by Alpheus Manghezi.

Gasperini, L., Mozambico. Educazione e Sviluppo Rurale (Rome: Edizioni Lavoro, 1989).

Geffray, C., La Cause des Armes au Mozambique. Anthropologie d'une Guerre Civile (Paris: Karthala, 1990).

Gersony, R., Summary of Mozambican Refugee Accounts of Principally Conflict-Related Experience in Mozambique (Washington DC: Bureau for Refugee Programs, 1988).

Hall, M. and T. Young, Confronting Leviathan: Mozambique since Independence (London: Hurst & Co., 1997).

Hanlon, J., Mozambique: The Revolution under Fire (London: Zed, 1984).

———, Mozambique: Who Calls the Shots? (London: James Currey, 1991).

———, Peace without Profit: How the IMG Blocks Rebuilding in Mozambique (London: James Currey, 1996).

Harrison, G., The Politics of Democratisation in Rural Mozambique: Grassroots Governance in Mecúfi (Lewiston NY: Edwin Mellen, 2000).

Henriksen, T., Mozambique: A History (London: Rex Collings, 1978).

———, Revolution and Counterrevolution: Mozambique's War of Independence 1964–1974 (Westport CT: Greenwood Press, 1983).

Hermele, K. Land Struggles and Social Differentiation in Southern Mozambique: A Case Study of Chokwe, Limpopo, 1950–1987 (Uppsala: Scandinavian Institute of African Studies, 1988).

———, Mozambican Crossroads: Economics and Politics in the Era of Structural Adjustment (Bergen: Chr. Michelsen Institute, Department of Social Science and Development, 1990).

Hoile, D., Mozambique: A Nation in Crisis (London: Claridge, 1989).

———, Mozambique, Resistance and Freedom: A Case for Reassessment (London: Mozambique Institute, 1994).

Honwana, R., and A. Isaacman (eds), The Life History of Raúl Honwana: An Inside View of Mozambique from Colonialism to Independence, 1905–1975 (Boulder CO: Lynne Rienner Publishers, 1988).

Hume, C., Ending Mozambique's War: The Role of Mediation and Good Offices (Washington DC: United States Institute of Peace Press, 1994).

Isaacman, A., A Luta Continua: Creating a New Society in Mozambique (Binghampton NY: State University of New York at Binghampton, 1978).

_____ and B. Isaacman, *Mozambique: From Colonialism to Revolution, 1900–1982* (London: Westview, 1983).

Isaacman, B. and J. Stephen, *A Mulher Moçambicana no Processo de Libertação* (Maputo: Instituto Nacional do Livro e do Disco, 1984).

_____, *Mozambique: Women, the Law, and Agrarian Reform* (Addis Ababa: United Nations Economic Commission for Africa, 1980).

Johnston, A., *Study, Produce, and Combat! Education and the Mozambican State, 1962–1984* (Stockholm: University of Stockholm, Institute of International Education, 1989).

Jouanneau, D., *Le Mozambique* (Paris: Karthala, 1995).

Katzenellenbogen, S., *South Africa and Southern Mozambique* (Manchester University Press. 1982).

Küppers, H., *Renamo. Über den Wandel der Mosambikanischen Rebellenbewegung zu Einer Politischen Partei. Ein Beitrag zur Transitionsforschung* (Hamburg: Lit, 1996).

Lindholt, L., *Questioning the Universality of Human Rights: The African Charter on Human and People's Rights in Botswana, Malawi, and Mozambique* (Aldershot: Dartmouth, 1997).

Marshall, J., *War, Debt, and Structural Adjustment in Mozambique: The Social Impact* (Ottawa: North-South Institute, 1992).

_____, *Literacy, Power and Democracy in Mozambique: The Governance of Learning from Colonization to the Present* (Boulder CO: Westview Press, 1993).

Mazula B. *Educação, Cultura e Ideologia Em Moçambique, 1975–1985. Em Busca de Fundamentos Filosófico-Antropológicos* (Porto: Edições Afrontamento, 1995).

Mazula B. (ed.), *Elections, Democracy, and Development* (Maputo: Embassy of the Kingdom of the Netherlands, 1996).

Mendes, J., *A Nossa Situação, o Nosso Futuro e o Multipartidarismo* (Maputo: the author, 1994).

Meyns, P., *Mozambique. Im Jahr 2d. Unabhängigkeit* (Berlin: Oberbaumverlag, 1977).

_____, *Befreiung und Nationaler Wiederaufbau von Mozambique: Studien zu Politik und Wirtschaft 1960–1978* (Hamburg: Institut für Afrika-Kunde, 1979).

Minter, W., *Apartheid's Contras: An Inquiry into the Roots of War in Angola and Mozambique* (London: Zed, 1994).

_____ (ed.), *Invisible Crimes: U.S. Private Intervention in the War in Mozambique* (Washington DC: Africa Policy Information Center, 1994).

Mittelman, J., *Underdevelopment and the Transition to Socialism: Mozambique and Tanzania* (New York: Academic Press, 1981).

Morozzo della Rocca, R., *Mozambico. Dalla Guerra alla Pace. Storia di una Mediazione Insolita* (Milan: San Paolo, 1994).

Mosca, J., *A Experiência Socialista em Moçambique (1975–1986)* (Lisbon: Instituto Piaget, 1999).

Munslow, B., *Mozambique: The Revolution and its Origins* (London: Longman, 1983).

_____ (ed.), *Samora Machel: An African Revolutionary. Selected Speeches and Writings* (London: Zed, 1985).

Myers, G., J. Eliseu and E. Nhachungue, *Security and Conflict in Mozambique: Case Studies of Land Access in the Post-War Period* (Madison WI: University of Wisconsin-Madison, Land Tenure Center; Maputo: Ministry of Agriculture, 1994).

———, *Security, Conflict, and Reintegration in Mozambique: Case Studies of Land Access in the Postwar Period* (Madison WI: University of Wisconsin-Madison, Land Tenure Center, 1994).

Newitt, M., *A History of Mozambique* (London: Hurst & Co., 1995).

Nilsson, A., *Unmasking the Bandits: The True Face of the M.N.R.* (London: ECASAAMA/UK, 1990).

Nordstrom, C., *A Different Kind of War Story* (Philadelphia PA: University of Pennsylvania Press, 1997).

Ratilal, P., *Emergency in Mozambique: Using Aid to End the Emergency* (New York: United Nations Development Programme, 1990).

Rocha, A., C. Serra and D. Hedges, *História de Moçambique*, 3 vols (Maputo: Cadernos Tempo, 1983).

Rudebeck, L., *Conditions of People's Development in post-Colonial Africa* (Uppsala: University of Uppsala, 1990).

Sachs, A. and G. Welch, *Liberating the Law: Creating Popular Justice in Mozambique* (London: Zed, 1990).

Sahlstrom, B., *Political Posters in Ethiopia and Mozambique: Visual Imagery in a Revolutionary Context* (Uppsala: Almqvist and Wiksell International, 1990).

Saul, J., *A Difficult Road: The Transition to Socialism in Mozambique* (New York: Monthly Review, 1985).

Serra, C., *Combates pela Mentalidade Sociológica. Crenças Anómicas de Massa em Moçambique, Seguido de Mitos e Realidades da Etnicidade e de para um Novo Paradigma da Etnicidade* (Maputo: Universidade Eduardo Mondlane, Livraria Universitária, 1997).

———, *Novos Combates pela Mentalidade Sociológica. Sociologia Política das Relações de Poder em Moçambique Seguido de Desafios de uma Medicina Bernardiana* (Maputo: Universidade Eduardo Mondlane, Livraria Universitária, 1997).

———, (ed.), *Eleitorado Incapturável. Eleições Municipais de 1998 em Manica, Chimoio, Beira, Dondo, Nampula e Angoche* (Maputo: Livraria Universitária, Universidade Eduardo Mondlane, 1999).

Singh, M., *Socialist Construction: The Experience of Mozambique* (Norwich: University of East Anglia, School of Development Studies, 1990).

Sogge, D., *Mozambique: Perspectives on Aid and the Civil Sector* (Oegsteest: GOM, 1997).

Souto, A. and A. Sopa, *Samora Machel. Bibliografia (1970–1986)* (Maputo: Centro de Estudos Africanos, Universidade Eduardo Mondlane, 1996).

Strachan, B., *Mozambique: The Quest for Peace: the Political, Social and Economic Context, 1980–1994: A Select and Annotated Bibliography* (Johannesburg: South African Institute of International Affairs, 1996).

Synge, R., *Mozambique: UN Peacekeeping in Action, 1992–94* (Washington DC: United States Institute of Peace Press, 1997).

United Nations, *The United Nations and Mozambique, 1992–1995* (New York: United Nations, Department of Public Information, 1995).

Urdang, S, *And Still They Dance: Women, War, and the Struggle for Change in Mozambique* (London: Earthscan, 1989).

Vines, A., *Renamo: Terrorism in Mozambique* (London: James Currey, 1991).

_____, *No Democracy without Money: The Road to Peace in Mozambique (1982–1992)* (London: Catholic Institute for International Relations, 1994).

_____, *Renamo: From Terrorism to Democracy in Mozambique?* (Oxford: James Currey, 1995).

Weimer, B., *Die Mozambicanische Aussenpolitik 1975–1982. Merkmale, Probleme, Dynamik* (Baden-Baden: Nomos, 1983).

Wilson, K., *Internally Displaced, Refugees and Returnees from and in Mozambique* (Uppsala: Nordiska Afrikainstitutet, 1994).

Yañez Casal, A., *Antropologia e Desenvolvimento. As Aldeias Comunais de Moçambique* (Lisbon: Instituto de Investigação Científica Tropical, 1996).

Zacarias, A. (ed.), *Repensando Estratégias sobre Moçambique e África Austral. Conferência Organizada em Maputo de 21 a 24 de Maio de 1990* (Maputo: Instituto Superior de Relações Internacionais, 1991).

Selected Mozambican literature

Cassamo, S., *O Regresso do Morto* (Maputo: Associação dos Escritores Moçambicanos, 1989).

Chiziane, P., *Balado do Amor ao Vento* (Maputo: Associação dos Escritores Moçambicanos, 1990).

Couto, M., *Vozes Anoitecidas* (Maputo: Associação dos Escritores Moçambicanos, 1986).

_____, *Cada Homem é uma Raça* (Lisbon: Caminho,1990).

_____, *Terra Sonâmbula* (Lisbon: Caminho, 1992).

_____, *Estórias Abensonhadas* (Lisbon: Caminho, 1994).

_____, *A Varanda do Frangipani* (Lisbon: Caminho, 1996).

_____, *Contos do Nascer da Terra* (Lisbon: Caminho, 1997).

Craveirinha, J., *Karingana Ua Karingana* (Maputo: Académica, 1974).

_____, *Xigubo* (Lisbon: Edições 70, 1980).

_____, *Cela 1* (Lisbon: Edições 70, 1980).

_____, *Maria* (Lisbon: África, 1988).

_____, *Hamina e Outros Contos* (Lisbon: Caminho, 1997).

Ferreira, M., *No Reino de Caliban*, vol. 3 (Lisbon: Plátano, 1985).

Honwana, L.B., *Nós Matámos o Cão Tinhoso* (2nd edn) (Porto: Afrontamento, 1972).

Khosa, U. B. K., *Ualalapi* (Maputo: Associação dos Escritores Moçambicanos, 1987).

Patraquim, L.C., *Monção* (Lisbon: Edições 70, 1980).

_____, *A Inadiável Viagem* (Maputo: Associação dos Escritores Moçambicanos, 1985).

_____, *Vinte e Tal Novas Formulações e uma Elegia Carnívora* (Lisbon: África, 1991).

Sousa, N. de, *Poemas* (mimeo).

White, E., *Amar sobre o Índico* (Maputo: Associação dos Escritores Moçambicanos, 1985).

———, *Homaíne* (Maputo: Associação dos Escritores Moçambicanos, 1987).

———, *O País de Mim* (Maputo: Associação dos Escritores Moçambicanos, 1989).

———, *Poemas da Ciências de Voar e da Engenharia de Ser Ave* (Lisbon: Caminho, 1992).

———, *Os Materiais do Amor Seguido de o Desafio à Tristeza* (Maputo: Ndjira, 1996).

Literary criticism

Chabal, P., *Vozes Moçambicanas* (Lisbon: Vega, 1994).

———, *et al.*, *The Postcolonial Literature of Lusophone Africa* (London: Hurst & Co., 1996).

SÃO TOMÉ E PRÍNCIPE

Cruz, C.B. da (ed.), *S.Tomé e Príncipe. Do Colonialismo à Independência* (Lisbon: Morães Editores, 1975).

Eyzaguirre, P., 'Small Farmers and Estates in São Tomé, West Africa' (PhD thesis, New Haven CT: Yale University, 1986).

Denny, L. and D. Ray and J. Torp, *Mozambique—São Tomé e Príncipe: Politics, Economics and Society* (London: Frances Pinter, 1989).

Henriques, I, *São Tomé e Príncipe. A Invenção de uma Sociedade* (Lisbon: Vega, 2000).

Hintjens, H., and M. Newitt (eds), *The Political Economy of Small Tropical Islands: The Importance of Being Small* (Exeter: University of Exeter Press, 1992).

Hodges, T. and M. Newitt, *São Tomé e Príncipe: From Plantation Colony to Microstate* (London: Westview, 1988).

Oliveira, J. E. da Costa, *A Economia de S.Tomé e Príncipe* (Lisbon: Instituto para a Cooperação Económica, Instituto de Investigação Científica Tropical, 1993).

Romana, H., *São Tomé e Príncipe. Elementos para uma Análise Antropológica das suas Vulnerabilidades e Potencialidades* (Lisbon: Universidade Técnica de Lisboa, Instituto Superior de Ciências Sociais e Políticas, 1997).

Schümer, M., *São Tomé und Príncipe. Ausbruch aus der Isolation* (Bonn: Forschungsinstitut der Deutschen Gesellschaft für Auswärtige Politik, 1987).

Seibert, G., *Comrades, Clients, and Cousins: Colonialism, Socialism, and Democratization in São Tomé e Príncipe* (Leiden University, Research School of Asian, African, and Amerindian Studies, 1999).

Shaw, C., *São Tomé e Príncipe* (Oxford: Clio Press, 1994·[World Bibliographical Series]).

INDEX

(for abbreviations see list on pp. xiii–xv)

333

www.ingramcontent.com/pod-product-compliance
Ingram Content Group UK Ltd.
Pitfield, Milton Keynes, MK11 3LW, UK
UKHW040729150225
455125UK00001B/75

www.ingramcontent.com/pod-product-compliance
Ingram Content Group UK Ltd.
Pitfield, Milton Keynes, MK11 3LW, UK
UKHW040729150225
455125UK00001B/75

9 780253 215659